CINEMA IN TURKEY

CINEMA IN TURKEY

A New Critical History

SAVAŞ ARSLAN

OXFORD
UNIVERSITY PRESS
2011

OXFORD

UNIVERSITY PRESS

Oxford University Press, Inc., publishes works that further
Oxford University's objective of excellence
in research, scholarship, and education.

Oxford   New York
Auckland   Cape Town   Dar es Salaam   Hong Kong   Karachi
Kuala Lumpur   Madrid   Melbourne   Mexico City   Nairobi
New Delhi   Shanghai   Taipei   Toronto

With offices in
Argentina   Austria   Brazil   Chile   Czech Republic   France   Greece
Guatemala   Hungary   Italy   Japan   Poland   Portugal   Singapore
South Korea   Switzerland   Thailand   Turkey   Ukraine   Vietnam

Copyright © 2011 by Oxford University Press, Inc.

Published by Oxford University Press, Inc.
198 Madison Avenue, New York, New York 10016

www.oup.com

Oxford is a registered trademark of Oxford University Press

Library of Congress Cataloging-in-Publication Data
Arslan, Savaş.
Cinema in Turkey : a new critical history / Savaş Arslan.
   p.   cm.
Includes bibliographical references and index.
ISBN 978-0-19-537005-8; 978-0-19-537006-5 (pbk.)
1. Motion pictures—Turkey—History—20th century.   2. Motion picture
industry—Turkey—History—20th century.   I. Title.
PN1993.5.T8A77 2010
791.43094961—dc22   2010009158

Printed in the United States of America
on acid-free paper

To my daughter

Acknowledgments

When a long process extending almost a decade comes to a conclusion, it comes down to memory. Like Zhuang Zi who dreamed of a butterfly or the butterfly who dreamed itself as Zhuang Zi, this work of memory and dreams involves making or carrying the traces of a history of acknowledgments and oblivion. Human to butterfly and gaze to identity is this list that moves back and forth.

I would like to start by thanking my adviser, Ron Green, for sharing my concerns and warmheartedly helping me in my graduate work; Stephen Melville, for his comments and intellectual support; and Victoria Holbrook, for offering me the opportunity to do graduate work at the Ohio State University.

In the Turkish academic world, I would like to thank Nezih Erdoğan, who shared my initial interest in film studies at Bilkent University; Deniz Bayrakdar, who created a lively environment of discussion through Turkish film studies conferences. At Bahçeşehir University, I am grateful for the support of our university's administration and would like to thank Enver Yücel and Haluk Gürgen, my colleagues, and our teaching assistants and students who helped me in various manners.

I also want to thank the staff and reviewers at Oxford University Press who helped shape this manuscript into its current form, and Emily Coolidge for copy-editing and for the camera obscura in the vicinity of Yeşilçam Street.

The images used in this book are borrowed from Burçak Evren's *Türk Sineması* (Turkish Cinema) and TÜRVAK's (Türker İnanoğlu Foundation) *5555 Afişle Türk Sineması* (Turkish Cinema in 5555 Posters). It is a pleasure for me to thank both Burçak Evren and Türker İnanoğlu, as well as Ezel Akay, for letting me use these images.

While I was doing research for this project, I received various travel grants from the OSU, which provided me with funding to interview several filmmakers and critics including Yücel Çakmaklı, Safa Önal, Kunt

Tulgar, Seyfi Havaeri, Bülent Oran, and Giovanni Scognamillo, and use the collections of the Mithat Alam Film Center, Türker İnanoğlu Foundation's (TÜRVAK) Film Museum and Library, and the Sermet Çifter Library.

Unfortunately, three of these filmmakers, Oran, Havaeri and Çakmaklı, are not among us anymore. As for friends and family who would have liked to read this volume, Sadi Konuralp, Metin Demirhan, and my former father-in-law embarked on eternal travel before I could share it with them. As for those who have not yet departed, my friend İlker, my parents, siblings, and Wendy are the backbone of this work. But this work came to life only after the first letter.

There are a lot of others in this process whose names, organizations, and institutions are not written but kept here, in me, by persistently embracing the ground like couch grass and idyllically flying above it like a butterfly.

Preface

The Heart of the Couch Grass

It was a couch grass living silently on the Anatolian plain
Before the famine.
It thrived from the smallest things
For example when a bird flew towards Kızılırmak
It was happy as if water had flooded its roots.
When a cloud passed overhead
It stopped being couch grass.
The earth, it would say, the earth
I would not change it for anything.
Now, it does not want to live.

İlhan Berk

Two important developments that fall within the reach of this book took place in 2008. İlhan Berk[1] passed away in 2008 at the age of ninety. In the same year, the first of the two highest-grossing films of contemporary cinema in Turkey, a sketch-based, episodic comedy film, *Recep İvedik* (dir. Togan Gökbakar, 2008), was released and seen by 4.3 million spectators, despite bad press from film critics (the other one is *Recep İvedik 2* [dir. Togan Gökbakar, 2009]). These two seemingly unconnected occurrences, one in the realm of poetry and the other in that of popular cinema, are illustrative of one of the premises of this book, that of a purported contradiction between cultural forms in Turkish cinema, between high art and low art, or art house and popular cinema.

My doctoral dissertation dealt with this dynamic through the analogy of couch grass that, according to the *Oxford English Dictionary*, is "a species of grass (*Triticum repens*) with long, creeping root-stocks, a common and troublesome weed in cornfields." Like cinema, it is native to Europe but quickly spread to the world. Its rhizomic form and aggression strengthen the analogy with popular cinema, producing links and connections across arts, cinemas, genres, and borders. As I delved more into couch grass, I also came across a painting by Jean Dubuffet, the infamous painter of *Art Brut* (i.e., raw art) titled *Door with Couch Grass*. For Dubuffet, the dominance of high culture over artistic creativity produced a sense of history that gave primacy to canonized works, at the expense of anonymous and innumerable examples of simple creative activity (1988, 14). *Door with Couch Grass* is a painting produced along these lines: it is made out of an assemblage of numerous paintings cut and pasted together with layers of paint and sand, and additional texture provided by the tines of a fork. Like this painting, popular cinema of Turkey from the 1950s to 1980s, Yeşilçam, can be characterized by a similar, assemblage- and collage-like act of simple creativity.[2] Thus I took a specific form of popular cinema similar to that of classical Hollywood cinema and introduced Yeşilçam as a comprehensive modality and form, growing and spreading aggressively from rhizome joints—by creating imitations, adaptations, hybrid structures, and cultural dislocations and relocations.

However, the scope of this book is different. The dissertation thesis pushed the analogy of couch grass to its limits. Instead, this book attempts to look at the entire history of cinema in Turkey. To this end, it examines how cultural forms, including cinema, have been exchanged, altered, and unendingly modified at different times and spaces. This is not just in relation to cultural forms but also the very existence of Turkey, which is chronically in-between and on the move. As I write these lines in Istanbul, in a city astride two continents, Asia and Europe, divided by a strait yet facing across, cinema in Turkey is also about Istanbul: it was born here, it has been mainly practiced here, and it has at least for four decades been named after a street in Istanbul. Yet Turkey, its culture, and its cinema have often been considered by many in terms of its connections to the West. Various accounts of cinema in Turkey have attempted to create passageways similar to those of Istanbul, connecting continents through bridges or tunnels. Instead of attempting to connect or bridge things, this book underlines separation—the separation inherent in the very in-betweenness of Turkey's cinema. It is neither Eastern, nor Western, but both and neither simultaneously. As much as it is about connections and similarities, it is also about clashes and differences because, as I will elaborate in the following pages, at the heart of culture lays separation.

When I started to work on this book in 2006, the first part of the manuscript's title was same with that of the dissertation, "Hollywood *alla Turca*," and it was borrowed from the last movement of Wolfgang Amadeus Mozart's *Piano Sonata in A, K331, Rondo alla Turca*, the Turkish Rondo, inspired by the beats of the Ottoman Turkish janissary bands. This analogy inscribes the eighteenth-century interest in Turkey in European music, opera, and theater, but also the movement and integration of cultural forms. Yet this analogy, while reiterated a few times in the following pages, also fell short of this volume's interests.

In addition, since 2006, two new volumes on the cinema in Turkey have been published: Gönül Dönmez Colin's *Turkish Cinema: Identity, Distance and Belonging* (Reaktion, 2008) and the English translation of Asuman Suner's 2006 book *New Turkish Cinema: Belonging, Identity and Memory* (IB Tauris, 2009). Both of these books focus primarily on recent cinema in Turkey through familiar tropes of identity and belonging by attributing the adjective "Turkish" to the cinema in Turkey and imagining cinema in Turkey as in search of an identity. Unlike these two volumes, this book deals with the cinema of Turkey without necessarily considering it as Turkish or expressive of national identity. Rather, it uses cinema to examine various movements, exchanges, and transformations as a staple of cultural production. The main theme of this book inscribes the multiplicity and multitude of any given cultural form as not limited to a discriminatory national framework, nor to Yeşilçam. Thus it addresses the history of cinema in Turkey, which is not necessarily covalent with "Turkish" cinema. Throughout the book, this rendering of cinema acknowledges both the nation and its others and the different interpretations of cinema underlining the coexistence and clash of the melodramatic and the realistic, the popular and the artistic, the forced and the spontaneous.

The bulk of this book concerns films of the Yeşilçam era, which represents the height of Turkish film production. However, this book goes beyond this period, offering a critical look at the broader history of cinema in Turkey both preceding and post-dating Yeşilçam. This history can be periodicized roughly into three eras: pre-Yeşilçam cinema until the late 1940s, Yeşilçam cinema from the 1950s through the 1980s, and post-Yeşilçam or the new cinema of Turkey since the early 1990s. Unlike the Yeşilçam era, which engulfed almost all filmmaking in Turkey, contemporary cinema in Turkey, considered here under the rubric of the new cinema of Turkey, encompasses a clear-cut distinction between popular cinema and art house or auteur cinema: while the former is intended for Turkish-speaking communities around the world, the latter may well fall in the realm of world or trans-national cinema often seen at film festivals and art house theaters by international cineastes. Perhaps the new cinema of Turkey is now the allegro: the lively tempo of Turkey's cinema is nowadays better heard than before. But to be able to account for this, it seems crucial to situate this cinema in terms of its history. As Berk said, the couch grass may not want to live anymore; hence Yeşilçam is passé. However, cinema in Turkey still persists and as post-Yeşilçam, it is inescapably set against Yeşilçam. Perhaps the death of Berk and the birth of post-Yeşilçam has a hidden meaning: regardless of your will to live or die, death and birth are about the same thing, about beginnings and ends; about a separation that is an unending repetition.

Contents

CINEMA IN TURKEY

1

Introduction

A three-minute Coen brothers' short, *World Cinema*, which was shown at the 2007 Cannes Film Festival along with thirty-four shorts under the title *Chacun son Cinéma* (To Each His Own Cinema), features James Brolin as Dan, a Texan cowboy, who in an art house film theater in Santa Monica, California, tries to decide between two films: Jean Renoir's *La Règle du jeu* (The Rules of the Game, 1939) and Nuri Bilge Ceylan's *İklimler* (Climates, 2006).[1] The theater employee Dmitri (Grant Heslov) helps him by giving information about both films. While there is an obvious play between the film buff who is expected to know better than a Texan cowboy, with regard to Ceylan's film, the employee makes two mistakes: he says that the film is Ceylan's second film while it is indeed Ceylan's fourth feature-length film, and despite calling it a Turkish film, he also mentions that the film is in Turkic with subtitles. After Dan watches *İklimler*, he wants to speak with Dmitri, but since his shift is over, he speaks with another theater employee (Brooke Smith) and asks her to tell Dmitri that he enjoyed the movie, adding, "There is a helluva lot of a truth in it."

A helluva lot of truth is what international filmgoers often find in Turkish films. Often, in the English-speaking world, when "Turkey" and "cinema" are mentioned in the same sentence, either some will think that *cinema* is a word that is mistaken for *delight* or some film buffs may speak about Yılmaz Güney, Nuri Bilge Ceylan, or *Midnight Express* (dir. Alan Parker, 1978). Both the films of these two filmmakers and the controversial Hollywood film involve a helluva lot of truth about Turkey and its cinema. However, once the expectation of non-Western filmmaking is set according to its representation of realities, oftentimes popular domestic films of such cinemas do not make it to the world scene. Instead, accounts of national cinemas cover only issue films or realistic dramas because of such expectations. Then, whenever one starts to speak of a broader, more popular, and perhaps more inclusive version of truth, one contradicts such established norms. While such a sense of truth or reality extracted from non-Western filmmaking is combined with a sense of exoticism, this may not necessarily reflect the more mundane realities that attract the vast majority of any population to the movies. Turkey and its cinema pose different problems for historians of international or world cinema in terms of their placement in geographical and film historical divisions. While, until recently, Yılmaz Güney had been almost unanimously the only figure covered by film historians, one may perhaps add the following directors in the forthcoming volumes on film history and/or world cinema: Nuri Bilge Ceylan, Fatih Akın, and Ferzan Özpetek. It is also very probable that the latter two names may be mentioned in discussions of German and Italian cinemas, respectively.

Despite such figures and their acclaimed films, the cinema of Turkey is quite an uncharted area in the English-speaking world. However, when one digs down a little, Turkish filmmakers and the cinema of Turkey have always been quite international and involved various coproductions and exchanges with Western and non-Western filmmakers at different levels. Not only did the first important Turkish film director, Muhsin Ertuğrul, make films in Germany and the Soviet Union in the early 1920s, there was also a far more extensive active exchange between the popular cinema of Turkey and countries such as Italy, Greece, Iran, and Egypt. Not only do such links and exchanges go unremarked upon, but the cinema of Turkey (which to date has produced almost 7,000 films) also poses problems in terms of its place in the history and geography of cinema. For instance, Aristides Gazetas's *An Introduction to World Cinema* (2000) does not even mention Turkey, and David Cook's *A History of Narrative Film* (2004) only mentions Turkey in a chapter on the "East European Renaissance" under the subtitle "Other Balkan Countries." *The Oxford History of World Cinema* has a short chapter on Turkish cinema under the section "Cinemas of the World" (Novell-Smith, 1997). Robert Sklar's *Film: An International History of the Medium* (2002) mentions Turkey in the chapter "The Global Advance of Cinema," which includes sundry countries from Australia to China, the Soviet Union to Spain. Sklar mentions Turkey in relation to four geographical locations: two countries, Turkey and Brazil, and two regions/continents, the Middle East and Africa, and notes, "The world has its share of 'unknown' cinemas—unknown not to their practitioners and audiences but to mainstream criticism and historiography" (479). For him, the cinemas of India and Turkey are among these "unknown" cinemas, only recognized through some figures such as Yılmaz Güney, whose name serves as the title of the section in which Sklar discusses Turkey.

While Turkey's location in relation to film history is a complicated matter, this is also the case for Turkey itself—a country neither Western nor Eastern, but between the two. This is one of my initial points about the cinema of Turkey, which started during the days of the Ottoman Empire, went through a nation-state that initially found itself between the stresses of the traditional and the modern, and recently between the global and the local. However, national cinema discourses often yearned for cultural specificity and authenticity, without approaching the in-betweenness of national cinemas. When one looks at recent scholarship on national cinemas, one finds Stephen Crofts noting that in the 1990s, with the influx of globalism and electronic technologies, Arjun Appadurai's five "scapes" (ethnoscapes, mediascapes, technoscapes, finanscapes, and ideoscapes) and Ella Shohat and Robert Stam's multiculturalist arguments reworked the earlier understanding of nationalism (1998, 385–86). Crofts proceeds to offer several categories of analysis to account for these recent developments: production, distribution and exhibition, audiences, discourses, textuality, national-cultural specificity, the cultural specificity of genres and nation-state cinema "movements," the role of the state, and the global range of nation-state cinemas. However, his understanding of the nation-state through eight characteristics relies upon modes of production that do not account for global economic structures. Instead, Crofts specifies four economic schemes (market economy, mixed economy, centrally controlled economy, and other), none of which can explain global cinematic flows and exchanges (1998, 389). In concluding his essay, Crofts situates national cinemas in terms of their cultural specificity in art film sectors and film festivals, while he also underlines the danger of homogenization of nation-state cinema labels due to globalization and international coproductions. Crofts's discussion separates arguments of the 1980s, national cinemas, from those of the 1990s, transnational cinemas, as well as distinguishing between popular and art cinemas. In addition, he demands cultural specificity from international art cinemas in a world where popular cinemas have become increasingly globalized.

Such a regressive placement of the (inter)national against the global not only attempts to restore national cultural specificities but also coincides with various Turkish commentaries on contemporary cinema in Turkey. When asked about such recent films as *Karpuz Kabuğundan Gemiler Yapmak* (Boats Out of Watermelon Rinds, dir. Ahmet Uluçay, 2004), which recounts the coming-of-age story of two cineastes, one of whom later becomes the director himself, *Gönül Yarası* (Lovelorn, dir. Yavuz Turgul, 2005) featuring a character moving from the southeastern Turkey to Istanbul, and the highly successful masculine melodrama *Babam ve Oğlum* (My Father and My Son, dir. Çağan Irmak, 2005), the founder of the Islamic *milli* (national) cinema movement, Yücel Çakmaklı says that these films could well be examples of *milli* cinema for they bear the characteristics of "our" culture, life, and values as homegrown, domestic narratives that do not come under the influence of what he refers to as *cosmopolitan* cinema, a mishmash of Western and westernized cinemas (2007).

This perspective is closer to what Stuart Hall identifies as the first moment of cultural identity that relies upon the creation of a "oneness," a shared culture that can be imposed from above and that may be superficial or artificial (2000, 704–5). For Hall, apart from the national identity that he feels Caribbean cinema must discover, there is another cultural identity, a uniqueness, that recognizes differences and that places one's self through the acknowledgment of the other: "It is only from this second position that we can properly understand the truly traumatic character of 'the colonial experience'." Relying on the "Other," to posit postcolonial cultural identity and its cinematic representation, Hall offers "a conception of 'identity' which lives with and through, not despite, difference; by *hybridity*" (2000, 706). This understanding of cultural identity, which posits a diasporic situation, focuses on hybridizations, syncretisms, and creolizations that are livable only through a Lacanian economy of representation, the Other, and "the return to the beginning," underlying an aim of "discovering who we are"; it relies on the construction of identifications and positionalities (Hall 2000, 714).

Hall's second moment of national cultural identity is commonly reproduced within the discourses of migrant, diasporic, transnational or Euro-Turkish cinemas. This view owes a lot both to film studies relying on postcolonial theory and to Hamid Naficy's rendering of "accented cinema," which focuses on the situation of filmmakers and the provenance of their films in exile or diaspora. For Naficy, it is through dominant cinema (the big Other or Hollywood) that we can determine the films of diasporic and exilic subjects as "accented" because of their "displacement" and "artisanal production modes" (2001, 4). Accented filmmakers, who often produce authorial or autobiographical films, not only turn the authorial function from the parental to the performative but also bring forward a presence on the "interstices" of their fictions and reality. The characteristics of "accented cinema" (fragmented, multilingual, and self-reflexive narrative structure; doubled and lost characters; themes of journey, displacement, and identity; feelings of dysphoria, euphoria, and nostalgia; and interstitial and collective modes of production), as outlined by Naficy, easily account for diasporic situations, but they are also amphibian, in large part applicable to various other situations and conditions, such as contemporary postmigrant and auteur cinema. While Naficy finely places accented cinema as both "a cinema *of* exile and a cinema *in* exile," this cinema's critical potential itself is contingent upon the condition of exile; its theory of criticism is imagined both *in* the exile and *for* the exile. Thus the dialogue of accented films with both home and host societies must be approached with care to understand how they touch on discussions, instead of how they present themselves in a limited world of exilic and diasporic dialogue and imagination.

Naficy, who attempts to move away from "postmodern theory's" textuality, claims to "put the locatedness and the historicity of the authors back into authorship" through fixing them into a diasporic or exilic situation and to some extent by casting them as a contemporary variant of Second Cinema in the non-Western world. Asuman Suner claims that accented cinema could be observed in "world cinema," as a contemporary rendering of national cinemas (2006b). However, for Suner, world cinema, bereft of such a critical potential, is indeed bereft of social, aesthetic, and political specification, and thus is a troubled concept like national cinema—a blank signifier (2006b, 376). By offering "accented cinema" as a genre and thus by extending its scope to directors such as Nuri Bilge Ceylan, Bahman Ghobadi, and Wong Kar-wai, she claims to reassess national cinema discourses, again by bringing them face to face with a conundrum of specificity and specification. To this end, she provides an overview of the arguments of several film theorists. She discusses Paul Willemen, who ties the national to the question of "cultural specificity"; Ella Shohat, who criticizes the unitary nation for concealed issues related to class, gender, racial difference, and cultural heterogeneity and who offers to see the nation as an imaginary construct; and Susan Hayward, who underlines globalization and thereby provides a way to reframe the conception of national cinema (2006b, 376–77). However, the problem again comes down to a fixing of the specificity of accented cinema's auteurs who are posited through the preconstituted categories of national cinemas and whose transnationality or hybridity is defined through an imaginary claim toward the unitary or originary conceptions of nations, which is itself produced in and by the critical discourses of these scholars.

In these discourses, while poststructuralism is seen as a "scholarly disease" concealing historical specificity, nationalisms are reiterated through national cinema discourse. For instance, with reference to Benjamin Barber's discussions on Jihad versus McWorld, Matte Hjort and Scott MacKenzie argue that nationalism is as valid as globalization when instituting an understanding of contemporary cinema and that recent studies on national cinemas and on new forms of nationalisms—"queer nationalism"—are important in accounting for contemporary cinema (2000, 2). Despite this incursion of globalization into their discourse, however, Hjort and MacKenzie still follow Pierre Sorlin in order to restore a definition of national cinema, demarcated by actual national borders and economic and juridical control, even though it may not denote a nation's specificity (2000, 5). While this is the definition of national cinema that Hjort and MacKenzie seem to choose in their introduction to the book *Cinema and Nation*, as they note, Andrew Higson's article in the volume seems to oppose their definition and, interestingly, to reiterate the very poststructuralist arguments they seem to reject. For instance, as Hjort and MacKenzie put it, Higson suggests a "text-based" "approach focusing . . . on themes and concepts of nationhood and national identity" instead of "economic-oriented," "criticism-led," and "consumption-based" conceptions (2000, 5).

Seen from this angle, then, national cinemas, especially those of non-Western or Third World countries, are imagined as self-constituted entities limited to their national borders and catering to historical specificities (one that, for the Western eye, is marked by a colonial past). The world of popular cinema in the non-Western world, which has not yet been extensively explored, involves various exchanges, interactions, and even coproductions on national, regional, and global scales handled by filmmakers from not only the non-Western world but also the Western world, and by practices outside of the claims of unitary nationalisms. However, when works such as *Accented Cinema* or *Cinema and Nation* focus on non-Western "national" cinemas, they frame them as territorially demarcated, traditionally determined, and nationally united. Hjort and MacKenzie see

Kevin Robins and Asu Aksoy's article on Turkish cinema in the volume as a political piece that runs against the Kemalist legislators who, according to them, made cinema into "an ideological instrument instead of the filmmaker's preferred means of mediating and acquiring knowledge about actual Turkish realities" (2000, 12). As will be explained in the following chapters, cinema in Turkey, despite governmental control and censorship, has not been made into an instrument of the government. Instead this comment is itself indicative of a very Western "nationalist" discourse projected onto non-Western national cinemas.

Robins and Aksoy's article, on the other hand, argues that the "deep nation," which is "the most fundamental aspect or level of belonging in any group," works against cultural diversity and change, and thus precludes the existence of a "national cinema" in contemporary Turkey (2000, 205). According to Robins and Aksoy, deep nation prevents the filmmakers' ability "to know and represent the social and cultural realities of their country" and forces them to "inhibit the cinematic knowledge" (2000, 211). However, in the same article, they focus on Yeşim Ustaoğlu's *Güneşe Yolculuk* (Journey to the Sun, 1999) and celebrate its exposure of Kurdish "reality" in Turkey. However, this line of argument again boils down to a relation of power/knowledge and "reality" that can only be mastered by Westerners or non-Western filmmakers who have acquired the capacity to think within Western tropes. Interestingly enough, in the same volume, after noting that nations are simultaneously things and masquerades and that in national cinemas identity coexists with differences, Susan Hayward warns about "an 'alternative' form of essentialism," which is offered as a solution and mirrors the practice of dominant ideologies (2000, 95). Thus demanding a "truly" national cinema or commenting on the cracks in national cinema discourses by way of art house or auteur films, as in this case, inevitably leads to a reproduction of existing national cinema discourses that expect a "helluva lot of truth" from non-Western cinemas. While such are the contemporary renderings of national cinemas, and specifically the cinema of Turkey, historians of cinema in Turkey also show a similar interest in cinema by linking film to reality and truth.

National Film History According to Turks

As one of the most acclaimed early historians of cinema in Turkey, Nijat Özön, notes in the preface to his history of Turkish cinema, many people who see a book on this subject would ask, "Is there such a thing" (1962, 6)? The question might have been a fair one to ask until the publication of Özön's book in 1962. For him, those who ask this question are divided into four groups: those who are pessimistic because of the weak progress of Turkish cinema as an art form; those who are influenced by negative interpretations of domestic cinema; those who have not seen or who do not know domestic films; and those who ask this question just to say something that sounds smart.[2] Özön remarks that all of these groups share one thing: a lack of knowledge about Turkish cinema. Özön's book addresses this lack and he proposes a periodization of Turkish cinema. For him, the initial steps of Turkish filmmaking date back to the Ottoman era, between 1914 and 1922. The period of the "theater-makers"[3] starts one year before the 1923 foundation of the Turkish Republic and continues to 1939, one year after the death of the founder and the first president of Turkey, Mustafa Kemal Atatürk. Between 1939 and 1950, in the period of transition, the theater-based producers/directors/actors gave way to the "cinema-makers," who did not necessarily have a background in another art form. The last period, between 1950 and 1960, Özön calls the period of cinema-makers. Even though the dates Özön gives are contestable, the late 1940s marks more or less the end of the dominance of Ertuğrul and a change in modes of film production and exhibition.

While the years of the Second World War saw a serious decline in the number of films imported from Europe, the war's outcome paved the way for the importation of American and Egyptian films. These were either examples of classical Hollywood cinema or examples of Egyptian popular cinema. Thanks to an early nationalization effort in the 1920s, Egyptian cinema was flourishing in the late 1930s and 1940s, peaking in the late 1940s in terms of film production (Shafik 1998, 12). In the meantime, the total number of films produced in Turkey before 1950 was around a hundred. The entry of Egyptian films and their surprising popularity among Turkish filmgoers of the 1940s marks a decisive moment in popular filmmaking in Turkey. According to Özön, this decade was the period of transition from theater-makers to cinema-makers while the existing studios of the period followed conventions set before them without adding much. Özön discusses Egyptian films as making it very difficult for the directors of the transition period because the consumers of these films were "a *backward* (my emphasis) group of spectators who had grown up with and who were used to Egyptian films or to the films of theater-makers" (1962, 145). Here, Özön discusses the relative insufficiency of cinematic culture on the part of both filmmakers and spectators and he underlines the importance of film critics and writers for such "development." For Özön, this pattern changed in the 1950s with the full control of cinema-makers who gave the first examples of a "truly" domestic cinema.

What is a "true" national or domestic cinema? How can one pinpoint the truth and essence of a nation and its cinema? Is it possible to realize a national cinema once that nation and its culture dispose of, or eliminates, the foreign influences? Often non-Western projects of modernization in the newly founded nation-states of the twentieth century disregarded various aspects of tradition and ethnicity as reconceived by the elite, often along artificial nationalist lines. Such projects of the elite arose from various strands of westernization, ranging from a colonial past to forms of self-colonization through the creation of cultural and educational models. These were often founded on positivist social science models and in the case of Turkey, the social engineering program of the republican elite primarily excluded the Ottoman and Islamic aspects of culture. A series of reforms in the 1920s replaced the sultanate with a republican democracy; abolished the caliphate, religious orders, and religious schools; gave control of religious institutions to the state through laicism; and westernized the education system. Republican reforms also worked through a visually coded system, with the replacement of the fez and traditional Ottoman-style clothing with hats and Western-style clothing, the replacement of Arabic with Latin script, and the creation of a new capital city in Ankara (a small town where a comprehensive project of city planning and concentrated architectural development contrasted with the capital of the Ottoman Empire, Istanbul).

Along with such sociopolitical reforms, a new definition of national "Turkish" culture attempted to create a modern, civilized nation in the wake of the Ottoman Empire's dissolution. This model of westernization, supported by the bureaucratic elite, evolved from late Ottoman models of westernization, especially the one proposed by a group called the Young Turks. The early republican cultural model was put out in the 1920s by Ziya Gökalp, who emphasized the limited German Romantic understanding of culture as *Kultur* over an integral understanding of culture that encompasses all aspects of human activity. This limited view of culture served to produce a vision of a reified and originary national culture that could be engineered. However, this required processes of categorization and segregation of what hitherto had existed within the realm of culture. Gökalp's book *The Principles of Turkism* had a strong political influence in the cultural realm (1968). Art and art policies were strictly defined in line with such Western conceptions as humanism, high art, canons and conventions, originality, authenticity, and artistic creativity. Gökalp's definition of culture and civilization appropriate for Turks involves Western culture and a modernized version of traditional folk culture in the arts, disregarding Ottoman and Islamic culture.

According to this classification, a synthesis between the West and the origin (i.e., traditional Turkish culture) should be sought while the East (i.e., the Ottoman Empire and Islam) should be disregarded (Tekelioğlu 1996). To illustrate this, Gökalp first delineated three types of music available in Turkey in the 1920s (Eastern music, Western music, and folk music) and then dealt with the national properness of each. Not surprisingly, Eastern music is what is foreign to Turks; folk music belongs to the Turkish *Kultur*; and Western music to the new civilization of Turks. Thus genres like classical Ottoman music or traditional folk music were banned from radio broadcasts in 1933 and 1934 while Western classical music and opera, tangos, waltzes, and polkas, along with modernized versions of folk music, were broadcasted. This also involved a new understanding of Turkey within its new borders, which were mostly determined in 1923. Under the influence of protectionist and defensive postwar policies, the young nation not only had to define itself within its new borders and in opposition to the lands beyond them but also to disseminate a new, homogenized national culture to all regions of the country.

Ziya Gökalp's project redefined all the arts in the creation of a new national taste. What is striking in Gökalp's arguments and their application during the republican period is the glaring absence of cinema, especially when contrasted with the concurrent use of cinema as a political tool in the young Soviet Union. One might relate this to the technological underdevelopment of Turkey at that time, but cinema was not absent from Ottoman and Turkish life. The first exhibition of Lumière films took place at the Ottoman court late in 1896, after which film theaters became an integral part of everyday culture. By the 1910s, the first documentary and feature films had been made. During the first two decades of the newly founded republic, Muhsin Ertuğrul, who was a dominant figure in cinema, shot his first film in 1922 and directed thirty films before his death in 1953. A theater actor and director by profession, Ertuğrul also helped encourage the republican disinterest in cinema. He considered theater to be the primary performing art, conceiving of film in relation to theater and partially as a means of producing filmed versions of plays acted by theater players. Thus not only was film ignored by the cultural reformers and policymakers of the republican regime, it was even relegated to a subordinate status by the country's dominant filmmaker.

Although cinema in Turkey started to proliferate during the one-party era from the 1920s through the 1940s, this period served as a formative era during which the films of Ertuğrul and others determined/established basic genres not dissimilar from their Western counterparts, such as action-adventure films, family melodramas, comedies, urban and village dramas, and adaptations from theater plays, vaudeville, novels, and foreign films. More important, the general disinterest in cinema allowed filmmakers to remain relatively independent from the concerns of westernization and high art, especially after the 1940s. This led to a rather spontaneous development of popular cinema that was unique and uncharacteristic in a country where everything, including cultural production, was centrally managed and mediated. "Cinema entered Turkey through private enterprise," says Giovanni Scognamillo, a Turkish film historian of Italian descent: "The earliest theaters and the first imported films were also the products of free enterprise" (1998, 97). The direct intervention of the state in other arts was not replicated in the case of cinema, except through a continually changing and politically volatile system of control and censorship, as I will elaborate below.

Unlike Gökalp's cultural projects and Özön's account of a history of cinema predicated upon an ideal Western example while disposing of non-Western influences, and which thus reads as progress toward realism, this book argues that the alterity of non-Western cinemas owes itself to such relations among Western and different non-Western forms of entertainment. When one deals with the history of cinema in a non-Western country, the story always starts with how cinema, as a Western medium, is first exhibited and practiced in this non-Western country. Since the technology is imported, any non-Western national cinema naturally reflects the films and equipment available to filmmakers. This socioeconomic history of cinema is also tied to cultural and political colonialism, not only in terms of the dominance of Hollywood or other Western popular cinemas but also in terms of the foreignness of the technology, which is coupled with a need to adapt, translate, and naturalize it. Thus, the entry of such foreign film sources may be taken as the harbinger of a filmmaking practice that is more of a diversity and difference, than that of one that is foreclosed under an ideal model. In this manner, while the examples of classical Hollywood cinema opened a path of "learning by watching" for these new filmmakers, the popularity of Egyptian films, in opposition to Özön's negative view of their low quality and exploitative character, suggested the possibility of producing economically viable homegrown popular films.[4]

Cinema in Turkey has both benefited and suffered from this general neglect. Since audience satisfaction was crucial to continued survival, cinema enjoyed an opportunity unique in Turkey to reflect a grassroots, rather than an elite, culture. On the other hand, as many filmmakers have often complained, it had to develop without state support for production, often leaving it bereft of funds as well as unable to experiment with nonpopulist forms. In fact, from its earliest days the Turkish film industry had to rely on private entrepreneurship and it was not until the 1950s that the film market truly took off. The post–Second World War era was marked by growth among the Turkish bourgeoisie due to relative economic liberalization coupled with U.S. economic aid awarded after Turkey's membership in NATO.

These changes in technical, economic, and political conditions for filmmaking and their effects on film production present an alternative route to construct a new periodization of cinema in Turkey. A very significant development that facilitated the burgeoning of Turkish filmmaking took place in 1948 in the form of a decrease in the municipal entertainment tax taken from ticket revenues. Four years after this tax adjustment, the number of films made in 1952 was fifty-six, more than three times the eighteen films made in 1948. This development culminated in a gradual increase in the number of films made throughout the 1950s. During this era, the initial turning point came through between 1958 and 1961, when approximately one hundred films were made per year. The number of films produced annually rose above one hundred in 1961, above two hundred in 1966, and peaked around three hundred in 1972, while remaining at around two hundred until the 1980 military intervention prevented the continuation of almost all independent cultural activity. Between 1980 and 1983, around seventy films were made annually. During the mid-1980s, the number of films made was around 150, followed by a fall from grace in the late 1980s. After the 1990s, the annual number of films made hovered around forty or fifty. Moreover, only 25 or 30 percent of the films made in the 1990s were exhibited in theaters, the majority of which were under the control of the U.S. production and distribution companies. In the mid-1990s, just around the centennial of the first exhibition of films both in France and in Ottoman Turkey, domestic cinema started to rise from its ashes. Throughout the last decade, domestic films in Turkey at times fare better in the market than Hollywood and other foreign films.

The periodization proposed in this book brackets the socioeconomic rise and decline of Yeşilçam. While referring specifically to a location, a street off İstiklal that originally housed offices of producers, "Yeşilçam" also came to indicate a certain type of popular filmmaking—in a way, comparable to the name "Hollywood," especially classical Hollywood cinema. The golden years of Yeşilçam, the 1960s and the 1970s, were marked by three military interventions: one of them opened a decade of limited artistic freedom after 1960; the second, in 1971, divided the two decades by limiting the openings created by the previous decade; and, in 1980, the last and the most reactionary intervention triggered a period of decline. Given these historical developments, this book will deal with three main periods: Pre-Yeşilçam (cinema in Turkey until the late 1940s), Yeşilçam (between the 1950s and 1980s), and post-Yeşilçam (1990s onward). The Yeşilçam era itself is further divided into three phases: "Early Yeşilçam," the 1950s, as a period of opening and laying out of a certain cinematic pattern of production, distribution, and exhibition; "High Yeşilçam," the 1960s and 1970s, as a period of "the classical" or "golden age" in popular cinema (hence the similarity to classical Hollywood cinema); and "Late Yeşilçam," the 1980s, as a period of change and of decline in film production, distribution, and exhibition—perhaps also a decline in a particular popular film form. Post-Yeşilçam, the period after Yeşilçam, not only gave way to novel avenues of filmmaking in and after the 1990s but also demanded a response from contemporary filmmakers as Yeşilçam represents the golden age of filmmaking in Turkey. Alternatively, this new period is coined as the new cinema of Turkey, indicating the changes in the understanding of sociocultural parameters and their effects on cinema.

Turkey in Transition

A year after the showing of the Coen brothers' short, at the very same Cannes Film Festival, when Nuri Bilge Ceylan received the best director award for his *Üç Maymun* (Three Monkeys, 2008), he made a short speech in Turkish saying, "I would like to dedicate the prize to my lonely and beautiful country, which I love passionately." While it is not uncommon to love one's country, and to find it beautiful, the word *lonely* was cryptic and elicited a cacophony of responses. Indeed, this cacophony is to some extent understandable for a country living with the specter of an imperial past, the ashes of which were mixed into the mortar of the new country and can be seen in its ideology of self-subsistence. This short speech was received quite well among the nationalists in Turkey and even the sports pages of Turkish dailies, which unanimously cover soccer, used these words in their tabloid style headlines after the Turkish national team or a Turkish soccer team won a game against another national team or a foreign club. Moreover, some thought that Ceylan addressed the winner of the 2006 Nobel Prize in Literature, Orhan Pamuk, who is known for his criticisms of Turkey's political and historical downturns.[5] Regardless of whether there is any truth in this association, the popularity of these words in 2008 points to a long-standing Turkish problem with its own image and with its image in the eyes of the West.

Who are Turks? Is "the Turk" an all-inclusive umbrella term for all of the people living in Turkey, or does it inscribe an ethnic allegiance? This book is about the cinema of Turkey, including the late Ottoman era and the republican era that started in 1923 after the foundation of the Republic of Turkey. According to a 2007 survey, being a citizen of Turkey has been identified first as loving Turkey (80 percent), then, saying "I am from Turkey" (62 percent), being Muslim (55 percent), and being Turk (46 percent) (Erdem 2007). As may be seen from this survey, while the nation-state's central republicanist ideology and its projects of modernization from above, which also involved the marginalization or elimination of the nation's others, have recently lost their momentum and influence, Turkey has still been imagined as being in-between different identity claims and nationalist surges.

Today, Turkey is between various identifications and stresses. As a country it is neither Western nor Eastern, neither modern nor traditional. In the eyes of various scholars of modernization, it was defined a transitional country. Framed by a positivistic approach, the discourses on the development and modernization of non-Western countries often involved the definition of countries such as Turkey as transitional. According to modernization theorists who also aligned themselves with the post-Second World War international policies of the United States, such as Samuel Huntington, W. W. Rostow, and Daniel Lerner, there were two main categories: the modern and the traditional. Whereas the Western countries are taken as modern, traditional societies were often defined as not having the characteristic traits of a modern country, including man's control over nature, scientific and technological advancement, rationalization, secularization, industrial growth, urbanization, and a liberal democratic political system.[6] Apart from its obvious positivistic and evolutionary sociological renderings, a significant problem with the U.S.-led modernization theory was its dictation of only one path toward modernization, a path that would bring together "undeveloped" or "traditional" countries with the United States and the First World.

As a country evolves in this unilinear route, it also passes through different stages between tradition and modernity. Such societies that lie between are called transitional societies. As Reşat Kasaba points out, while Samuel Huntington views Turkey as a country torn between "the West and the rest," this view of Turkey as caught between two things has a more complex historical backdrop than is immediately apparent. In his *The Passing of Traditional Society*, which focused on the village of Balgat in 1950 and a suburb of Ankara in 1954, Daniel Lerner commented on Turkey's situation as transitional, between the traditional and the modern (Kasaba 1997, 23). However, instead of focusing on anomalies such as the segregation of some migrants, while others found themselves in the middle of Islamic brotherhoods or leftist unions and still others were learning and adapting to life in urban areas, Lerner tried to limit this dynamism to a categorical frame (Kasaba 1997, 23). For Kasaba, Lerner's Balgat grocer, the marginal figure between the pious figures of the chief and the shepherd in Balgat of 1950, was someone who loved to see American movies for their excitement and for their engaging plots (1997, 33). In other words, if the Balgat grocer was not categorizable, if he was a transitional figure who was neither quite modern nor traditional, it would be tempting to ask: what if we consider him not as the exception, but as the standard?

Often, scholars of Turkey who are critical of these modernization theories also place the republican process of modernization from above in the "gray zone" between the modern and the traditional. In the eyes of modernization theorists, the republican modernization came to a halt in the 1990s, with the rise of religious and ethnic political movements. By commenting on market capitalism, human and civil rights, and individual protectionism as tenets of modernization in the 1990s in Turkey, Kasaba maintains that the demise of top-to-bottom state modernization does not mean the collapse of modernity in Turkey. Instead Turkey has perhaps found its own route of modernization staying in between the stress zone of the traditional and the modern. Today, while the capital city of Turkey is in Ankara, the majority of businesses and arts and cultural life is centered in Istanbul, a city with "a cultural conflict, revolving around the definition of locality and identity, between the globalizers and the localizers—somewhat akin to the modern-traditional clash" (Keyder 1999, 23).

By taking into account such stresses created by the in-betweenness of Turkey, this book takes Turkey's transitional status with a twist. Instead of following either the modernization theorists' unilinear trajectory or the republican modernization-from-above, it deals with the history of cinema as being in continual "trans-ing," continual transition, translation, and transformation. Ravi Vasudevan argues that regardless of whether transition is understood in terms of linear progress from one historical stage to another or from traditional to modern, this view implies that these cinemas are destined to follow the Euro-American examples, given the fact that cinema's technological and perspectival history is intricately linked to the West. However, this transitional state presented different solutions to the problems that might have already been experienced by Western cinemas. In other words, though they are transitional, "Third World" cinemas offer various methods of translating, transforming, and mirroring the West, and these societies and cinemas simultaneously claimed, at times violently, their national identity and culture. "At issue, then, is how traditions of identity, aesthetic form, and cultural address are deployed for a politics of creative adaptation and interrogation of social transformation in a colonial and postcolonial world" (Vasudevan 2000, 131). On the other hand, when one looks at the history of cinema in Turkey, while its transitionality inscribes an in-between state, this state also falls into and apart from the categories of national cinemas seen through the national and the transnational.

What Was Yeşilçam?

In the 1990s, Yeşilçam films became a staple of the daytime and late-night television that took the place of film in many people's entertainment practices. Today, some of these films—produced as regular, popular entertainment—have gained cult status among some spectators, particularly young, educated, and often ironic cineastes, precisely for their low-budget effects. A reemerging interest in these films both nationally and internationally is at hand, as suggested by some recent Turkish films that mock Yeşilçam's popular melodramas and historical adventure films. But what was that industry? What made Yeşilçam films popular and what were the characteristics of popular film that made them so controversial at the same time? What does this discomfort with the popular reveal about the interests of various spectatorial groups in Turkey? What was different about Yeşilçam that still makes contemporary spectators ironically humiliate and nostalgically embrace these films?

While the problems of Yeşilçam film are apparent in nearly all of its productions, perhaps an award-winning film made under far better conditions best illustrates the stark contrast between Yeşilçam and the Western cinemas it was supposed to emulate. In 1983, a year after gaining international renown by winning the Golden Palm at the Cannes Film Festival for the film *Yol* (The Road, 1982, dir. Şerif Gören) Yılmaz Güney, the Kurdish actor-writer-director known as the "ugly king" of Turkish cinema, made a film in France, *Duvar* (The Wall, 1983) with the support of 2 million French francs. This was far beyond the budget of any Turkish film at that time. So what did Güney do with this opportunity? *Duvar* presents a story about the harsh conditions of correctional facilities for children in Turkey at that time. Since he was in exile in France, the film was shot at a French monastery using Turkish actors and crew. A documentary about the making of the film shows a tracking shot in which one of the kids carries coal in a wheelbarrow. At the premier of the film, after seeing this scene filmed with a rocking camera attached to the wheelbarrow, director Atıf Yılmaz notes, "I could not understand why this scene was not shot with a steady-cam or a crane but with a camera attached to a wheelbarrow with wire." After noting the sheer strangeness of such equipment Atıf Yılmaz adds, "But given that he [Güney] had good finances and vast technical resources in France, and that he knew that this scene was not ok, I could not understand why he did not consider these [technical] possibilities" (1995, 215). In addition to such technical deficiencies, on an ideological level, Güney scandalized the leftist community in France, which had previously supported him when he warmly invited the ostracized director Elia Kazan to the set. Perhaps less well-known but more shocking, Güney scandalized the parents of his child actors when he sought realism by slapping and verbally abusing them on the set so that their tears would look real.

Figure 1.1. Photograph taken during the filming of *Umut* (Hope, Yılmaz Güney, 1970); actor-director Yılmaz Güney "directing" the cameraman

Despite the exceptional circumstances of its production in France, ample financial resources, and reception as a politically charged art film, the previously mentioned problems with the film's production present a very telling story from which to understand the Yeşilçam tradition out of which Güney emerged. It shows how a filmmaker of the period understood and experienced the making of a film and technological incompetence resulting from shooting chronically low-budget films in Turkey. In Yeşilçam, all films were dubbed to save on audio equipment costs, all films were shot very quickly (in a period ranging from a couple of days to a few months), and all involve a seemingly endless number of technical "mistakes" when compared to contemporary notions of "proper" filmmaking, particularly in the Hollywood tradition. Many of the films have a very simple storyline that narrates the eternal clash between good and evil, staying true to a melodramatic modality.

Technically, many Yeşilçam films were made with handheld cameras without the assistance of dollies, cranes, or other professional equipment. Even if some technical gadgets were in use, they were either very limited in number or invented on the spot, with a number of shortcomings as a result. For example, Seyfi Havaeri, the director of *Kara Sevda* (Unrequited Love,[7] 1968), talks about one of his inventions that served as a substitute for the crane shot (2002). When the zoom became a part of regular cameras in the 1960s, many films employed a highly distracting, even amateurish, use of the zoom for close-ups. In terms of editing, continuity editing with shot distribution and orientation was the underlying practice without much attention paid to rules such as the 180- or 30-degree rules of classic Hollywood film. Kunt Tulgar, the director of various action-adventure films in the 1970s and 1980s, mentions that the director of the first Turkish Tarzan film, Orhan Atadeniz, was an editing guru (2002). While shooting, Atadeniz carried single frames from the original Hollywood Tarzan or wildlife documentaries in his pockets and before shooting a scene, he took out a frame in order to arrange the *mise-en-scène*. By specifically blocking the players for orientation, he could make the actors fit into scenes of the footage already in hand and then edit the frames from this footage into his own production.

Film staging and production was fraught with budget-related difficulties from beginning to end. Most of the star actors did not have a formal education, but were recruited either through star contests organized by popular magazines, through connections, or even chance encounters with filmmakers. Except for period films, the actors frequently brought their own costumes. Even the action-adventure star Cüneyt Arkın says that he had to provide his own trampoline, fireman's net, and even his own horse to shoot such scenes (2002). Around 1970 when color films became widespread, it was rumored that some film production companies brought clothes for their star players from Paris. Inspired by the idea of shooting in color, they bought clothes in solid, bright colors to take advantage of the new technology. All of these films were dubbed at the studios during the postproduction stage, in many cases by professional theater players temporarily working as dubbing artists for foreign films. In order to save film, according to Tulgar, filmmakers would cut normal 35mm film in half, making 17.5mm filmstrips with which to edit the dubbed sound onto visual footage (2002). Matching reels were then sent to Italy to be edited together. Thus, problems of lip synch arose, as well as distortions in the image quality.

Film production companies did not use established studios, with the exception of some scattered attempts such as a Western town set. Instead, they rented lavish bourgeois houses in and around Istanbul mainly for melodramas and used actual historic sites for historical films. Many of the desert scenes in different films were shot at the beach of a small town close to Istanbul. The lighting equipment was simple and basic; natural light was often preferred. Because the camera equipment was not very well maintained, Havaeri tells how, during the 1950s, he and his cameraman unsuccessfully attempted to make a wooden box covering the old, damaged camera to prevent exposing the film to light (2002). Since the amount of fresh film was so limited and domineering producers were so prone to scold over every wasted frame, filmmakers rehearsed a scene many times before shooting it.

While production quality was often low, the period of high Yeşilçam has a wide typology, from mainstream films with or without stars, low-budget productions, to auteur or art films. This diversity includes a variety of filmic genres, such as family melodrama, action, adventure, comedy, and fantasy, as well as spaghetti (or "kebab") Westerns, sex, and horror films. Though many of these films rely upon the Turkification of Western films, they also present a melodramatic modality that enmeshes elements of a melodramatic narration with an authentic practice of realism. In this respect, as I will elaborate below, poor *mise-en-scène* or poor quality of shooting and editing did not present a problem on the part of spectators because the traditional performing arts in Turkey, such as theater-in-the-round, did not rely upon the sets but primarily on the explanation of the situation and the start of the play through a series of descriptive instructions. Similarly, Yeşilçam's presentation of its stories was based on oral cues rather than visual narration. It was the story that was of interest and therefore the deficiencies of visual narration were eliminated through oral narration.

Thus Yeşilçam, viewed from a Western and westernized perspective, did not present a realistic language or high-quality filmmaking, but instead was a series of discontinuities and failures. This has changed in the post-Yeşilçam era: the situation created a dual status with regard to film criticism. Whereas a more political and intellectual line of criticism took Yeşilçam as a popular film industry intoxicating the masses with ideologically conservative or mute content, the popular press, such newspaper columns and magazines, intended primarily to promote major films and stars. When film critics or filmmakers produced lists of the five or ten best Turkish films, often these films were social realist dramas. Similarly, the mainstream histories of cinema chose social dramas and helped create a canon of cinema in Turkey that is often understood as films departing from Yeşilçam's drawbacks.

In this book, while acknowledging the existing historiography and criticism of film in Turkey, I propose two departures from the understanding of Yeşilçam and distinctive or canonical Turkish films. Instead of postulating Yeşilçam as a category of a culture industry or popular filmmaking, Yeşilçam is the name given to the filmmaking practice in Turkey roughly between 1950 and 1990. Thus, Yeşilçam is understood as both a hub of cinema having a specific set of distinctive characteristics in terms of production, distribution, and exhibition network, and a specific filmic discourse and language developed by bringing together different films under one umbrella. For instance, that is why it is argued below that the post-Yeşilçam era is of a separation between popular filmmaking practices and art house or international film circles. On the other hand, the choice of the films in this book may seem striking for its purported disregard to the canonical films in Turkey. However, the films I deal with in this book attempt to provide a representative sample of the cinema of Turkey by inviting into discussion regular products of the industry ranging from tearjerkers or low-budget action-adventures. My selection of films is thus a conditioned practice in the sense that I plan to illustrate my arguments with films that have not been considered in detail by the majority of film writers in Turkey and abroad.

In this book, I argue that Yeşilçam may be seen in relation to the following notions: Turkification, *hayal*, melodramatic modality, and *özenti*. In the following chapters, I will introduce these notions in relation to the historical processes of cinema in Turkey. As I will elaborate in the next chapter, the history of the traditional performing arts and the history of cinema in Turkey will present a convergence of the two screens, that is, some Western Lumière films were shown on the Eastern screen of Karagöz shadow play, called *hayal* (lit. image, imagination, dream, and specter). Cinema developed in Turkey by interweaving two screens, the traditional and the modern, the realistic and the spectral. To this, the history of Yeşilçam, as it attempted to be a "small" Hollywood, also appends a dream of making films similar to those of Western cinemas. However, the makeup of cinema in Turkey, the presence and use of a Western medium in a non-Western land, brought about its own particularities and peculiarities through practices of translation, transformation, and restitution.

Hayal underscores a transitory state enmeshed with the drama of nation building, which involved attempts to invent a nation and its culture, an aggressive attempt to unify all the multiplicities of a country under a single, unitary national umbrella. This also had its effect on the production and consumption of the cinematic products in Turkey. In this respect, the dubbing of domestic films in Turkish by professional dubbing artists created an uncanny combination of the actor's image with the dubbing artist's voice. In Yeşilçam, sound was not recorded live during filming. But during this dubbing process, while foreign films were Turkified through a series of modifications or omissions of characters, dialogues, and storylines, Yeşilçam films were also frequently modified during the postproduction stage. Moreover, Yeşilçam utilized not only cinema as a Western medium, but also Western films themselves through remakes and adaptations. Thus I will deal with Turkification not only as a translation and transformation of the West through Yeşilçam's own terms and terminology but also as a practice of nationalization that carries with itself the violent and aggressive elements of nationalism. I will call this latter meaning of Turkification "Turkification-from-above." But such practices of Turkification in Yeşilçam are not limited to a non-realistic, postsynchronized filmmaking, but also to an active (mis)translation and transformation presenting a popular cultural synthesis. In this manner, Turkification may be thought of as a process of coexistence between the West and the East, with various failures, novelties, and aggressions.

Enmeshed with the practices of *hayal* and Turkification, I will introduce the notion of *özenti* (imitation or pretension) in an attempt to understand the meeting of the Eastern and two-dimensional Karagöz shadow play with the Western and three-dimensional Punch puppet play. Yeşilçam's *özenti* is about a perpetual movement from self to other in an attempt to be like the other, that is, the Western popular cinemas, especially Hollywood. *Özenti* is about desire—a desire to be like the other, the West, the superior instances of the cinematic practice. Yeşilçam's filmmakers were always aware of the impossibility of being equals with Hollywood, though they strove toward equality regardless. In this movement from self to other, a return to the original self is impossible and through *özenti*, Yeşilçam maintained a double existence, not being one nor being the other but in continual movement between the two.

While *hayal*, Turkification, and *özenti* will give clues to Yeşilçam's workings and being, its "melodramatic modality" will help understanding how Yeşilçam constructed its filmic texts. This analysis will not rely on a limited view of melodrama as a particular genre, but rather as a spectral genre, a modality that encompasses a particular history of entertainment and arts through the practices of filmmaking. Thus, Yeşilçam's melodramatic modality will be tested in films chosen from a variety of genres. Certainly, the discussion of modality will raise problems of boundaries and analytical classifications or categories in relation to strict modes, but instead of offering first a mode or model and then looking for the dissolution of it through subversions or excesses, the arguments on genres of high Yeşilçam will deal with the above-cited doubling between ground and altitudes, between overlappings across different generic instances and the specificities of particular films. Moreover, the period of late Yeşilçam will deal with how various aspects of Yeşilçam have been recycled and transformed, not only through the changes in terms of the socioeconomic and cultural milieu but also the cinematic practices and the consumption of films. In discussing these films, I will trace the persisting elements (those related to the ground) of the melodramatic modality of Yeşilçam, as well as the changes (the new altitudes) that came about in the vanishing years of Yeşilçam.

Post-Yeşilçam or the New Cinema of Turkey

Yeşilçam died one of many deaths before coming back to life in television. But with television came a change in film culture that also changed Turkey's contemporary cinema, leading to post-Yeşilçam (Evren 2005) or the new cinema of Turkey. While new American cinema's or new Hollywood's birth is comfortably located in the early 1970s, the timing/periodization of new cinema in Turkey is debatable. Indeed, if Yeşilçam was a "Turkish" cinema characterized by Turkifications, nationalism, and the republican *hayal* and *özenti*, what has come to be termed "new Turkish cinema" has the capacity to be more of the "new cinema of Turkey" rather than a cinema limited to and defined by its "Turkishness." Recent discussions about ethnic identities, reform programs initiated toward full membership in the European Union, increasing class differences as a result of the capitalist economy, and a decrease in the rural population have all helped the movement toward such changes.

The post-Yeşilçam era not only presents a challenge in terms of understanding what happened to and what happened after Yeşilçam but also how to name this period: new "Turkish" cinema or new cinema of Turkey? I suggest the use of new cinema of Turkey rather than as the new "Turkish" cinema, in an attempt to move from a limiting, nationalistic framework to an understanding focusing on multiplicities and pluralities, as well as with the transnational and global characteristics of contemporary cinema in Turkey. The post-Yeşilçam era brings to the fore various changes in the production, distribution, and exhibition network and in storytelling conventions. Thus instead of combining various separations in a melting pot by calling this phenomenon "new Turkish cinema," either post-Yeşilçam or new cinema of Turkey will be used in this study to account for the separations and differences of the contemporary cinema in Turkey.

In the post-Yeşilçam era, a clear-cut separation between the world of popular cinema and art and festival films came to the fore, as well as with various convergences and exchanges between cinema, television, and advertisement markets. There was tension between popular cinema in Turkey and the state broadcasting company TRT (Turkish Radio and Television) throughout the 1970s and 1980s and later between cinema and the private television channels that started in the early 1990s. Unlike the TRT's television channels, which until the demise of Yeşilçam gave at best a very limited broadcast time for domestic films, private broadcasting companies started showing Yeşilçam films in the early 1990s. Additionally, with the rise of private channels, television commercials became an important venue for filmmakers and young film school graduates. Lastly, after private channels started to invest in television series following the tropes of Yeşilçam, these also created a very active market for the filmmakers. In the meantime, with the changes in the world of contemporary cinema, the crews of the television series and commercials started to not only make films but also they often considered cinema as a more respectable business than what they were doing because they found cinema, even if the financial stakes were lower, more sophisticated.

Another important post-Yeşilçam attribute is related to the issue of globalization, the changing profile of population, and migration. The 1950s saw a remarkable increase in migration from rural areas to urban areas, which continued gradually throughout the four decades of Yeşilçam. This internal migration was also complicated by a wave of immigration to European countries, mainly Germany, starting in the mid-1960s. The largest wave of migration interacted with a period of Yeşilçam filmmaking in the second half of the 1970s, during which the patterns of family spectatorship declined due to the rise of television as entertainment and to economic hardship felt especially by migrant families from the countryside. It gave way to the rising popularity of 16mm sex films aimed at a young male group of spectators primarily from migrant families in the cities. A later wave of migration created a videotape market for the films shot in the 1980s, initially in Europe and later also in Turkey. Thus a remarkable number of films made in the 1980s were not exhibited in theaters but went directly onto the videotape market, during which the distribution companies of Hollywood and their films dominated the film market. Especially after the 1990s, not only the second- or third-generation migrants living throughout Europe started to produce films but also various domestic filmmakers either moved abroad or started to produce coproductions with filmmakers from different countries.

Apart from an internationalization or globalization of the contemporary film world of Turkey, the post-Yeşilçam era experienced higher production and promotion costs, live recording of sound in the majority of films, extensive use of digital technologies at different levels of filmmaking, and an all-around level of professionalism. The new generation of filmmakers and filmgoers is comparatively younger and well educated. This brought about an increased awareness of global developments in cinema and a change in demand from the spectators who increasingly compared the films made in Turkey with those made abroad. The separation between the world of popular cinema and art house films, on the other hand, brought about a differentiation of demands and expectations on the filmmakers and a concurrent change in filmic narration. Not only have the issues of technical incompetence been eliminated to a great extent but also narrative content has changed. While popular films adopted a storyline that calls to mind examples of global popular cinemas, especially those of Hollywood, and remade some of Yeşilçam's successful genre films, the art house films and independent cinema explored alternative avenues ranging from modernist and minimalist to multifarious and layered postmodernist storylines.

Finally, I will address a question frequently asked in Turkish cinema circles throughout the late 1980s and the 1990s: "Is Turkish cinema dead?" In response to this question, I will outline the transformation of post-Yeşilçam cinema, which in this instance might be compared to an amphibian existence in a new world of private broadcasting companies. Into this discussion, I will integrate the recuperation of Yeşilçam cinema after its alleged death. This recuperation appears in two forms: nostalgia and cultist and ironic revival, which may indicate Yeşilçam's postmortem presence, as an inescapable reference point for its aftermath. I will also develop an understanding of the post-Yeşilçam era through a discussion of global cinema, transnationality, and new media. In this, I will underline the change in cinema through the integration of Turkey into the global economic system, the changes in the production, distribution, and exhibition networks, and the influence of other media, including television and new technologies. In understanding the post-Yeşilçam period, I will also focus on the transnational characteristics of the new cinema in Turkey. In this hyphenated form of the national, I will emphasize a shift from the national to the transnational through multiplication of identities, border crossings, and alternative avenues of filmic narration. At the same time, I will foreground the persistence of the national in this new picture in opposition to its transnational occurrences.

2

Pre-Yeşilçam
Cinema in Turkey until the Late 1940s

Periodization

While the true development of cinema in Turkey as a popular industry did not begin until the 1950s, the roots of its unique cinematic language developed from its inception in the late Ottoman era and during the early years of the republic. The first fifty years of cinema in Turkey coincide not only with the two world wars but also with a long war for independence that resulted in the inception of the Turkish Republic in 1923 and the ensuing westernization and modernization.[1] As a country on the margins of Europe, Turkey had a little-known but extremely popular cinema especially during the 1960s and 1970s. However, the history of this cinema has not been covered well either in Turkish or in other languages. Instead, existing histories often reiterated an unchanging outlook without paying much attention to the plurality and versatility of this cinema. To understand the popularity of cinema in Turkey and its specific characteristics it is crucial to look at the origins and early years of cinema in Turkey, its reception and its original path that carried the stresses of a country that is simultaneously non-Western and Western.

The first extensive study on the history of cinema in Turkey was Nijat Özön's 1962 book, which proposed the following periodization:

1. The initial steps of Turkish filmmaking, which date back to the Ottoman era, between 1914 and 1922.

2. The period of the "theater-film-makers" starting one year before the 1923 foundation of the Turkish Republic and continuing to 1939, one year after the death of the founder and the first president of Turkey, Mustafa Kemal.

3. The period of transition, which he situates between 1939 and 1950, indicating the beginnings of the era of the "cinema-makers" who did

not necessarily have a background in another art form. While these filmmakers continued to produce films after 1950, this sharp delineation was created in light of the first elections in Turkey, which led to a change in the dominant party and politics in the country.

4. The period of cinema-makers, between 1950 and 1960, during which filmmakers who did not have background in theater started to produce films and better examples of a film language free from theatrical influences.

In a recent piece, Özön updated this commonly used periodization,[2] by extending the period of cinema-makers to 1970 and adding a new period named Young/New Cinema between 1970 and 1987 (1995a). On the other hand, a recent study by Rekin Teksoy (2007) offered another periodization that describes Muhsin Ertuğrul as the founding father of Turkish cinema, the 1950s as a period of transition, the period between 1960 and 1980 as Yeşilçam, and the period after the 1990s as the era of new filmmakers. Instead this book offers a novel periodization by moving the Yeşilçam era, between the 1950s and the 1980s, to center stage. The early years of cinema in Turkey are thus considered as the pre-Yeşilçam era, while the post-Yeşilçam era is rendered as the new cinema of Turkey.[3]

The first five decades of Turkish film are a developmental period informed by crucial economic and political changes culminating in a prolific popular film industry. Most significantly, after a long period of single-party leadership, extended due to the uncertainties surrounding the Second World War, Turkey held its first multiparty elections in 1946. While upholding the reforms instituted by Mustafa Kemal Atatürk, the Democratic Party that came to power in 1950 paid more attention to popular desires, traditions, and voices. The instatement of the Truman Doctrine in 1947 led to the Marshall Plan in 1948, which suffused the Turkish economy with American aid during the 1950s. The resulting growth in infrastructure, particularly roads, coupled with the upsurge in industry led to the beginning of mass migration to the cities, creating a wider and more diverse audience for cinema, formerly the province of urban elites. Ties between Turkey and the United States grew even stronger as Turkey sent troops to the Korean War and thus secured its membership in NATO. After decades of postwar economic struggle, the population had risen to 21 million by 1950, from a little over 10 million in 1923.

The world of Turkish cinema was hampered, however, by protectionist economic programs designed to ensure competitive prices for Turkish products. In 1948, the reduction of the sales tax from 75 percent to 25 percent on tickets for locally produced films made them more affordable. Concurrently, film production companies began to gather around Yeşilçam Street, which gave its name to the post–Second World War popular film industry. Among the twelve film production companies listed in 1947 in *Filmlerimiz* (Our Films), a publication of the Domestic Filmmakers Association (*Yerli Film Yapanlar Cemiyeti*), seven were located in the vicinity of Beyoğlu while five were on it. While the first Turkish association for theater owners, film importers, and producers was established in 1932 (*Türkiye Sinemacılar ve Filmciler Birliği*, Turkey Filmmakers and Theater Owners Association), the Domestic Filmmakers Association was founded in 1946 and organized the first domestic film contest in 1948. Basically, before Yeşilçam became prominent in the late 1940s, cinema in Turkey was predominantly experienced through imported films. Hollywood dominated the cosmopolitan and elite theaters of upscale Beyoğlu in Istanbul, where during the 1947–48 season, 100 of the 118 films shown were Hollywood films. Egyptian films, however, were more popular in the periphery. This chapter will outline the roots of Turkish popular cinema as a foreign form merged with local performing and visual arts within a political context that experienced two world wars: the first being a catalyst for revolution that led from empire to a republican nation-state; the second, in which Turkey remained neutral, becoming an important political nexus in the post–Second World War era, allowing Turkey to benefit from closer ties with the United States.

Early Turkish Cinema: The Problem of Origins

First Film Screenings: Beer Halls to Coffee Houses

In 1897, in the heart of the Ottoman Empire that would later become the Turkish Republic, the earliest known public screening of *"photographie vivante"* (living photography) took place in Salle Sponeck, a beer hall in Pera (contemporary Beyoğlu), the most cosmopolitan quarter of Istanbul. Before that, in 1896, there had been a number of private screenings of Lumière films that took place at the Ottoman Palace and probably at some other aristocratic residences, making it possible that some female viewers may have seen them as well.[4] Since Sultan Abdulhamid II forbade the use of electric generators in Istanbul, these first public screenings relied on oil lamps to project the films—one can imagine the scene: the heavy smell of burning oil in a small, dark screening room. Ercüment Ekrem Talu, who attended one of these screenings at the Salle Sponeck, remarks that he and his friends discussed cinema at school, noting that it had become a popular conversational subject throughout Istanbul society (Özön 1962, 22). While some claimed that to watch films was a sin, others were happy that another element of "civilization" had arrived in Istanbul. Such reactions are typical to the ongoing cultural debate between Islamic conservatism and westernization and modernization processes.

After the initial screening at the Salle Sponeck, other places in Pera, like the Concordia Entertainment Palace, soon offered screenings too. There is some debate concerning the sponsor of the screenings. While many suggest Sigmund Weinberg, a Polish Jew from Romania, who was the representative of Pathé Fréres in Istanbul (Güvemli 1960; Özön 1962; Scognamillo 1998), others suggest an unknown man named Hanri (Henry) (M. Gökmen 2000, 59; Evren 1995, 34).[5] In addition, a recent study notes that this first exhibition was handled by Henri Delavallée, a French painter who lived

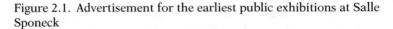

Figure 2.1. Advertisement for the earliest public exhibitions at Salle Sponeck

in Istanbul at the time (Özen 2007, 74). In 1897, soon after these early screenings in Pera, *"projections animées de grandeur naturelle"* (animated projections of natural size) were introduced into old Istanbul, where the population was predominantly Muslim. This time, however, Hanri showed the film on a Karagöz shadow play screen in a coffee house, the *Fevziye Kıraathanesi* (Çalapala 1947). The technology of traditional shadow puppetry is based on projection of semitransparent, two-dimensional puppets to create moving effects on a screen. This gradually gave way to a new technology, cinema, which unlike the non-illusionistic characteristics of Karagöz, created a lifelike effect. While there are no records discussing the motivation of those who projected Western films on puppet screens, it is tempting to infer the mind-set of those who mingled the two traditions. The obvious similarity between Karagöz and cinema even led Cecil B. DeMille, after seeing a Karagöz show in his 1931 visit to Istanbul, to say that cinema had possibly been born out of shadow plays (M. Gökmen 1989, 54).

Yet while both are story-based forms projected on a white screen, one from the back and the other from the front, the relation between Karagöz and cinema is more interesting in terms of their differences. One offers a non-illusionistic, presentational Eastern entertainment, while the other is a product of Western technologies of vision rooted in the Renaissance. Rather than presenting film as a new medium on a fresh screen draped against the wall in mimicry of Western screenings, however, those who presented the show at the Fevziye Kıraathanesi made a deliberate choice to use an existing setup—and, presumably, a smaller screen—so as to incorporate film into existing spectatorial practices. Thus the import became local, in much the same way as many Ottoman families sat in traditional cross-legged fashion on their newly purchased Western-style armchairs.

Pera was also the site of other entertainment practices augmenting traditional forms of theater and festivities popular during Ramadan, the Islamic month of fasting. During these early years, cinema became one of many such entertainments available during the evenings of this festive month, in which the day's fasting gave way to entertainment and celebration after dark. At the Fevziye and other venues where film was shown alongside shadow plays or other entertainment programs, an interesting relationship developed between the two. Like the coalescing of early film shows with vaudeville in the West, cinema in Turkey existed concurrently with shadow plays. Noting that Karagöz and cinema belong to two different worlds, Özön nonetheless claims that the elements of traditional theater, from shadow puppetry, outdoor theaters in town squares, to other forms of public narration (such as *Tuluat*, storytellers, and other forms of mimicry, which I will address later), led to a "cinema of Karagöz," employing common stock characters and speaking style. For Özön, Turkish cinema would become "true" cinema only to the extent that it escaped from these elements of traditional entertainment (1995a, 11–12). Yet, as I will argue in the following chapters, Turkey's national cinema emerged, not despite the incorporation of these traditions, but because of them.

Traditional and Modern Theaters and Performance Styles

Özön's ideal of a "true" cinema is not very different from that of André Bazin—a continual evolution toward complete realism, defined as perfect illusionism. However, apart from the stock characters of traditional theater, what remained intact in the cinema of Turkey is *hayal*, which literally means not only dream but also shadow, specter, imagination, and mirror. "Theatrically speaking, it means nothing more than imitation or mimicry; plays or acting based on imitation. It is a general term, such as *wayang*,[6] used for many forms of the performing arts" (And 2002, 998). Thus *hayal* indicates a close relation to shadow plays, and Karagöz shadow play masters are often called *hayali*. Özön considered Yeşilçam as the cinema of Karagöz, which is non-illusionistic and nonrealistic, and therefore tied to non-Western forms of shadow play. In other words, Özön's aspiration for the "Turkish cinema" is not what "popular Turkish cinema" achieved. The preservation of this tradition was directly opposed to the aesthetic expectations of Kemalist intellectuals[7] who may have felt that popular Turkish films' failures were related to its traditionalism, in contrast to the modernization attempts in other arts. Other modern arts in Turkey generally presupposed a departure from their traditional counterparts. For example, the emergence of watercolor and oil painting in the nineteenth century signaled the demise of miniature painting; classical music was imported to construct a culturally elite form, supplanting Ottoman court music and existing in contrast to folk forms. However, despite the republican project's attempts, various popular art forms maintained ties to the traditional arts at different levels, by creating distaste on the part of the cultural elite who defined their tastes according to modern, Western art forms. Thus, in contrast to Özön's and the republican project's interpretation of an art that failed to achieve equivalence with its Western models, cinema in Turkey often incorporated traditional forms into a specifically local and popular cinematic vernacular. As will be made evident, this is not only a symptom of the tensions created by rapid modernization coupled with westernization but also reflects the complicated position of intellectuals and elites in relation to the arts, both of the West and those native to their own country.

One could argue that while film incorporated traditional theatrical arts, it also maintained relationships with arts otherwise relegated to museums. For example, miniature paintings use a mode of realism distinct from that of the Western perspectival tradition. While in post-Renaissance Western art, the truth of representation relies on a singular focal point, in miniatures realism is often depicted through its use of content or the story. Thus, in the miniature genre, the interior and exterior of a building are equally visible; a scene can be simultaneously viewed from across and from above. Thus, a single image can incorporate more than can be encompassed by normal human vision; it is not realistic in terms of everyday temporal experience. The miniature genre is a narrative realism, in which the conventions of expression supersede those of positivistic experience (not unlike Western modernism).

Likewise, traditional theatrical performances shared an eclectic narrational sequentiality. Rather than having a single storyline, shadow plays and theater-in-the-round are composed of a series of loosely knit performances. Traditionally, an introduction is followed by a dialogue based on two characters, but not limited to them, and at times only loosely related to the story that follows the dialogue. Generally those performances develop through wordplay, misunderstandings, and puns, which often carry double entendres and prurient appeal (And 2000, 52). Before the principle story is introduced in the theater-in-the-round, a transition is accomplished with music and dances involving all the players (Kudret 2001, 28). In these performances, the characters would already have been familiar to the spectators and they would assume a role based on the main story. Most of the time the stories come from culturally prevalent folktales, but performances were eventually adapted from various sources, including some Western plays. After the central storyline, the performance would bring in a concluding section reminiscent of the introduction. In shadow plays, these structural frames involved a repartee between the duo of Karagöz and Hacivat, and in the theater-in-the-round, between Kavuklu and Pişekar. Apart from these two primary characters, Ottoman citizens were represented through their ethnic identities: the Greek, Jew, Arab, Albanian, Kurd, and so on. In addition, there were no women actors in the theater-in-the-round, which led male actors, called "*zenne*," to play roles like the female lead, wives of main characters, and black nannies.

Theater-in-the-round is set in the open air, often a town square, and "with minimal sets and props, they summoned up a world in which the spectator's imagination had free rein." For Metin And, "when the hero climbed up on a chair, the audience understood that he had reached the second floor of a house" (2002, 1007). Language was of primary importance and the dialogue reflected local vernacular, often including slang and obscenity. Without any storyline, "meaningless words, fabricated sayings, and cacophonous sounds" came together to make the language itself the instrument of laughter (And 2001, 143). Both in the dialogue sections and the main story, non-diegetic intrusions to the story and illusionism created an effect of alienation. "Trickster" characters incongruent with narrative frequently undermined the realistic illusionism of the stories. This brings an element of surrealism into the narratives, which at times are themselves enmeshed with dream sequences and minor storylines. As in dreams, exaggeration and false conflicts produced between the lead characters were intended to elicit laughter from the audience. But such practices did not spread into the world of modern, westernized theater in Turkey; instead, intellectuals and the reformers of the republican era criticized these traditional forms of theater as antiquated and tried to replace them with the practices of performing arts of the West. But in terms of cinema, such aspects of *hayal*, non-illusionism, and presentationality of miniatures or shadow plays persisted to some degree in the popular films of Yeşilçam.

While Ottoman citizens started to translate and perform popular texts, such as those of Molière, European theater and opera troupes performed periodically in Istanbul and other metropolitan areas. The earliest Western-style theater buildings with a proscenium, intended for traveling European circus troupes and theater plays, were built in the 1830s. Though Turkish actors and writers participated, many of these early Ottoman theaters were founded and run by non-Muslim minorities and performances were either in Ottoman Turkish or in the troupe's own language. One such theater, the "Ottoman Theater," founded by the Armenian Güllü Agop (Vartovian), performed traditional works and popular European plays in both Armenian and Turkish (And 1999, 22). Rather than creating direct translations of European performances, these theaters often adapted them to Ottoman life. Such adaptations were done from the works of Molière, Victor Hugo, and Voltaire.[8] While both Muslim and non-Muslim authors had begun to produce domestic plays in Western genres, at this time most of the staged works were still direct translations from European works.

Tuluat was a combination of Western and traditional theatrical forms, utilizing adaptations and borrowings from Western texts and staged in a Western style theater building. Similar to commedia dell'arte and the-ater-in-the-round, *Tuluat* used improvisational music and dance, vivid narration, and mimicry. The Ottoman Theater of Güllü Agop not only per-formed examples of Western theater but it also was partly a *Tuluat* theater, which coupled its improvisational character with slapstick-like comedy and obscene language (And 1985). What was important in *Tuluat* was the cultural grounding of the familiar characters, the genre and the general storyline of the text to be performed on stage. However, due to the impro-visational nature of the performance, the dialogue, the names and traits of the characters, and even the storyline were all subject to change based on the flow of a specific performance or the audience's reaction. The per-formance was often interrupted by a series of musical interludes that were only occasionally related to the story. In accordance with the Western texts contributing to these performances, characters were updated with con-temporary references and the increasingly Western-style clothing of the last quarter of the nineteenth century. Among these characters were İbiş (servant), Tirit (old man), Sirar (son), Kız (girl), and Tiran (tyrant) (Nutku 2000). İbiş, the main character, is a buffoon-like simpleton who is in love with the maid Fatma of the mansion of the wealthy miser, Tirit. Tiran is generally the villain of comedies and melodramas, while the love between Sirar and Kız provides romantic motivation. Other characters included Tirit's wife, and the mansion's cook, steward, and gardener, similar to the puppet plays of İbiş (Oral 2002, 23). While theaters devoted to *Tuluat* were opened throughout Istanbul in the late nineteenth century, the plays were also performed in more traditional venues like coffee houses and appeared in other towns through the efforts of traveling troupes. *Tuluat* presented a correlate to cinema that was later combined with the film screenings in venues combining Western and Eastern İbiş entertainment practices. Like shadow plays and theater-in-the-round, *Tuluat* also had a narrative struc-ture that would be adopted by the cinema in Turkey.

The First Film Theaters

In old Istanbul, especially during the month of Ramadan, film screenings quickly became a part of the longer entertainment program that involved these traditional forms of Ottoman theater and shadow plays. However, as Özön puts it, these screenings remained a "refugee" (*sığıntı*), "a foreign-made entertainment" (*gavur işi eğlence*) (1962, 24). In Pera, the screenings of this "*spectacle merveilleux et saisissart*" (marvelous and amazing spec-tacle) took place alongside variety theaters, circuses, and other popular entertainments. The majority of ads and other printed announcements of film screenings were in French, Greek, Armenian, and German, which is also indicative of early spectators' ethnic background (Scognamillo 1998, 18) who were either the non-Muslim inhabitants of Pera or the upper-class Muslims who lived in or frequented this part of town.

Although film screenings were very popular, spectators in Istanbul had to wait until the fall of the conservative Sultan Abdülhamid II in 1908 for the first film theater, which was opened by Weinberg under the name of *Cinéma Théatre Pathé Fréres* (Çalapala 1947). Before the construction of such a permanent venue, all of the projection machines were transportable and the venues were only open to men. While many early theaters opened in Pera during the 1910s, including the *Ciné Éclair*, *Ciné Cosmographe*, *Ciné Centrale*, *Les Cinémas Orientaux*, *Ciné Gaumont*, *Ciné Lion*, and *Ciné Palace* (Scognamillo 1991, 20), film theaters were eventually opened in other parts of Istanbul as well as within other major towns of the empire. One of these film theaters, the *Milli Sinema* (National Cinema), was opened in 1914 at the former location of the *Fevziye Kıraathanesi* and was run, for the first time, by Turks (Çalapala 1947; Özön 1962, 25). Before its establishment Ottoman general Ahmet Muhtar Pasha opened another film screening hall at the new military museum. Mustafa Gökmen notes that Pasha tried to encourage film viewing and promoted this new medium in old Istanbul (1989, 37–38). By having the Ottoman military band play the accompaniment for silent feature films, the new cinema also created a specific domestic, nationalistic intervention into the film screenings. After the opening of such theaters and some other open-air screening venues, regular daytime screenings on specially reserved days of the week for female spectators of the middle classes became popular (Çalapala 1947). Thus, by including a previously untapped audience, theaters increased their spectatorial base and added to the range of activities available to women in the empire by mimicking existing practices of temporally segregated gender inclusion already commonplace in spaces such as public baths. These early cinemas also had spaces allocated for orchestras, which performed musical scores during the films.

Cinema, first as a side attraction to other shows, began in the beer halls of Beyoğlu (Pera) and then moved to the coffee houses of old Istanbul. Indeed, Gökmen claims that the *Fevziye Kıraathanesi* was right at the geometric center of the historical citadel marked by a column that stood by the coffee house (1989, 27). In this context, beer and coffee represent opposite tracks of socialization, the one Western in style, and the other Eastern. After noting that coffee houses were "taverns without wine" (or beer) Ralph Hattox argues that coffeehouses provided masculine places for political and cultural conversations, gaming, storytellers' performances, shadow plays, and musical bands (1996). Like cinema, coffee and coffee houses were initially taken as *bid'a* (a religiously improper novelty) in contrast to *sunna* (customs and traditions with a religious grounding). However, this was not the case for beer halls, which, because they were located in cosmopolitan Pera, did not infringe on the traditional and conservative parts of the city. Cinema was a novel form of entertainment for the cosmopolitan part of Istanbul, which would then become the center stage for first-run theaters and the film production companies of Yeşilçam.

Figure 2.2. Advertisement for the film show of Manaki(s) Brothers in four different languages (French, Ottoman Turkish, Anatolian Greek, and Armenian)

The First Turkish Film

Perspective, the illusion of a three-dimensional world on a two-dimensional surface, much like Bazin's "myth of total cinema" (Bazin 1967) or Özön's ideal of cinematic realism, was introduced to the Ottoman Empire much later than in many other regions. Although perspective painting had been available to Ottoman lands since the Renaissance, it did not emerge until the early nineteenth century when Ottoman artists trained by the military, the avant-garde of Ottoman modernizing reforms, began to use the practice. With the increasing popularity of positivist ideology among reformers in the military, perspectival depiction became a necessity for teaching basic logistical maneuvers, cartography, and modern weapon technology (Cezar 2003, 91; Tansuğ 1996, 51). Likewise, the military was among the first institutions to take a formal interest in film. When the Ottoman Empire allied itself with the Germans in the First World War, an enormous popular upsurge of religious and nationalist fervor led to an attack on a building in Hagia Stephanos (Yeşilköy) commissioned by the Russians to commemorate their march on Istanbul in 1878. Despite zealous attempts to burn it down, the building survived the attack more or less intact. When Ottoman army officers decided to dynamite its foundations, they saw an opportunity to film the event for nationalistic propagandistic purposes. According to an often-repeated story, they hired an Austrian film company, Sascha-Film Gesellschaft, to film the event, though to increase the propaganda value of the film, a Turkish citizen was asked to use the camera once it had been set up by the foreign crew (Özön 1962, 37–38; 1970, 3–5).[9] Fuat Uzkınay, the first Turkish filmmaker, had worked as a projectionist for Weinberg and others. However, despite his interest in filmmaking, he had never used a camera. He got a crash course from the Austrian Sascha-Film's crew and shot the *actualité* film, *Ayastefanos'taki Rus Abidesi'nin Hedmi* (The Demolition of the Russian Monument in Hagia Stephanos).[10] It is very difficult to retrieve the exact details of what happened during the filming of the demolition because neither copies of the film nor any witnesses to the event has survived. However, as will be elaborated below, what is more interesting is the possibility of a Turkish film when there was no Turkish state. Since the film was made during the late Ottoman era, is it possible to argue that the Turkish cinema predates the Turkish Republic?

Between 1910 and 1914, Uzkınay ran a cinema society at Istanbul High School (Sultani), where he was the director of internal affairs (Çalapala 1947). There he worked with Şakir Seden who later founded the first Turkish film import and production company with his brother Kemal (Scognamillo 1998, 32). After the start of war, following the German example, the Ottoman Army also initiated a photo and film center in 1915. Uzkınay took over the operation of the center in 1916, after Weinberg's Romanian citizenship necessitated his abdication (Scognamillo 1998, 30). The center produced various propaganda and newsreel films during the First World War, as well as two feature films. Uzkınay remained as a documentary filmmaker for the Army Photo and Film Center until 1953. He documented various stages of the War of Independence, yet distanced himself from the popular film industry developing without the patronage of state. The presence of Uzkınay as a documentary filmmaker with state support who remains an outsider to the nascent film industry emphasizes the independent path that the industry was to take.

Although Uzkınay's first film is lost, in the last couple of years another film has been touted as the first film shot by Ottoman citizens: a documentary by the Manaki brothers depicting the visit of Ottoman Sultan Reşat Mehmet V to Salonica and Bitola (Evren 1995, 94). The names of these filmmakers were either written as Milton and Janaki Manaki (Macedonian version), Miltos and Yannakis Manakia (Greek version), Milton and Yanaki Manaki (Turkish version), or even Milton and Ianachia Manachia (Aromanian version). While it is unclear whether or not they were Turkish, they were both Macedonian and citizens of the Ottoman Empire. For Evren, the Manaki brothers' 1911 film about Sultan Reşat's visit may be accepted as the first "indirectly" Turkish film.

Monument Russe à St. Stéphano, Constantinople.

علی انتقام
آیاسطانوسنده روس آبده ساه قدری
۲ - ۵ تشرین ثانی ۱۲۷۰

Figure 2.3. Photographs of the Monument at Hagia Stephanos

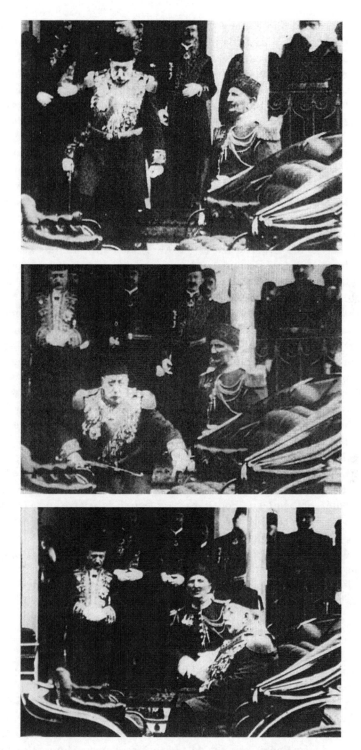

Figure 2.4. When being filmed by Manaki(s) Brothers in 1912, Sultan
Reşat supposedly says, "Let the boys play with it."

However, that film was not the first film done by the Manaki brothers. According to the Macedonian Cinema Information Centre, the brothers bought their first film camera, a Bioscope, in 1905 and shot their 114-year-old grandmother weaving: *The Weavers* is then the first Macedonian film. While another Macedonian source states that their films were "the first filmed scenes in the Balkans, on Macedonian soil" (Vasilevski), a Greek source states that "they were born in Abdela, a tiny village in the Ottoman Empire that was annexed to Greece in 1913" (Constantinidis 2000, 3) and for another Greek source, it is "the first Greek film... made in 1905 by the Manakia Brothers, whose work would be the subject of Theo Angelopoulos's *Ulysses' Gaze* (1995)" (Georgakas 2002–3, 2). Interestingly, Angelopoulos's film indirectly places the Manaki brothers at the beginning of Greek cinema and this disagreement led Macedonian filmmakers to protest the film during the Cannes Film Festival, where it was shown in 1995 and received the Grand Prize of the Jury. But Constantinidis also adds that their Greekness depends on how one defines the Greek nation and that "they lived and worked in a multi-ethnic environment, and they spoke Vlach, Greek, Romanian and Turkish" (2000, 3).

While Ottoman identity was based on religious and multiethnic communities, the dissolution of the empire resulted in the creation of a number of nation-states throughout the Balkans and the Middle East. The imagination of national communities based on ethnic identities and languages, as well as religious differences, entered the consciousness of Greeks, Macedonians, and Turks in the eighteenth and nineteenth centuries. Coupled with territorial demands, these nation-states experience continuing difficulties due to the fictive territorial divisions that have failed to meet the ethnic demands of conflicting nationalisms. While Macedonian lands were divided among Bulgaria, Greece, and Serbia during the Balkan Wars of 1912–13 (Roudometof 1996, 264), various territorial claims arose from Macedonian nationalists, while the neighboring nationalists countered with claims of their own. "For Greeks, Macedonia is a name and a territory that is an indispensable part of the modern Greek identity. For Macedonians, it provides the single most important component that has historically differentiated them from Bulgarians" (Roudometof 1996, 285). How is this relevant to Turkish film history, which is only tenuously related to the films of Ottoman citizens? This question underlines the complexity of Turkish national identity and its representation in the cinema of Turkey.

Nationalism and Belated Modernity

Since 1996, November 14th has been generally accepted by film organizations as "Turkish Cinema Day," which is based on the date of Uzkınay's lost first film. Alternative dates have been proposed: the date of Manaki brothers' 1911 film about Sultan Reşat's visit to Salonica and Bitola (or Selanik and Manastır, one now a Greek town and the other a Macedonian town); Mustafa Gökmen's suggestion of the date of the founding of the Army Photo and Film Center; and the date of the first film screening, December 13, 1896, at the Salle Sponeck (Bozdemir 2001). The variance of these dates is indicative of the debates surrounding the origins of a film history referred to as "Turkish," despite the fact that these dates predate the foundation of the Republic of Turkey in 1923. These formative events for the cinema in Turkey all took place during the slow collapse of the multiethnic and multicultural Ottoman Empire demarcated along religious boundaries. Now there are many nation-states spread around the Balkans and the Middle East, all of which developed national identities and cultures based on their common ethnic, linguistic, and religious backgrounds. Despite different relationships with the West, these states share various modernizing and westernizing interventions with the intention of catching up with the West.

The persistence of such problems of territoriality and nation building might be related to what Gregory Jusdanis calls "belated modernity." The belated and incomplete modernization in non-Western countries is symptomatic of the imitation and duplication of Western models. "The imported models do not function like their European counterparts. Often they are resisted. The project of becoming modern thus differs from place to place" (1991, xiii). While the West is perceived as the ideal model, newly formed nation-states waver between the traditional and the modern without completely creating a Western duplicate and also without totally destroying the indigenous culture. Coupled with this relation to the West in terms of modernization, the building of national cultures goes through fictional lines based on invented and constructed histories. An imagined community in Benedict Anderson's (1991) terms owes its identity to intentionally constructed fictions about a national myth that binds its members to one another with a common history and cultural heritage. As with the discriminations and exclusions integral to this originary myth, there is an inherent violence attached to nationalism based on a shared suppression of the excluded tales about the silenced communities and ethnicities.

Figure 2.5. Advertisement for Cemil Filmer's film theaters

The origins of a national cinema—the first screenings, theaters, and films—all are part of a narrative of national culture. Therefore, discerning the location of the first Turkish film and tying it to a particular canonical history of a national cinema is deeply important to a history of the national cinema. The placement of the origins in the respective histories of nation-states involves various discriminations and exclusions that serve well with individual claims of identity in respective nation-states. Under these circumstances, the first Turkish, Greek, or Macedonian film in a land of nascent nation-states needs to be considered the product of a multicultural environment from which various national cultural myths have arisen. Moreover, the archaeology of early film is still open to the possibilities of finding new "origin films" of a given national cinema. Regardless of what the different nationalist myths narrate, these films might also be seen as illuminating records of a life shared by different communities tangled in wars that defined and redefined the borders of these countries.

Given that this study is about the history of feature films in Turkey, is it necessarily confined to Turkish cinema? Should one include documentaries or other forms of recorded film? How should one define "Turkish" in this context, given the complicated national history? These are the questions that will be addressed throughout this study. To begin with, this study is limited to a consideration of feature films. While one may talk about "Turkish feature films," one may also talk about "the feature films of Turkey." The first incorporates the national history of feature films while the second one implies a discussion of "the national" and what the concept comprises. Until recently, films related to oppressed ethnicities and suppressed languages were excluded from the discussions of Turkish feature films. In a nation-state that came to become partially aware of its internal "others" only in the recent years, films made within Turkey that include identity claims outside the nation-state are also a recent phenomenon. Unfortunately, until recently very few such films had been made. After Yeşilçam migrated to television series, the world of cinema in Turkey was renamed as either "New Turkish Cinema" or "New Cinema of Turkey." As will be discussed throughout this book, Yeşilçam not only Turkified non-Turkish films but also helped the Turkification of popular culture, in perhaps a more effective way than the republican reforms. In contrast, the post-Yeşilçam era offers various avenues to dismantle this propensity toward nationalism.

Early Turkish Feature Films and Film Import

The Army and Cinema: The First Feature Films

How, then, did film become properly Turkish? In the West, film emerged after photography, which in turn emerged through a perspectival tradition of representation within the medium of painting. This tradition in large part informed the evaluation of both photography and film as art and as documentation. Film emerged in Turkey in the absence of such a

tradition. Perspective drawing and early Western-style painters of the Ottoman Empire learned Western techniques in a military school, combining
the positivistic urges and necessities of westernization. While maintaining
a distance from cinema throughout the pre- and early republican era, the
army nonetheless had a close interest in the propaganda potential of cinema. It shot newsreel *actualités* and produced a handful of documentaries
and feature films both of the army fighting the war for independence and
as internal propaganda.

Sigmund Weinberg and Fuat Uzkınay were involved in the making of
the purportedly first Turkish feature film through the army's photo and
film center. Weinberg began working on two feature films, one, *Leblebici
Horhor* (Nutmaker Horhor, 1916), that was not completed due to military
conscription of its actors, and the other, *Himmet Ağa'nın İzdivacı* (The
Marriage of Himmet Ağa, 1916–18), that was completed by Uzkınay due
to Weinberg's departure from the center. The former was an operetta produced and performed by the then-popular troupe of the Armenian Arşak
Benliyan. The second one was an adaptation, in the style of *Tuluat* theaters, of Moliere's *Le Mariage Forcé*, again performed by Benliyan's troupe
(Özön 1970, 14). Naturally, these early films, like those of Western countries, were based on theater plays. But, like the theater performances, they
were "Turkified" adaptations of the popular Western performances.

Though primarily interested in supporting the armed forces, the National
Defense Organization (*Müdafaai Milliye Cemiyeti*), founded in 1911, also
funded and aided in the production of "culture." Toward this end, Kenan

Figure 2.6. The studio of Army's Photo and Film Center, 1915

Erginsoy shot *actualités* about the war and panoramas of the Bosporus. Not surprisingly, payoff from theater owners was not enough to cover production costs. According to Muzaffer Gökmen, the films screened in theaters at that time fell into three broad categories: sights/landscapes, short comedies, and feature/narrative films (Scognamillo 1998, 34). All of the feature films were adaptations of the Western cinema, which shifted the interest and expectations of early spectators from a "cinema of attractions" to the beginnings of a conventional, narrative film. To cover the waning influx of foreign, especially European, films during the war, the organization accepted Sedat Simavi's offer to make a feature film (Çalapala 1947). It opened a studio to this end and made three full-length feature films: *Pençe* (Claw, 1917), *Casus* (Spy, 1917), and *Alemdar Mustafa Paşa* (1918). The first two were shown in film theaters, making *Pençe* the first locally made film ever screened. However, due to the Allied Forces' invasion of Istanbul in 1917, the editing of the third one was not completed.

Following the closure of the National Defense Organization's studio, equipment from the old studio was used to outfit a new studio formed by the War Veteran's Organization (*Malül Gaziler Cemiyeti*). Upon his return from military service, Uzkınay worked on a series of films in this new stu-

Figure 2.7. Sigmund Weinberg

dio along with Ahmet Fehim and Fazlı Necip: *Mürebbiye* (Governess, dir. Ahmet Fehim, 1919) and *Binnaz* (dir. Ahmet Fehim and Fazlı Necip, 1919). He also worked on a short comedy, *Bican Efendi Vekilharç* (Mr. Bican the Butler, 1921), directed by Şadi Fikret Karagözoğlu and another short film *Istanbul Perisi* (Fairy of Istanbul, 1922) directed by Fazlı Necip. After a number of screenings in Istanbul, *Mürebbiye* was banned by the Allied Forces because the portrayal of the French governess in the film was considered too loose for public mores, and thus was perceived as belittling the occupying nations (Özön 1970, 19). Like their earlier counterparts, these films were also inspired by or based on popular theater plays of the era. While they were for the most part made with the use of sets similar to those in theatrical production, they also included some scenes shot on location. Despite the unavailability of a copy of *Mürebbiye*, Özön notes that it was influenced by theater (1970, 25). Apart from a few close-ups and general views of Istanbul, these films were mostly composed of long or medium long shots, much like the French *films d'art* or filmed plays. In 1927, after making various short comedies and propaganda films, this studio reverted to army control, now under the aegis of the Republic of Turkey and its short stint of making feature films came to a permanent end, allowing narrative cinema in Turkey to develop on its own without the direct involvement of the state.

Cinema and the Republic

Filmmaking in Turkey remained limited in scope until the end of the Second World War—only sixty feature films were made before 1945, while fifty-five films were made in the four years following the war (six in 1946, twelve in 1947, eighteen in 1948, and nineteen in 1949) (Özgüç 1998). When the Republic of Turkey was founded in 1923, there were only about thirty theaters. This number rose to around 130 by 1939 and 200 by 1949 (Özön 1995a, 49). In 1923, almost 80 percent of the population was rural and 90 percent was illiterate. This may have been a great incentive for the republican reformers to produce domestic films through state institutions and studios for educational and propaganda purposes, as was the case in the Soviet Union.

However, the republican elite did not focus on film production. Instead, they halfheartedly supported film exhibition through the People's Houses, which were the centers for adult education and the dissemination of the republican reforms throughout Turkey. When the elite were shut down by the Democratic Party in 1950, there were 474 houses and 4,036 smaller branches called People's Rooms. Özön notes that almost all of the houses had a screening hall while some of the People's Rooms had the small 16mm projection machines that ran on oil. These screening rooms were primarily used to show foreign films, and there was even an *agit-train*,[11] based on the Soviet example, organized by the People's Houses in 1933, which traveled between Ankara and Samsun. However, these film screenings were poorly planned and showed whatever films were readily available. Though there were some tax cuts intended to facilitate dissemination of educational documentaries and a law requiring private theaters to show them before the main features, private film importation companies and theaters did not benefit financially from these laws and, with the exception of showing newsreels, were reluctant to adhere to them.

Among the most commonly shown films at the People's Houses were two documentaries shot by Soviet filmmakers invited to Turkey by the republican rulers: *Ankara, Türkiye'nin Kalbi* (Ankara, the Heart of Turkey), by Sergei Yutkevich and Lev Arnstam during and after the tenth anniversary celebrations of the republic in 1933, and a documentary by Esther Schub, *Türk İnkılabında Terakki Hamleleri* (The Leaps of Progress in Turkish Reforms, 1934–37). Other documentaries about the republic in the 1920s and 1930s produced by Turkish film companies were heavily criticized in the parliament for their focus on box office success rather than towing the party line (Özön 1995a, 56). Yet while republican reformers put effort into the education of Turkish artists in other fields of art, cinema was largely ignored: no film schools were opened, no studios were founded.

Film Importation and Hollywood

Under such conditions, cinema in Turkey was primarily based on the consumption of imported films until the late 1940s. After German films' brief period of dominance during the First World War due to the exigencies of alliance, American films started to corner the Turkish film market as they did elsewhere, though Western European and Soviet films were also imported. Giovanni Scognamillo notes that American companies started to dominate the Turkish film market after 1925, a dominance that continued during and after the Second World War when European cinemas literally came to a halt (1991, 53). While films from the French, German, and British companies such as UFA and Gaumont were also shown in the 1920s and 1930s, all of the Hollywood majors such as Metro, Paramount, Fox, United Artists, Warner Brothers, Universal, and First National were participants in the Turkish market in the 1930s, either independently or through Turkish distribution companies. A list provided by Scognamillo indicates that more than 60 percent of the films shown in Beyoğlu theaters during the 1935–36 season were Hollywood films (1991, 133–36). In 1931, a weekly film magazine by the name of *Holivut* (Hollywood) was established and continued until 1937. Coverage of Hollywood films and stars was not just limited to this magazine, but proved to be a primary interest of other film magazines and newspapers as well. The addresses of Hollywood stars and film production companies were published regularly in these magazines. There were even photo albums devoted to Hollywood stars published at the time, such as *Sinema Yıldızları* (Cinema Stars) in 1934. Later the Hollywood star system became a driving force and four-walling[12] was employed by the majors in their film sales to Turkey.

Despite the enormous economic and cultural gap between Turkish film and Hollywood, Hollywood became a dream destination for Turkish filmmakers as early as the 1920s. Not only did magazines promote American films, they also organized contests to send Turkish actors to

Figure 2.8. The front and back cover of the bilingual film magazine
Le Ciné Turc, 1927

Hollywood. Many actors and directors tried their luck in Hollywood, with little success. This intense, perhaps excessive interest was motivated by the desire to remove the stigma as the sick man of Europe, to represent Turkey as a developed country equal to Western nations. In keeping with this dream, star contests were organized to send actors to Hollywood or a Western European country. In 1929, *Sinema Gazetesi* announced, "We will Send Two Young People, a Man and a Woman, to Hollywood, the American Capital of the Kingdom of Cinemas." As stated in the magazine, "almost every nation has film stars known by the world, but we do not have one yet" ("Amerika Sinemalar Paytahtı..." 1929, 8). The drive to address this absence led to a system in which readers were asked to send in personal photographs to be published in the magazine and rated by other readers. Those who received the highest number of votes would be judged by journalists, filmmakers, and the representatives of German and American companies in Turkey. Two successful contestants, a young man and a young woman, would then purportedly be sent to Hollywood, though no winning contestants ever actually made it to California.

Hollywood was not a dream above all criticism. There was still some belief in the might of European cinema, and the involvement of European filmmakers in the ranks of Hollywood gave some power to such arguments. Still, despite criticism of Hollywood's factory-style production, which was thought to be based on the assembly-line production of the Ford Company, Hollywood's influence remained strong. Nuri Ahmet notes, "In the stories of American films, the names of characters, the place where the story takes place and the date may change but not the main traits of the story" (1929, 3). He describes a typical plot in which two people fall in love, break up, then reconnect, and as they kiss each other, the film finishes with a happy ending. But this "moldism" (*kalıpçılık*) was not limited to plot. There were many actors who modeled themselves on Charlie Chaplin, Douglas Fairbanks, and Emil Jannings: "These moldists wear clothes like their examples, grow moustaches like them and finally they act like them" (1929, 3). But he also noted that these model actors, who were mostly foreigners, started to return to Europe with the advent of sound film. Because of this, he believed American sound films would be stagnant copies of silent films until new models were established. What makes this assertion particularly ironic is that such critiques of standard film categories have been one of the most constant critiques leveled against Turkish cinema pretending to be a "little" Hollywood.

The Advent of Sound Film and Dubbing

In silent films, intertitles were almost immediately problematic. Though the bilingual intertitles intended for the cosmopolitan filmgoers of Istanbul were criticized, and though that problem was eliminated with the development of sound technology, dubbing "talkies" posed new challenges. While it was relatively easy to replace written segments with translations, sound technology required extensive translation, specific pronunciation, and in many cases adaptation. Sound films were consumed in Turkish, which necessitated the development of a dubbing industry and caused dissemination of a mainstream Turkish accent, used by Istanbulites and the Turkish actors of Istanbul theaters. While the importers and theater owners exploited dubbing for increased profits, the process offered further possibilities of Turkification, akin to what had happened in *Tuluat* theaters. The adaptational potential of dubbing, which disturbed the borders between cultures and blurred identity claims, while lowering the costs for domestic films, became the mainstream practice of cinema in Turkey after the mid-1940s. This section traces the advent of sound and dubbing and discusses its advantages and disadvantages, both real and perceived, as well as how these correlate with Turkification-from-above.

The Senses of Turkification

In doing this, I will introduce "Turkification-from-above" in an attempt to account for the republican reform programs. As a term that appeared in social sciences, the notion of Turkification harbors a variety of meanings, ranging from a model or ideal of nationalization and the creation of a nation-state to a critical conception of such policies that dismantled the others of the nation. The concept of Turkification surfaced in the Ottoman intellectual circles in tandem with the rise of nationalism. The rise of Turkification may be seen as a response to the ongoing process of the dismantling of the empire when different ethnicities that lived under the empire started to pursue the ideas of creating their own nation-states. A study that understands Turkification to be a policy to create a national core for the empire argues that Turkification aimed to nationalize a geographical center (Anatolia) and exerted assimilative and exclusionary practices (Ülker 2005, 615). While initially championed by the Young Turk movement, Turkification came to be at the core of the late Ottoman and early republican nation-building process. In an article on three movements in the late Ottoman politics, namely "Turkification, Islamization, and Modernization," published in 1912, Ziya Gökalp notes that these three ideals are not in conflict with one another (1976, 12). Instead, aligning these ideas into one model in which modernization is emphasized as a necessity by placing the nation at center stage and limiting religion to morality, he underlines the primacy of Turkish identity over the Ottoman one.

Turkification is not limited to one of the renderings above. Instead, it is one of the driving motives of a cumulative modernization project of a newly founded nation-state that had multiple repercussions on the social, economic, political, and cultural life of the republic. While the existing literature on Turkification is often published under the auspices of the social sciences and history, Turkification is inscribed in terms of historical turning points, including the dismantling of the empire and the ensuing violence and ethnic cleansing of the empire's geographical core, the early republican population exchange with Greece in the mid-1920s, the capital tax levied on the non-Muslim population during the Second World War years, and the riots and the mob attacks against non-Muslims on September 6–7, 1955. To these one may add the early republican reform programs that limited the non-Muslim economic capital and the purification of the Turkish language.

This sense of Turkification, as "Turkification-from-above," is associated with a series of reforms and changes that may be spoken of in relation to modernization and westernization of Turkey. By calling the Ottoman-Turkish political elite's project "modernization from above" and by linking it to westernization, Çağlar Keyder notes that modernization from above involved the imposition of the elite's own understanding of modernity (its institutions, beliefs, and behavior) on the people of Turkey, whereas modernization is a "self-generating societal process" (1997, 39). Similarly, after emphasizing modernization through "the expansion of markets" (the elimination of traditional obligations), the spread of protective ideologies and movements" (the redefinition of families, the recasting of identities, and the creation of national and international institutions), and the regulation of the "relations between people and their rulers" (freedoms, human and civil rights, and popular sovereignty), Reşat Kasaba also notes that the application of such a project in Turkey turned out to be a "top-down process" that was "narrow and sterile" (1997, 19–24).

Indeed, both Kasaba and Keyder's renderings are borrowed from different scholars of modernity and modernization including Marshall Berman and Karl Polanyi. For instance, Marshall Berman sees the building of St. Petersburg as "probably the most dramatic instance in world history of modernization conceived and imposed draconically from above" (1983, 176). For him, while the creation of the city is handled by the rulers and it is thus "a symbolic expression of modernization from above," modernization from below came to the fore when the people started to define the public space and the political life according to themselves (1983, 181). It is this rendering of "Turkification-from-above" that is reworked in this study, indicating a limited view of change and progress that created an active process of segregation and discrimination to modernize and westernize the country. When it is considered in terms of the cultural realm, this process involves not only a translation and transformation of the source but also a limited adaptation of it based on the premises of the republican modernization and westernization programs. In this respect, Gökalp's cultural model for the republic, which revolves around the creation of a Turkish essence using Western sources and denies Ottoman sources, is at the core of the Turkification-from-above. Below I try to outline how Turkification-from-above surfaces in the dubbing of early sound films and in the early republican domestic feature films. On the other hand, a different sense of Turkification, perhaps a Turkification-from-below, in relation to translation, adaptation, and piracy of Western texts, will be introduced later as one of the defining traits of Yeşilçam.

Silent Films and the Problem of Intertitles

Until the mid-1920s, when the influence of Hollywood became apparent, cinema had served as entertainment only for the urban cosmopolitan upper classes, while the majority of the population, in rural areas, remained unexposed. Like the films themselves, film magazines were mostly bilingual. Regardless of the site of production of the film, intertitles were most often in French, sometimes in English, and were usually followed by bad Turkish translations in smaller fonts, shown for a shorter duration. When no Turkish intertitles were available, spectators who were unfamiliar with the foreign language were given a written synopsis in Turkish before the show ("Sinemalar ve Seyirciler" 1929, 4). Because of the high illiteracy rate in some areas, a staff member read intertitles to the spectators, a disputed practice particularly after the introduction of Latin script in 1928 and attempts to increase the literacy rate. For the writers of *Sinema Gazetesi* (Cinema Newspaper), the dissemination of the Latin script was a critical reform and they urged film importers to use bigger fonts for the Turkish intertitles and do away with the French ones altogether ("Sesli Filmlere Dair" 1929, 7). They also criticized the conditions of film theaters in Istanbul including the high price of both first- and second-class tickets, the placement of seats very close to the screen, the poor quality of the light, the dim and out of focus images projected on the screen, the absence of fire exits, and the French intertitles ("Sinema Biletleri Pahalıdır!" 1929, 10). The coming of sound, which put an end to intertitles, was a beneficial development in the eyes of these reformers, despite the subsequent development of the more dubious dubbing industry.

Sound Film

By the time sound film arrived in Turkey, Beyoğlu theaters had already cornered the entertainment market. Fikret Adil notes that the Beyoğlu of 1930 was known for "internationally famous nightclubs, variety theaters, and the competition between film theaters to have the best galas, to show the first sound films, and to import the best projection machines" (Scognamillo 1991, 59). When the first sound films appeared, theater owners were aware of this novelty, and it was no longer considered a transgressive innovation, but a new incentive to attract or even exploit unwitting spectators. In one such instance, a writer with the pseudonym *Seyirci* (spectator) criticizes Beyoğlu Şık Theater for its sound films, which were "created" with the help of a gramophone for music, and a couple of kids to provide "sound effects." These kids knocked on a piece of wood when someone knocked on a door in the film, or whistled when a train was seen on the screen (1929, 4). Until the late 1930s, due to the lack of proper sound equipment, many film theaters offered a "variety programming format" with a music concert attached to the exhibition of a film (Gürata 2007, 338). Such tactics soon became an important device for popular filmmakers who claimed to present their spectators with things that were otherwise unavailable to them, be it in the form of a supernatural world or a new technology that had not yet arrived in Turkey.

It is clear that the exploitative nature of the popular film industry was present in its earliest days. While, for instance, *Sinema Gazetesi* claimed a distaste for nudity, it simultaneously promised to publish examples of the nudity trend claimed to be spreading around the world (1929, v. 13, 5). Hollywood films and other Western films presented a Western style of life that was emulated and often adapted by the principal filmgoers, the urban middle and upper classes. Yet such cultural novelties were also taken with a grain of salt, like the bilingual intertitles. The advent of sound film raised issues of identity that had remained literally unspoken in the silent film era. The first sound films were not dubbed, which gave rise to a discussion of nation building and the creation of pure Turkish; some critics/reformers were naively afraid that with the aid of sound film, English and German cultures were going to "invade the earth." Still the writers of *Sinema Gazetesi* assured their readers that a solution would be found ("Tenkit" 1929, 3). That solution came about when Elhamra film theater premièred *The Jazz Singer* (1927) and when the first sound film studio was opened by İpek Film in 1932. Thus the practice of Turkish dubbing became a standard element of film exhibition. In the meantime, the names of Beyoğlu theaters were also Turkified in line with the republican language reforms and the "Citizen Talk Turkish" (*Vatandaş Türkçe Konuş*) campaign developed in 1933 (Özuyar 1999, 34).

Dubbing: (Mis)translation, (Re)writing, and "Turkification"

The creation of scripts to be used in dubbing foreign films involved two stages: first, the original scripts were translated into Turkish; then the translations were worked over by dialogue writers who adapted them for a new audience. The process of rewriting and adaptation, inevitable in all translations enhanced by this double process, is reminiscent of postcolonial states of mimicry, where the colonized native must act the part of belonging to the colonizer while never being quite able or willing to step into his shoes. While Turkey was not formally colonized by the Western powers, the nation-state exhibited a self-colonizing cultural mentality built upon the premises of an anti-imperialist outlook presupposing unevenness between empires and colonies. Indeed, no foreigners had politically colonized the country, yet, as in colonized countries, the elite who led modernizing reforms had Western educations and development ideals. The republican elite first presupposed a national belatedness and then found the cure in the westernization and modernization of the country. As Rey Chow points out,

> In the history of Western imperialism, the Chinese were never completely dominated by a colonial power, but the apparent absence of "enemy" as such does not make the Chinese case any less "third world" (in the sense of being colonized) in terms of the exploitation suffered by the people, whose most important colonizer remains their own government.... While the history of Western imperialism relegates all non-Western cultures to the place of the other, whose value is "secondary" in relation to the West, the task of nationalism in the "third world" is that of (re)inventing the "secondary" cultures themselves as primary, as the uncorrupted origins of "third world" nations' histories and "worth." (1993, 9)

Like Chinese intellectuals, those in Turkey remained obsessed with constructing a nation through their educated and urban imagination and stayed blind to the ethnically and religiously diverse and rural population. The movement of nationalism, which turned inward and sought an originary mythology, involves a violent oppression of its internal others. Chow considers how the narcissism of nationalism usually (mis)translates into an oppositional stance toward the West. Cultural production based on the idea of an essential nation, then, is based on the assumptions of the local elite who themselves are westernized and alienated from their own people. In reading cinema in Turkey, then, one sees how dubbing is not just a matter of rewriting and adapting the othered West, but is also bound up with internal mechanisms involving the violent aspects of nationalism, in terms of both ethnic identities and class positions. By not simply translating but also adapting these films to emphasize and disseminate Turkish cultural codes (i.e., Turkification-from-above), Western films began to provide models of a modernizing ideal and suggest that they did indeed represent the Turkey of the not very distant future.

As indicated above, while many of the reforms in the cultural field did not touch on cinema, control and censorship were commonplace. But there was also some self-control and self-censorship involved in manifestations of republican ideology. The Turkification-from-above, which involved the process of the rebirth and purification of a language, westernization in the field of arts and culture through the use of the Latin alphabet, and films translated, adapted, and rewritten in Turkish, might be thought of as simultaneously oppositional and accommodationist. While nationalism's internal othering worked toward a violent unification and standardization of national identity, the elite's modeling of westernization and modernization undermined traditional social life, thus creating a double bind on the lower classes. In this way, among others, a positivist national project in social engineering solidified the westernized elite's class position through its own reforms. In this respect, filmmakers and producers, who belonged to the elite (though in differing degrees), either controlled their own texts or remained cautious about censorship. However, beyond these predictable and intentional controls, the process of dubbing introduced nationalist urges through a vernacularization. While the value of this vernacularization may be contested in its own borders, it is attractive in terms of cultural exchange. The naive anxiety about the invasion of English and German languages not only resulted in tactical rewriting but also led to a readjustment of the language, providing for an internal center and external other, positioned as the enemy. But given its hegemonic status, this other, whether it was the West or Hollywood, was itself adored by those who presupposed an oppositional alterity. While the reification of the West as exemplary created a love-hate relationship, it has also created ambivalent responses. As the Turkey of republican reformers moved away from its Arabic or Ottoman characteristics by employing the West in place of the East, this project of Turkification-from-above also found its reflection in dubbing.

Dubbing Hollywood

One of the renowned dubbing artists, Ferdi Tayfur, remembers his first foray into sound, dubbing Adolphe Menjou's character Major Rinaldi in *A Farewell to Arms* (dir. Frank Borzage, 1932). Even though he held that lip-synching and correct translation were the most important aspects of the business, when an interviewer from *Son Saat* newspaper asked in 1951 which character he liked the most among those he "created," he did not seem to think that the creation of new characters out of original films contradicted his emphasis on accurate translation. For instance, he expressed pride in creating Arşak Palabıyıkyan, a bushy-mustachioed Armenian version of Groucho Marx. "This character has become so famous that even some Armenians in Istanbul claimed that they are his relatives. But our Arşak is indeed Jewish Kruso Marks" (Tayfur 1985, 82). For Nezih Erdoğan, apart from serving as a means of translating foreign films, dubbing "was also the means by which adaptations and imitations were assimilated, creating identifiable characters and plots for the audience" (2002, 237). But Erdoğan's insightful analysis ends there, without discussing what is made identifiable and what is assimilated. Similarly, Gürata notes with reference to Alim Şerif Onaran that international films were retitled and "altered in order to give the impression that the movie was set in Turkey." Ahmet

Gürata, who calls this "a cheap way of catering to local tastes," also does not pursue this practice's relation to Turkification (2007, 337). This practice of dubbing is not just a translation but also a mistranslation tied to a proposed national cultural model. This (mis)translation not only produces an intercultural adaptation marked by a resistive potential to the West but also provides intimates about what happened to the minorities in Turkey's nation-building project. In this respect, "Turkification-from-above" is a double mechanism that "others" the West and its own minorities simultaneously, by turning a Jewish American character into an Armenian Turk. Nationalist claims inherently bring about the questioning of its others, be it the Americanness of Jews or the Turkishness of Armenians who share a precarious position at the margins of national origin myths.

Another story told by Tayfur suggests an additional imperialist aspect of dubbing. Seeing that Laurel and Hardy films were box office failures, Tayfur proposed a solution after seeing a French copy of *Bonnie Scotland* (Lorel-Hardi Hindistan'da, dir. James W. Horne, 1935) where Laurel and Hardy were dubbed with a British accent. Tayfur went to Robert College, an American high school in Istanbul, to talk with a British teacher in Turkish and to secretly pick up the teacher's accent (Tayfur 1985, 82). He replaced the original jokes with completely new, culturally specific ones that would speak to his audience, and provided the voice for both Laurel and Hardy (Cimcöz 1970, 8). *Bonnie Scotland* was part of a series of Anglophile films that Hollywood released before the Second World War. M. T. Bennett sees the film as an attempt to capitalize on the success of *The Lives of a Bengal Lancer* (dir. Henry Hathaway, 1935), which openly supported British imperialism through the story of a Scottish Canadian fighting against the Indian resistance (1997). Not only was the film officially denounced by the Indian authorities, it was also rejected by the censor boards of Muslim North African countries, though it was shown in Egypt and Turkey with slight alterations. Similarly, by producing stereotypical images of Scots with heavy accents, *Bonnie Scotland* served as an escape from the economic powerlessness of depression-era Americans through identification with the popular imperialism of its allies (Richard Hofstadter, in Bennett 1997, 5). While the imperialist text is explicit in this film, the republican elite had inherited an imperial past and altered it to fit a narcissistic nationalism, unfamiliar to the Indian cause and to the Third World in general. They proposed that Turkey set an example for Third World countries by creating an independent state, but they simultaneously imagined themselves as above other Third World countries, closer to Western countries, and only slightly less developed. It is no wonder that while sending troops to Korea in return for NATO membership, Turkish politicians never showed interest in participating in the Bandung Conference of 1955. Therefore, Turkification-from-above is not quite an anticolonial stance; instead, it is a rewriting that gives primacy to the Western example. This aspect of Turkification-from-above, however, would ultimately produce further discord between the westernized Kemalist intellectuals who led the republican regime and popular filmmakers.

Dubbing and Censorship

In the first decade of the republican regime, there were no central control mechanisms concerning film production or exhibition. Instead, governors were responsible for controlling films within their jurisdiction, while filmmakers, as members of the republican elite, often practiced self-censorship resulting in very few films were made during this era. While little is known about them, it is likely that the content of Turkish intertitles in foreign films was probably controlled, particularly where they touched on issues of national identity and culture. However, with the advent of sound films and the development of dubbing practice, a need for more comprehensive control emerged. In a report presented to the parliament in 1929, Naci Bey stated that imported films were infected by Christian and Jewish propaganda and detrimental to public morality (Erkılıç 2003, 37). In 1932 Mustafa Kemal Atatürk specifically requested that importers stop showing *All Quiet on the Western Front* (dir. Lewis Milestone, 1930). According to Pars Tuğlacı, after watching Milestone's film in 1930, Atatürk had first talked about how touching and accurate the film was in its portrayal of the effects of war, but went on to say that it would not be helpful for the Turkish nation, which had recently emerged from war, to see it (Scognamillo 1991, 36). The republican elite's reforms always took a paternalist attitude and attempted to dictate a correct education for the Turkish people. While the republican reforms instigated the secularization and democratization of the country, the country was nevertheless controlled by a single party, the Republican People's Party, until 1950. Thus, limited attempts to establish multiparty regimes in these early years were quickly abandoned, demonstrating the failures of what Erik J. Zürcher calls "tutelary democracy" (1994, 185). The control and censorship of films started within this context of popular tutelage.

In 1932, "The Directive concerning the Control of Cinema Films" (*Sinema Filmlerinin Kontrolüne Dair Talimatname*) was released, motivated in large part by the concern with educating the nation. As a part of the law demarcating general police duties, a new regulation, prepared in 1934 and finalized in 1939, established a board of controllers to be selected from public officials. This board had a double standard: while foreign films were loosely controlled, strict oversight of domestic films began with the film script, and the board's verdict on them was permanent (Özön 1995a, 61). Controllers did not usually know foreign languages and did not generally bother to read the Turkish translations of the films. Instead, they looked for antimilitarism, religious propaganda, communism, anti-Turkey sentiments, and obscene scenes that antagonized traditional customs and mores (Onaran 1968, 60). Moreover, while film importers were responsible for making any necessary changes, a lack of established controls during the screening of films led to most of these films being screened as shipped. In reality, this was the case for many of the Turkish films as well. The censors banned 4.5 percent of the 9,097 foreign films shown, while asking for revisions for 7.9 percent of them (Gürata 2007, 345). The censorship board's primary concern was monitoring political content based on the current government's political attitude.

Despite discrepancies in the degree of oversight, domestic or foreign social realist and leftist films were consistently the most highly censored. While there were some changes made to the regulation in 1977, 1979, and 1983, it remained in effect more or less until 1986, when a new law transferred the duty of control from the jurisdiction of the Ministry of Interior to the Ministry of Culture. The current law introduced some changes in content, adopted ratings system, and added representatives from the film industry to the board. Despite a few highly controversial decisions, the degree of censorship has been far less restrictive since that time.

Official censorship policies were strengthened by a self-censorship born of the ideas of tutelage and loyalty to Kemalist principles, especially during the early years of foreign film post-synchronization (dubbing). Sacide Keskin, a dialogue writer and dubbing artist during the years of the Second World War when there were lots of American, Arab, and Indian films on the market, reported that she would receive translated scripts and write new dialogue for them tailored to meet cultural and political expectations. As dubbing actors worked from these rewrites, they often made further spontaneous modifications to enhance synchronization. She also explains that she used to make changes in the dialogues by altering anti-Turkish statements in a Bulgarian film or completely rewriting the story of *Çanlar Kimin için Çalıyor* (For Whom the Bell Tolls, dir. Sam Wood, 1943) to eliminate its pro-communist slant (Keskin 1985, 82). While the Turkish censors strictly controlled Eastern Bloc films in the 1950s, Turkey's (and Turkish film importers') increasing debt to the United States due to currency devaluations gave the United States Information Service (USIS) the opportunity to control American film exports to Turkey. The USIS's Information Media Guaranty Program banned Hollywood films such as *Rebel without a Cause* (dir. Nicholas Ray, 1955), *Around the World in 80 Days* (dir. Michael Anderson, 1956), and *Baby Doll* (dir. Elia Kazan, 1956) (Erdoğan and Kaya 2002).[13]

Until the system began to change in the 1980s, those foreign films that had passed the censorship board were subjected to an intricate process of preparation, from dubbing to a political filtration process supported by the Turkish Right and Turkey-based U.S. agencies that combined republican nationalism and anticommunism. The post-synchronization of films was not just a process of (mis)translation, (re)writing, and Turkification, it also acted as a catalyst for the subsequent instruction and creation of a new public divided between a westernized, modern identity and an Eastern, traditional one. This public would continue to interact with Turkish cinema despite the obstacles placed in its path.

Early Feature Films

In 1952, Vehbi Belgil claimed that Turkish films were instruments for publicizing Turkey abroad. If Turkish films reached a high standard of quality, they would attract Western spectators and the rest of the world would learn that "the Turks were clothed like civilized men, they were not blacks, and that Turkish girls had unmatched beauty" (21). But, for Belgil, this ideal would only become possible if the state took the following measures: reduce taxes on films, build modern studios, open a film institute to rival the State Theater and Opera, limit the dubbing of foreign films, and provide incentives for producers to export films and for filmmakers to develop their craft. A constant theme in reviews of Turkish cinema is a desire for direct involvement of the state along these lines. Not only does such a desire reflect support of statism, a faith in centralized state control inherent to the Kemalist ideology of the Republican People's Party, it also reflects a belief that official support will elevate the status of film as an art and emphasizes the cultural project of the republic to raise the level of the arts to standards set by and measured against the West. However, such direct support failed to materialize from either the republican elite or from the center-right parties that came to power after the institution of the multiparty system. This situation created a safe haven for popular filmmaking outside the purview of the conventions of cultural westernization that limited other arts, despite a practice of control through the censorship board. Even more effective was the self-censorship of filmmakers who reflexively supported republican norms. Nonetheless, the reliance on private capital ensured that cinema became a profit-driven industry that placed audience desires above all else.

Early Film Studios

For cinema in Turkey, as in early Western cinema, commercial interests were of the utmost concern from the very beginning. The first Turkish film production company, Kemal Film, was established in 1919. While initially it only imported films, in 1922 the company built a studio and hired the established theater director and actor Muhsin Ertuğrul, who had already made three films in Germany. One of the first films shot by Kemal Film was *Ateşten Gömlek* (Shirt of Flame), an adaptation of a novel by one of Turkey's first women novelists, Halide Edip Adıvar (Çalapala 1947). Around the same time, İpek Film opened a film theater and began to import films, eventually producing them as well. In 1928, it hired Muhsin Ertuğrul to direct the first Turkish sound film *İstanbul Sokaklarında* (On the Streets of Istanbul). Because the first Turkish sound studio did not open until 1932–33, this film was dubbed in Paris with the presence of all but one of the actors, thus making this the first partly dubbed film in Turkey, a practice that was rapidly standardized by Turkish films (Muvahhit 1973a, 91). İpek Film also produced many short films, including straightforward recordings of Karagöz shadow plays, theater-in-the-round shows, and musical performances of singers such as Münir Nurettin and Deniz Kızı Eftelya (Onaran 1981, 140). A third film company established in 1938, Ha-Ka Film, also moved into the production business from the exhibition track. An important practice instigated by this studio was a "Turkified" post-synchronization, which combined the dubbing of foreign films with a montage of short sequences shot in Turkey (Çalapala 1947). Three such

Figure 2.9. Kemal Film Studio in the 1920s

films are *Yeniçeri Hasan* (Janissary Hasan), *Zeynep*, and *Memiş*: "Turkified" foreign films dubbed into Turkish with a few added dramatic scenes played by Turkish actors and musical scenes with Turkish singers. In addition to these fiction films, a documentary using a similar style, *Türk İnkılabında Terakki Hamleleri* (The Leaps of Progress in the Turkish Revolution), combined footage taken from foreign and Turkish newsreels worked into a narrative scheme visualized by a history teacher.

This overview of the earliest studios establishes a number of cues with which to understand the discussion of cinema in Turkey continued in the next few chapters. First of all, none of these studios were comparable in size to those in the United States, Germany, France, or Italy. They opened with minimal equipment and worked primarily with Muhsin Ertuğrul or other theater actor-directors who saw cinema as a secondary business. Unlike in the United States, where the nickelodeon boom resulted in the association of film with lower-class entertainment, in Turkey film production and consumption were primarily upper-class activities in the early years of cinema. Nonetheless, cinema's secondary social role and limited budget resulted in a low quality of film production. Not only was film technology imported as a Western product, few early filmmakers were specifically trained in European standards and techniques of filmmaking. Upon their return, even those who had studied in Europe did not fully benefit from their travels, either because of limited resources or modest skills. Naturally, the strained economic conditions of filmmaking affected the product, and restricted budgets were central to the experience of filmmaking in Turkey from its inception. Writing in 1918, Ertuğrul claimed that it was not possible to make films in Istanbul because there were no cameramen, no studios, no directors, limited stages and costumes, and only inept artists (Özön 1962, 57–58). While the history of cinema in the West is rooted in the late nineteenth century, the first films made in Turkey were produced almost two decades after the invention of the medium.

The republican elite, who espoused a positivist, evolutionary model of society and history, considered this belatedness to be the sole culprit behind the poor quality of Turkish cinema. However, when figures affiliated with the republican reformers made films in the first two decades of the republic, their films also reflected the pitfalls of the republican discourse.

Muhsin Ertuğrul—The "One-Man" of Turkish Cinema

The reign of the Republican People's Party and the career of director Ertuğrul seem comparable when one looks at the political and cinematic histories of Turkey. Historians of cinema in Turkey generally accept Nijat Özön's (1962) criticism that Ertuğrul was more successful in creating a "one-man rule" in cinema, in preventing others from making films, than as a director. Several directors who started their careers during Ertuğrul's last years talk about his unwillingness to let City Theater actors act in other directors' films (Kamil 2000, 19; Kenç 1993, 27; Havaeri 2002). Entering the world of film as a stunt player for Istanbul theaters, Ertuğrul lived briefly in Paris, Berlin, and Moscow. While his first trip abroad was only for the theater, he shot a number of films in Germany and Russia, in 1919 and 1925, respectively. However, according to his own accounts, he worked in the cinema business in Europe only to support himself while trying to develop a career as a theatrical artist (Scognamillo 1998, 61). In accordance with republican cultural models, he did not favor such Ottoman theater forms as theater-in-the-round or shadow plays. Instead, he favored Western-style plays performed and directed by non-Muslims during the Ottoman era and also by Turks, especially after the 1910s. Ertuğrul's conservative position led him to reproduce the cultural ideology of the republican elite and thus his interest in cinema was secondary at best, and was largely motivated by a desire to fund the high art of the City Theater through money earned from the popular art of film. While he ultimately became better known for his films, his interest in cinema never really developed. This prejudice against film by Turkey's first continuous film director is indicative of the perception of Turkish film in general as a second-rate cultural form.

In 1953, Muhsin Ertuğrul made his last movie, *Halıcı Kız* (Carpet Weaver Girl). Funded by a bank, it was the first color film in Turkey (processed in Germany) but did poorly at the box office, and Ertuğrul retired from directing. In the same year, he was also preparing a remake of Hugo Haas's 1951 film, *Pickup*, but the project was later completed by Baha Gelenbevi under the title *Kaldırım Çiçeği* (Sidewalk Flower, 1953). Nijat Özön notes similarities between the directors, Ertuğrul and Haas, but he did not elaborate. Instead he simply says: "To introduce Ertuğrul to Americans, saying the 'Turkish Haas' would suffice and Haas to Turks as the 'American Ertuğrul'" (1962, 109). In the *All Movie Guide*, Hal Erickson notes that Haas was a Czech-born movie Renaissance man who is generally excluded from scholarly auteur film histories. Already a scriptwriter and actor of Czechoslovakian comedies, Haas escaped to the United States from the

Nazis during the Second World War. While in the United States during the 1950s, he wrote, directed, and acted in various melodramas. Erickson characterizes them as "a lonely middle-aged man (Haas) lured into an ill-advised sexual relationship with a blonde trollop (nearly always played by Haas' protégée Cleo Moore) with fatal results" (2005).

In *Pickup*, after his puppy dies, an old man marries a young blond who later plans to kill him for his money and run away with her lover. In the meantime, the old man experiences psychosomatic hearing loss but regains it in a car accident! In the end, he gets a divorce from his vamp wife and finds himself a new puppy. Despite being the dominant figure of early Turkish cinema, directing films in Germany in 1919 such as *Samson, sein eigener Mörder* (Samson, His Own Murderer) and films in the Soviet Union in 1925 such as *Spartakus*, and having the best available conditions to make film in Turkey, Ertuğrul's last project was an ambitionless remake of a melodrama with mundane intrigue, tawdry coincidences, and sleazy sentimentality—a film modeled after those of Hollywood's East European trash filmmaker Hugo Haas. Why would Ertuğrul produce remakes of a low-budget Hollywood melodrama when as early as 1924 he had written of the Ottoman Melodrama Company's melodramas: "Today there is no more taste and patience left to see any of these works" (Sevinçli 1990, 126)?

Ertuğrul was the director of Istanbul City Theaters that dominated the theater world of the early republican era. City Theaters had a drama and comedy department under Ertuğrul, in addition to an operetta or revue department that produced popular plays. Ertuğrul preferred playing and directing classical and serious plays, an activity in line with his education in the West and with the republican cultural projects that aimed to nurture the high culture of the West in Turkey. He also did not feel close to traditional theatrical forms, which were suppressed by the republican cultural reforms. Moreover, he claimed that he was not under the influence of the West and the lowly genres of Western theaters, distinguishing himself from popular Ottoman theater-makers. Such a distinction between the traditional, Eastern, and lowly Ottoman culture, and the modern, westernized, and higher republican culture is presupposed by the republican elite. Eastern theaters were not in any way within Ertuğrul's purview—even Japanese theater, which was valorized and utilized by Sergei Eisenstein, was not of interest to Ertuğrul (Scognamillo 1998, 61). In short, like his counterparts in other areas of republican culture under state control, he reproduced the ideology of the republican elite despite his actual independence from the state. Last but not least, Ottoman theaters modeled on Western examples either involved mostly non-Muslim actors because there were no female Muslim actors, or were directly run by non-Muslims. Ertuğrul's criticism of these theaters was also based on their absence of nationalism. When asked about the acting style and pronunciation in early Turkish films done by others, Bedia Muvahhit, an actress both of City Theater and Ertuğrul's films, says that the mainstream style was that of late nineteenth-century Ottoman theater, especially of

Figure 2.10. *Halıcı Kız* (Carpet Weaver Girl, Muhsin Ertuğrul, 1953)

the Ottoman Melodrama Company, but not that of the City Theater. This
style was based on Ottoman syntax incorporating the influences of Arabic,
Persian, and French, and, more important, of the accented speech of Ottoman Armenians (1973b, 94). The claim of a more "clear" pronunciation, in
"purer" Turkish, should be considered part and parcel with the republican
reforms concerning the creation of a national culture.

Figure 2.11. *İstanbul Sokaklarında* (On the Streets of Istanbul, Muhsin Ertuğrul, 1931)

While he criticized melodramas, Ertuğrul nonetheless made a number of black and white adaptations or remakes of Western melodramas including *Halıcı Kız* (Carpet Weaver Girl, 1953). As mentioned previously, this melodrama, which is filmed as stiffly as the silent French *films d'art*, is representative of Ertuğrul's oeuvre as a filmmaker. Ertuğrul's proximity to the republican elite and his respectable position as a man of theater provided him with relatively good support for his films, also giving him the opportunity to be the director of the first sound and first partly dubbed film, *İstanbul Sokaklarında* (Streets of Istanbul, 1931).

Like the historians of Turkish cinema, filmmakers such as Şadan Kamil, who had been to film school in Germany and worked at the RCA Studios in England and Pathé in France, saw Ertuğrul's films as theatrical and historical, with actors entering the scene as they did on a theater stage (2000, 15). Like the operettas, light operas or musicals of late Ottoman and early republican popular vaudeville and variety theaters with spoken dialogue, Ertuğrul produced a number of films modeled on German operetta films and French vaudevilles as well as famous Turkish operettas. These films were just "filmed vaudevilles" or "filmed operettas" that served to bring the Istanbul City Theater to the screens of film theaters throughout Turkey (Onaran 1973, 82). For instance, concerning his *Söz Bir Allah Bir* (One Word, One God, 1933), Atilla Dorsay noted that the camera was fixed, allowing little to no movement. There were pans during dialogues and no shot-reverse-shot editing, but these pans were not even done with care: they frequently showed the silent actor while one heard the other actor talking off-screen. In the scenes with singing, Ertuğrul typically shot just the singer, ignoring peripheral action (1986, 110–11). Thus Ertuğrul's films were a combination of adaptations, remakes, and theatrical elements. However, he also adapted a number of Turkish novels about the War of Independence and the building of a new nation; these were the films that strengthened his position both as a filmmaker and a favorite of the republican elite.

Still, reviewing his career as a filmmaker, apart from his highly criticized insistence on dominating the film scene in Turkey, his films consistently reflect the dualities and dilemmas of cinema in Turkey. In line with the dicta of republican cultural projects, many Turkish filmmakers claimed that they wanted to make realist films about sociopolitical and economic issues that would aid in the education of the masses and the dissemination of republican reforms, but they were unable to do so due to insufficient infrastructure and the profit-driven economics of the cinema market. Ertuğrul's films share these qualities and, given the trying conditions of the era in which he worked, his contribution remains notable and set the stage for Yeşilçam.

Turkification-from-above as Hayal

Writing on *Söz Bir Allah Bir*, Atilla Dorsay criticized Ertuğrul for not domesticating the French vaudeville play on which the film was based; the husband-wife-lover triangle, notes Dorsay, was not at all suitable for

Turkish customs. The idea of suitability had to do with the modernization efforts of the republican elites, including modifications of social life (1986, 111). The republican elite did not merely attempt to take the technology of the West, as did other early westernizers, but tried to adopt a Western lifestyle, beginning with the elites and intended to trickle down to the masses. Republican reforms concerning civil law and clothing, and the introduction of various cultural novelties, such as republican balls featuring Western dance music like the tango or waltz, can all be viewed as elements within an encompassing visual revolution that attempted to alter the very look of the country. The visual reforms, such as the replacement of fezzes with hats, the banning of headscarves in official public spaces, and the dissemination of Atatürk portraits and statues as an integral part of the interior and exterior decoration of public buildings, were also introduced in films and influenced those in control of the censor boards. This led to naive reactions against showing arid lands of the Anatolian plateau rather than representing rural life with a mechanized agricultural practice.

While imagining scenery that would be comparable to the industrialized West was merely a trifle in contrast with the harsh realities of a country exhausted by decades of war, such a focus was not only about "dreaming" and "imagining," but rather mirrors the reality of being an underdeveloped non-Western country and was a specter continually haunting the republican elite. The manufacture of the West in a non-Western country had to be captured in the spirit of its own non-Western environment if it was to be effective. While this environment was an idealized rural, backward country, it was constructed through an image of the picturesque

Figure 2.12. *Leblebici Horhor* (Nutmaker Horhor, Muhsin Ertuğrul, 1923)

and industrialized Western countryside. Dorsay's criticism of Ertuğrul for not "domesticating" French vaudeville bears the mark of this duality—the image of the West versus the West itself—which cannot be easily reconciled. In its relation to the West and its cinemas, Ertuğrul, and the filmmakers, film historians, and film critics who came after him all shared a common dream that was foiled by the films themselves, which continually reminded them of their belatedness, their not-yet-there status. Their dream is spectral: whenever you come close to it, it vanishes by reiterating the state of not-yet-being-there. This is shared by republican intellectuals and filmmakers—a primordial situation that conditions artistic production either by incessantly attempting to be there (westernization) or by attempting to deny the attempt to get there (anti-westernization). Yet cinema, a product of Western technology and an imported Western medium, is inscribed with its Western identity. It is a humanistic history of visual technologies since the advent of perspectival vision. In this vein, "Turkification" will be taken as not a schlocky way station but rather as a defining trait of cinema in Turkey. Like Ertuğrul and his contemporaries, Yeşilçam filmmakers also tried to translate, adapt, remake, vernacularize, and domesticate a medium that is inherently Western and demands a response simply on the grounds of its otherness. In doing this, they produced a different sense of Turkification, a Turkification-from-below, rooted in the idiosyncrasies and coincidences of a self-serving film industry.

3

Early Yeşilçam
The Advent of Yeşilçam in the 1950s

The *Trans-ing* of Yeşilçam

Two different screens informed the cinema of Turkey: one in the non-Muslim, westernized, and cosmopolitan space of the Sponeck beer hall and the other in Muslim, Turkish, old Istanbul's Fevziye coffee house where Western films were exhibited on a Karagöz screen. The republican reformers imagined a national culture bereft of non-Muslim minorities, as they simultaneously dreamed of westernization, of a secular, modern society with cosmopolitan entertainment practices. However, the traditional and Muslim Istanbul that was initially closed to the traditional entertainment practices, later embraced a popular cinematic practice, Yeşilçam, that offered an alternative path for translating or transforming the West.

In this cultural current flowing from the Fevziye coffee house, there are two different ways of "trans-ing,"[1] that is, transferring, translating, or simply moving across or outside, while finding yourself in an intermediate state, between waking and sleeping—perhaps, in the most Orientalist sense, between an awake, enlightened West and a sleepy, dark East. The republican elite's claim to Enlightenment and their positivistic social engineering project attempted to modify daily life and cultural practices, bringing them closer to Western ideals. Kemalism relied on a metaphor of light: the republican officials, teachers, and soldiers, bringing enlightenment to the farthest parts of Anatolia, where traditional and backward forces of religion, feudal economic and social systems, and rural life persisted. This process required translations and transformations, because unlike the republican "Turkification-from-above," the people's translation, adaptation, or transformation of republican reforms produced another response to the West and westernization—a "Turkification-from-below." This popular Turkification may be observed in Yeşilçam cinema or *arabesk* music, both of which, remaining outside the realm of high culture, offered accessible cultural routes.[2] These alternative modes of translation involve a sociological sense of "transitions," similar to Bollywood's narrative form that has a special resonance in "transitional" societies. Thus, various ways of *"trans-ing"* are at stake in this intermediate state between the West and the East—neither entirely one nor entirely the other; once the presence of the West is felt through its colonial presence, technology, or through the westernization and modernization projects of the non-Western elite. This transitional state, at the same time, produces a continual transfer, translation, or transformation of the West. By naming this "Turkification," this chapter elucidates the links between popular cinemas of the West and the non-West, and places Turkification in relation to cinematic adaptations, domestications, imitations, and melodramatic modality.

Toward Yeşilçam: Egyptian Films and *Arabesk*

The Organization of the Friends of Turkish Film was founded in 1952. The following year it organized the first Turkish film festival, following a contest organized in 1948 by the Domestic Filmmakers Association to determine the best Turkish films. Among the friends of Turkish film were writers, filmmakers, and journalists such as Burhan Arpad, Lütfi Ö. Akad, Aydın Arakon, Orhon M. Arıburnu, and Hıfzı Topuz. Later, in 1959, Arpad wrote that the first indications of cinema as an art form evolved in the years between 1947 and 1953. For him, among the things that occurred during this time that contributed to this evolution were the reduction of sales tax on domestic films from 75% to 25% in 1948, the severe decrease in exhibitions of Egyptian films, the increase in the number of people expressing dislike for American and European films, an increase in the number of films involving artistic realism that shied away from the influences of theatrical filmmaking (such as *Vurun Kahpeye* [Hit the Whore, dir. Lütfi Ö. Akad, 1949], *Yüzbaşı Tahsin* [Captain Tahsin, dir. Orhon M. Arıburnu, 1950], *Vatan İçin* [For the Motherland, dir. Aydın Arakon, 1951], and *Efelerin Efesi* [The Best Buccaneer, dir. Şakir Sırmalı, 1952]) (Scognamillo 1998, 137). Arpad was not fond of adaptations, Turkifications, and other domestic films presenting a complete form of entertainment for spectators. Instead, he identified originality and authenticity as the criteria of propriety within the republican reform program. Arpad makes three important points in this short quotation. The first is related to the economics of filmmaking. With the help of the tax cut, various investors established film production companies for instant returns. The second point concerns Egyptian films, which were ostensibly present in the Turkish film market during the Second World War and produced a differentiated pattern of spectatorship in Turkey dependent on socioeconomic class and political position. Arpad's last point concerns the choice of films based on quality and artistry. He preferred films with nationalist sentiment, especially those about the War of Independence that led to the foundation of the Turkish Republic.

Complying with the republican cultural reform programs, Friends of Turkish Cinema announced that their aim was "the advancement of Turkish filmmaking in terms of art and to raise its level of respectability

Figure 3.1. The cover of Domestic Filmmaker's Association's booklet which features Rakım Çalapala's short overview of the history of Turkish cinema until 1947

in the world of international filmmaking, as well as determining the best domestic films of the year" ("Türk Film Dostları..." 1952, 11). Arpad is careful to note that the tax cut was made possible by the government of the Republican People's Party (RPP), which ruled the country until 1950. With the 1950 elections, the Democratic Party (DP) came to power, and with them, more liberal economic policies deviating from the republican elite's statist measures. The DP was supported by the traditional and more religious peripheral political forces, which started to migrate to major metropolitan areas like Istanbul and Ankara, making the limitations of republican reform projects immediately apparent. The proponents of the RPP saw this as the embodiment of regressive forces. This indeed was the early construction of what Reşat Kasaba called "the Turkish experience," of "the old and the new–existing side by side and contending with, but more typically strengthening, each other" (1997, 17). The binaries of the Turkish experience are not very different from those of modernity and modernization processes in many nation-states: Western and non-Western, Turks and non-Turks (Kurds and other ethnicities), secular state and religious masses, center and periphery, urban and rural, wealthy and impoverished. With this in mind, Arpad's choice of films and belief about the potential of Turkish cinema become more specifically meaningful: he was yearning for an artful, realistic cinema that idealized the republican regime, its reforms, and its fight against its enemies, perceived as the others of the nation-state, both external and internal. The tax cut and the increase in film production inaugurated a popular film industry that ran parallel to the increased visibility of the others of the republican regime. This latter thread, then, created an alternative path of westernization and modernization. Thus, whereas republican cultural forms mimicked the Western perspectival and illusionistic tradition, traditional theatrical forms persisted in Yeşilçam, which placed such non-illusionistic and nonrepresentational practices together with the Western ones.

In line with the Turkish experience, which has involved the old and the new simultaneously, the rise of Turkified popular cultural forms is visible in a number of films made in the 1940s. These pre-Yeşilçam films were not simply adaptations; they were comedies and melodramas presenting a complete venue of entertainment. One such film, started by Muhsin Ertuğrul but finished by dubbing artist Ferdi Tayfur, *Nasreddin Hoca Düğünde* (Nasreddin Hodja at the Wedding, 1940), made use of different performances such as traditional Hodja jokes[3] narrated by Reşit Gürzap, songs of Müzeyyen Senar filmed during a circumcision ceremony, the shows of magician Zati Sungur, and Tayfur's performance of his dialogues from Laurel and Hardy films (Özön 1962, 108). While such pre-Yeşilçam films combined aspects of traditional and modern to entertain urban lower and middle classes, the early Yeşilçam developed a seeming narrative coherency by knotting the early films' episodic aspects. However, Yeşilçam's Turkified melodramas supported by song scenes were produced after the Second World War, after Turkey's filmmakers had been exposed to Egyptian, and to some degree Indian, popular films.

The Popularity of Egyptian Films in the 1940s

During the Second World War, the importation of feature films, celluloid films, and equipment from European countries came to a halt, which led to an alternative importation route through Egypt. Along with Hollywood films imported through Egypt, Egyptian films were also introduced to the Turkish market and soon became very popular. Nijat Özön notes that in the years between 1938 and 1944, while only seventeen domestic feature films were made, sixteen Egyptian films were shown. While there were around 100 or more Egyptian films shown in Turkey during the 1940s (Cantek 2000, 34), the wave was started by *Dumu al-hubb* (Tears of Love, dir. Muhammad Karim, 1936). According to Özön, when this film was shown for the first time, Turkish spectators who had not seen a domestic feature for three years at the time, rushed to Şehzadebaşı in old Istanbul, stopped traffic on the street, and broke the windows of the film theater in anticipation of seeing famous Arab singers and people in fezzes and robes (1962, 117). While in the early years the song sequences of Egyptian films with Muhammad Abd al-Wahhab and Umm Kulthum were not dubbed, Turkish singers later started to dub them. This practice kept the melody relatively intact although the lyrics were altered by the Turkish singers, an act supported by the Film Control Commission, which banned songs sung in Arabic. In 1942, the general secretariat of the RPP warned the Ministry of Internal Affairs about the number of Arab-language films, noting that Arab films were a threat to the Turkish language in the areas bordering Syria (Cantek 2000, 35). This ban, then, was not just a reflection of wartime conditions, but more important of Turkish nationalism, which had become increasingly fervent during the war, as evidenced by the ethnic and religious discrimination accompanying the creation of a "secular Turkish" country, similar to the exclusion of internal others of the Turkish nation who were subjected to a special wealth tax in the same year.

The popularity of Egyptian films coincided with an increase in the number of film theaters in Anatolian cities and in the peripheries of urban areas. Therefore, beginning with Egyptian melodramas, film content developed toward the tastes of an increasingly rural, lower-class spectatorship. As they watched Egyptian films, in Hürrem Erman's words, the practice of filmgoing for entertainment was born in its most "primitive" form (1973, 26). It was the melodramatic modality of these films that attracted the spectators who became the driving force behind Yeşilçam films. However, this modality differs from what Viola Shafik calls "musical melodramas" in relation to *Dumu al-hubb*, which features lengthy performances of popular singers. Shafik tied this genre to a tradition stemming from pre-Islamic Arab culture of singers reciting or singing poetry (1998, 109). For her, musical melodramas carried elements of traditional Arabic music that intended to produce specific moods and emotions. However, this argument is undermined by Egyptian director Ahmed Badrakhan, who notes that *tarab*, excitement or delight attained through repetition, tied to *maqam*, or the melodic mode of traditional music, is detrimental to spectatorial motivation because such an incessant repetition of the most exciting part until the attainment of *tarab* is not viable in popular cinema (Shafik 1998, 112). Indeed, what Shafik called musical melodramas were not quite musicals, for the songs did not generally serve a narrative function tied to the plot, but were there to set the mood or were used as an entertaining interlude. Much like Bollywood or Yeşilçam films, these scenes with singing, which in formalist terms mark narrative discontinuity, were extra attractions or spectacles. Similar to the distinction between Bollywood and Calcutta or between Yeşilçam and the republican cultural project, Egyptian cinema was not devoid of such an ideological controversy between what is and what should be: "Since its emergence, Egyptian cinema has preferred to produce (or reproduce) emotions rather than the real," writes Abbah Fadhil Ibrahim (Shafik 1998, 110).

The melodramatic is contrasted against the realistic, for the latter is frequently understood by Third World intellectuals as the true and proper form of producing culture. Yet processes akin to Turkification introduced the element of *hayal* or *wayang* in the context of popular cinemas in a geography ranging from Arab countries to Iran, India, and Southeast Asia. The significance of this extensive geography for Turkish film emerges through a variety of recurring themes: colonial experiences, projects and violent practices of nation building, definitions of a national culture, attempts to realign the limits of the modernity, and the fight against traditional elements. In these geographies, the products of popular cinema were consumed not only in their native country but also in their regional vicinity, suggesting that they resonated not simply within national or cultural borders, but in societies that shared a particular relationship to modernity.

Throughout this geographic spectrum, traditional forms of storytelling (both folk and religious) and performances that shared a similar narrative formation have persisted. As traditional performance forms, w*ayang* or *hayal* relied upon performers who told anecdotal stories with narrative gaps and breaks, repetitions, and minimalist symbolic props. Coupled with their nonrepresentational *mise-en-scéne* and non-illusionistic narrationality, such performances had very flexible plots based on a minimal set of recurring themes and narrative elements. Common to these forms is an element of the journey that is more or less related to the journey of spirits (or specters) without much loyalty to spatiotemporal consistency. Such presentations were divided into integral narrational units that were not necessarily related. It was up to the performer or puppeteer to improvise elements from the basic frame. In particular, the Egyptian melodramas popular in Turkey in the 1940s and later some Bollywood films involved various musical scenes that were unrelated to the plot. Instead, those scenes were singular units or episodes that in many cases stood on their own and did so by breaking the representationality and illusionistic characteristics of cinematic realism, reclaiming *hayal* as their defining quality. This spatiotemporal irrelevance to the story is a reminder of both the journeys of spirits across time and space and the offer of a spectatorial attraction through music promising entertainment and ecstasy, rather than mere narrative closure.

In the cinema of Turkey, there was not only a controversy between realist and melodramatic modalities but also between approaches to westernization: one from above and the other from below. Film producer Hürrem Erman claimed that his first film, *Damga* (Stamp, dir. Seyfi Hava-eri, 1948) ran against Muhsin Ertuğrul's *Halıcı Kız*, which was in concert with republican reformism. He also added that during the gala of Ertuğrul's film in a first-run theater in Beyoğlu, a spectator from the second balcony, after hearing a long tirade by a shepherd in the film, shouted sarcastically: "Oh man, are you a shepherd or Shakespeare" (1973, 27)? The republican project was about creating Shakespeares, Mozarts, and Swiss villages throughout the war-torn, barren lands of Anatolia. Hence the cultural violence associated with the attempt to dismantle what ran counter to their project. Anatolia was the site of the republican dream. In this respect, Egyptian, Indian, or popular Turkish films complicated and hindered this project by presenting ambivalent and alternative routes of westernization.

The Response to Egyptian Films and Arabesk

Despite the bans and other reservations of the republican elite against Egyptian films, these films were not merely popular but also had a role in the rise of *arabesk* (Arabesque, or deemed to be like Arab cultural forms) music and culture, which became a truly widespread cultural response of the migrants living in the peripheral parts of the urban centers, especially Istanbul after the late 1960s. As noted earlier, Ziya Gökalp and the republican elite modeled an idea of synthesis between the West and the "Turkish" folk culture, while disregarding elements of the East, represented by the strains of Islamic and Ottoman culture. Thus they preferred Western musical forms over local forms and attempted to synthesize Western classical music with Turkish folk music, for instance, by inviting Béla Bartók to modernize and polyphonize the monophonic Turkish folk music (Tekelioğlu 1996). As much as *arabesk* music and culture was deemed backward, rural, and fatalistic and therefore excluded from state radio and television broadcasts during the 1970s and early 1980s, its arbitrary but effective combination of Western and Eastern musical instrumentation and singing styles produced a hybrid form representing the ever-present clashes and controversies of Turkish culture. In its ambivalent relation to the West, *arabesk* culture grew with migration from rural areas to shantytowns or squatter settlements (*gecekondus*) that popped up in urban peripheries and then started to infiltrate urban centers. However, though the form initially responded to internal migration and protested urban culture, it later came to be associated with and even incorporated aspects of urbanism. Slowly becoming mainstream, *arabesk* culture eventually came to be incorporated into the upper-class urban practices. The increased visibility of *arabesk*, initially a protest about the conditions of urban life, did not succeed in producing much change in class positions and patterns. The lower classes of Turkey still reside in the peripheries of urban centers and commute to the center for work.

Arabesk seems to have a double significance in relation to Turkish culture: if it is not totally exterminated, whatever is repressed by the projects of a national culture returns as a "specter" and haunts these projects in one or another form. The presence of *arabesk* music coincided with the increased "visibility" of Kurds in supposedly Turkish urban centers, where the clash of ethnic identities subsumed by the national narrative became apparent. Seen from this perspective, *arabesk* musicians are portrayed as a crisis in the republican cultural project through the backdrop provided by the much-disliked influence of Egyptian cinema, Arab music and culture, and Indian cinema; and by the ever-present attempts to "purify" the Turkish language through omitting Persian or Arabic words. Today some Turkish or Kurdish *arabesk* musicians have become incorporated as cultural "classics," much like the earlier Turkish performers who translated and then performed Arabic songs in Egyptian films, and also much like the earlier representatives of Ottoman court music. Today such popular musical forms exist together with other high and low Western forms, such as classical music and pop or rock.

The resonance of Yeşilçam and *arabesk* against a backdrop of Egyptian films and their "Turkified" songs exemplifies the popularity of this alternative route of cultural modernization and westernization. This is not surprising, as the songs in Egyptian films also involved a practice of westernization and modernization: Muhammad Abd al-Wahhab—who helped produce, acted in, and performed songs in *Dumu al-hubb*—was responsible for various innovations and changes in music. "He introduced various dance rhythms, like tango, rumba, samba, and foxtrot, and was the first to use song duets...derived from the conventions of operetta" (Shafik 1998, 113). This was not very different from popular musical forms and Yeşilçam, for both presented a hybrid of West and East; not as dictated from above, but emerging in their own flux. Thus Egyptian films not only reflected a similar response to the West, but their popularity was also easy for filmmakers to exploit.

Aside from Egyptian films, the influx of non-Western cinemas also involved Indian films that entered the Turkish market after 1947. During the mid-1950s, popular Indian melodramas such as Raj Kapoor's *Awara* (Vagabond, 1951) were hits, as was the case in many non-Western countries (see Iordanova et al. 2006). Unlike social realist Indian films, such melodramas also resonated with the practice of Turkification. Ahmet Gürata notes that various Indian films that arrived in the Turkish market after *Awara* were retitled to include the word *Awara* (2008). Moreover, several remakes of *Awara* were made in Yeşilçam until the 1980s. These entertainment schemes involving film and songs were later integrated by Yeşilçam initially with folk music but later on with *arabesk*. Starting in the early 1970s, *arabesk* singers such as Orhan Gencebay or Ferdi Tayfur produced films that repeated the narrative formulas of 1950s and 1960s folk singer melodramas. As a result, Yeşilçam's process of Turkification is not a clear-cut linear and progressive project but an ambivalent, heterogeneous, and ruptured practice that cannot be reduced to a genealogical model, but thrives with a pragmatics of modality marked by multiple and illimitable performances.

Toward Yeşilçam: Film Industry "Turkified"

"Why are our films not as perfect as those of America, Europe, and even our neighbor Egypt?" The Domestic Filmmakers Association's answer to this question was: "Our domestic films are forced to gather financial returns to compensate for production costs, only from domestic box office revenues" (Yerli Film Yapanlar Cemiyeti, 1947). While Hollywood films were exhibited internationally and Egyptian films were exhibited in other Arab countries, very few Turkish films were exhibited outside of the country and the films' cost was only recouped by domestic ticket sales. However, following the end of the Second World War, there was some activity in filmmaking, which persuaded some filmmakers to invest in domestic films. To further their profits and to increase the number of films made in Turkey, the organization demanded that the government reduce the income tax on domestic films and filmmakers, cut the tax on ticket revenues from 75 percent to 20 percent, and cut the taxes on the importation of film equipment. According to the organization, this would improve the abilities of Turkish filmmakers and artists and make the nation proud of its cinema, and lead to increased exportation of film. Not surprisingly, the Domestic Filmmakers Association saw cinema as a combination of art and business that could make a nation both proud and rich.

Such lobbying by film producers who were members of this organization was also voiced and supported in film magazines. Sezai Solelli, the editor of *Yıldız* (Star) magazine, noted that the Turkish filmmakers were not asking for the direct support of the state, as in Egypt, but only for a cut in the numerous taxes imposed on the film industry in Turkey, including filmmakers' contracts, ticket prices, and the revenues of production companies (1948, 38). Under such conditions, even the cheapest Turkish movie cost three times more than the importation and dubbing costs of an Egyptian film, which left the Turkish filmmakers in a disadvantaged position. To protect its own industry, Egyptian taxes on domestic films were lower than those in Turkey, and Egyptian theaters were required to show a set number of domestic films, as was the case in some European countries at the time. That very year, a new tax regulation created a crucial impetus for the popular Turkish film industry, which led to a remarkable increase of domestic films in the following years.

A Short Note on Cinema Organizations and Laws

One of the complicating factors for the cinema in Turkey was the multitude of organizations established, often unsuccessfully, to promote and support filmmaking. In addition to the Domestic Filmmakers Association, the Cinema and Filmmakers Organization (*Sinemacılar ve Filmciler*

Cemiyeti) was established in 1946 by a group of producers, importers, and filmmakers. Parallel with emerging organizations and associations, the evolution of cinema into a more defined business took place in the late 1950s through the clarification of production, distribution, and exhibition networks as distinct entities. As the industry stabilized, a number of other filmmaker organizations were founded, such as the Producers Organization in 1962 and the Union of Cinema Workers (*Sine-iş*) in 1963. Despite a number of attempts at unionization, the Turkish film industry, much like some of the other industrial sectors, has fervently fought against workers' rights and unionization. Several organizations founded in the1970s, including the Film Industry Foundation (*Film-San Vakfı*, 1975) and the Film Workers Union of Turkey (*Türkiye Film İşçileri Sendikası*, 1978) ceded their functions to organizations established in the 1980s, such as the Film Producers Organization (*Film Yapımcıları Derneği*), the Professional Association of the Owners of Cinema Works (*Sinema Eseri Sahipleri Meslek Birliği*), the Film Actors Organization (*Sinema Oyuncuları Derneği*), the Modern Film Actors Organization (*Çağdaş Sinema Oyuncuları Derneği*), the Cinema Workers Union (*Sinema Emekçileri Sendikası*), and the Film Critics Organization (*Sinema Yazarları Derneği*). As seen from the proliferation of such organizations, the Turkish film industry was not a very clearly regulated and organized industry in terms of relations between production companies and workers, and in terms of the basic workers' rights, including fair contracts, insurance, and the like. Mahir Özerdem, who acted in a Turkish-Italian coproduction, *Safiye Sultan* (La sultana Safiyè, dir. Guiseppe di Martino and Fikri Rutkay, 1955), wrote in 1954 that Italians worked with strict contracts; moreover, actors and crew, all of whom were unionized, were always on schedule (6). In Turkey, however, actors worked on multiple contracts at the same time, and went from one film set to another. Such differences between the work habits of Western and Turkish film industries were always striking for the Turkish filmmakers, yet even as they bemoaned the different standards, nothing changed: such changes would have run the risk of increasing the cost of films and thereby decreasing profits.

Likewise, the first Turkish law concerning cinema and films (other than censorship laws) as well as videotapes and audiotapes was passed in 1986, when Yeşilçam was already fading. This law reflected a meeting point of various interests: filmmakers and importers were not happy when their films were pirated in the videotape industry and shown in public places such as coffee houses, bars, and restaurants without their permission; and the state was not happy with the circulation of pirate videotapes of films with "divisive ideologies," such as the later films of Yılmaz Güney that were banned in Turkey at the time (Özön 1995a, 58). In this respect, while filmmakers were happy to openly steal from foreign sources, they didn't appreciate it when others pirated their films. The state represented its usual interest in cinema, which focused primarily on taxation, control, and censorship, thereby letting the industry evolve on its own.

The Conditions of Filmmaking

The disorganization that continued throughout the early years of the Yeşilçam industry had its roots in the world of instant profit created by the 1948 tax cut that allowed them to try their luck at large-scale businesses. Like the early years of cinema in the United States, filmmaking in the early Yeşilçam era was not an attractive profession for the elite, so the film industry relied upon instant capital from various sources. Film production companies, which started to gather in the vicinity of Yeşilçam Street, sprouted like grass during the 1950s, from around ten in 1948 to more than one hundred in 1961 (Sason 1961a, 101). However, this increase in the number of production companies was not accompanied by an increase in the technical qualities of filmmaking. The available infrastructure of film production and exhibition remained ineffectual, which was also the case for film distribution until the late 1950s when distributors became increasingly important.

There were no state-funded or state-controlled film studios in Turkey, nor well-developed or technologically sound studios in the private sector that would be comparable to Western studios. Unlike Hollywood, which emerged from a constellation of film companies and studios, the Turkish film industry was named after a street that housed the offices of several film production companies. The increased number of films and film production companies did not translate into an increase in the number of available studios or postproduction laboratories. Throughout Yeşilçam's rise in the 1950s, the films were mostly shot *en plein air* in Istanbul or at one of several lavish former Ottoman aristocratic mansions and middle-class houses, which were rented to the filmmakers and used repeatedly as sets in several films. In 1951, *Yıldız* magazine reported that Istanbul was turning into Hollywood thanks to filmmakers shooting outdoor scenes and drawing the attention of crowds as they worked. "Throughout this summer," the report continued, "we came across such scenes in places such as the beaches, Sirkeci station, the slopes of Mühürdar, the Babıali incline, the shores of the Bosporus, the Princess Islands and the Dolmabahçe pier" ("Hollywood'a Dönen şu İstanbul" 1951, 9). The films that took place outside of Istanbul were generally shot in nearby towns and villages to reduce the transportation and lodging costs. The only existing film studios at the time were those used for dubbing foreign films, some of which turned into low quality postproduction studios. Director Şadan Kamil said that in the 1940s the film laboratory of Marmara Film Studio had a number of handmade wooden tubs that were five feet deep and one foot wide and used to wash the rolls of negative film. The machines used by Western studios for this process were beyond their means (Kamil 2000, 19).

It was not just the equipment that was extremely expensive for the filmmakers but also raw film stock, which throughout the history of Turkish film was always imported. For instance, in the early 1950s, Faruk Kenç mentioned that import regulations imposed by the Democratic Party government made it very difficult to get raw film (1993, 27). The DP government also attempted to control filmmaking indirectly by distributing raw film through its Media and Publishing (*Basın Yayın*) institution. This is again indicative of the relationship of the Turkish state to cinema: let it develop on its own but simultaneously retain control through regulatory limitations. For film producer Hürrem Erman, Turkish governments always saw cinema merely as a form of entertainment and failed to see its industrial potential. For him, cinema was an industry employing many people with the potential to be turned into an exportation sector (1973, 26). The state was not interested in opening film schools, film libraries, or *cinematheques*. The only existing places that might have served such functions were the screening theaters established by the RPP at the People's Houses, which were closed under the DP government. This situation continued until the mid-1960s, when the first *cinematheque* and film archive were established. The first film school opened in the mid-1970s.

Filmmakers also learned how to make films, and the tricks of the trade, through practice and individual innovation. In the years following the Second World War, directors who claimed that they had visited Hollywood or other European film industries started directing films (Havaeri 2002), actors were gathered literally from the street, and films were made with any available equipment. Director Faruk Kenç claimed that he used the traveling shot for the first time in Turkey in his 1940 film *Yılmaz Ali* (Perseverant Ali), but because they used an old, heavy camera, moving it on the rails that they built proved quite difficult (Kenç 1993, 27). Another director, Seyfi Havaeri, talked about how, while shooting his second film, *Damga*, they filled the hole on the camera's film cartridge with gum, and imitated a crane shot by asking his cameraman with a camera on his shoulder to shoot a scene from on top of a moving truck (2002). Such experiments and practical innovations might have been experienced by Western filmmakers in the early years of cinema when it was a new invention. But in Turkey, filmmakers tried to understand and analyze the cinematic narration of Western films while adding local, domestic elements. İlhan Arakon and Kriton İliadis, both of whom were respected directors of photography, examined lobby cards and stills of Western films to learn how they did lighting and *mise-en-scène* (Arakon 2004).

Similarly, Erman, an active producer from the late 1940s on, recounted how his independent group rented a repaired wooden camera with one lens to make his first film (Erman 1973, 23). Havaeri mentioned that a major film company of the period, İpek Film, which worked with Muhsin Ertuğrul, would not lend its equipment to them and instead they found a Greek photographer, Coni Kurtdeşoğlu, who helped them rent a camera (2002). In return for his help, Kurtdeşoğlu, who did not have any experience in filmmaking, did the camera work for this film, which was based on a story about the life of a young girl in Istanbul after the loss of her Greek mother and Ottoman Turkish father. While Erman credited the story to Fikret Arıt, Onaran claimed that the story belonged to an unknown Greek writer (Özgüç 1998, 52). Erman offered the role of the young girl to a

Ms. Mensure after being impressed by her variety show at a bar. They promptly changed her name to the more glamorous Sezer Sezin. Then Erman, in search of a lead actor, met Memduh, to whom he gave the surname Ün, meaning fame. However, more significantly, Ün was supposedly the surname of the Hollywood actor known as Turhan Bey, known in Turkey as *the* Turkish actor in Hollywood, despite being only half-Turkish with no ties to Turkey. For another role, Erman recruited his Armenian dentist, Arşavir Alyanak, who later became a director.

Although most of the film was shot under the direction of Havaeri, a couple of remaining scenes were shot by another director, Lütfi Ö. Akad, also new to the filmmaking business. After the completion of shooting, Erman and his companions realized that they did not have a studio for postproduction. They hired a carpenter in Adapazarı, a small town close to Istanbul, where Erman owned some film theaters. The carpenter made four or five tubs, all of which leaked the chemicals used to wash the negatives. Their misadventures continued when they printed the film and discovered that most of it was out of focus and the renowned editor-director Orhan Atadeniz was hired to edit the film with the available footage. The last touch involved rewriting the dialogue and dubbing the film in the studio. Although this film is no longer available, it is clear that the film must have been quite low in quality. Surprisingly, the film was extremely successful and despite the criticisms of Erman's urban, educated friends, the film was a favorite weepie among the doormen and janitors of his studio.

Thus, filmmaking in those years was not as standardized or predictable a process as it was in the West. Instead, it was spontaneous and arbitrary in terms of the constitution of a cinematic narrative and discourse. As an integral part of its transitional character, it involved various ways of mirroring and reinventing Western experiences of early cinema. In addition, even though some filmmakers went to the West for film education, upon their return they did not necessarily put their training faithfully to work. Instead, partly due to the unavailability of Western-style studios and necessary technical equipment, filmmakers were forced to create their own practical solutions and inventions. But it was also due to other conditions of filmmaking in a non-Western, underdeveloped country that they had to develop their own ways of responding to and transforming the technology and language of cinema. Given this, filmmakers practiced a "Turkified" filmmaking that is translated through mirroring, mimicking, and transforming Western cinema.

Film Exhibition

During the late 1940s and early 1950s the problems of filmmakers were not limited to the conditions of filmmaking, but extended to the exhibition of their films. Because the rise of domestic cinema took place over a mere couple of years, the infrastructure of filmmaking was not fully developed. Director Faruk Kenç, when discussing the limited availability of film theaters for domestic films, noted that many first-run theaters in

Figure 3.2. The façade of Süreyya Film Theater (aka. Majik and Taksim), 1950

Istanbul were booked in advance for foreign films (1993, 27). Such theaters could only allot one or two weeks to domestic films, a period that might be extended to three or four weeks if the film was making a significant profit. Although the exact number of film theaters in operation during these years is not known, reasonably reliable estimates give a sense of what was available. Oğuz Özdeş, very optimistic about the rise of Turkish cinema, was concerned about the number of film theaters in 1951, which was close to 300. Özdeş recounted that half of Istanbul's ten first-run theaters were controlled by İpek and Lale film companies, while foreign film importers were unwilling to show domestic productions (1951, 24). Özön noted that the number of film theaters, around thirty in 1923, had risen to 130 in 1939 and 200 in 1949 (1995a, 49). In the years following the 1948 tax cut, there was a steady increase in the number of theaters. In 1950, 23 domestic and 229 foreign films were exhibited to almost 12 million spectators, and in 1959 95 domestic and 246 foreign films were exhibited to 25 million spectators. These numbers peaked in 1970 with 224 domestic films and 2,242 film theaters selling 246 million tickets to a population of 35 million.

During the 1950s, producers had relative control over the exhibition of films. Production companies had to rely on their relationship with the owners of first-run theaters that were partly controlled by major film importation companies before distributors started to control the market in the

Figure 3.3. The interior of Süreyya Film Theater

high Yeşilçam era. However, in other theaters the producers created their own distribution network either by renting films to theater owners or by four-walling these theaters for a few weeks to a few months, depending on the number of films produced and the company's financial power. Tuncan Okan noted that to four-wall a theater, the producers paid a guaranteed amount of money and shared the profit with theater owners. In many cases, from ticket sales, theater owners received 35 to 45 percent of the net profit after taxes (1958, 37). Similarly, Erman noted that, for *Damga*, they initially rented a first-run theater for a week, but due to its success, the film was shown for two more weeks and a few more copies of the film were printed for distribution to Anatolian cities. Although there was a system of profit sharing through a percentage given to Istanbul theater owners at the time, Erman noted that they also gave percentage shares to some Anatolian theater owners for the first time (1973, 23). Due to the lack of a distribution system, they sold the film's rights to theater owners for a fixed price. In short, much like the conditions of production, the distribution and exhibition of films were not yet based on a clearly defined system: both production and exhibition worked spontaneously and independently.

Film Criticism and National Identity

With migration and the spread of film theaters to small towns in Anatolia, both the patterns of spectatorship and film criticism were transformed.

While the majority of spectators were from the lower and middle classes in peripheral locations (both urban and rural), their relation to Western cinemas was limited to and conditioned by dubbing. Their taste was deemed "primitive" by director Şadan Kamil: "People used to go to see a film as if they were going to coffee houses or night clubs. They listened to music and watched famous singers and dancers." People favored these films because, according to Kamil, they enjoyed looking at a star player, listening to a couple of songs, or crying at a few touching scenes. He marveled at how these spectators never tired of watching the same subjects time and time again (2000, 22). Such comments became standard fare among filmmakers and critics throughout the history of cinema in Turkey; an assumption of believing spectators to be primitive, naive and underdeveloped is shared by both the elite and intellectuals. As Ravi Vasudevan notes, "[T]he middle-class are bearers of a rationalist discourse and the attributes of responsible citizenship and...the popular cinema...is the domain of first a pre-modern, and then a decultured, lumpenized mass audience" (2000, 135). Likewise, in Turkey, the republican modernization discourse also propagated class distinctions based on sociopolitical positions. An urban, educated, westernized, and mostly Kemalist bourgeoisie and petty bourgeoisie carried the modernizing ideology of novelty and linear historical progress, favoring Western cinemas and domestic "realist" films. Alternatively, as Vasudevan notes with reference to Ashish Nandy, commercial or popular cinema "attracted spectators to a narrative which ritually neutralizes the discomfiting features of social change, those atomizing modern thought-patterns and practices which have to be adopted for reasons of survival" (2000, 135). This may be why an alternative route of Turkification was adopted by both Yeşilçam and *arabesk* music.

Along with the popularity of Egyptian films and the rise of domestic film production, various film magazines changed the focus of their coverage. Earlier popular film magazines covered Western cinema by using Western popular film magazines and materials supplied by the distributors of Western films, in which the international dominance of Hollywood is clearly visible. In the 1940s, Egyptian films and stars were also covered in these magazines. Starting in the late 1950s, on the other hand, two types of film magazines emerged: one followed the earlier tradition of covering popular films and stars with sensational and gossipy material while the other considered cinema as a form of art, publishing serious articles about the possibility of making realist films. However, before this partition, film magazines of the late 1940s and early 1950s were optimistic about Turkish cinema's future despite heavy criticism of its existing films. In 1949, one film critic, Sami Onat, wrote: "Belly dancing music, bar amusement, the costume film trend, the caprice of melodrama, the desire for bland surprise and some other differences in outlook turn film into nonsense" (Onat 1990, 52). For him, to attract more spectators, producers forced directors to continue churning out such films. Such vehement criticism was not universal. In 1954, before its coverage shifted from Hollywood to domestic cinema, *Yıldız* (Star) magazine announced a victory for domestic films in its editorial section: "Until five or six years ago, nobody believed in the progress of filmmaking in Turkey" ("Yerli Film-lerin Zaferi" 1954, 3). The report, which noted that 300 of 350 imported films were American, asked why, despite the dominance and quality of American films, local spectators nonetheless flocked to the technically incompetent domestic films. The answer is simple: people saw themselves in these films. Unlike the foreign, unfamiliar stories and morals of the American films and reliance on characters like television artists, bankers, and gangsters, domestic films reflected people's own lifestyles, issues, and music. Through Turkish films, spectators could dream about being artists like those on the screen, whereas the Los Angeles gangster was outside of their experience. According to the magazine, the first victim of the rising popularity of Turkish cinema was Egyptian film; the second blow was felt by the French and British films, which were fading out of the market; and the third blow was yet to be gradually felt by American films. While companies that used to import began to produce, film magazines shifted their attention from foreign to local products.

Amid this national optimism, other magazines criticized popular films, while forgetting that imported realist or political films were either censored or had a limited viewership. While this allowed many to deem the Turk-ish public, almost paternalistically, as backward and underdeveloped, for them, many of the domestic films were traditional and premodern. Reşat Kasaba noted that both the modernizing elite in Turkey and scholars of Turkish modernization, such as Bernard Lewis and Daniel Lerner, imag-ined Turkey to be eliminating its traditional elements. Yet such discourses of modernization, when faced with the realities of Turkey, demanded new categories allowing for the contradictions both of modernization and of those unaligned groups in society that were neither modern nor tradi-tional. Daniel Lerner, in his 1958 book *The Passing of Traditional Society*, describes the city as a modernizing landscape that contains various fig-ures, including migrants living in miserable conditions who never pen-etrate into the urban environment; those who find a satisfying life through industrial discipline; and still others who "are infused with new dreams and glory—imagining themselves at the head of an Islamic brotherhood, or of a proletarian union" (Kasaba 1997, 23). Yet, according to Kasaba, such uncertainties or ambiguities did not prevent them from claiming that "Turks are the happiest people in the Middle East," for Turkey was, above all else, modernizing. In this process of modernization, religious groups, Kurds, and non-Muslim minorities contradicted the promise of a singular national identity and culture. While until the 1950s many non-Muslims escaped, were deported, or were subjected to population exchange, a con-siderable part of the remaining non-Muslim population found itself pay-ing special wealth taxes or having their businesses attacked in the riots of 1955. As the production companies and magazines that made up Yeşilçam cinema settled into Beyoğlu, they entered the previously cosmopolitan spaces being slowly abandoned by non-Muslim minorities. Ironically, both Yeşilçam and *arabesk*, as popular and alternative "Turkifications" (or "Turkifications-from-below") in the cultural field, resonated with the republican nationalist ethos in its aggression toward non-Muslim and non-Turkish minorities. Yeşilçam not only made various movies in support of Kemalist ideology but it also reproduced the aggressive nationalist ideology. At the same time, it countered the projects of the Kemalist state by introducing elements of tradition and religion side by side with modernity. Nevertheless, Yeşilçam's existence is marked with an ambiguity and transitionality, not amenable to the models of modernization as prescribed by the modernizing elite and scholars.

Yeşilçam's Turkification of Western and non-Western films furthered this ambiguity. In some cases, such Turkifications did not quite fit the scheme of Turkishness: they reproduced Western models or brought in elements of tradition and religion or tropes of non-Western cinemas. But ultimately, they were Turkifications, bearing the traits of both a transformation or translation and a cultural aggression or exclusion. Although numerous adaptations were made, as Giovanni Scognamillo points out, only 230 of 3,100 films made before 1973 were adaptations of Turkish literature, due to strict censorship, copyright payments, and the intellectual investment that such adaptations required (1973c, 62). In 1965, according to an unnamed critic, the tempo of making 150 films with a limited number of production companies and filmmakers made plagiarism of foreign films a pragmatic necessity (Scognamillo 1973c, 67). While the critics of early Yeşilçam defended domestic films, especially the realist ones, they were critical of adaptations and remakes. Yet on a more fundamental level, cinema, a Western medium with its particular technological and ideological history, demanded a creative response from non-Western filmmakers and spectators. The most prevalent of these responses are vernacularization, domestication, adaptation, reinvention, imitation, mimicry, and simple plagiarism, all of which are different ingredients of Yeşilçam's Turkification ("from-below").

Turkification and the Melodramatic Modality

The *auslands journal* (foreign lands) section of the Web site of the German television channel ZDF (www.zdf.de) ran a news story on March 4, 2004, titled: *"Alles getürkt,"* meaning all or everything is *"getürkt,"* by "the book pirates of the Bosporus." It is a story about street vendors selling pirated copies of bestseller books such as the Harry Potter series and Orhan Pamuk's novels. The piracy was not limited to books, but also extended to CDs, VCDs, and DVDs of copyrighted software and movies. Although in the last couple of years, the copyright laws have been strengthened in an attempt to match European Union laws, the piracy of copyrighted materials remains common in Turkey. The story also indicated that some of the vendors saw themselves as "Ottoman Robin Hoods" with an "anti-imperialistic" sensibility. However, they are not "Ottoman" anymore, but "Turkish," with nationalist fervor enmeshed with religious and ethnic identities. In German, *getürkt* is a word literally meaning "Turkified." But following the recent exposure of Germans to the Turkish migrant community, the contemporary usage of the word gained an extra, derogatory meaning indicating corruption, fakery, or falsification, or as used in this story, piracy.

According to the *Oxford English Dictionary*, "to Turkify" or "to Turkicize" means "to render Turkish" and "Turkish" means "pertaining or belonging to the Turks and Turkey." The verb "to turkish" means "to transform, especially for the worse; to pervert, to turn into something different" and it has been used since the early sixteenth century. While the etymology of words like *turken*, *turquen*, *turkin*, *turkess*, *torcasse*, *torkes*, *turkiss*, or *turkess* is uncertain, it would not be difficult to believe they originate from the word *Turk* and suffix "-en" by "referring to the action of the Turks in transforming Christian churches into mosques, or from the Koran being regarded as a transformation or perversion of the Bible." Words such as *turken* or *turkess* mean "to transform or alter for the worse; to wrest, twist, distort, pervert" or "to alter the form or appearance of; to change, modify, refashion (not necessarily for the worse)."

If not from religious sources about a conversion from Christian into Muslim, the contemporary usage of the word may have originated from a famous eighteenth-century chess-playing machine by the name of "the Turk" that was created by a Hungarian baron, Wolfgang von Kempelen. This chess machine was "a mechanical man, fashioned from wood, powered by clockwork, dressed in a stylish Turkish costume—and capable of playing chess" (Standage 2002). Originally created for the entertainment of the Austro-Hungarian empress Maria Theresa, this machine challenged such famous figures as Benjamin Franklin, Catherine the Great, Napoleon Bonaparte, and Edgar Allan Poe. Though a long-standing curiosity for many, the Turk, named for the wooden figure's costume, functioned through trickery; it faked, falsified, or simulated a real machine with the capability of playing chess, yet it was still a curious and exotic invention. Thus the image of the "Turk," ranging from perversion to falsification, is still at stake in the digital age, thanks to piracy. Put differently, "Turk" serves as an "other" to the West as much as the West is the other of Turkey.

The contemporary German usage of the word emerged from contact with the Turkish population in Germany, who originally arrived as guest workers but settled, creating a large diasporic population. Thanks to them, things are Turkified (*getürkt*) either by being transformed in a Turkish way or manner or by being made unruly or unlawful. In other words, Turks create ways of getting along with rules and laws by ruining the validity or legality of civil life and the civic virtues of the Western tradition of democracy and civility. That is why things are transformed, altered, changed, modified, refashioned, twisted, simulated, invented, falsified, faked, distorted, wrested, corrupted, perverted, and pirated. Turks in Germany or elsewhere are *getürkt*, *alles getürkt*! Turkification does not stop there; films and filmmaking are also *getürkt*.

The earlier drama of nation building, which is placed through *hayal*, runs parallel to Turkification with its vernacularization of purifications and exclusions. While *hayal* emphasizes a *transition* from "shadow" plays and traditional performing arts to cinema by bringing together shadow plays and cinema on a screen of dream and imagination, Turkification amasses protocols of imitation, adaptation, translation, and transformation. In the case of Yeşilçam, Turkification accommodates a range of relations to Western cinemas, from Hollywood to art cinema and auteur films. There is not a single dreamed West, nor is there a single Western cinema. With these issues at hand, Yeşilçam's Turkification marks various practices, ranging from facile to complex, of translating, transforming, or rendering Western cinemas.

While *hayal* and Turkification help us to understand what Yeşilçam is and how it works, "melodramatic modality" of Yeşilçam emphasizes how such protocols work in films and how Yeşilçam films offer melodramatic modality common to various popular cinemas. The concept of modality emerges in multiple analytic realms, particularly in the study of poetry and music, and has recently been applied to the study of film as well. The concept of modality is reminiscent of metered poetry that involves a rhythmic flow of meter and accent. Following the conventions of Eastern poetry in general, Ottoman and early republican poetry in Turkey relied on meter as well as a determinate set of themes such as the everlasting love between the rose and the nightingale. Traditional Turkish shadow plays or theater-in-the-round had a similar structure of a ground-setting modality and the actual performances of players or puppeteers. Similarly, classical Turkish music has a similar form that involves a modality or a rhythmic pattern preserved during the performance, even if the sounds of the instruments or the voices of the singers have a chance to float or fluctuate at different "altitudes" or pitches. Modality sets a basic pattern or ground by providing a set of aesthetic articulations, while specific performances float in, on or around the boundaries of this ground. Words such as *altitude*, *accent*, or *performance* mark particular instances of the reproduction or transformation of this ground.

In "Remapping Hollywood," Christine Gledhill notes that modality "defines a specific mode of aesthetic articulation adaptable across a range of genres, across decades, and across national cultures. It provides the genre system with a mechanism of 'double articulation'" (2000, 229). Yeşilçam relies upon the articulation of a melodramatic modality that not only has a particular history in the Western countries but also has a variety of traditional occurrences in Turkey.[4] In this respect, Yeşilçam combines melodramatic modality with the storytelling conventions of Turkey that rely upon oral narration. Its synthesis of a two-dimensional way of seeing with a perspectival one works through its translation and adaptation of a Western medium into a domestic visual set of practices, that is, Turkification. In this respect, a variety of visual and oral storytelling conventions coexisted in Yeşilçam. As I will elaborate below, melodramatic modality presents a sphere for the coexistence of the modern and the traditional, involves mechanisms of coexistence with and in other genres, and facilitates a dialectic of pathos and action and a Manichean conflict of good and evil through a predictable storyline that resolves with the morality of the common man after a series of spectacular and dramatic confrontations.

Grades of Turkification in Yeşilçam

From production to consumption, Turkish filmmaking is often *getürkt*. Although copyright laws or concerns were not applied within the cinema of Turkey, the filmmakers demanded their own intellectual rights when they had an opportunity to sell films internationally. The first Turkish Tarzan film, *Tarzan İstanbul'da* (Tarzan in Istanbul, 1952), was shot by Orhan Atadeniz and exported to countries including Spain, Portugal, France, and several Arab countries. Kunt Tulgar, whose father, Sabahattin Tulgar, produced and did the camera work on the first film, made a second Tarzan film, *Tarzan Korkusuz Adam* (Tarzan the Mighty Man, 1973). Just as the 1952 script was credited to Kunt Tulgar, who was only four years old at the time, he credited his film to his son, Kaan Tulgar, then just a year old. According to Kunt Tulgar, the first film was an adaptation of Richard Thorpe's *Tarzan's New York Adventure* (1942), though the film actually utilized earlier Tarzan films like the W. S. van Dyke classic, *Tarzan, the Ape Man* (1932). Kunt Tulgar also mentions that, apart from a couple of scenes featuring an elephant, the first film was shot in Turkey by "borrowing" scenes from documentaries and other Tarzan films (2002). Orhan Atadeniz, as a renowned editor and director, cropped frames from different films and carried them in his pocket during the shooting so that he would be able to give instructions to the players about how to enter the frame and where to look and move. Thus Atadeniz followed rules of continuity editing as he Turkified Tarzan creating a homegrown Turkish hero in place of a Hollywood import: Tarzan was *getürkt*.

The translation of the West implicit in Turkification does not simply take place between two languages, but also through other elements of cultural multiplicity. It is not reducible to a transfer from one set to another, each clearly coded and decodable. Here the West and the East are not identifiable totalities with a firm set of elements; they are surfaces on which various particularities float. Nonetheless, most discussions on adaptation have instead assumed properness and originality through the introduction of a supposed universality of both language and culture. For example, Giovanni Scognamillo offered three different categories: "true" adaptations, vernacularized subjects (*yerlileştirilen konular*), and subject matters put in Turkish language (*Türkçeleştirilen konular*) (1973c, 69). Scognamillo called Selim İleri's adaptation of the Graham Greene novel *This Gun for Hire*, which was made into a film by Lütfi Ö. Akad by the name of *Yaralı Kurt* (Wounded Wolf, 1972), a "true" adaptation and a canonical film. To this Scognamillo adds "mere" adaptation in which a foreign film is remade without making any changes to the setting or characters. On the other hand, when material is borrowed from a foreign film and adapted, there are two avenues. The

Figure 3.4. *Tarzan İstanbul'da* (Tarzan in Istanbul, Orhan Atadeniz, 1952)

better and more successful one is vernacularization in which the filmmaker adeptly transfers the original story's elements into a Turkish context such as Zeki Ökten's *Bitirim Kardeşler* (Badass Brothers, 1973), which is an adaptation of *Lo Chiamavano Trinità* (My Name Is Trinity, dir. Enzo Barboni, 1970) and *Some Like It Hot* (dir. Billy Wilder, 1959). However, when the filmmaker borrows elements from a foreign film and adapts them without

Figure 3.5. *Drakula İstanbul'da* (Drakula in Istanbul, Mehmet Muhtar, 1953), *Left*: scriptwriter-actor Bülent Oran, *Right*: Atıf Kaptan

much focus—for example, Hulki Saner's adaptation of *Damdaki Kemancı* (Fiddler on the Roof, 1972)—then, Scognamillo calls it *"Türkçeleştirme"* (lit. Turkishification). In other words, for Scognamillo, there are good and bad examples of borrowing (i.e., stealing) from foreign sources. For him vernacularization is different from *Türkçeleştirme* because when foreign settings, characters, and traditions are changed for Turkish ones, vernacularization is "more realistic" and "closer to our society" (1973c, 72). In other words, Scognamillo's better model aligns him with Özön or Turkification-from-above, whereas *Türkçeleştirme* is seen more in line with a lesser example of Turkification. However, unlike Scognamillo's hierarchical categorization, the notion of Turkification proposed here suggests that all of these different ways of dealing with foreign sources lurks back to the very existence of cinema in Turkey, a Western form of entertainment and art whose presence in Turkey is inescapably linked to unremitting Turkification.

Turkification and Melodrama

Turkification relied on melodramatic modality in Turkifying Western texts. Often the foreign sources are put into the functional mold of melodrama: pure evil and pure good, an intrigue, a spectacular clash. Safa Önal (2002), one of the most prolific scriptwriters of cinema in Turkey, stated that there were some fundamental texts that many Turkish films relied upon in one way or the other, such as *Stella Dallas* (dir. King Vidor,

Figure 3.6. *From left to right*: director Adolf Körner, actor-director Talat Artamel, and director Faruk Kenç, 1941

1937). Another highly sought after scriptwriter, Bülent Oran, noted that Bernard Shaw's *Pygmalion* is another such story incessantly reproduced by popular Turkish cinema (2002). Although the "original" adaptation of *Pygmalion* in the cinema of Turkey, *Sürtük* (Hussy, 1942), was made by the Czechoslovakian director Adolf Körner, director Ertem Eğilmez's adaptation of *Pygmalion* shows the complexities involved in the process of Turkification. After failing to adapt the story, Eğilmez decided to have a look at Mahmut Yesari's novel *Sürtük*. Similar to *Pygmalion*, this novel was about a man who culturally educates a prostitute, who eventually cheats on him and leaves him once again alone. They also read Garson Kanin's *Dünkü Çocuk* (Born Yesterday) in which a journalist culturally educates a low-class woman. Eğilmez, following these examples, eschewed a happy ending (Eğilmez and Şendil 1974, 18–19). According to Agah Özgüç's film dictionary, Eğilmez's *Sürtük* (1965) is a marriage of *Pygmalion* and Charles Vidor's 1955 film *Love Me or Leave Me* (1998, 277). In addition to his 1967 sequel *Sürtüğün Kızı* (The Daughter of Hussy, which according to Özgüç is a remake of King Vidor's 1937 film *Stella Dallas*), Eğilmez also remade *Sürtük* in 1970 with different actors. Interestingly, Cemil Cahit of *Yıldız* magazine noted at the time that Adolf Körner's adaptation might not be shown in theaters because of its close relationship to Hollywood's *Pygmalion* (dir. Anthony Asquith and Leslie Howard, 1938), which was playing in Turkish theaters (Gürata 2001, 27). In the same year Körner made another film, *Kerem ile Aslı*, based on a traditional love story starring two famous singers of the time, Müzeyyen Senar and Malatyalı Fahri.

Although many of these films from the Second World War years are lost, the nuances they involved aptly illustrate aspects of Turkification, combining traditional forms with Western references with variations achieved through successive alterations of the same themes. For instance, the Turkification of spy or crime stories often involved the addition of both a motivational "love story" and a number of scenes with songs (Oran 2002). Yet these melodramatic interventions carried such Turkifications away from Scognamillo's "true" domestications. Thus Turkified stories such as *Pygmalion*, Xavier de Montépin's *La Porteuse de Pain* (The Bread Peddler), and Billy Wilder's *Some Like It Hot* were not "true" because realism was absent in them (Scognamillo 1973c, 70–71). Interestingly enough, realism is again a Western form, to be imported and adapted.

The link between realism and melodrama is worth noting here. Peter Brooks's study on the novels of Balzac and Henry James, *The Melodramatic Imagination*, delineates melodrama as "a specifically modern mode, which evolves out of the loss of pre-Enlightenment values and symbolic forms, in response to the psychic consequences of the bourgeois social order, in which the social must be expressed as the personal" (Gledhill 1987, 29). In a post-sacred modern society, melodrama fills a void created by secularization, individualization, and westernization efforts such as those demarcated by the positivistic republican reforms. Like the relationship between romance stories and the European realist novels, nineteenth-century Ottoman novels appropriated the style of Western novels while also utilizing traditional love stories from both idealized folktales and more down-to-earth *meddah* (storyteller) stories and imitations (*taklit*). According to Berna Moran, folktales such as *Kerem ile Aslı*, *Tahir ile Zühre*, and *Emrah ile Selvi* were composed of four parts: "1. the start of a love between young woman and man, 2. the unavoidable falling apart of the lovers, 3. the struggle of lovers to get together, and 4. the ending with marriage or death of both" (1995, 24). The highest virtues in these stories are the lovers' fidelity to each other, moralism, and the ultimate triumph of love. In early Turkish novels, writers like Ahmet Mithat and Şemsettin Sami aimed to incorporate analyses and information on human nature and psychology, transforming these stories into Western-style realistic texts (Moran 1995, 30). These novels introduced two types of women: one angelic, victimized by love, and the other a femme fatale, victimizing for love. Moran interprets the victimized woman as a victim of the traditions and customs that modernization and westernization efforts attempted to eliminate. He also suggests that such characters are not borrowed from Western novels but from traditional stories since Ottoman morality and ethics frowned on extramarital relationships and womanizers (1995, 35). Though such novels seem to oppose the patriarchal system, in their conclusion, they reinstate the romantic elements of folktales and the heterosexual relationship of protagonists with a Hollywood-style happy ending or with the death of the lovers.

Before cinema, these traditional stories were the principle material for late nineteenth- and early twentieth-century shadow plays and theatrical forms, especially the marriage of Western and Ottoman theaters in *Tuluat*. Similar to Western performing arts and literature, which inherited melodrama from earlier popular traditions, the late Ottoman rise of melodrama and realism involved westernization in the arts and the combination of popular traditions and literature. While *Tuluat* relied upon a generic storyline and characters, it also contained improvisation freely modified by actors during performance. The generic aspects of these late Ottoman forms, later adopted by Turkish films, resonated with the post-Enlightenment realist tradition of capturing, representing, and modifying the world in two ways: in relation to the contrast between reform and restoration (or positivist republican reform projects of westernization and modernization) and through a view of melodrama as a modality inscribed in different genres of popular cinema in Turkey.

Melodrama and Modernity

As Peter Brooks suggests, the relationship between melodrama and modernity is tied to melodrama's roots in the traditional or what preceded the modern, that is, "melodrama's search for something lost, inadmissible, repressed" (Gledhill 1987, 32). The melodramatic imagination inscribes this other side of modernity, which is lost and continually repressed by positivist projects and belongs to the realm of the masses rather than that of high art. However, this distinction should not situate the classical realist text normatively in opposition to the excessive melodramatic; instead, the melodramatic is "a basic element of popular cinema" (Williams 1998, 44). Brooks's argument underscores a response to the Enlightenment's projects, its modernism that was countered in the post-Enlightenment era through a romantic reaction attempting to restore the pre-Enlightenment truth and morality. In this line Brooks construes Gothic novel, an early Romantic form, as a reaction to desacralization and rationalism (1976, 17). Yet this is not merely a binarism between progress and regress, realism and melodrama, but instead elucidates the infusion of the melodramatic into the realist novel and the persistence of the melodramatic side by side with other modern forms, such as the coexistence of liberty and the libertine in an Enlightenment framework.

Early melodramas of the late eighteenth century also coincided with the rising bourgeois consciousness struggling against feudalism and aristocracy. Thomas Elsaesser recounts that Restoration melodramas replaced tragic endings of prerevolutionary melodramas with happy ones, and that "they reconciled the suffering individual to his social position, by affirming an 'open' society...the victory of the 'good' citizen over 'evil' aristocrats, lecherous clergyman and even...the lumpen-proletariat, was re-enacted in sentimental spectacles full of tears and high moral tones" (1987, 46). Despite their conformism and submission, these melodramas still conveyed political sympathies and indicated social evils. This contested existence and experience of melodrama, including filmic melodrama, for Elsaesser, is ambivalent: "melodrama would appear to function either subversively or as escapism—categories which are always relative to the given historical and social context" (1987, 47).

Brooks's historical overview of the tensions between cultural forms interacts with modernity that, like melodrama, carried contrasts integral to its existence. Ben Singer argued that scholars such as David Bordwell, Miriam Hansen, and Tom Gunning conveyed cinema's concurrence with modernity through urban experience, novelties, and changes in human perception (2001). Referring to this modernity thesis, Singer relates melodrama to six basic aspects of modernity: "modernization, rationality, discontinuity, mobility, individualism, and stimulation" (2001, 35). As part of this examination, Singer brings in Baudelaire's arguments about art and modernity, setting the "ephemeral, fugitive, and contingent" against the "eternal and unchangeable" of art. While Singer only takes the ephemeral, contingent, and fugitive aspects of modernity as denoting a fuzzy novelty, he does not pursue the other side of modernity. Alternatively, as Stanley Cavell points out, Baudelaire discusses modernist painting, particularly that of the realists such as Courbet and Manet, who were asked to *make* "these natural and historical and phenomenological transformations" that involved new "attirements, physiques, posture, gaits and nudity" (1979, 42). But Cavell asks: "why was he (and it is the poet Baudelaire in question) willing to forgo serious art in favor of modest draftsmanship?" Baudelaire's "despair of happiness," "disgust with officially made-up substitutes" for paintings, and estrangement from the present and the past leave him longing for photography and motion pictures: "the wish for that specific simultaneity of presence and absence which only the cinema will satisfy" (1979, 42). For Cavell, Baudelaire was "the prophet of the modern," "perverse and superficial," and he chose dandies, fashion, cosmetics, crowds, women, and courtesans, all of which became parts of the stories of cinema.

Cavell understands cinema to be a medium through which someone makes sense and discovers ways of making sense of the world. Once filmmakers started to speak this language, there was no longer anything unknown. Cinema came with the persistence of what Cavell, with reference to Panofsky, called "fixed iconography"—"the well-remembered types of the Vamp and the Straight Girl...the Family Man and the Villain" (1979, 33). Aside from not sharing Panofsky's presupposition about the public, who would grow accustomed to and then leave behind such devices, Cavell perceived these types to be integral to cinema's way of creating individuals who are not individuals but *individualities*: "For what makes someone a type is not his similarity with other members of that type but his striking separateness from other people" (1979, 33). These individualities, existing through repeated incarnations, inflect mood and release fantasy.

Cavell's view of cinema as a photographic medium whose subject is reality is also related to a crosscurrent that puts forward the capacity of the medium to magically reproduce the world. For him, we connect with the world "through viewing it, or having views of it" and viewing a movie makes this "automatic, takes the responsibility for it out of our hands. Hence movies seem more natural than reality. Not because they are escapes into fantasy, but because they provide relief from private fantasy and its responsibilities" (1979, 102). Thus movies avoided the consciousness and seriousness of modernism. Cavell expounds this in the postscript to *The World Viewed*, by noting, "Movies from the beginning have existed in two states, one modern, one traditional, sometimes running parallel to and at varying distances from one another, sometimes crossing, sometimes interweaving" (1979, 219). Cavell does not deny the possible absence of a relationship between cinema and modernism, yet he sees movies as myth, inherently anarchic, and thus irreducible to the consciousness and rationality of modernist projects: "Their unappeasable appetite for stories of love is for stories in which love...must find its own community, apart from...society at large" (Cavell 1979, 214). Thus movies' myth is concerned with a human gathering that does not belong to society (*gesellschaft*), but to some "origins and comprehension which lies behind the grasp of human history and arbitration" (Cavell 1979, 214). For Cavell, the experience of movies is what the spectator consents to in front of a movie; it is in that myth of democracy that becomes livable in the land of romance—not in the land of secular politics or of American literature.

It is this aspect of movies that belongs to the melodramatic modality of popular cinemas. It is what is left from *gemeinschaft* (community)—which runs parallel to *gesellschaft* (society). Yeşilçam relies on a coexistence of the traditional and the modern, on a carnivalesque ground where different members of the filmgoing community share a communal sense of transgression. As family entertainment, spectatorship in the 1960s and the early 1970s involved partaking of pathos, laughter, and noise. It is what modernization from above (i.e., the republican reform projects) could not altogether eradicate or repress, like the drama of the primal scene. As Peter Brooks notes, "melodrama refuses repression," a repression also broken by its own narrative, in such "moments where repressed content returns as recognition, of the deepest relations of life, as in the celebrated *voix du sang* ('You! My father!'), and of moral identities ('So you are the author of all my wrongs!')" (1994, 19). Brooks views melodrama as a silent revelation of good and evil invested in the spectacular and sensational. This conflict between villain and hero, between types as individualities, constitutes the dramatic narration of melodrama that is "a *mise-en-scène* whose system of figuration is caught between restoration and reform" (Browne 1994, 168). Modernity, with its culture industries and class-based ideological positions, functions through these projects that distinguish between high and low culture, reform and restoration, progress and regression. Thus linear models of modernization applied to non-Western countries, such as those of Lewis and Lerner, see modernity as a model achievable through continual development and progress and complete elimination of the traditional. However, much like the dramatic narration of melodrama, Yeşilçam is caught between restoration and reform, progress and regress—in a constant state of transition. Turkification, as translation and transformation, emerges from a transition that cannot be fixed in a rational path of linear progression, and thus runs parallel and counter to the republican reform projects. Though it is not a Turkification-from-above, Yeşilçam's Turkification-from-below carries the stresses of such transition.

Melodramatic Modality

The second aspect of melodrama as melodramatic modality is a founding element of Yeşilçam's popular cinematic presence. Historically, melodrama originated in two different renderings of opera: "In France the idea that music might be interpolated between passages of speech to indicate what characters were feeling and representing pantomimically" (Wickham 1992, 184). Jean Jacques Rousseau took this sense of melodrama to describe his monologue in *Pygmalion* (1771). A second rendering of the term emerged in Germany: Jean Brandes and Georg Benda "applied the term to their *Ariadne auf Naxos* (1775), where speech was backed by music to heighten the emotional quality of the scene" (Wickham 1992, 184). Both of these evolved into theatrical practices throughout Europe, where a new entertainment practice, composed of new entertainment settings such as taverns or pleasure gardens, offered diverse performances including songs, dances, and other spectacles. For Glynne Wickham, morality (virtue of the common man and the happy ending rewarding the good), the spirit of revolution (Rousseau's noble savage and the lower-class fantasy of upward mobility or revolt), romantic novels (an inherently good hero tortured in the dungeons of Gothic castles by their evil owners, serving for the visual enrichment of the spectacle), and circuses (fairground attractions and spectacles of epic size imitating the Roman ones) are all aspects of melodrama. Gilbert de Pixérécourt merged these with a large orchestra, stereotyped situations, characterizations of circus tableaux, intrigues, and sensationalism, which were later adapted by Anglophone writers. The last contribution to melodrama came with the fantasy of gold-seeking pioneers advancing to the Western frontier, which gave melodrama a moral framework: "the spectacular reversals of fortune which acquisition, or loss, of this precious metal could itself effect, coupled with the part that women could play in precipitating such reversals" (Wickham 1992, 189).

Melodrama, then, emerged in popular entertainment practices of the modern era and, maintaining the sentimental and spectacular aspects of entertainment, moved to cinema. Thus it carries traces of not only a transformation from tradition to modernity but also pre-cinematic entertainment forms involving theater, fairground attraction, and carnival. Beyond the confines of the genre of women's or family melodramas, melodrama is a parasitical term coexisting with a variety of other genres by supplying them with pathos, action, laughter, and a moralistic story. Instead of being a "pure" or "proper" genre that is fixable at a specific time and place, Rick Altman construes melodrama, with Russell Merritt's term, as a "phantom genre," "a slippery and evolving category" (Altman 1999, 71). In the early years of American cinema, melodrama developed in association with a variety of genres that blended pathos, romance, domesticity, action, adventure, and thrills. "Richard Koszarski emphasizes the villain-hero-heroine triangle, true-to-type characters, and visually powerful dramatic confrontations" as basic elements of melodrama (Altman 1999, 72). This view reiterates the combination of popular entertainment and modernity in early theatrical and literary melodrama. Melodrama, then, can be seen as a "cultural form inherited from the nineteenth-century stage, in tension with and transformed by realism and the more realist techniques of cinema" (Williams 1998, 50). This is also relevant to Yeşilçam, which not only inherited a similar literary and theatrical tradition but was also transformed by the modernist reform programs by eventually stitching those traditions together in its modality.

Early film melodrama, in the period of silent cinema and early sound film, was not limited to a specific genre but ran through a host of genres: Western melodrama, crime melodrama, sex melodrama, mystery melodrama, and comedy melodrama (Altman 1999). Melodrama, as a modality, in Yeşilçam, presented a mode of storytelling that promised sensation, excitement, and continual motivation in the fight between good and evil presented with a spectacular *mise-en-scène* and with sentimentality and morality that realigns the melodramatic with a "realistic" message. "It is this basic sense of melodrama as a modality of narrative with a high quotient of pathos and action to which we need to attend if we are to confront the most fundamental appeal of movies" (Williams 1998, 51). As Cavell argues, it is this "appeal of movies" that does not belong to the post-Enlightenment secular society, but to a community that found itself in modernity through a myth of egalitarianism livable only in the land of romance. It is this sense of Yeşilçam that has been nostalgically reiterated in contemporary Turkey. But what is this nostalgic sense of melodrama or of Yeşilçam and what is the melodramatic modality of Yeşilçam?

Discussions on melodramatic modality (or on melodrama as a phantom genre), which grows with and persists in other genres, are based on a revision of early cinema's history. In her chapter "Melodrama Revised," Linda Williams reiterates Tom Gunning's rendering of the term *attraction*, borrowed from Sergei Eisenstein. Gunning's reading of early film spectatorship considers a combination of narrativity with spectacles and emotions, differentiating it from the linear narrative described in *The Classical Hollywood Cinema* of David Bordwell, Kristin Thompson, and Janet Staiger. While such formalist renderings of classical Hollywood cinema or classical realism inscribe linear and continuous narrative, the departures from such texts are automatically placed against the norm and interpreted as excess or transgression. However, as Williams points out, Staiger's later studies introduce the coexistence of narrativity and spectacle, demanding the emotional response of spectators regardless of their class backgrounds. Lastly, Williams, through Rick Altman's arguments, questions the dominance of the classical through melodrama that accommodates "ephemeral spectacle, showmanship and moments of artistic motivation," and thus leads to an admiration of the show, beyond the classic text's "cause-effect linear progress toward narrative resolution" (1998, 57).

Williams traces melodramatic modality in various films ranging from D. W. Griffith's *The Birth of a Nation* (1915) and *Broken Blossoms* (1919) to social issue films (*Salt of the Earth*, dir. Herbert Biberman, 1954), action films (*First Blood*, dir. Ted Kotcheff, 1982), and blockbusters (*Schindler's List*, dir. Steven Spielberg, 1993). She equates the melodramatic character of *Schindler's List* with the false consciousness that relieved Americans and Germans of their guilt by identifying with the moral good of the ordinary people typified by Schindler. By articulating Peter Brooks's argument about melodrama that emphasizes the retrieval of innocence and good in a post-sacred world where such moral and traditional binds were lost, Williams claimed: "However, what we think and what we feel at the 'movies' are often two very different things. We go to the movies not to think but to be moved" (1998, 61). Williams's reading of the melodramatic modality in relation to false consciousness may lead one to dismiss film as "movie" and cinema as "entertainment" by retreating to a more familiar contradiction that has been long embedded in film criticism. But beyond that contradiction, the myth of democracy and freedom lies at the heart of the melodramatic modality—a romance of utopian social existence where justice and equality prevail.

Williams offers five melodramatic features traceable in films from diverse genres and times. D. W. Griffith's *Way Down East* (1920), a film about the mythic world of melodrama taking place in a space of innocence, illustrates the first feature. The film creates, following Brooks, its own idyllic *mise-en-scène* of nostalgia and conservatism. Williams notes, "Nostalgia for a lost innocence associated with the maternal suffuses this film. Pathos arises, most fundamentally, from the audience's awareness of this loss" (1998, 65). The second one is, following Elsaesser, melodrama's focus on virtuous victim-heroes through a story narrated through the victim-heroes. Third, "melodrama appears modern by borrowing from realism, but realism serves the melodramatic passion and action" (Williams 1998, 67). Here, with reference to Christine Gledhill, Williams notes that melodrama is tied to the past, unlike realism, which searches for a renewed truth and stylistic innovation. Fourth, "melodrama involves a dialectic of pathos and action—a give and take of 'too late' and 'in the nick of time'" (Williams 1998, 69). Finally, in line with Brooks's argument, "melodrama presents characters who embody primary psychic roles organized in Manichaean conflicts between good and evil" (Williams 1998, 77). Williams then ties melodrama to a specific articulation of American democracy: the myth of a democracy, based on equality and freedom, carries middle-class morality envisaging a Manichean conflict where the good necessarily triumphs. Thus the polarities articulated in the film's narrative serve a double purpose: moral polarization helps the narrative construction of action or pathos and the happy ending resolution promotes conventional morality and an insistence on inherent innocence and goodness. As previously discussed, such values and morality underpin the secular, bourgeois characteristics of melodrama. But does such a modern capitalist frame have a particular national reference limited to the American case, or does melodramatic modality have a comparable relevance in other national contexts?

Is There a Nationality of Melodramatic Modality?

The melodramatic modality inscribes various national identities and traditions through nationalization and modernization. The convergence of the nation-state and modernization involved not only the development of national culture and identity but also the effects of modernization itself: mass education, urbanization and migration, mass communication and culture, industrialization, bureaucracy and policing, modern professions, the construction of family, and individualism and consumerism in capitalist societies, as well as the amplification of nonaristocratic class distinctions. Following Ernest Gellner, nationalism is not related to an inferable consciousness and rationality but to an invention of them, a projection of a nationality onto a community regardless of its heterogeneity (1983). For Benedict Anderson this invention involves the self-definition of nations as imagined political communities that are limited and sovereign (1991). While an imaginary communion is supposedly shared by all members of a nation despite their inequality and differences, such ties construct an inclusive imaginary fraternity and equality. Nations are invented but real, imagined but practiced, and pure yet rife with conflict. Nation-building involves the cultural constituents of modernity with a secular state apparatus, legal system, language, and education, that led to the creation of a high canonical culture of the nation distinct from the culture of past. Yet the imaginary bind of nations emerges through that which is lost in the process, a sense of community and ethnic communion outside the rationalist and materialist world of modern societies. This mythical origin is meant to bind the nation together. Williams's argument about the democratic character of melodrama in the American context resonates with a myth of "representational" democracy articulated in a unitary nationality. Melodrama, if taken as coincident with democracy, not only conveys the claims of innocence and purity attached to a national identity (which Williams associates with Americanness) but also inadvertently makes these claims for nationalism itself. Contrary to Williams's nationalization of melodrama, melodrama can instead be understood as part and parcel of the process of purification, pitting us against them and good against evil, that makes up the drama of nation-building, through which its violence and crime became coded as for the greater good and thereby erasable.

Thus, instead of reading melodrama as a distinctively American modality in the footsteps of Williams, but as a modality that shares the same topos with other modern national cultures and that persists in this topos of high and proper culture, it may be possible to view melodrama's coup as persistent and widespread. If one may talk about a pragmatics of storytelling, the melodramatic modality is right at the heart of such a practice. Melodrama is entwined with modernity; it belongs to a greater picture of the modern era, accommodating in its own contradictions and transitions. The break with the past and tradition proposed by modernist projects creates various discontinuities and seizures—yet it is impossible to remove them completely from culture and the arts. In this respect, melodramatic modality is indicative of the failures of modernist projects of high and proper culture. At the same time, although initially tied to a bourgeois revolt against aristocracy, it was later deemed not useful. Melodrama does not, in the non-Western world, cater to modernization projects. Because it is not actively cultivated, it exists by not belonging; it exists spontaneously and persists independently. Such presence through exclusion makes it clear that melodrama is particularly vital in geographies outside of the Western cinemas, such as Japanese and Mexican cinemas (Elsaesser 1987), Chinese cinema (Browne 1994), Egyptian cinema (Shafik 1998), or Bollywood (Vasudevan 2000).

Cinema in Turkey was left out of republican cultural reforms that also determined what belonged to high and proper culture. These reforms, enforcing a correct model of modernization and westernization, were partly successful and led to the coexistence of a variety of cultural and artistic practices. Therefore Yeşilçam's melodramatic modality with its aspects of *hayal* and Turkification-from-below became eloquent in its relation to the republican cultural project: it offered not only an ambivalent and alternative "Turkification" with all of its political and national disputes, it also belonged to that imaginary world of nationality that the republican establishment attempted to impose from above. Integral to its melodramatic modality and its national and democratic myth, Yeşilçam cinema also presented a *dream* of Turkification-from-below that is simultaneously traditional and modern, Western and non-Western. Thus Yeşilçam's melodramatic modality expounds the general context of modernity and nationality, both of which resonate with the melodramatic modality of Hollywood or other national cinemas through a morality and ethics of good and evil, myths of democracy, rationality and romanticism, a nostalgia for lost innocence, a dialectic of pathos and action, spectacular and sensational attractions, types or individualities, dramatic conflicts and spectacular reversals of fortune, intrigues, and triangles of hero, heroine, and villain.

How, then, did films of the later decades of Yeşilçam take up these issues and move forward in keeping with both republican ideology and popular tastes? As will be elaborated in the next chapter, Yeşilçam, through aspects of Turkification, *hayal*, and melodramatic modality, produced a language and aesthetic that, attempting to balance conceptual frameworks with economic and technological exigencies, diverged from the desire of many filmmakers and critics.

4

High Yeşilçam I
Industry and Dubbing

Yeşilçam's *Hayal*

The key issues of the interdisciplinary character of film studies, as identified by Christine Gledhill and Linda Williams in the introduction of the anthology *Reinventing Film Studies*, are particularly relevant: "the massness of cinema," film as both a "sensory" and a "significatory" medium, and the conception of cinema as constituting an "alternative public sphere." Through these tropes, this chapter will consider cinema's mediation between rationality and romanticism, meaning and feeling, attraction, spectacle, and entertainment as well as business and education. The rise of Yeşilçam cinema to a dominant position within the Turkish national market during the 1960s and 1970s invited considerations about its commercial and popular cinematic appeal and its opiate effect on the masses. However, when reexamined it also contains a resistive potential, both against the West as represented by Hollywood, and by the republican establishment intent on reproducing the West. Yeşilçam cinema presents an ambivalent response to westernization and modernization, simultaneously siding with it and against it. Yeşilçam offered a path of Turkification-from-below entangled with the *hayal* and the melodramatic modality of a popular cinema in its translation and transformation of modernity and that which constitutes "the West."

Gledhill and Williams propose a new perception of "the significance of the 'image' and 'imaginary' as sites of cultural construction," thus requiring a rethinking of cinema at the heart of the social imaginary, relocated in the complexity of cultural forms, practices, and effects (2000, 2). In this cultural construction, it becomes imperative to maintain the relationship between tradition and modernization, as mediated by *hayal*, which denotes popular cinema in Turkey in its complexity and ambiguity. The use of the word *hayal*, derived from Arabic, does not suit republican language reforms intended to purify the Turkish language by substituting many

Arabic and Persian words with Turkish ones fabricated by bureaucrats and intellectuals. Thus, to account for all of its connotations, *hayal* is also replaced by several words. For instance, *görüntü* or *imge* and *imgelem*, for image and imagination, introduced new words resonating with "image," betraying the republican establishment's westward outlook. The uses of *düş* for dream and *gölge* for shadow mark the authentic cultural model of the republican project, that of Turkishness, which has its roots in Central Asia. The remaining two meanings, *ayna* as mirror and *hayalet* as specter, remained untouched: *ayna* is a Persian word and *hayalet* an Arabic one. While the first two sets of words indicate the republican model's ideal synthesis of the West and the Turkish folk cultures, the latter couple of words demarcates the republican cultural project's limits between its imaginary and proper self, and its others (Islam and the non-West). Interestingly, when one sees his/her *hayal* in the mirror, this very spectral image appears: it is simultaneously you and your inverted self, that is, your other. Thus it stands as a perfect metaphor of the republican regime's project: even if you try to change and westernize yourself and your country by erasing what has hitherto been a part of your culture, you would not be able to erase it altogether—hence the sublation. Instead it would stand out in the mirror when you see yourself, your image, your other. It is the specter in the mirror that is you but simultaneously also not you.

Considered together, these words are all embedded in a politics of language signifying the multifaceted coexistence of disparate and oppositional entities in republican Turkey. In the relationship between language and power, purified Turkish words denote Kemalism, while Arabic and Persian words, commonly used in the Ottoman language, indicate an anti-Kemalist, often Islamist political stance. Here *hayal* is used not to imply either of these positions, but to lay out the intricacies of signification and sensation, to point to cultural choices that signify positions and concerns about the relation between being politically correct and taking advantage of the natural intricacies of language. *Hayal*, like many other Persian or Arabic words, is still in use because even the best cultural projects or purifications cannot totally control the language. Instead they may have a life of their own by staying a part of the everyday culture and by staying apart from authoritarian pressures. Similar to Yeşilçam cinema, *hayal* is used here to highlight the analogous interplay of hegemonic claims, as well as the ambivalence of responses and practices. Intermingled with ambivalent identity claims, the commercial and industrial shortcomings of Yeşilçam transformed various inputs into profitable tactics. Thus political positions such as Kemalism or Islamism, and social aspects of morality or sex were both profitably exploited by Yeşilçam.

Yeşilçam is not bereft of the perennial contradictions and uprooted systems produced by Turkish politics, where intense nationalism discriminated against its sociocultural others, radical republican reforms have coexisted with conservative and Islamic powers, and three military interventions—in 1960, 1971, and 1980—have interrupted and mediated the production of national discourses both by government and at the grassroots level. Erik Jan Zürcher called this period the Second Turkish Republic—between the 1960 military intervention that ended the First Turkish Republic (established in 1923) and the 1980 military intervention (1994, 253). The Second Republic introduced a more "liberal" constitution in 1961 that remained in effect until 1982. In terms of film production, Yeşilçam's most prolific years took place between the military interventions of 1960 and 1980. In this period, the number of feature films made was in excess of 3,500, approximately half of the films made in the history of cinema in Turkey. While at the beginning and end of this period the annual number of films made was around 100, at the time of the 1971 military intervention this number peaked at around 300 films. During these years, the film industry worked smoothly, with a defined network of production, distribution, and exhibition. Despite the political upheavals and ambiguities that characterized these decades, Yeşilçam was able to thrive as a popular mass medium because of cinema's ability to produce a dual presentation of sense and meaning and its creation of an alternative public sphere of *hayal* against and within the real public sphere of politics. This will be elaborated on two levels: Yeşilçam's system of production, distribution, and consumption will elucidate the specificities of this period and the process of filmmaking from preproduction to postproduction, and the practice of dubbing or post-synchronization will be elaborated in terms of Turkification and *hayal*.

The Periodization of Yeşilçam's Golden Age

Had life in Turkey not been interrupted by the 1960 coup, it might have been possible to conceive of Yeşilçam beginning immediately after the Second World War and developing gradually in concert with Turkey's multiparty democracy. However, both the violence of the 1960 intervention itself—resulting in the execution of the Democratic Party's political leaders—and the constitution instituted by the same military regime the following year, radically changed the possibilities available to Yeşilçam and to Turkey as a whole. The military represented statist Kemalism, while throughout the 1950s, the Democratic Party (DP) represented a more populist path toward modernization and westernization that catered to the conservative, Islamic identity of the people. Despite the army's claims to be outside of party politics, the coup attempted to eliminate the incorporation of such populism into the programs of top-down reform. Nonetheless, despite its fervent nationalism and moderate Islamism, it was also the DP that promised a millionaire in every neighborhood and the creation of Turkey as a small America under the patronage of the United States during the cold war. While the 1960 military intervention attempted to "restore order," the capitalist wave of economic liberalization initiated by the DP was partially slowed. Similarly, Yeşilçam narratives commonly assert a dynamic between central and peripheral sociopolitical forces: the DP, addressing peripheral traditionalist and conservative forces, threatened the reformist Kemalist center. However, this is not a clash between westernization and anti-westernization, or modernization and anti-modernization. Instead, both political forces shared the dream of westernization and modernization and what was at stake was the control over the locus of power, the center, and the ways of realizing their dreams. The irony of the military intervention was that while the Kemalist center yearned for unchallenged political power, the Western examples ran counter to that, with a democratic political discourse that was not administered by the military. It was also during the 1960s that migration and socioeconomic modernization of the peripheral forces started to become more visible in the center. During the 1960s, thanks to the 1961 constitution, novel challenges to Turkish politics were introduced by unions and other civil societal organizations demanding socioeconomic equality, and by socialist parties represented in parliament. Filmic narratives echoed these demands with social realist films about urban life, migration, and also the melodramatic fantasy of vertical class movement. Yeşilçam echoed the hegemonic power relations of the state, filmmakers, and its audience.

Even though the 1971 coup coincided with Yeşilçam's peak years, it cut through Turkey's political and social life. Generally regarded as a more right-wing intervention than its predecessor, the 1971 intervention was a military memorandum demanding the resignation of the government. It was followed by elections rather than by military governance, but did not stop there and ultimately led to the execution of three leftist guerillas and a violent and bloody manhunt for other leftist factions in the country. These aftereffects resonated powerfully in the world of cultural production. In the meantime, Yeşilçam's production pattern was shifting, initially with a rise in low-budget production and ultimately with a decline in both the quantity and purported quality of the films. Much as the increasing politicization of the masses in the late 1960s was impeded in 1971, another such era of politicization and violent interactions among left-wing, right-wing, and Islamist political groups in the late 1970s concluded with the 1980 military intervention. This coup, under the governance of a three-year junta, brought political life to a halt and greatly diminished the number of films made in the country. While the 1961 constitution was slightly modified following the 1971 military intervention, the military junta created a new constitution in 1982, thus starting the period of the Third Republic (Zürcher 1994). This constitution reduced political rights and freedoms, intending to limit separatist movements, especially those of Kurds, leftists, and Islamist radicals. After jailing many and executing some of the political activists of the late 1970s, the junta placed a ban on the political parties and leaders of the late 1970s that remained in effect until 1987. In 1983, elections were held to choose Turkey's prime minister and new ruling party, while the leader of the junta secured the office of the presidency. This complex era bracketing Yeşilçam's peak and decline cannot be separated from the workings of the industry itself.

The period of the Second Republic saw, on the one hand, internal migration and increased urban visibility of peripheral forces, and on the other, the emigration of guest workers first to Germany after their invitation in 1961, and later to other European countries. Immigration was a result of slow economic and industrial growth, which was protective, subsidiary, and insufficient to compensate for large increases in population. Both population and industrial growth in Turkey were substantial during this period. By 1960, the 1923 population of Turkey had more than doubled, reaching 28 million; by 1980, it reached 45 million. After the 1950s, the U.S. government, often in collaboration with NATO, established a number of military bases in Turkey to monitor the Soviet Union. Along with the bases, a new way of life and Americanization were introduced to Turkish culture, particularly in urban centers among the upper middle class. For example, the first Coca-Cola plant in Turkey opened in Istanbul in 1964. In the meantime, television broadcasting started in 1968 in Ankara, and then in 1971 in Istanbul. However, Americanization was countered by anti-American sentiment voiced especially by leftist organizations. But with the rise of television, especially after the 1974 establishment of state television's national broadcasting, not only did the world of filmmaking change but also Americanization found a new niche through U.S. television series and films.

All of these developments had enormous effects on cinema. With the increasing urbanization and modernization of the Second Republic, cinema became one of the main avenues of family entertainment. As an entertainment industry, film's dominance persisted during the 1960s and 1970s, only waning as a result of competition from television in the late 1970s. According to Nijat Özön, the average of seven to eight tickets bought per person in 1970 fell to less than one per person by 1985. He also notes that while the total number of tickets sold in 1970 was almost 250 million and the total number of televisions in the same year was 30,000, by 1984 total ticket sales decreased to 56 million and the total number of television sets increased to 7 million (1995, 50). More important, during these two decades domestic films did better in the box office than foreign films. While this trend came to an end in 1982, with the twenty-first century rejuvenation of the domestic film industry, domestic films have again started to be on par with foreign films at the box office.

The most immediate solutions in the late Yeşilçam era involved turning some centrally located theaters into small shopping malls or closing them down entirely. While this was the solution preferred by theater owners, it was of little use to filmmakers who wanted to continue producing films. On the other hand, the late 1970s decline in family spectatorship led filmmakers to augment the doses of action and sex in their films in order to attract urban male spectators. This popularized the genre of sex films in the second half of 1970s with a specific visual makeup and pattern of spectatorship. While many Yeşilçam scholars have considered the sex film industry as aberrant from Yeşilçam's earlier patterns, these sex films maintained Yeşilçam's filmmaking patterns and filmic texts and are therefore not discounted in this study. Then, in the 1980s, though theaters lost their appeal for the filmgoing public, the videotape industry helped Yeşilçam persist. Although in a different medium and form, television series in the post-Yeşilçam era continue to reproduce such basic elements of Yeşilçam's melodramatic modality.

The transformations in filmmaking in the mid-1970s have led some to situate the golden years of Yeşilçam between 1960 and 1974 (Abisel 1994), while others have suggested different periodizations based on auteur directors and changes in the language of filmmaking.[1] This book extends this period to 1980 and addresses the era of the Second Republic as the period of high Yeşilçam. Undoubtedly, as a form of popular filmmaking, Yeşilçam's best years in commercial and artistic terms were during the 1960s and 1970s. While the specific dates may differ to an extent, all of the film historians cited above participate in nostalgic remembrance of a golden age of a naive and innocent filmic world of melodramatic modality, though this period also involved intense sociopolitical and cultural change. Today Yeşilçam films, which continue to be consumed by spectators of various contemporary television channels, represent a bygone era. Framed by nostalgia, this era is interpreted with the "innocence" of not belonging to the global and modern world of capitalism that has been altering Turkey with increasing rapidity since the 1980s. In an entry on an open air theater in Izmir in an online user-driven dictionary, *Ekşi Sözlük* (Sour Dictionary), the users noted the theater's nostalgic value making the audience feel like as if they are in Yeşilçam film and likened it to *Cinema Paradiso* (Guiseppe Tornatore, 1988, http://sozluk.sourtimes.org/show. asp?t=bornova%20hayat%20sinemas%C4%B1). Similarly, Abisel calls the 1960s and the early 1970s the "happy years of Turkish cinema" (1994, 98). Such an image and imagination of happiness, romanticism, innocence, and purity disregards the period's social and political turmoil. These were years of the often-violent socioeconomic transformation of Turkey, marked by military interventions, political oscillations, and violence.

The acceleration of Turkish modernization during the high Yeşilçam era resulted from numerous factors: the expansion of mass education, mass communication, and culture; import substitution–based industrialization; urbanization, migration, and immigration; the advance of the nuclear family and individualism; consumerism within an increasingly capitalist economic system slowly replacing the state-centered planned economy; and the amplification of class distinctions. While the First Republic achieved sociopolitical modernization, the Second Republic brought about more of a socioeconomic modernization entangled with capitalism. Yet both processes of modernization and westernization were far from complete and a third process was initiated by the 1980 military intervention and new constitution in 1982, which gave way to a more authoritarian power structure coupled with depoliticization, privatization of the economy, and the integration of Turkey into the global capitalist system, especially after the 1990s. All of these produced various consequences for mass culture and entertainment, and fostered nostalgia for the "happy," "pure," and "innocent" years of popular filmmaking in the high Yeşilçam era. Perhaps rather than looking through such rose-colored glasses, it might be useful to examine Yeşilçam's system of production, distribution, and exhibition and how this produced an industry of popular or commercial cinema in Turkey.

The Popular Film Industry

Toward a Working System of Production

The system of production was determined by an intricate process that, in director Kunt Tulgar's words, started at the table and ended on the table (2002). The first table referred to is in a business office where a producer and a distributor met to decide upon what films to make for the upcoming season. Other participants of this cinematic roundtable meeting were the director, the scriptwriter, and the stars. While Tulgar's claim reflects the preproduction stage of many films, the distributors' role in determining the films produced varied based on the power of the production company involved. Major filmmaking companies had a greater say during the preproduction stage, while some minor operations relied mainly upon the money that distributors would bring them. In the case of minors, distributors had a say in selecting actors and the genre of the film, preferences that were based on their expectations concerning the region in which they distributed films. In other cases, star actors, directors, and scriptwriters could influence decisions made during the preproduction stage.

According to Tulgar, the process of filming was conducted quickly, culminating at the second table, that of postproduction, where a film was edited and dubbed. In many cases, the flaws arising from poor sets, poor film quality, and lightning-speed filming could be partially eliminated during the postproduction stage. This was not an occasional or temporary phenomenon: Hürrem Erman brings our attention to the fact that despite the increased number of films, the technology of filmmaking remained constant during the 1950s and 1960s. For instance, he notes that equipment such as editing tables or an almost half-century-old Debrie Matipo printer that he bought secondhand in the late 1940s were still used in the early 1970s. He also mentions that there were no dissolves or fades in color films, just cuts from one scene to another, due to the lack of proper equipment (1973, 25). Erman also acknowledges that even though the costs of filmmaking almost doubled with the advent of color films, revenues did not increase accordingly (1973, 30).

The transition to color films came around 1970, and while only 56 of 229 films made in 1969 were color, 138 of 226 films in 1971 and 178 of 208 films made in 1973 made use of the new technology (Abisel 1994, 103). Apart from increased costs of filmmaking and the use of different brands of color film stocks for the same film, even different copies of the same film differed remarkably in quality thanks to a discrepancy in the conditions of postproduction studios. The varying quality of film development was due to a number of factors, from the equipment and staff to the urgency and speed of development. In light of these factors, Tulgar's assertion of the importance of the postproduction stage is understandable. Yet even as filmmakers tried to eliminate the failures of the filming process, the postproduction stage was nevertheless marked with its own incompetence.

Bonds, Loan Sharks, and Taxes

The system of production, distribution, and exhibition was intricate during the high Yeşilçam era. Three important factors influenced the industry: the financing of filmmaking with bonds and checks, the role of distributors, and four-walling of theaters. Because of inconsistent accounts and limited, unreliable data left from the period, it is difficult to ascertain exactly when these practices became standard. Erman mentions that the "bond system" came into frequent use after the mid-1950s, when the number of films produced rose (1973, 28). But producer Nusret İkbal of Be-Ya Film contends that in 1960 he was the "first" one to use bonds to finance his films (Türkali 1974, 47). Unlike state bonds, those used by Yeşilçam filmmakers were more like postdated checks or legally valid certificates of debts to be paid at a specific due date. Türkali also mentioned that the initial use of bonds by film producers did not coincide with the dominance of regional distributors, which was strongly felt during the second half of the 1960s. Bond use became standard practice when regional distributors started to give them, or other forms of financial credits, to help film production companies gain an advantage over other distributors working in the same region.

As a result of this system, the first half of the 1960s was witness to quite a lot of competition between distributors. Film production companies started to pay actors and other filmmakers with these bonds, eventually leading film industry workers to get the bonds cashed by illegal bankers, or loan sharks, at a reduced or discounted rate. Both production companies and filmmakers wanted to create artificial financial guarantees in order to reduce their financial risk. While film production companies wanted a guarantee that filmmakers, including star actors and directors, would be available for their films, filmmakers were equally concerned with guaranteeing themselves a job and a certain amount of advance payment. Yet this system soon led to a false economy in which nobody worked for cash, only for promises of future payment. Türkali asserts that the system was also corrupted by raw film importers supplying the market with cheaper raw films to increase their revenues, and also by ambitious loan sharks (1974, 48). As the system of bonds became a widespread practice in the mid-1960s, these loan sharks and regional distributors became the most important actors in the industry. In 1967, the magazine *Sinema Postası* reported that four main "loan sharks" of the film industry (Adnan Karadayı, Ferdinand Manukyan, Metin Alper, and Necdet Barlık) claimed that if they had not cashed bonds, Turkish cinema would have only produced twenty-five films a year—one-tenth of its annual production at the time. The article also noted that loan sharks often ignored the legal limit on the amount of interest that could be charged while cashing bonds.

However, these four bankers also threatened filmmakers because banks later protested one-fifth of the bonds that they cashed ("Sinemanın Para Babaları" 1967, 10).

A subsequent issue of the same magazine announced an urgent need for legal regulation of the film industry's finances, since many of the production companies ran the risk of going bankrupt over protested bonds ("Sinema Kanunu..." 1967, 9). These companies paid their workers with bonds rather than regular salaries and benefits. The minor workers of the film industry—technicians, stunt performers, and stage workers—worked, without any form of insurance, under difficult conditions, for extra hours, and without holidays. Due to the absence of unions or extremely limited unionization in the film industry to this day, this lack of job security remains a serious problem. The head of Turkey's Film Workers Union, Nazif Taştepe, mentioned in 1974 that while he was the head of the union for four years, they had been able to get basic social security plans for only 35 of their 1,500 members, and the premiums for these were paid only during filming (Taştepe 1974, 17). Erman recounts that the "bond system," the advance cash and bonds coming from the distributors, drastically reduced the amount of capital that production companies invested in films, to only a quarter of the film's budget. Despite being vulnerable to fluctuating market conditions, the absence of big investors, and the reluctance of national banks to give credit to producers made the industry dependent on bonds (Erman 1973, 32).

The tax system, on the other hand, encouraged producers to recoup their tax payments by making even more films. Taxes on films were based on the five-year projection of amortization. Sixty percent of the total amount was charged in the first year, 20 percent in the second, 10 percent in the third, and 5 percent in both the fourth and fifth years (Erman 1973, 28). Thus a film's financial success was dependent on the money grossed in the first year of exhibition. However, after 1973, very few films ran for more than a year. When Erman mentions the first year, he is referring to the calendar year, while the film season was assumed to start in early autumn and continue through late spring; films exhibited early in the season had a greater chance of bringing more revenues. In addition, Erman and some other producers mentioned that they sold some films to distributors in Greece, Italy, Germany, Cyprus, Iran, and other Middle Eastern countries. However, such sales were not factored into the projected revenues of a film but were, rather, unexpected bonuses. Nevertheless, more films made by film producers meant more taxes to be paid. This bond and tax system, coupled with increasing costs due to color film and hiring star actors, the chronic devaluation of the Turkish lira, and the delayed arrival of ticket sales revenues through regional distributors could easily force a production company into early bankruptcy.

Regional Distributors and Four-Walling

In such a network of production, distribution, and exhibition, distributors were particularly influential in the decision-making processes of small production companies between the mid-1960s and mid-1970s. Lots of new entrepreneurs who invested in films for instant profit made this an excessively dynamic market, while some major companies persisted. Of the seventy-five film companies that made films in 1962, only nineteen were still active ten years later. The others either left the market, or in some cases continued under different names. Until 1995, only 17 companies were producing more than 49 films and the most active company was Erler Film, which has made 169 films since 1960, while Er Film produced a total of 150 films after 1961. Kemal Film, Saner Film, and Erman Film also made more than 100 films, while the remaining 12 companies made between 49 and 98 films. These major companies often four-walled film theaters in Istanbul, leaving small companies out of first-run theaters especially. In 1962, while only 5 production companies made 5 or more films with a total of 30 films, the remaining 70 companies were responsible for 101 of the 131 films produced. A similar pattern is also visible in 1972, when only 17 of 124 production companies made 5 or more films, totaling 120 out of 300 films, while the remaining 107 companies made 180 films. Major film production companies that stayed in business for more than two or three decades produced around 25 to 30 percent of the films each year. While the percentage of companies that produced more than 5 films was 22 percent in 1962 and 40 percent in 1972, 17 major companies produced 1,471 films, which is close to a quarter of the films made in Turkey in that span. Thus, minor companies that produced the majority of films became increasingly dependent upon distributors.

Regional distributors, who took control by eliminating competition and thus had an economic monopoly over film distribution in their region, were also able to channel the spectatorial demands thanks to information gathered from theater owners. In this system, Turkey is divided into six regions: Istanbul, Samsun, Adana, Izmir, Ankara, and Zonguldak. This division resonated with the geographical division of Turkey by the republican regime, to disperse the central power of the state and to reframe a fictive cultural reordering of Turkey through the association of a characteristic folk culture to each region. There were seven regions in this scheme: the two Western regions, Marmara and Aegean, were the most developed parts of Turkey with Istanbul and Izmir as their respective centers. While the Mediterranean region lay along the southern coast of Turkey, the Black Sea region lay along the northern coast and the barren lands of central Anatolia housed the capital city, Ankara. The mountainous and arid lands of eastern Turkey were called the Eastern Anatolian and Southeastern Anatolian regions, the latter of which is mostly populated by Kurds. In this partitioning, Turkey was imagined as a unified entity bereft of ethnic and lingual diversity. While Yeşilçam's regional divisions were also based on the commercial viability of regions, the content and theme of films shown in different regions varied depending on where a film was sent. In a sardonic article, Çetin Özkırım recounted this process using the example of a production company that, after making a contract with a star actor, leaks the information to the press in order to attract the interest—and thus bonds—of regional distributors. Later the company, with the regional distributors of Adana and Izmir, determines the film's plot and where to insert standard scenes of belly dancing, a funeral, and songs (1959, 3).

Compared to other regions controlled by distributors, Istanbul and the Marmara region generated a considerable amount of revenue for a film and the distribution of films stayed principally under the control of production companies. The following chart outlines Nilgün Abisel's annual estimates of the consumption market around the beginning of 1970 (Abisel 1994, 100).

Table 4.1. Number of Theaters and Spectators in the Regions

Region	Number of Theaters	Number of Spectators
Adana (21 towns)	463	37,335,472
Izmir (12 towns)	646	51,427,031
Ankara (6 towns)	216	29,474,552
Samsun (16 towns)	238	20,420,363
Zonguldak (2 towns)	82	13,149,007
Marmara (9 towns)	343	27,288,164
Istanbul	436	67,402,721
Total	2,424	246,497,310

Given this information, the distributors, visiting Istanbul during the spring to make deals with producers and relaying spectatorial demands as reported by regional theater owners, influenced the number of films, genres, and stars for the upcoming season. However, for the major companies, this was the case only if the company was in dire financial straits (Erman 1973, 34). Major producers like Erman also forecasted the trends for the upcoming season and attempted to introduce some novel plots or genres. For instance, if a film gained remarkable success during one season, other producers tried to exploit this by making films in the same genre, with the same or similar star actors, and so on. However, while in such a case other producers continued to produce adventure films, for example, Erman, in the 1973–74 season, devoted his efforts exclusively to producing "lighter" films, "comedies or sentimental comedies" (1973, 34). In addition, the production company's existing contracts with star actors and directors in part determined the genre. Stars preferred to repeat similar roles and typecasting was based on a star's performance in specific genres. While producers evaluated the stories brought to them by their contracted directors or scriptwriters, they also kept an eye on recently released foreign films to determine how they could benefit from them. Thus, all of these factors determined stories, directors, and actors.

The regional distribution system, directed by the distributors' demands, reflected the tendencies of spectators in different regions of Turkey, at times influencing their identity and culture. Erman mentions that while spectators in Adana and Ankara preferred action films, films about *efes* (local bandit heroes) had a higher appeal in Izmir (1973, 33–34). Alternatively, religious-themed films brought more revenue in Samsun, Ankara, and Adana. Whereas these differences are indicative of unverified observations, they reflect regional variations in rural and urban levels of modernization, the interest of spectators and their educational level, and the interplay of nationalistic, ethnic, and religious fervor. For instance, unlike the urban areas of the same region, the rural population around Izmir region was fond of religious films. In 1961, a theater in Söke, a small Aegean town, exhibited a religious documentary with edited footage from different films. The theater moved out all the chairs to put rugs on the floor to mimic the interior of a mosque and during the ten-minute intermission, they offered nonalcoholic and religiously proper rosewater to the spectators ("Haberler" 1961, 29). In another case, Musa Özder, a traveling cinema projectionist with a 16mm projection machine, traveled to remote villages in southern Turkey's Taurus Mountains to show religious films. During the summer he traveled with two donkeys, riding one, with the projection machine in his hand, while the other carried an electric generator. He projected films on school walls, if available, or on a screen that he strung up between two trees, though strong wind occasionally complicated things. Özder recounts that the villagers liked religious, historical, and rural-themed films. When he had problems with village imams claiming that cinema is "immoral and the work of the devil," religious films threw them off and even made some villagers stand up during the call to prayer in films (1974, 50–53). While such regional identities played out in exhibition patterns, the collaboration of producers and distributors produced another tactic in which separate scenes—including fighting, romantic exploits, or religious themes—were shot for the same film and were edited in depending on the region to which it would be sent. Furthermore, majors produced several films in different genres to cater to film preferences in different regions.

The four-walling of theaters in Istanbul by major production companies increased the minors' dependence on distributors. Before four-walling became a common practice, the majority of first-run theaters in major cities showed foreign films; for instance, in 1958, almost 90 percent of those were Hollywood films. The devaluation of the Turkish lira that year, however, made American companies warn Turkish importers that they had to pay their debts in order to continue importation ("Filmcilik..." 1958, 32). While this economic crisis also made raw film extremely expensive, domestic filmmakers were still able to produce films at a lower cost than that associated with imported Hollywood A-movies. As domestic films gradually moved from second-run theaters to first-runs, even second-run theater owners started to demand more domestic films ("Sinema: Meydanı..." 1958, 30). While the floodgates for Yeşilçam films were opened, four-walling, known in Yeşilçam as the "foot system" (ayak sistemi), became a standard fare in Istanbul. Four-walled theaters, called the "feet" of the production companies, were generally rented by an alliance of companies. In the late 1960s and early 1970s, there were three "feet" networks that guaranteed exhibition for approximately 110 to 120 films. The alliance of producers paid theater owners an advance fee for four-walling, thereby ensuring that only their films were shown. During this time, almost three-quarters of the 200 to 300 films made annually did not participate in the system of four-walling (Erman 1973, 28). While first-run film theaters in Istanbul were reserved by majors, in order to four-wall theaters outside Istanbul, producers either sold the films directly to theater owners or paid them 25 percent of ticket revenues. However, as distributors became more powerful, producers in these locations gradually moved away from four-walling Anatolian theaters.

Majors and Minors: Quality Films and Quickies

In this system of production and distribution, majors controlled first-run theaters in and around Istanbul, while distributors were effective in the decision-making process of smaller production companies. Forced to stay outside the four-walled theaters and unable to work with star actors under contract with majors, minor production companies sought their fortune in quickies, reminiscent of Hollywood's B-movies or independent exploitation films. The practice of producing quickies, such as action-adventures, fantastic films or science fictions, Westerns, adaptations of comic books or Hollywood serials, and sex comedies, closely resembles the history of Italian cinema, which experienced a similar situation during those years.

Indeed, there was an active exchange between the popular film industries of both countries; some Italian companies came to Turkey to make films and at times to make coproductions, while Turkish filmmakers sent many films to Italy for postproduction. Pierre Sorlin noted that in Italy, as in Turkey, there was a distinction between two types of film: "quality films" and "quickies." In Italy, while quality films were booked to national distributors at exorbitant prices and therefore expected to bring a high return from first-run theaters, quickies were booked to regional distributors who sold them to peripheral and rural theaters (Sorlin 1996, 120). Sorlin also explains that the quality and sophistication of films became more important for Italian intellectuals who formed cinema societies and cine-forums that led to a distinction between "elite" or "high" and "mass," "popular" or "low" forms. While this distinction was operative in relation to the work of majors and minors, or between Yeşilçam's mainstream and its low-budget filmmakers, with reference to Christopher Wagstaff, Sorlin notes that spectators living in suburban, peripheral, and rural areas "confronted with loosely constructed stories full of thrills and excitement, let their attention fluctuate, carefully following the fights or chases but began to chat as soon as there was a pause in the action" (1996, 121). However, in Yeşilçam, this aspect was indeed a characteristic of film spectatorship in general, valid for both quality films and quickies.

In Turkey, nearly all spectators attended open-air summer theaters with wooden chairs, brought their food and purchased drinks from theater tea gardens, and chatted during the film, enjoying the film as much as the social event. At the time filmgoing was a family experience as much as it was the experience of young male spectators. Thus apart from major and minor, and first-run and second-run differences, there was another binary of Yeşilçam. In addition to the nostalgically remembered family experience, action-adventure quickies catered to young male spectators who, after the mid-1970s, became the main consumers of sex films. In the late 1970s, the economic and social turmoil of devaluation and inflation, unemployment, security crises due to political polarization and violence, and the concurrent popularization of television sets among middle-class families were all factors that drove the family audiences to stay home, and gave leeway to sex films. However, such low budget, poor-quality films have always been part of the film scene. Quickies of various genres coexisted with films perceived as higher quality, and young, undereducated, lower-class males had long been their primary demographic.

Exploitation Cinema as a Survival Tactic

Yeşilçam films, in comparison to Western popular cinemas, had undeniable problems with technical quality and narration due to the economic conditions of filmmaking. In comparison to major's films, Yeşilçam's quickies were even worse in this respect. In 1972, one producer of quickies, Mehmet Karahafız's company Osmanlı (Ottoman) Film, produced 22 films, and like other minors, he chose a faster and cheaper way of making films with the cheapest available equipment and without established actors or renowned directors and scriptwriters. Perhaps influenced by their education in Italy, figures such as Mehmet Karahafız and Kunt Tulgar produced and directed films in a manner reminiscent of Italian cinema practice.[2] One of the 22 films produced by Karahafız was *Bombala Oski Bombala* (Bomb Oski, Bomb!), directed by the prolific Çetin İnanç, who directed almost 200 films in a period of little over two decades. İnanç, who regularly completed films in 10 to 15 days, worked even faster with this costumed superhero flick, completed in just two days: one day for shooting and another for editing. He also noted that they often shot 3 or 4 films at the same time, simply traveling from one set to another (1999, 346). Quickies, as survival tactics of minors, offered attractions, fantastic spectacles, and thrills for their spectators. In the late 1970s, many of these minors started to produce sex films that also fall in the ranks of low-budget, exploitation cinema.

Quickies resonated with American and Italian exploitation cinemas. As in other genres, directors such as İnanç or Tulgar were following other popular film industries and Turkifying some of their examples. İnanç mentioned that they Turkified Dutch, German, and Italian erotic movies (1999, 348). Another hasty director, Yılmaz Atadeniz, famous for Turkifying Hollywood serials, comic books, and Westerns, read the Italian photonovel *Killing* (first published in 1965 in Italy by Ponzoni) in a Turkish paper and shot two Kilink movies simultaneously to utilize the same sets and costumes, *Kilink İstanbul'da* (Killing in Istanbul, 1967) and *Kilink Uçan Adama Karşı* (Killing against the Flying Man, 1967). "It was interesting. There was eroticism, adventure; there was mask and thus mystery. I told myself that it suited my style and I immediately decided to make it into a film" (Atadeniz 1999, 328). When his friend İrfan Atasoy liked the idea, Atasoy gave him bonds to finance the movie in return for the distribution rights in the Adana region and for being the lead actor in the movie.

While minors adapted such tactics to survive, in the late 1970s, majors continued to introduce new stars through their conventional melodramas and popular comedies. The exploitative tactics that the minors used to create sex films were considered by many to be crude, obscene, and "pathological." In the first issue of an Islamist film magazine, Fatih Şen called sex films "an epidemic that highlighted a load of diseases, a load of economic crises which ranged from the disinterest in the state to the insufficiency of thought, morality, and aesthetics" (1977, 11). On the other hand, starting with the 1960s action-adventure films, female nudity had already been a part of Yeşilçam even before the wave of sex films. However, as in the Western world, sex films' overtly erotic content and pornographic elements came at a time when television created considerable competition, and the market was trying to adapt to major demographic changes resulting from urban migration. The lower class or lower middle class, peripheral clientele of these films, who had previously flocked to action-adventure films with limited erotic content and female nudity, started to watch sex films, as middle and upper classes were at home enjoying their television sets.

Sexploitation Films

In such an environment, the Turkification of an Italian film, Öksal Pekmezoğlu's *Beş Tavuk Bir Horoz* (Five Chicks One Rooster, 1974), the first film of the wave of sex comedies fit right into the mold of low-budget, exploitation cinema. In the Italian original, *Homo Eroticus* (aka Man of the Year, dir. Marco Vicario, 1971), Sicilian Michele (Lando Buzzacca) is of "simple peasant stock, lower-class, a Southerner, yet he is being seduced, desired, and bedded by many wealthy Northern women" because he is "extremely virile, is in possession of an enormous penis and has been nick-named after his three testicles" (Gavin). In the Turkish version, the Sicilian servant is turned into Kazım (Sermet Serdengeçti), a villager, who migrates to Istanbul following a doctor's discovery of his extraordinary sexual power. Kazım becomes famous in Istanbul and five sexually unsatisfied high-society women have intercourse with Kazım before his compulsory marriage to a girl whom he sexually assaults (Özgüç 1974, 70). This film was not just a simple sex comedy but, like its counterparts, echoed mainstream Yeşilçam films' melodramatic modality through the heterosexual relationship between peripheral, lower-class and urban, upper-class characters. At the same time, sex films, aimed at male spectators, transformed heterosexual romance into cruder and more obscene forms.

The 1970s saw two distinct waves of sex films. The first wave came in 1974 with the influence of other European cinemas, especially Italian sex films. While the earlier action-adventure films of the late 1960s and the early 1970s involved nudity as a part of the "thrill" of action directed

Figure 4.1. *Beş Tavuk Bir Horoz* (Five Chicks One Rooster, Öksal Pekmezoğlu, 1974)

for male spectators, sex comedies integrated nudity into their storylines. Giovanni Scognamillo and Metin Demirhan claimed that nudity in the earlier films was a kind of "fishing" that demonstrated that films incorporating nudity brought more money (2002, 144). Made without any of Yeşilçam's star actors and directors, the first wave of sex films was initially produced by low-budget filmmakers who had previously worked as directors of action-adventure quickies. Their actors included low-

Figure 4.2. *Ah Deme Oh De* (Don't Say Ah, Say Oh, Nazmi Özer, 1974)

rank Yeşilçam actors and extras, as well as newcomers from theater and women eager to enter the film world in any guise. At the inception of the sex comedy wave, only about 5 percent of the 189 films made in 1974 integrated nudity into the narrative. However, the success of films such as *Ah Deme Oh De* (Don't Say Ah, Say Oh, dir. Nazmi Özer, 1974) or

Beş Tavuk Bir Horoz encouraged other low-budget filmmakers to exploit their popularity; more than half of the 225 films made in 1975 were sex films. Although this early wave, characterized by gratuitous nudity and obscene jokes as well as comical "bed scenes," lost its allure in the following years, it nevertheless made way for an increasing percentage of sex films during the late 1970s. Sex films of the late 1970s became increasingly obscene, without being explicit enough to qualify as hardcore pornography. During this second wave, sex films gained new impetus with the use of thrifty 16mm films. In 1979, two-thirds of the 193 films made were sex films and almost all of those were shot on 16mm; all of these 16mm sex films, as well as many of the films of the first wave, were shorter than regular feature films in order to allow projectionists at film theaters to insert hardcore footage that had been shot separately or spliced from foreign films.

Even though Turkey experienced two conservative Nationalist Front coalition governments during these years, increasing political rivalry and violence allowed sex films, as well as political films from both the left and the Islamist right, to escape the attention of censor boards. The 1980 military intervention and the subsequent three years of military rule put an end to these films, yet the production of sex films had a lasting effect on the film industry. While many theaters closed during this period, some of those that remained began to show Turkish and foreign sex films, often two or three films for the price of one. Thus the sex film industry created a continuing forum for the local film industry when political limitations, as well as the television-driven shift in spectatorship, had severely curtailed its viability.

Deemed the dark years of Yeşilçam, the sex film wave between 1974 and 1980 was also coupled with an increase in the importation of foreign, principally European, sex films. Thus low-budget filmmakers competed with the foreign sex films by producing Turkified examples. Stephen Heath, seeing pornography in opposition between liberation and repression, mentions the dilemma of the "sexual fix" that disguises the relations of power embedded in sexuality (Williams 1989, 14–15). Instead of taking sides with relation to this dilemma, a look at the constructions of sexuality and their relation to pornography would imply the conditions of Turkey in 1970s. The 1980 military intervention put an end not only to political extremism but also to sex films, a form of sexual extremism sullying morality in the eyes of the soldiers. As Williams notes with reference to Walter Kendrick, "[P]ornography is simply whatever representations a particular dominant class or group does not want in the hands of another, less dominant class or group" (1989, 12). In the case of Turkish sex films, the dominant classes' assumption that the lower classes would not be "responsible" enough with politics or with such representations was instrumental in the Kemalist army's intervention; the military intervention took on the responsibility of protecting the people from themselves by "fine tuning" politics and morality, as they suppressed political voices and sex films.

Contrary to the popular label attached to the late 1970s Yeşilçam sex films, though many were made, they did not become the filmmaking norm, and mainstream melodramas and comedies continued to be produced. Nevertheless, sex films had the effect of making onscreen nudity possible and in the muted and apolitical world of the post-1980 military intervention era, this perhaps led various male directors to speak for women and their sexuality in a series of "art" films generally referred to as "women's films." These were not melodramas, but rather dramas addressing women's identity and female sexuality. Thus one of the ironies of Turkish sex films, directed toward a male audience, was their subsequent effect on quality male directors' addressing of female sexuality. Tied to the sex films of the 1970s was a shift from action, adventure, and fantasy toward soft-core sex comedies. As İnanç mentions, there was no difference between sex films and religious films for the filmmakers; if religious films were more lucrative they would have been equally happy to produce those instead of sex films (1999, 348). Taken in this vein, sex films, that is, "sexploitation films," belong to the second grade of Yeşilçam industry, a broader range of low-budget, exploitation films produced by minors.

Although one may see the period of sex films as one in which the popular film industry experienced severe crisis both in terms of form and content, an alternate reading of *Beş Tavuk Bir Horoz* is also possible. Rather than emphasizing its sexual content, one could instead focus on its Turkification of an Italian film, its presentation of a lower-class dream of vertical class movement, and its use of Yeşilçam's melodramatic modality. Like the Sudanese Mustafa Said in Tayeb Salih's novel *Season of Migration to the North*, who went to Britain for education and had relationships with British women in an attempt to "liberate Africa with his penis," or like Fabián of Buenos Aires in José Luis Marquès' *F—kland*, who travels to the Falkland Islands to impregnate British women and let future children of Argentine blood dominate the island, both Sicilian servant Michele of *Homo Eroticus* and villager Kazım of *Beş Tavuk Bir Horoz* represent masculine violence directed toward the female members of a dominant class. Both films reveal the latent threat of the return of the other as more powerful than those with actual power. Despite its ill-conceived strategy of resistance, besides reproducing patriarchy, Kazım's masculine terror is also quite politicized. In this respect, sex films resonated with the comedy films of the 1970s, especially those with actor Kemal Sunal, which introduced a frequent use of obscene language and street vernacular tied to the texts of resistance against dominant class. While comedy persisted through the 1980s, the production of sex films came to a halt with the military intervention; nonetheless, cheap theaters continued to screen them and the advent of the VCR in the 1980s made them a common part of the video market, facilitating their informal export for the enjoyment of immigrant workers.

Melodramatic Modality, Turkification, and *Hayal*:
Knotted in Dubbing

Sex films carried Yeşilçam's tropes with its melodramatic modality, Turkification, and *hayal*. Like their predecessors, they investigated different tactics of Turkification-from-below while maintaining a consistent pattern of melodramatic modality. Despite variations and changes, this process involved various levels of translation and transformation. The exploitation of Italian photo-novels or Hollywood melodramas, even Soviet socialist realist films, had been a constant theme of filmmaking in Turkey. Such Turkifications contained a permanent postproduction element, dubbing, that, as in a carpet, knotted together various threads of Yeşilçam. Above, dubbing is introduced in tandem with the dubbing of foreign films, which involved both a translation and a rewriting of the stories of Western films, as well as with the replacement of the opening credits of foreign films. For example, the opening credits of Raj Kapoor's *Awaara* (1951) named only the lead roles (Nargis and Raj Kapoor) and the director (Raj Kapoor), while giving full credits to those who "Turkishified" (meaning "put into the Turkish language," a variant on the more ethnically inflected Turkification) the film, that is, a full list of dubbing artists, dubbing director, translator, voice synchronizer, and the dubbing studio.

Earlier Practices of Turkification and Dubbing

The Turkification of foreign films involved not only the dubbing of Western films but also of the Egyptian or Indian films that were particularly popular in the 1940s and 1950s. This process of Turkification involved (mis)translations, the Turkification of characters, and muting of ideological aspects of films by giving them a "Turkish" voice, similar to the practice of Turkification-from-above. In the 1940s, Ha-Ka Film imported socialist realist Soviet films and then dubbed and "Turkified" them, adding locally made scenes to make them "fit" with the realities of Turkey. This ideological purification was, in the words of the owner of the company, Şadan Kamil, a form of "domestication" (*yerlileştirme*): shooting some new scenes, montaging them into the Soviet films, and dubbing them (2000, 16). Interestingly, such scenes frequently involved songs and dances performed by famous Turkish singers and dancers, as well as the scenes that altered the narrative flow. Faruk Kenç, a director who started directing in late 1930s, referred to scenes acted by famous comedians as "Turkification" (1993, 25). The last element of such "Turkified" films was dubbing, guided by a new script composed of the translation, transformation, and alteration of the original Soviet text. To provide narrative "coherence," the Turkish dubbing artist who dubbed the hero of the Soviet film also dubbed the domestic-made scenes with the Turkish actor who acted in place of the Soviet character. Thus, if there was another Turkish artist acting in the scene, she or he was voiced by the dubbing artist who spoke for their character in other portions of the film. Ha-Ka Film did not stop there, and later "domesticated" German, American, and French films, before eventually starting to make "Turkish" films.

In the cinema of Turkey, sound was recorded live during the filming of most films before the Second World War and in almost all films since the mid-1990s. The five decades in between are marked by dubbing or post-synchronization, which in many cases was done by professional dubbing artists who began their careers dubbing foreign films. In an anecdote that appeared in *Artist* film magazine in 1960 (vol. 18, p. 30), a journalist asked Adalet Cimcöz, who, with her brother Ferdi Tayfur, voiced many Yeşilçam stars, about her views on a theater to be opened by the stars of the era. Cimcöz's reply to the question was caustic: "Excuse me, but who will dub that theater?" Had this theater come to fruition, it would have reversed the normal pattern of movement from the world of theater to that of film, revealing the artifice of the latter. While the theater never became a reality, Cimcöz's point is obvious: prompters were not enough for Yeşilçam stars, they needed dubbing artists or they had to dub themselves. Her reply also implies that the people on screen were visual actors incapable of carrying their own voices on a stage. In post-synchronized films, Yeşilçam films either worked with professional dubbing artists or had actors dubbing their own parts. Dubbing was instrumental in making the process of filming fast and inexpensive; by eliminating the need for rehearsals through dubbing, actors repeated their lines for the camera immediately after a prompter read them during filming. This allowed filmmakers to take only one shot of many scenes by decreasing the chance of audio continuity problems and thus decreasing the amount of raw film used for filming.

Turks Voicing Their Own Films!

During the early sound film era, only a few films were made and film sound was recorded live on the set. Because many early film actors were theater actors and some also worked on the dubbing of foreign films, the transition from silent to sound films in Turkey did not create the problems it did in Hollywood, where the advent of sound films required some film stars to have voice training. Though the transition to sound film went smoothly for the cinema of Turkey, one of the preconditions for the rise of Yeşilçam was not this transition, but a transition from live sound recording to post-synchronization. For this reason, any history of Yeşilçam cinema is inherently tied to Faruk Kenç's *Dertli Pınar* (Troubled Spring, 1943), which was the first fully dubbed film. Because İpek Film did not let Kenç use their studios for making this film, he decided to shoot the film without sound and then dub it at producer Necip Erses's sound studio, where foreign films were dubbed at the time (Sekmeç 2001, 6). Leon Sason claimed that this was partly due to the cost and import restrictions that made finding raw film stocks and other equipment difficult during the Second World War years (1961b, 32). Kenç claimed that both the success and the significantly reduced costs of his film led others to follow his lead, but also added that he did not like post-synchronization (1993, 27). Like it or not, dubbing became standard practice in filmmaking and contributed to Yeşilçam in terms of both Turkification and *hayal*.

While "Turkification," in the case of (mis)translations of foreign films and the process of dubbing, involved mechanisms of othering, including the West and the others of Turkish national culture, the dubbing of Yeşilçam films by Turkish dubbing artists produceed an ironic non-illusionism. Due to the existing practice of dubbing foreign films, it may be argued that the dubbing of Turkish films did not demand a change in the auditory expectations of filmgoers. A common cliché about the dubbing artists is that they all belonged to a tradition of the City Theater of Istanbul; directed for many years by Muhsin Ertuğrul, these actors disseminated speech based on the Istanbul accent. Thus, this new practice supplemented the earlier, Turkifying one, of dubbing foreign films. The interest in maintaining an appropriate adherence to republican linguistic mores meant that villagers were usually represented with preternaturally proper, Istanbul Turkish; equivalent, perhaps, to a Midlands farmer speaking Oxford English. Such dubbing created a linguistic identity for the masses to adopt that was in keeping with the formulation of an increasingly uniform pan-Turkic national identity.

According to Erman Şener, during the high Yeşilçam era, voice artists were generally paid based on their work for three-hour sessions (1968, 37). şener noted that based on sessions that took place in the dubbing studio, a film was cut into 150 to 300 parts to ease the recording work. Before recording a part, dubbing artists watched that clip a couple of times to ensure lip synchronization, and then rehearsed their parts. When the dubbing directors signaled the start of the process by uttering the number of the part, the sound engineer began recording. Dubbing actors used the same microphone placed at a standard distance without any concern for the depth of sound of the characters in the film. Using this method, all of these parts were dubbed and the dialogue of a movie was recorded on film. The last part of the process involved moving the film to an editing table to synchronize the sound copy of the film with the silent image copy. If there was a separate recording of sound effects and film music, it was also edited together with the two other copies. As suggested by Erman Şener's description of the dubbing process, such a sterile sonic environment created a rather cold and senseless voicing of many films, lacking the ambient noise of everyday life. While the technique and infrastructure of sound remained similar during the period of Yeşilçam cinema, this practice of voice artists dubbing was not universal and there were some film actors who voiced themselves in the 1950s and 1960s.

His Master's Voice, His Slave's Body

While dubbing was financially beneficial for Yeşilçam, it remained an obstacle to cinematic illusionism or realism by creating breaks and discontinuities in the diegesis. Such a use of sound is comparable to American musicals and sex films, both of which raised issues different from those of the early sound films' experiments. In contrast to Eisenstein's or later avant-garde uses of sound, Hollywood's transition to sound led to more dialogue and increasingly realistic effects. In most narrative or feature films, sound—in the form of dialogue, music, or sound effects—was used to foster a realistic illusion of the diegetic world. According to Williams, while music helps to establish the mood and the rhythm of bodies and to fill in the gaps of editing, sound effects add to the spatial dimension of diegesis, and "synchronous speech ties the body to the voice" (1989, 122). For her, this illusion of realism in mainstream American cinema was not replicated by the use of sound in musicals and sex films. Instead, in hardcore sex films, lip synch often failed and the use of post-synchronized close-up sound "disembodied" the female voice. But like musicals with post-synchronized musical scores recorded in sound studios, the clear and close-up sounds in sex films offered an effect of closeness and intimacy. Instead of increasing the realist effect, Williams argued that they produced more of a "surreal" effect, breaking up a film's "continuity" or "realistic illusion." Such gaps and discontinuities are among the reasons that Yeşilçam is generally considered bad or low quality.

Nezih Erdoğan notes that "the discrepancy between the visual and the aural" involves a variety of situations (2002, 239). These include the invisible presence of the prompter; the voicing of actors by professional dubbing artists; in the case of an actor voicing himself/herself, the matching of an image recorded earlier with a voice recorded later; problems of lip synch; the distortion of the first syllable of words in some films; and the use of music. In addition, songs performed by actors complicated dubbing further because an actor who was voiced by a dubbing artist during his or her dialogues would be voiced by a different singer. So an actor might be doubly dubbed! Sadi Konuralp noted that the use of music in films was widely based on a practice of using musical scores from vinyl records, "upholstery music" (*döşeme*) as it was called by the industry (2004, 63). In the period between the 1950s and 1980s, the majority of films used such records and to this end, the industry employed a number of composers or musicians, who were well aware of Western and other musical traditions and who often had a good collection of records from which to upholster film music. Certainly, the use of these musical selections had a broad range: from original Western movie soundtracks to traditional and modern Turkish musical genres, as well as various Western musical genres, including but not limited to classical music, jazz, blues, rock, and pop. Stitching these together, Erdoğan noted, "The soundtrack of Yeşilçam appears extremely impoverished" (2002, 239) and asked whether all Yeşilçam actors spoke in the same voice:

[T]hey do not speak at all. Their bodies are given over not to homogenous thinking subjects but to Logos expressing itself through voices that were only slackly attached to bodies. Hence Yeşilçam is like the shadow-play master whose voice remains the same by way of the differences it produces. It might well be suggested that the voice *in* Yeşilçam is the voice *of* Yeşilçam; the utterances are instances of

Logos which dictates its moral universe and orchestrates the unfold-
ing narrative. (2002, 243)

Erdoğan claimed that through post-synchronization Yeşilçam muted bodies while disembodying voices and that, by making actors "be-spoken,"
Yeşilçam's film scripts describe action without articulating dialogues
into the flow of everyday life. For him, then, the bodies of actors become
vehicles for the mediation and the disembodied voices belonging not to a
theocentric space, that of Logos, but to an Islamic one that penetrates all
bodies. This, for him, blurs the line between a Cartesian body-soul duality
and also between diegetic and nondiegetic worlds that diffuse the "Divine
Presence" throughout the soundtrack. Erdoğan concludes his article by
noting that though Yeşilçam appears to separate two domains "by giving
body to the service of Logos and by denying the characters the 'look,' and
therefore the sight of the body, this body-soul duality is resolved by the
condition of the existence of body for the mediation of voice and thus
truth" (2002, 249). This may be argued in relation to the Kemalist projects of secularization and to mainstream dubbing marked by an Istanbul
accent that became the standard accent of Turkish through radio and
television. While on a "theocentric" level the body is muted and the voice
is disembodied, Erdoğan's analogy of Yeşilçam in relation to a Karagöz
master whose voice is the only voice throughout a play does not work
on a fundamental level. Instead Yeşilçam is about a multitude of voices,
a cacophony more than an orchestrated regime of sound and voice. It
does not present a single, omnipotent, and godlike voice, because it caters
to ambivalent and contradicting voices. This "dream" of having a single
voice that would be "be-spoken" for all is also shared by the Kemalist
reformers.

Cinematic Sound and the Illusion of Voice

Still on an imaginary level, the muting of bodies in the name of a voice
speaking the truth has also been the dream of projects of modernization
from above. Nostalgic for his melodramas, comedies, and sex films of
the 1960s and 1970s, Armenian Yeşilçam director Aram Gülyüz currently
directs films and television series that have prolonged Yeşilçam's practice
of post-synchronization. He relates a story of a guest from France in the
early 1970s whom he took to a couple of films at different theaters. After
watching the films, his guest ironically pondered the dubbing: "Just think
how interesting it would be if all of our stars also had the same voice"
(2004). Gülyüz had an epiphany: in Yeşilçam films, a small number of dubbing artists were voicing many of the stars. However, the bodies were not
simply muted, instead they had gestures, star texts, and they were types
or individualities. One of the most acclaimed realist directors of Turkey,
Lütfi Ö. Akad noted that in choosing actors he did not care much about
their acting but "their facial and bodily makeup, their 'type' as the French
call it" (2004, 59) In many Yeşilçam films from the 1950s and 1960s, there

are blatant looks of the bodies that address the spectators. In particular, happy endings are often indicated not simply by the coming together of the happy couple but by the attention the actors pay to the viewer— through a look or a wave not seen by the rest of the characters, that is, by deliberately addressing the nondiegetic world. Alternatively, as the happy couple walks off, an auxiliary character either gestures for the closure of a stage curtain or waves good-bye to the spectators, signaling their return to the nondiegetic world. As Peter Brooks argues, we can understand "melodrama's constant recourse to acting out, to the body as the most important signifier of meanings," as "the genre's frequent recourse to moments of pantomime." Though not given a chance to voice themselves, noble savages communicated with the Europeans in gestures—they offered "a set of visual messages, pure signs that cannot lie, the undissimulated speech of the body" (Brooks 1994, 19).

However, the play of gestures in Yeşilçam did not necessarily come at a point when verbal language became inadequate. Instead, dialogues were mostly descriptive or even at times instructive, perhaps similar to early sound films. As scriptwriter Bülent Oran said, "Turkish spectators watch films with their ears" (Türk 2004, 219) and they were very aware of the types of stars: "A *jeune* cannot be an evil man and *jeune dames* cannot intentionally be prostitutes. Only fate can lead them to such flaws" (Türk 2004, 217). Moreover, Oran added that such habitual identifications of types of actors, such as comic, evil, or femme fatale, were related to types in *Karagöz* plays. "For example, when Necdet Tosun appeared on the screen, the film theater was ready to laugh before he did anything" (2004, 225). Even if you turned such comic types into evil characters, Oran claimed that the spectators laughed at the most dramatic parts of the films. In this respect, Yeşilçam's melodramatic modality belongs to fluid dualities, at times spoken by the dubbed voice of truth and at other times the autonomous gestures of a savage, that is, both modern and traditional or both civilized and primitive. Thus seeing Yeşilçam in terms of diegesis or continuity, or of a religious morality, is complicated due to its continually recurring nondiegetic elements, its discontinuities and coups, and its attempt to come to grips with a Western bourgeois morality that coincides with an Eastern traditionality. Viewing dubbing only in terms of muted bodies and disembodied voices implies gestured bodies given to savagery or pantomime.

In considering the sound of Yeşilçam, and voice as such, one also must consider what voice is—what do the voice of the dubbing artist, the actor, and the singer add up to in a single film? For example, the most legendary, acclaimed, and stereotypical female star of Turkish film, known as the "sultana," Türkan Şoray, was initially dubbed by several dubbing artists, but eventually was dubbed almost exclusively by Adalet Cimcöz. In her later films of the 1970s, she chose to dub her own lines. However, in all of these films, her songs were exclusively dubbed by singer Belkız Özener. Thus Türkan Şoray spoke and sung with different voices in her different films, yet the absence of realism in this multiplicity of voices never threatened her singular star image. While communication through speaking, through the word, is one aspect of voice, the truth of voice is not just limited to the word or to "articulate signs." Though Erdoğan interprets voice in the service of religious morality and truth, Yeşilçam's voice, which was constantly recorded and played in "mono," is more complicated in its give and take, its realism and spectacularity, or its "ah" and "oh," its pain and pleasure. Should we then assume that Yeşilçam's use of post-synchronization is integrated in a monotheistic tradition bringing about a mediation of voice and truth by ousting the body? Or should we ask whether cinematic sound (music, sound effects, and the voice of actors or dubbing artists) belonged to a realm of the spectacular and the savage? How should we place Yeşilçam's sex films such as *Ah Deme Oh De* (dir. Nazmi Özer, 1974) or *Oooh Oh* (dir. Aram Gülyüz, 1978) into this frame of Logos?

Close-Up on Noise

Williams argues that hardcore sex films involve various close-ups of both sound and image. However, she also notes that a close-up shot of a body part or an act differs from a close-up sound of pleasure. Following Alan Williams, she argues that a close-up sound in the manner of a close-up shot is not possible; the soundtrack and the image track are not commensurable. Still, though it may not be useful in increasing realist effect, the post-synchronized sounds of pleasure in hardcore films, similar to close-up shots, offer the "spectacular." But still this spectacularity in "the aural 'ejaculation' of pleasure" does not match with the truth of the close-up shot of visual ejaculation. In this respect, she argues that aural voyeurism is subject to failure because the foregrounding of the sound of pleasure is very different from the image of pleasure. Following Mary Ann Doane, she notes, "Sound cannot be 'framed' as the image can, for sound is all over the theater, it 'envelops the spectator'." While it may be possible to show male pleasure on the image track, the sounds of pleasure (especially of women) are often not "articulate signs," but they come from "deep inside," by being attributed to "primitive pleasures" (Williams 1989, 124–25). However, Yeşilçam's sound in sex films, asking women to moan not in pain ("ah") but in pleasure ("oh"), was not just dubbed to increase the realist effect like American hardcore sex films or musicals. Rather, a film was completely dubbed to knot it together during postproduction. A give and take of pleasure and pain was supposed to culminate in *Oooh Oh*, the sound of total pleasure: entertainment. As for entertainment, what was offered was a package: not only a realistic and rational narrative and its placement into a coherent and continuous cinematic language but also a complete entertainment program that involved attractions, spectacularity, pleasure in pathos or action, and tears in pain and laughter.

When discussing Yeşilçam, this state of being neither one nor the other, but both at the same time must be emphasized. Perhaps it would, then, be wiser to comprehend Yeşilçam in relation to Turkification, as translation and mistranslation, a transformation and a perversion or vulgarization.

Though this may not be articulated in terms of a politics of emancipation, at the same time, it is not simply reducible to a cinema of escapism or intoxication. Beyond this problem of savagery or vulgarity, an integral question attached to Yeşilçam and its Turkification is *hayal*. While the Turkification of Western technologies involved various avenues of quick but imperfect solutions as well as mirroring and outright plagiarism, the dream of filmmakers was to create films equal in quality to Western ones even as their technological and cultural makeup prevented this from ever becoming a possibility, let alone a reality. While they participated in dubbing practices at the time, looking back, almost all Turkish filmmakers were critical of dubbing, for it was non-illusionistic and nonrealistic. Nobody considers that it was perhaps reasonable, even natural, within a particular spatiotemporal configuration of film production and consumption. Instead of reading Yeşilçam as a mythic narrative of gradual accomplishment of realism and considering dubbing as one of the prime obstacles before such realism, Yeşilçam's dubbing might be viewed not as what seems "real" but a solution that seems "natural" to the conditions of its production. As noted above, Oran claimed that Turkish spectators watch movies with their ears. He relates the story of the man who shined his shoes and used to take his family to a tea place right by an open-air theater first to listen to the film and then to decide whether or not they should buy tickets to watch it. If what they heard was showy or thrilling enough, they bought tickets to watch the film (2004, 219). Should we then claim that Yeşilçam's consumers were more of an "audience" than they were spectators? Had this been true, there would have been no incentive to go into the film theater to "see" the film, which was there and which stayed there. Inside such theaters, there was a carnivalesque environment filled with spectators from all ages talking with family and friends during the film, bringing food and eating or sharing with others. Sodas and tea were sold, and children ran around and made noise as others cursed them. Parallel to this world of family carnival, film theaters showing sex films offered another, darker environment of carnivalesque masculinity marked by masturbation, and at times by homosexuality and pedophilia. It was an underground carnival that fostered darker pleasures. How important was the illusion or realism of a diegetic world, both in terms of soundtrack and image track for such spectatorship within the distraction of open-air summer theaters that constituted half of the theaters in Turkey during the golden age of Yeşilçam cinema?

Above, an alternative rendering of cinema, as an interweaving of the real and the magical, traditional and modern, and appearance and apparition, is laid out. Popular films do not offer reality to their viewers, but only visual and sonic images of it that allows them to naturalize myths without making them more civilized. Demanding reality from popular cinema and then criticizing it for its lack of reality is inherently against the nature of popular film. Viewed and heard as mythic and anarchic, popular films belong more to a carnivalesque world. Seen as apparitions in appearances or heard as moans or noises among discrete voices, film's naturalness may be understood in relation to our presence in nature that is tied to the unnatural and that involves not only a civilized, canonical beauty but also an ugly, savage, or irrational beauty. The voice of Yeşilçam is inescapably coupled with its noise. This noise is neither mono nor stereo or polyphonic, but cacophonic. It is in this cacophony that one may find what Yeşilçam Turkified with post-synchronized sound: not only voices, musical scores, and sound effects but also the noise of the theater, of the projection machine, and of its spectators. The nostalgia for the golden age of a popular cinema is not just for its sounds and images, but for an image and imagination of its precapitalist, carnivalesque laughter and crying, which is lost in the process of modernization and westernization, like the precapitalist, carnivalesque Karagöz or other traditional forms of entertainment.

5

High Yeşilçam II
Genres and Films

Every minute provides scenes of captivating astonishment
A spectacle house of cautionary tales is our screen
                                        —prologue to Karagöz plays

Karagöz and Punch

In March 2005, the Little Angel Theater in Islington, London, put on a new puppet play, *The Grass Is Always Greener*. In the play, which begins in a two-dimensional Karagöz format and transforms into three-dimensional Punch style, Karagöz is inspired to visit London when he sees his cousin Punch on television (Awde 2005). The artistic director of the theater, Steve Tiplady, explains how Punch "takes him up in the London Eye and offers him the world, if he becomes a 3D glove puppet" (Wright 2005). But in this Faustian storyline, as Punch, that is, Mephistopheles, brings Karagöz into the "real world," Karagöz realizes that the real world put before him and of which he dreamed, is not as he had imagined. According to Tiplady, "Like Turkey itself, half-European and half-Asian, the show is a mix of ethereal Eastern shadow puppets and knockabout Western Punch and Judy" (Wright 2005). In Turkey, Karagöz is considered a traditional, two-dimensional and basically vocal art outside the world of perspectival representation that has been slowly fading out over the last fifty years. But in this fade-out, is there a fade-in of Karagöz into other arts? Should it remain a pure, traditional art? Nowadays, not only do such questions persist in relation to Karagöz but they are also relevant in terms of Yeşilçam cinema, which by and large faded out of the contemporary world of filmmaking in Turkey while persisting in television series. What *The Grass Is Always Greener* "did" to Karagöz stands as a metaphor for Yeşilçam cinema that aspired to the more realistic Western cinema. But once it incorporated Western forms, there was no return, and instead a new existence emerged that is neither quite Western nor Eastern, but in-between.

Some Turkish film critics and writers noted that cinema, as a modern medium, is the output of technological and visual inventions allowing for a mechanical representation of the three-dimensional reality of the world; Karagöz had no place in this representational world and was instead relegated to a pre-modern mode of representation and entertainment and disregarded by film historians such as Nijat Özön. Alternatively, filmmakers such as Halit Refiğ considered Karagöz, if no longer visually viable, as one of the sources for Turkish cinema. Yet he did believe its form to be usable in the creation of a "national" cinema intended to produce homegrown perspectives and narratives. Both writers considered cinema as an essentially "serious," acculturating art. Set in this context, the Karagöz quote with which Refiğ opened his 1971 book *Ulusal Sinema Kavgası* (The Struggle for National Cinema) is indicative of how Karagöz and later Yeşilçam was consumed: above all, both forms provided its spectators with "scenes of captivating astonishment." While they presented cautionary tales, they did so within a house of spectacles involving both spectatorship of and participation in a world of dreams and escapade. Yeşilçam not only utilized traditional narratives but also overcame technological or visual shortcomings with the help of verbal communication, as did traditional theatrical forms. Thus while its sources and methods shared a specific relationship to both filmic and local traditions, as a popular film industry or as a mass entertainment industry by and large producing commercial films, Yeşilçam did not have a project or agenda mirroring that of the republic. Instead it repeated several well-established formulas to increase profits and produced genre films and cycles of films in the same genre. In doing so, the majority of Yeşilçam's filmmakers did not look for a "true" or "good" way of making films; instead they searched for the most profitable formula for filmmaking.

Yeşilçam's texts, which oscillate between realism and non-illusionism, are put together with the help of dubbing. They often introduce not only visual discontinuities and failures but also incoherent and discontinuous narratives; however, whenever the visual language became insufficient for conveying the story, filmmakers relied on dubbing or overdubbed narrative to eliminate these shortcomings. Similar to traditional theatrical forms that relied on limited sets and stages, they solved the problems of visual language with verbal language. Such solutions also brought about narrative formulations and genre-based practices based on the repetition of established formulas.

Genrification and the Recycling of Genres

Discussions of genre focus on analyzing aspects of films' production and consumption: film industries refer to genres before and during production as "genre films"; spectators are aware of genres; and critics interpret genres' significance within economic, sociopolitical, and cultural conjunctures. Genre criticism and popular cinema studies are also relevant to film criticism and film studies; while the former evaluates films through earlier examples of the same genre, the latter traces the development of and transformations in genres. At the same time, the borders and topography of film genres involve continual negotiations and alterations in different spatiotemporal contexts. Rick Altman notes that the earlier conception of melodrama has been undermined by recent film scholarship and that genres are subject to considerable redefinition (1999). This redefinition involves a continual alternation between the initial creation of genres (genrification) and their subsequent recycling in different periods and in other genres.

Yeşilçam producers took into account genres and generic choices that determined the following season's films through socioeconomic and political clues, tips from regional distributors, thorough knowledge of the market, and the surmised plans of other production companies. Scriptwriter Bülent Oran mentioned that producers had an annual period of indecision at the end of each season: "What films were they going to make in the incoming season? What was the public bored with? What was the public demanding" (1973, 22)? While producers initially gathered distributors' demands regarding particular stars, genres, and ingredients such as fight scenes, nudity, or lots of tears, they then considered the socioeconomic and political conjuncture: "Is the public experiencing hardship? Are they comfortable? Based on these factors, comedies or dramas are considered" (Oran 1973, 22). Filmmakers responded to the popularity of genres through the production, distribution, and consumption process, and through finding efficient and creative solutions to unstable conditions.

Altman's model of genre-cycle involves a constant process of genrification and recycling, of mapping and remapping: "Just as our knowledge of the changing borders of France underlies any current use of the term 'France,' so categories like *poetry*, *drama*, and *comedy* coexist with *the musical*" (Altman 1999, 69). Instead of presupposing an originary or specific point of reference for each discussion of France, it would be more commensurable to understand borders as being fluid, as subject to redefinition or remapping. Genres belong to a multiplicity of locations instead of a specific and definable locus, similar to Altman's argument about the relationship between genres and nation. While for some, the nation stood for "a single coherent concept referring to a single coherent referent... the very notion of nation appears to depend on constant conflict among multiple competing but related notions" (Altman 1999, 86). According to Altman, as systems and processes interconnected with one another, genres, like nations, suggest complex and interconnected communities and a presupposition of Benedict Anderson's notion of "imagined communities" and the Habermasian rendering of "a bourgeois public sphere" (1999, 196). "All genre formation... begins with a process of cycle-making creolization, combining gypsy adjectives with established, land-owning generic substantives" (Altman 1999, 199). Altman's view of genre/nation also presents a center-periphery conflict that continually shifts the borders and involves attempts to capture the center. Instead of arguing for a fixed center that is pure and originary, Altman's argument involves a dialectical operation that leads to continual transformations, as well as recyclings and regenrifications. This conception is commensurable with readings of Third World or postcolonial cinemas that moved from an understanding of national cinemas based on origins, essences, and purity to ambivalences, hybrids, and subversions. While this view inscribes Yeşilçam to an extent, its relation to Turkification, *hayal*, and melodramatic modality is also evocative. Yeşilçam is a site of demand and desire that presented complex and contradictory identity claims that oscillate between the East and the West; and thus such protocols of identity formation and identification are at stake in Yeşilçam's genre films.

Yeşilçam's *Özenti*

The Islamist director Yücel Çakmaklı remarks that the narratives of "cosmopolitan cinemas" (Hollywood and Western cinemas in general) are not "our" stories, those of a Turkish-Islamic identity (2002). For him, "cosmopolitan films" involve all film genres ranging from "adventure or comedy" to "historical action or comedy" and "Turkish cinema took these, initially tried to adapt them, but later started to imitate—even in the 1960s and 1970s, it started serial production by copying both scripts and films" (2002). Similar to Özön and Refiğ, Çakmaklı also yearns for a "national" cinema placed against Western cinema, incorporating and reflecting the traditions and mores of Turks. For him, even Ertuğrul's films about the War of Independence and all other social realist films are "imitations" of Italian Neorealist films. Likewise, he claimed that Satjayit Ray or Youssef Chahine's films emerged from an *özenti*, a demand and desire to imitate. Apart from his obvious distaste for leftists and the westernized elite, Çakmaklı's choice of words reiterates aspects of nation/genre. Regardless of their political views, for educated film critics and filmmakers, Yeşilçam is a cinema characterized by *özenti*.

The word *özenti*, which denotes a desire to imitate somebody, is a fabricated word and its root, "*öz*" means self or essence. *Özenti* is the noun form of the verb *özenmek*, which does not have a direct counterpart in English and which, according to the *Redhouse Turkish-English Dictionary*, means 1. to take pains (to do something), 2. to want to imitate (someone), and 3. to try to (do something one knows little about). In other words, it involves contentious effort, imitation, and novelty. According to İsmet Zeki Eyüboğlu's *Etymological Dictionary of the Turkish Language*, the "*en-mek*" suffix denotes a "self" that moves toward itself, and in *özenmek*, "*öz* (self) is self-reflexive. It thus makes itself closer to another self, it enters into a relationship with another self. *Özenmek* is, for a self, to try to do something done by another self by moving towards itself." The double meaning of the word *öz* is informative, for it resonates with the Turkish nation's relation to the West and its cinema's relation to the West. When one takes *öz* as "essence" and "pure or genuine," it refers to all claims of national identity that presuppose an essential, pure, and original Turkishness——even though such presuppositions vary between disparate communities under the imagined unitary rubric of a nation. Alternatively, *öz* refers to self: *özenmek* describes a relationship of desire between self and other (selves). Whenever one self desires to be another self, *özenmek* involves a movement that starts at the self, enters another self, and returns to itself. However, in this movement, in this process of "trying to do something one knows little about," the "essential, pure, and original" self is lost. When Çakmaklı calls Yeşilçam a cosmopolitan cinema and therefore a cinema of *"özenti,"* he indeed means a cinema without "essence, purity, and original-ity." Thus he demands a return to an "essence" found in Turkish-Islamic culture, the Islamic aspect of which is excluded from republican cultural reforms. More important, Çakmaklı's films, as products of Yeşilçam, are also not devoid of melodramatic modality, and are far from reproducing an *"öz"* because his claim to "return to our *öz*" is no longer pure and essen-tial, but "purified" and "essentialized."

Nationalism, Colonization, and the Third World

The most influential intellectual and political positions that relate to Yeşilçam involve leftist, Kemalist or Islamist ideologies. Besides their ideological differences, all of these purportedly original syntheses that intended to retrieve the lost, but pure Turkish essence overlook cultural colonization. Frantz Fanon stated that the native artists' production of visual arts is based on national works that are "stereotyped reproductions of details." For him, native artists working on modern, nonfigurative art forms in a pre-independence setting ironically refused foreign culture, intending to institute a national culture in the post-independence era. "After independence his anxiety to rejoin his people will confine him to the most detailed representation of reality. This is representative art which has no internal rhythms, an art which is serene and immobile, evocative not of life but of death" (Fanon 1967, 181). Fanon asks whether the truth of these artists is reality in a post-independence setting. In Turkey, which bears an imperial culture in its history and which was not colonized per se, but invaded and then engaged in a successful War of Independence, formations of a Turkish national culture accommodated elements of a colonized culture in its relation to the West, and those who yearned for an essential national identity developed cultural self-colonization. The national cultural project initially formed a myth of striving to meet the standards of the West through modernization from above and westerniza-tion, and then supported the myth with a secondary claim of being true to a national culture with an imaginary return to its essential and pure state. It was not coincidental that, when I contacted Metin Erksan for a possible interview in 2002, he refused to talk with me after I called Turkey of the Yeşilçam era a Third World country. For him, Turkey's place is not next to "those" Third World countries but next to the Western countries, as their equal. Yet Turkey as a Third World country easily suits the following definition:

> The fundamental definition of the "Third World" has more to do with protracted structural domination than with crude economic categories ("the poor"), developmental categories (the "non-industrialized"), racial categories ("the non-White"), cultural categories ("the backward"), or geographical categories ("the East," "the South"). (Shohat and Stam 1994, 25)

Such structural domination holds the essence of *özenti*: a nation never able to actualize because its structure is always being fed through an external system of essential identity and linear progress. However, asked to imagine a "Third World" country, Kemalist-nationalists only think about the poor, the nonindustrialized or the backward, something that the Turks should not be. It is because of such a nationalist sentiment that many intellectuals—leftists, Kemalists, and Islamists alike—have found themselves in a state of blindness that carries the impenetrable fog of a nationalist and an imperialist past. It is because of this that Turkish politicians did not find themselves in a position to attend the 1955 Bandung Conference that led to the Nonaligned Movement in 1961 and culminated in the conception of "Third World" terminology (Koçak 1995). Instead, Turkey conceived of itself within a frame of nationalist discourses in the Third World that assumed "an unquestioned national identity. But most contemporary nation-states are 'mixed' formations" (Shohat and Stam 1994, 26). Neither earlier Third Worldist initiatives nor perspectives, nor a contemporary postcolonial theoretical stance was proper for the national culture projects of Turkey that dreamed of being equal to the West.

As a Yeşilçam director producing many popular films generally referred to as "business films" (made just for profit), Erksan, like Refiğ, yearned for a proper national cinema that would be simultaneously modern and able to utilize such elements of Turkish culture as Sufism. Following Fanon, in yearning for a representative art, native artists stereotypically reproduced details in the name of reality. Such details proved lifeless and undecipherable not just to the foreign spectators but also to the domestic masses. Moreover, when Erksan heard that I was going to do a study on his film *Şeytan* (Satan), a "Turkification" and even an "Islamization" of *The Exorcist* (dir. William Friedkin, 1973), he refused to talk about this film, which, in his words, has no respectable place in his oeuvre. Assuming that it was not I who caused his anger during our very short telephone conversation, his attitude is likely a result of his position as a Kemalist, nationalist director staying true and proper, rather than indulging in the impurities and business aspects of a Turkified film. In his book on the possibility of making a film about Mustafa Kemal Atatürk, Erksan claimed that a film about him cannot be done in Turkey because it would concretize the concept of Atatürk and thus limit people's freedom in imagining Atatürk. Instead, Erksan proposed that "a big and real American filmmaker such as Martin

Scorsese, Steven Spielberg or George Lucas" must make this film (1989, 76). But one such big and believable American director had to come up with the idea independently, without incentive or requests from Turks because Hollywood had the best capacity to create "myths and legends" that would avail themselves to one's freedom to "image" and "imagine" Atatürk and his thoughts. The power of Kemalist ideology comes from its "image" of Atatürk as the savior of Turks and founder of the Turkish nation-state and the film has to represent the "inner truth" of the father of Turks. Taken in this vein, the inner truth reflects the genuine state of a self bereaved of fallacies. Instead of viewing national culture in terms of continual change and transformation, such a film and models offered by filmmakers offer stable and pure states of originality and essentiality without considering the split inhibited by the very presupposition of a national culture.

Colonial Selves, Postcolonial Others

The concept of *özenti* challenges such presumptions about unitary and originary selfhood because it introduces a movement that starts from the self, goes to the other, and then assumes a return to self. What this movement fundamentally marks is the impossibility of a self to which one can return or that would stay intact once such a movement occurred. In his article "Remembering Fanon," Homi Bhabha quotes Fanon who said that he, himself, "had to meet the white man's eyes" and see his "cannibalism, intellectual deficiency, fetishism, and racial defects." According to Bhabha, Fanon thus understood himself as far from his own presence marked by amputation, excision, and hemorrhage (1994, 115). Fanon's colonial subject is placed into vision and representation; while being "over-determined from without," Fanon sees this process as taking place in the colonial condition through image and fantasy. The ideas of civility and progress, the move from nature to culture, and the myth of man and society, according to Bhabha, are all undermined by the delirium and perversions of the colonial condition. In other words, post-Enlightenment Man's "dark reflection, the shadow of colonized man," disturbs and divides its being (Bhabha 1994, 116). For Bhabha, this "idea of Man *as* his alienated image, not Self and Other, but the 'Otherness' of the self inscribed in the perverse palimpsest of colonial identity" is transferred by Fanon onto the historic condition of colonial man. "The process of identification in the analytic of desire" is based on three arguments: to exist in a colonial condition is about a demand on the place of the Other; colonial otherness is "caught in the tension of demand and desire" as a space of splitting; and this identification is about "the production of an 'image' of identity demanded by the subject."

> The demand of identification—that is, to be *for* an Other—entails the representation of the subject in the differentiating order of Otherness. Identification…is always the return of an image of identity which bears the mark of splitting in that "Other" place from which it comes. (Bhabha 1994, 117)

Having listed these three conditions, Bhabha quotes Fanon's narration of the moment he was seen by a white French kid: "Look a Negro.... Mama, see the Negro! I'm frightened." Orhan Koçak wrote about two republican intellectuals, the republican reformist Nurullah Ataç and the traditionalist Cemil Meriç, who wrote on Shakespeare's *The Tempest* and were blind to Caliban's identity. For Koçak, instead of seeing this play/character in terms of a clash between two cultures, both saw it/him as parts of the same culture within a post-Enlightenment framework of universality and civility (1995, 228). After reading Edward Said's *Orientalism*, Meriç admitted that he would not be able to write a study like Said's, yet still claimed that he was familiar with the bulk of Said's sources. According to Koçak, Meriç, resorting to a form of Occidentalism, totally disregarded the real West as he made it into a single, unified entity with which he had a relationship of demand and desire: "If we burn all the Korans, if we demolish all mosques, we are still Ottomans in the eyes of the Europeans; Ottoman, in other words, Islamic: a dark, dangerous and enemy mass" (Koçak 1995, 241). Meriç's search for identity led him to dig into Eastern sources, including those of Buddhism. However, he favored sources in the French language. Though in his relation to the West, Meriç found himself in a relation of love and hate: of desire. He never imagined himself in the position of Caliban, the inferior slave whose island was conquered by a superior master, Prospero. Though he saw an inherent darkness, danger, and enmity in his identity, he tried to identify with what was enlightened and astute, instead of using his darkness, his shadow, toward political subversion. It was not just a coincidence but also an irony of history that Ernest Renan served as a source for the claims of national identity fostered by Ziya Gökalp or others who envisaged Turkey's national cultural projects. Renan's nationalism had to be stripped of its inherent racism in a search for a nationality based on a spiritual principle that links the past with the present.

Much like China, which could not quite place itself in the Second World or the Third World and which experienced a process of self-colonization by its own governments, the Turkish intellectual climate stayed away from Fanon, Said, and other postcolonial theorists until the 1990s. As noted with reference to Rey Chow, though both countries never experienced colonial rule per se, both countries were in effect colonized and both peoples suffered exploitation thanks to their own governments' modernization programs. Thus, postcolonial thought's stress on "deterritorialization, the constructed nature of nationalism and national borders, and the obsolescence of anticolonialist discourse" is significant in understanding this situation of colonization (Shohat and Stam 1994, 38). For Shohat and Stam, postcolonial theory involves transcending the earlier understanding of Third World and Third Cinema, inscribed by nation-building attempts and proximity to nationalist ideals of linear progression. Instead, "postcolonial theory, in so far as it addresses complex, multilayered identities, has proliferated in terms having to do with cultural mixing: religious (syncretism); biological (hybridity); human-genetic (*mestizaje*); and linguistic (creolization)" (Shohat and Stam 1994, 41). This shift from essentialism, nationalist originary models, and racial purity to hybridity and ambivalence may bring about a useful path of analysis in understanding cinema in Turkey.

Yeşilçam and Özenti

In the world of cinema, including that of filmmakers who yearned for a national, art, or political cinema, such a relationship with the West was not fostered. Instead Hollywood is rendered through a *dream* of the inversion of roles, to be in the place of the other, of Hollywood, to possess a phantasmic space that cannot be literally occupied—hence it is a dream. Such filmmakers are like Karagöz, who sees Punch on television and decides to go to London. There, Punch offers him the "world," to be like him, in a three-dimensional world of puppets. For this, Karagöz has to identify with Punch and accept the latter's three-dimensional world by leaving the two-dimensional world behind. Nezih Erdoğan, who has written on the problem of identification in relation to the construction of a national cinema in Yeşilçam, argues that both the defenders of westernization and its critics in Turkey placed the West both as the other and at the center of those arguments (1995, 180). While Yeşilçam understood its norms to be set by Hollywood, the proponents of a political or art cinema saw something like French New Wave or Italian Neorealism at its center stage.

In any case, the other had to be mirrored; the image of the desired other was outside and *özenti* involves a dream of being in the place of the other, possessing its space, and being the master. In this dialectical inversion of roles, however, the place of identification is marked by a tension of demand and desire. The dynamics of *özenti* are critical for understanding Yeşilçam. While Yeşilçam was called *özenti* by its critics who longed for a "true" national cinema, Yeşilçam produced ambivalent responses not simply to such yearnings but also in relation to the West. Yeşilçam's *özenti* thus involved a dialectical movement in which it is impossible to return to an originary self already lost in the process of modernization and westernization. Erdoğan argues that "melodrama as a popular genre which plays on desire" provided us "with valuable insight into the ambivalent nature of national identity" (1998, 264). This is indeed so, but extends past Yeşilçam melodramas to Yeşilçam's melodramatic modality and its genrification. Turkification and genrification are both processes of nation- or genre-construction. The dynamics of such processes are not reducible to clear-cut categorical identities.

Instead, Yeşilçam's *özenti* produced ambivalent and contradictory responses to both West and East, and to both reform projects and antireformist tendencies. *Özenti* demonstrates two distinct but related flaws of Yeşilçam: one in its relation to Western cinema and the other in its relation to the westernized elite and their reforms. Yeşilçam is also divided in itself in terms of films produced by majors and minors. United, these complex inputs create multiple and ambivalent realms of response and criticism, muting the possibility of a single path from a colonizing West to a colonized and traditional East. Instead, this is also coupled with another convergence between the westernized elite and the West and between the self-colonizers and the doubly colonized masses. While the elite's *özenti* is mediated through high culture and was at the focus of early republican reforms, popular cinema was bereaved of this focus. Following Fanon's arguments, such a relation to the West eventually resulted in the alienation of the elite and westernized intellectuals from the masses. This presupposed a demand and desire to reach the level of the West, to be equals, on a path of *özenti* that claimed to possess the place of other without giving up its own self. As Bhabha quoted from Fanon, this has to do with the colonizer's invitation of a shared identity based on education and status: "You are a doctor, a writer, a student, you are *different*, you are one of *us*" (1994, 117). Sold on such a claim to distinction, they repeatedly enacted their differences through the hierarchy constructed through self-colonization.

This relationship with the West, generally mediated by high culture, became more complicated in terms of cinema. While the masses were subjected to reforms, they were also aware of Western cinemas, mainly of the same Hollywood that the elites sought to emulate. The masses were marked not only by the dream of possessing the colonizer's place but also by the dream of stepping into the role of the self-colonizers who locally stood in their stead. They are not only presented with a double "image" of identity but also are asked to incorporate both. As doubly colonized, they were traditional, rural, and multiethnic and were asked to negate their identity, the multiethnic and multicultural aspects of their-selves. In terms of cinema, they consumed Hollywood culture through a certain mode of "Turkification" thanks to dubbing and at times reediting. The popularization of Egyptian and Yeşilçam cinema, with the rise in the number of film theaters and with migration to urban centers, created ambivalent identities and identifications, both in terms of the films of major and minor production companies and of their response to the West and westernizing reforms. In this manner, taken as a cinema of *özenti*, Yeşilçam's self is not just itself but a spontaneous and ambivalent movement from it-self to its others (i.e., dream-selves) before its return to it-self, which is distorted and transformed (i.e., "Turkified") in the process. But it is the distance between selves and others that underlines the "movement" of *özenti*, which involves the effort to create something novel in its imitation. But should one find in this process an antagonistic relation between the West and the East, the colonizer and the colonized, and the master and the slave? Should one presuppose a return to the self?

Özenti also introduces self and others, and the Lacanian "Other." In presenting "the place of the native [i.e., the colonized] as that of the image and the silent object," Chow notes that "a kind of 'lack' in a pejorative" sense is at work (1993, 48). Fanon attempted to fill this with an antagonism by claiming natives' subjectivity through an anticolonial envy and violence. Beyond this imagination of the native subjected to a Manichean ethics, to a melodramatic antagonism between good and evil, that limits the native to a field of the impure (i.e., *getürkt*), by following what she called "the

Lacanian language," Chow offered "the Other" (*Autre*), "that is before 'separation,' before the emergence of the *objet petit a*, the name for those subjectivized, privatized, and missing parts of the whole" (1993, 49). While a relation between the Subject and "object a," the object of desire, would lead one to a direct positioning of both, according to Bhabha or Chow, the introduction of the Other as the locus of speech and truth (i.e., the law of the father), puts representation into ambivalence by disclosing lack. Bhabha places this metaphor as "a process of substitution and exchange that inscribes a normative, normalizing place for the subject." However, this is simultaneously "the place of probation and repression, precisely a conflict of authority" (1994, 119). In this sort of identification, Bhabha underlines doubleness and suggests that the identity is assigned by a person into the place (of the Other). Instead of locating an antagonistic relationship between the West and the East, the ruler and the ruled, and the white and the black, both in terms of colonization and self-colonization, what Bhabha underscores is the ambivalence integral in the identification, the distance between the self and the Other: "the strategic return of that difference that informs and deforms the image of identity, in the margin of Otherness that displays identification" (Bhabha 1994, 120). While this reveals the identity and identification of colonized subjects and their complicated objectification of the Other, this postcolonial stance invites a completely different frame of reference in cinema. Echoing Bhabha, Erdoğan noted that the big Other of Yeşilçam is Hollywood, the external and unattainable entity that sets the rules:

> The Big Other plays on difference and the disavowal of difference, mimicry, departing from the denial of difference, will crash at the barrier of difference anyway. Hollywood is what Yeşilçam can never be....Difference signifies lack in this context. So, in order to make this lack "good," Yeşilçam, hopelessly produces excess....There is a paradox here; excess is not only a consolation for the lack, but it also justifies mimicry retrospectively. (Erdoğan 2001, 127)

Though this is a fair model of Yeşilçam, it also places Oedipal drama at the center stage through an analysis not only of the discourse of the colonized but also that of Yeşilçam. Even before that, this view of cinema relies on the idea of "excess," which is only possible, in Yeşilçam, through a presupposition of film language based on classical Hollywood cinema's "realism" and its continuity editing. Only after such grounding can one speak about the breaks and gaps (i.e., the excesses) that disturb classicism and continuity. However, as argued with reference to traditional performing arts, Yeşilçam's filmic language and narratives are demarcated by discontinuities and nurtured by such breaks; its non-illusionism is its defining character. Instead of wrestling with the problem of reality or a realistic illusion, Yeşilçam accommodates the naturalization of such non-realism.

But there are still other questions in relation to "the Other": do films claim an identity or is it the analyst, the Subject, who places cinema accordingly in the Oedipal drama? Alternatively, seeing Yeşilçam through "delirium" presents another rendering of the Oedipal drama, because "cinema is able to capture the movement of madness, precisely because it is not analytical and regressive, but explores a global field of coexistence" (Deleuze and Guattari 2003, 274). Instead of attaching the Oedipal guilt to the child, what if the father is guilty? Instead of Oedipus's story, what about Abraham's story? Marked by an analytical urge and an "infinite regression" in terms of the child's relation to the father [a father's relation to a child, who then becomes another father], the beginning of this delirium is based on a father's Oedipalization of a son. For Deleuze and Guattari, "every delirium is first of all the investment of a field that is social, economic, political, cultural, racial and racist, pedagogical, and religious: the delirious person applies a delirium to his family and his son that overreaches them on all sides" (2003, 274). While psychoanalysis places the real actions and passions of the mother and father into the "fantasies" of the child, and places that child into a scheme of infinite regression, it also does so in relation to a family, which is above all else a social field. After relating the familial field to, and placing delirium at the heart of, every unconscious social investment, Deleuze and Guattari mention two major types of social investment: segregative and nomadic. They also note two poles of delirium:

First, a paranoiac fascisizing (*fascisant*) type or pole that invests the formation of central sovereignty; overinvests it by making it the final eternal cause for all the other social forms of history; counterinvests the enclaves or the periphery; and disinvests every free "figure" of desire—yes, I am your kind, and I belong to the superior race and class. And second, a schizorevolutionary type or pole that follows the *lines of escape* of desire; breaches the wall and causes flows to move; assembles its machines and its groups-in-fusion in the enclaves or at the periphery, proceeding in an inverse fashion from that of the other pole: I am not your kind, I belong eternally to the inferior race, I am a beast, a black. (Deleuze and Guattari 2003, 276)

While the first pole advises reforms, the second withdraws, escapes by erasing a portion of the system. Yeşilçam's *özenti* does not presuppose an *öz*, an origin or essence; it does not attempt to establish a unity; and it does not follow republican reforms or claims to institute a "proper" national cinema. Instead its pragmatics dictates growth and aggressive expansion. Thus Yeşilçam explores a global field of coexistence, of the West and the non-West, of the colonizer and the colonized, of the paranoiac and the neurotic. However, this coexistence, seen in delirium, in "the general matrix of every unconscious social investment," involves the "astonishing oscillations of the unconscious" from one pole of delirium to the other. *Özenti* is about desire—a desire to be like the superior race and class, like the colonizer, the West. But it also engraves the impossibility of this, a return to self and thus an escape from desire: "I am not your kind," I am inferior, I am the colonized, black, Eastern, and *getürkt*.

Yeşilçam is neither revolutionary nor fascist. Instead its existential condition, *özenti*, is marked by the coexistence of two kinds—"Yes, I am your kind" and "No, I am not your kind." Yeşilçam's rhizomatic form "operates as an immanent process that overturns the model and outlines a map," despite its hierarchies and despotism: "It is a question of a model that is perpetually in construction or collapsing, and of a process that is perpetually prolonging itself, breaking off and starting up again" (Deleuze and Guattari 1994, 20). Seen in this regard, *özenti* is a perpetual movement between self and other without a return to original self or without a refuge at its other. Instead, as a rhizomatic form, it is always in the middle, in-between things and positions, by not being filiation but alliance, by not imposing an existence but a perpetual movement (Deleuze and Guattari 1994, 25).

Melodrama and Genre

While Yeşilçam integrates Turkification, *hayal*, melodramatic modality, and *özenti*, it is also a cultural entertainment machine that brought about "a mechanism of double articulation" in which unlikely combinations occurred through perpetual mapping and remapping. In this process, melodramatic modality is tied to genrification and recycling of genres. "Genre is first and foremost a boundary phenomenon" (Gledhill 2000, 221). While early scholarship "mapped" genres, defining its territories and boundaries, the contemporary understanding of genres suggests their hybrid, cyclical or amorphous existence, the processes genrification and recycling, mapping and remapping. Thus melodrama is reevaluated through its combination of action, pathos, and laughter, as "an early cultural machine for mass production of popular genres" and as a "modality...a culturally conditioned mode of perception and aesthetic articulation" (Gledhill 2000, 227). Melodrama, to exploit a broad public appeal, accommodates traditional forms with modern ones, bourgeois realism with romantic and sentimental dramas and comedies. Having its roots in a post-Enlightenment process of modernization and democratization, melodrama's "aesthetic, cultural, and ideological features coalesce into a modality" that "defines a specific mode of articulation" adaptable across genres, decades, or national cultures (Gledhill 2000, 229). Its double articulation in genres provides interchanges and overlappings, coexistences and alliances. "Thus melodrama thrives on comic counterpoint, can site its fateful encounters in romance, and keeps pace with the most recent of modes, realism, which first worked in cooperation with melodrama and then disowned it" (Gledhill 2000, 229).

Yeşilçam is also suffused with the following characteristics of melodramatic modality: it is a slippery and evolving category, a phantom genre; it is sensational and spectacular, and sensory and significatory; it may flow toward revolution or fascism; it is ambivalent and parasitical; though it grows aggressively, it coexists with other genres as well; in its replacement of a religious frame in a post-sacred world, it involves a nostalgia for a pure and innocent past; it enacts an endless fight between good and evil enmeshed with a middle-class morality; it serves well for an imaginary community of virtuous common men (i.e., noble savages) that constitute a nation; in this, it is stereotypical; it presents a myth of democracy that is livable in the land of romance and fantasy though it is marked by the return of the repressed by demanding a recognition; it demands emotional response through its spectacles and attractions as well as with its dramatic narrative shifts; it does not build its characters in their contradicting and complex selves, instead it enacts contradictions through a differentiation of stereotypical characters, through types or individualities; this aspect of individuality serves well with stars whose presence on the screen denotes singular individualities; it involves a hero-heroine-villain triangle; it works with dramatic and spectacular confrontations; in this, it is about intrigues, plays, and massive obstacles; in its working, there is a dialectic of pathos and action, a give-and-take of tension and relief; and lastly it resolves through a lifting of intrigues or obstacles. With all this in mind, how do these notions of Turkification, *hayal*, *özenti*, and genrification play out in a sampling of Yeşilçam films? The following sections offer an in-depth analysis of Yeşilçam films that cover a wide spectrum of types, from star-based business films to low-budget quickies in the 1960s and 1970s. These examples will help in constituting a thread of Yeşilçam's identity and provide concrete examples through which both devotees of Yeşilçam and those who have never seen its films may consider Yeşilçam with a fresh eye.

Hayat Bazen Tatlıdır (Life Is Sometimes Sweet, 1962)

Hayat Bazen Tatlıdır (hereafter HBT, dir. Nejat Saydam) was a major production with several stars and some color scenes. Summarized as "salon comedy" in a dictionary of Turkish films (Özgüç 1997), the film opened in sixteen theaters simultaneously, fourteen of which were mainly Istanbul's first-run theaters, while the other two were in Çanakkale and Bursa. HBT's advertisement in *Yıldız* magazine (Star, 1962, vol. 11) states: "Zeki Müren says that *Life Is Sometimes Sweet*. Life will not withhold the sweetest hours of itself from those who will see this film.... [HBT] is the most beautiful film of not only this year, but of many years...embellished with in-color revue scenes, the most beloved artists of our screen." As indicated by this ad, the "bureaucrat director" of the film, Nejat Saydam, who was employed to make business films in a systematic way and without personal glory, was not in the limelight. Before HBT, he directed another successful "salon comedy," *Küçük Hanımefendi* (Little Lady, 1961), which then became a film series starring Ayhan Işık and Belgin Doruk as the little lady of a rich mansion. Acting in various films at the time, Doruk was one of the three finalists for a popular acting competition in a 1951 issue of *Yıldız* film magazine along with Ayhan

Figure 5.1. *Küçük Hanımın Şoförü* (Little Lady's Driver, Nejat Saydam, 1962), *Left*: Ayhan Işık, *Right*: Belgin Doruk

Işık, the "king" of Yeşilçam. Doruk and Işık were arguably the first "stars" of Yeşilçam.

While Doruk and Zeki Müren's participation indicates a hit film by a major studio, Müren was also an acclaimed singer of Turkish classical music. Turkish classical music, a republican rendering of the Ottoman Palace music, combined elements of traditional Arab and Persian musical traditions. Like Egyptian melo-dramas (musical-films) with famous singers, HBT is a "singer film" following a familiar storyline: a singer with a lower-class or rural background falls in love with an upper-class woman and the obstacles to their relationship are eliminated with the singer's rise to fame in Istanbul. Müren, who acted in a limited number of big productions, said, "I am not at all ambitious in cinema. When I am not on tour I act in one film annually because I cannot refuse the insistence of my fans in Anatolia" (Müren 1963, 13). Instead of focusing on the plot, Müren's films principally presented the experience of Istanbul's music halls to Anatolian spectators and thus the opening credits of HBT focus on lists of songs performed in the film and credit the compiler of background music.

As for color scenes, the opening credits explain their limitation due to exorbitant costs. Before HBT, there were only four color films made in Turkey: an unfinished, partly color, animation film of 1951 (*Evvel Zaman İçinde* [Once Upon a Time], dir. Turgut Demirağ) and three color films (*Halıcı Kız* [Carpet Weaver Girl], dir. Muhsin Ertuğrul, 1953; *Salgın* [Epidemic], dir. Ali İpar, 1954; and *Ahretten Gelen Adam* [The Man Who

Figure 5.2. *Evvel Zaman İçinde* (Once Upon in Time, Turgut Demirağ, 1951)

Comes from the Hereafter], dir. Turgut Demirağ, 1954). After HBT, color film gradually became more common.

HBT, as indicated by its title, promised a "sweet film" with songs for the enjoyment of its spectators. As a light romantic comedy that takes place at a lavish bourgeois mansion with undeveloped cardboard characters (hence the name "salon comedy," which is often used for romantic comedies), HBT also promises a complete program of entertainment, involving music, a give-and-take of sensuality and spectacularity, attractions and astonishment. HBT opens with Zeki Müren (hereafter Zeki), who plays a character by the same name, hitchhiking with a suitcase and his dog. On a truck that picks him up, he meets another hitchhiker, Müsellim (Kadir Savun), also on his way to Istanbul. HBT automatically inaugurates the standard tropes of migration from Anatolia to Istanbul (i.e., periphery to center) and a promise of vertical class movement (i.e., from lower to upper class). In Istanbul, Müsellim goes to the lavish bourgeois mansion where Rasim, again played by Müren, works as a servant. Rasim, a comic character, contrasts with Zeki, a proper lower-class factory worker. Rasim is in love with Yeşim (Belgin Doruk) whom he peeks at at the neighboring mansion. HBT revolves around these two studio-constructed mansions, indicating an unusually high expenditure because Yeşilçam would usually have rented houses for sets. The following chart lists the main characters in the two mansions by their class backgrounds:

Table 5.1. Characters in *Hayat Bazen Tatlıdır*

	Mansion 1	Mümtaz's Mansion
Upper Class (Urban)	Father Grown-up childish son (mad, comic effect)	Yeşim Mümtaz (Yeşim's uncle) Semih (Yeşim's fiancé)
Lower Class (Rural)	Maid Rasim (Müren the comic) Şaban (cook with a regional accent) Müsellim (assistant cook) Servant	Maid Ayşe (Rasim's comic counterpart) Feleşen (Yeşim's black nanny) Zeki (Müren the lover, Yeşim's friend)

These stock characters are taken from the standard *Tuluat* theater mansion, but split between two mansions. HBT also replicates *Tuluat*'s typical storyline of love and performances of comic characters and singers. As Zeki's comic reflection, Rasim reproduces *Tuluat*'s *İbiş* character as a buffoonish simpleton servant perennially in love with the maid *Fatma* (Ayşe in HBT), despite Rasim's platonic love for Yeşim (the *girl* in *Tuluat*). The mansion owner's son (*Sirar* in *Tuluat*) is replaced by Zeki Müren, who eventually falls in love with Yeşim. This class difference is interpellated when Zeki is revealed to be Mümtaz's son by his ex-wife. Similar to *Tuluat*'s romance between *Sirar* and the girl, HBT offsets Zeki and Yeşim's relationship, with Yeşim's villainous fiancé Semih (*Tuluat*'s *Tiran* [Tyrant]). Finally, as in *Tuluat*, there are other stock types of a mansion such as the cook, gardener, and nanny.

Etched by melodramatic modality, HBT amplifies its pathos through Yeşim's wheelchair confinement and Semih's (Sadri Alışık) attempts to incarcerate her to take control of her uncle's money while cheating on her. As expected, Yeşim finds the emotional support necessary to recover in Zeki. Yeşilçam's melodramatic modality tirelessly repeats this trope of sickness or castration (e.g., characters who are crippled, blind, deaf, or diagnosed with heart failure or tuberculosis), even to the extent of being extremely comical, such as going blind after falling off of a chair. The "hired gun" scriptwriter of Yeşilçam, Bülent Oran, compared these tricks to "heroin." "At times, we were in the mood to pump up the dose. I do not remember its name now, but there was even one film in which we made both protagonists blind" (Türk 2004, 216). Oran even claimed to invent inexplicable and unnamed fatal diseases, only to have them healed through some sort of emotional or divine intervention: "I used to find various ways of committing suicide for protagonists.... If it was an emotional film, I made them take pills, if it was a thriller, I made them to go to a cliff and jump off" (Türk 2004, 216). The power of love, the divine intervention, also heals Yeşim in HBT.

Promising vertical class mobility, Yeşilçam's melodramatic modality incessantly underscored the inherent virtue and purity of its lower-class and lower-middle-class protagonists. Such social mobility is triggered by various events, including interclass marriage, winning the lottery, inheriting money from a distant relative, and, as in the case of this film, discovering a long-lost rich father. Instead of the personal flaws of protagonists, as in Shakespearean tragedies, the obstacles and intrigues are usually created by villains or evil as such, similar to the gods' involvement in worldly matters as in Greek tragedy. This externalization of evil facilitates the restitution of lower- and middle-class morality. Indeed, the most clichéd repartees of Yeşilçam present clear examples of such class- and tradition-based morality. Consider, for example, the following lines frequently associated with Yeşilçam films and easily recognizable to its aficionados:

Lovers, to each other: "When we get married, we will have a house with pink shutters" (with the connotations of a white picket fence);
Poor protagonist to rich one: "I may be poor but I am honorable," "We are from two different worlds," "You are as hostile as you are beautiful," or "Do you think you can buy me with money?";
Protagonist recognizing his/her long lost lover: "My God, this picture, this picture...," or "This voice, this voice....No, it cannot be";
When a protagonist goes blind: "Oh my God, I cannot see, I cannot see, I am blind," and later in the film, "Thank God, I can see, I can see";
A fallen mother assuring her son/daughter: "I will put you through school, even if I have to carry stones on my back";
Female protagonist to the villain: "You can have my body, but you can never have my soul";
Worker to his/her boss: "No, you cannot fire me. I resign";
Kid who does not know that he is talking with his/her real father: "Mommy, I liked this uncle very much. Can I call him, daddy?";
Mother to son: "Son, do not leave your father's blood on the ground" (announcing a blood feud, meaning that the son must kill his father's murderers);
Turkish hero against a Western or Byzantine evil lord: "O Justinius, this is what they call the Ottoman slap" (referring to a slap on the ear and neck that is supposed to kill at a single blow);
Turkish hero sacrificing himself: "You run away, I will take care of them";
Turkish hero coming to the rescue: "I have arrived, buddy"

Anyone who is familiar with Yeşilçam films not only recognizes the characters, but automatically identifies the storyline and genre of films solely from these one-liners. For instance, the last three examples are from historical dramas introducing a Turkish hero's love affair with a Byzantine or non-Muslim woman (not necessarily resulting in a happy ending, but at times serving as a metonymic means of capturing foreign lands) and the one before these three recounts a rural drama with feudal codes of honor. Such phrases illustrate the morality that Yeşilçam offers to the lower classes and Yeşilçam's cliché-based, stereotypical plots remaining true to

Figure 5.3. *Hayat Bazen Tatlıdır* (Life is Sometimes Sweet, Nejat Saydam, 1962)

the melodramatic modality that also reproduced stars through types or individualities. Stars identified by good or evil types cannot alter their types; that is, good types are always good, and a femme fatale or an evil womanizer must repeatedly act in such roles. As Oran mentions, "Indeed, we write characters according to the actors" (Türk 2004, 217). Therefore, at the beginning of HBT, Müren and Doruk are automatically identified as protagonists. Interestingly, though, Sadri Alışık, who was not yet a comedy star when this film was made, is the villain in HBT.

While the sentimentality and pathos is handled by illnesses and intrigues, HBT embedded its spectacularity with revue scenes that ran against realistic illusionism. Zeki's rise to fame in the film introduces various scenes in a nightclub or music hall (*gazino*) where Zeki reorganizes the stage through the introduction of novel revue programs shot in color. This switch from black and white to color, as an instance of spectacularity and attraction, introduces the film's oscillation between realism and non-illusionism. HBT, beyond telling a story, addresses its spectators directly by presenting them with performative attractions and musical entertainment. As melodrama combining music with drama, in HBT, Müren's songs interrupt the drama and the illusionistic narrative. *Hayat Bazen Tatlıdır* is the song sung by Müren during the opening credits. The image of migrant Zeki carrying his suitcase in the opening is mirrored in the closing scene by two suitcases, those of Zeki and Yeşim, about to fly abroad for their honeymoon. While the first suitcase is decorated with stickers spelling out "Bon Voyage," the second one replaces it and carries the sticker spelling out "The End." Thus a prop belonging both to diegetic and non-diegetic worlds directly addresses the audience and eliminates realistic illusionism.

As much as this ambivalent end stitches the filmic and the real world together and indicates the "sweetness" of life through the film's title and theme song, the last two in-color revue shows by Zeki implicitly address musical performance, its cultural politics, and Müren's double personality. Before Müren's popularity as a performer of a reformed version of Ottoman Palace music, various singers altered this music and also Turkified vaguely similar Egyptian songs. While Ottoman Palace music introduced a longer musical form with both instrumental and vocal parts in a specific *maqam* to trigger a particular mood, the republican form of it isolated and highlighted only the shorter vocal part. As the first solo singing star, Müren not only epitomized this later form but also changed the face of musical performance. The tropic instance of Yeşilçam's response to the republican reform of musical modernization that attempted to polyphonize traditional musical forms is evident when Müren performs his song in the company of a piano played by Yeşim. Alternatively, one of Müren's in-color revue scenes updates a classical song by a nineteenth-century religious and palace musician, Dede Efendi, who felt the pressures of westernization during his own time. Zeki calls this revue show the "*Şehzade Revüsü*" (Prince Revue) and he acts the part of an Ottoman sultan's son, wandering around his harem full of reclining odalisques while a black servant fans him with a large-feathered fan. Complete with thin mustache and earring, Müren reminds one of a Rudolph Valentino in an Oriental harem, Turkifying Hollywood's Orientalist fantasies and reiterating the imperial past of Turkey. Another reminder of this past is Yeşim's black nanny, a common character in Yeşilçam films of the 1950s and 1960s, a remnant of the slowly fading Ottoman aristocratic mansion life in Istanbul involving rural Turkish servants, cooks, and former black slaves. Fitting well with Yeşilçam's dream, HBT reconstructs the Ottoman past through the eyes of Hollywood, addressing the complicated nature of Turkification and özenti, demanding not only a revival of a strong country but also the recognition of that country as subject to westernization and the colonization of its own visual imagery. Much like Yeşilçam itself, Müren also noted that he knew his limits; he was limited by the borders of Turkey, for he sang his songs only in Turkish and not a major European language (Müren 1992).

HBT is intricately associated with Hollywood in both its Turkification of Hollywood and its concealment of identity issues. Writing about *Singin' in the Rain* (dir. Stanley Donen and Gene Kelly, 1952) with reference to Rick Altman and Peter Wollen, Steven Cohan notes the binaries in the film: masculinity/femininity, innovation/obsolescence, naturalness/engineering, body/voice, and image/sound. While Don (Gene Kelly) and Lina (Jean Hagen) star as the singing and dancing happy couple in *Singin' in the Rain*, the coming of sound and the ensuing innovations make Lina's shrill voice a complicating factor and allow Kathy (Debbie Reynolds) to team up with Don. Kathy comes to "embody the perfect synchrony of body and voice, dancing and singing, which marks the achievement of the talkie, just as the talkie's technological matching of sound and image mirrors the couple's off-screen harmonious blending of masculinity and femininity" (Cohan 2000, 57). Cohan then tries to introduce a "third term" to "deconstruct" this sound/image dichotomy. For him, *Singin' in the Rain* tries to "wed" the rift between sound and image through the introduction of dance, that is, performance. However, the film's self-reflexive emphasis on the instability of dubbing and its attempt to "wed" this rift "in the married print and the married couple" highlights the dance to stabilize the rift, but opens itself up to deconstruction (Cohan 2000, 61). This issue of "dance" and its relation to "coupling" offers an interesting resonance with HBT.

In HBT, when Mümtaz gives a dinner to celebrate the end of Yeşim's illness, though Yeşim wants to have her first dance with Zeki, Semih claims that Zeki had not actually helped at all and does not allow it. So while dance represents both overcoming castration and the novel possibilities of coupling for Yeşim, it is also crucial in revue scenes. In HBT, Müren's last revue show introduces issues related to "coupling," "doubling," and "dubbing": because Zeki and Yeşim have only twenty minutes to catch the plane for their honeymoon, Zeki has no time for the encore for which his fans are clamoring and he asks Rasim, who becomes Zeki's assistant at the music hall, to go on stage for him just for the spectator's applause. However, the owner Rıfat plays a record of Zeki Müren performing *Hayat Bazen Tatlıdır*, forcing Rasim not only to mime singing while a record plays but also to dance with the song, "to perform the song as if he is Zeki Müren." However, during his performance, Rasim fails—he can neither lip-synch nor dance. Instead, all of his gestures and mimics present an unruly combination of failure to mimic Zeki Müren. But he who is on stage at the end of the film is the "real" Zeki Müren, while Zeki Müren in the film has left for his honeymoon. While Gene Kelly's uncanny combination of a lower-class character with middle-class morality in his star persona was perceived to present problems of virility in a male dancer, Zeki Müren's singing, dancing, and attire brought about a wealth of meanings beyond a contrast of masculine virility and a male dancer. There are indeed three Zeki Mürens according to the film: two in the filmic world, and one in the real world. The "real" Zeki Müren, who belongs to the nonfilmic or extra-textual world, complicates the picture further.[1]

Both Zeki and Rasim in HBT reverberated through the "real" Zeki Müren, knotting the filmic with the real. In a peculiar sequence in HBT, after speaking with Rasim in front of the mansion, Ayşe leaves for work at Mümtaz's mansion. On the way, she comes across Müsellim carrying a candied apple. Without much talk and looking back and smiling, Ayşe takes off as Müsellim arrives at the entrance of the mansion where the mad son of the mansion owner (Sadettin Erbil) comes out and demands the apple. Then, as he starts to literally "lick" the apple, Rasim and Müsellim, standing on either side of him, also start licking it with great gusto. The son stops at times and glares angrily at Rasim and Müsellim, before resuming his lustful licking (of the "forbidden" fruit). This sequence, ripe with homosexual undercurrent, is indeed effectual through HBT's entertainment protocol based on a carnivalesque comedy. Yet the laughter, located around the comic persona of Erbil, has extratextual repercussions, informing Zeki Müren's double identity, perched on the border between the secrecy of his private life and the publicity of his transgressions, through lavish costumes and cross-dressing, or between the popular and sensational straight singer and the privately gay man. Taken in this line, when HBT introduces Rasim's failure to impersonate Zeki, this failure also implies extratextual and real failures in Müren's life. Thus, HBT's realism is not situated in its illusionism, but instead in its in-betweenness. While both Zeki and Rasim carry fragments of the "real" Müren, they are not able to match the lonely and gloomy Müren of well-kept secrets.

In addition to the heterosexual coupling of both Zeki and Rasim in HBT and the doubling of the filmic and the real identities of Müren, dubbing presents a further complication. Yeşilçam post-synchronized a film's soundtrack and image track with the help of professional dubbing artists or the actors themselves. Though this practice instigates prob-lems of realism, Yeşilçam films are watched by naturalizing dubbing, without attaching it to an issue of reality. In HBT, while Zeki and Rasim are not seen together in a single frame until the very late moments of the film, their similarity is implied earlier by other characters mistaking one for the other. While one of them is named as Zeki Müren, claiming to be the "real" Zeki Müren, Rasim is only referred to by his first name. In Yeşilçam, such a play with names is common, and in various films the stars portrayed characters answering to their actual first names and first and last names, or even corrupted versions of their actual names, such as Hülya Koçyiğit becoming Hülya Çokyiğit. While these names offer various crosscurrents between the filmic and the real, they also introduce the issue of naming in relation to the republican reform programs. There were no last names during the Ottoman Empire; instead it was customary to add the father's name as well as titles related to one's profession or heritage. This changed under the republican regime after a 1934 law made Western-style last names obligatory. Thus, being denied a last name, Rasim nominally and narratively embodies Zeki's rural, backward, uncivilized, and comic alter ego. Compared with the worldly and talented Zeki, Rasim's failure in performing Zeki Müren is amplified by his futile performance and unsuccessful attempt to lip-synch. The failure of lip-synch, however, is also Yeşilçam's perennial failure; its practice of dubbing constantly undermines realistic illusion. Thus when the "real" Müren fails to impersonate Zeki while he is acting as Rasim, it is indeed Rasim who epitomizes failure. Indeed, Rasim's situation is highly reminiscent of Yeşilçam, which has a dream of being an internationally renowned film industry, and thus reproduces *özenti*. In Yeşilçam's movement toward the West and then its return as an altered self, Yeşilçam's filmmakers claimed the "real" Yeşilçam as they mimicked their "ideal image" of Yeşilçam (i.e., of an artifice, of Hollywood). But Rasim is destined to fail in lip-synch or impersonation, for it is Müren who dubs his own reality (between Zeki and Rasim and between his secret and public lives) as Müren doubles his own image (both in film and in reality). Such is Yeşilçam's "reality" of dubbing and doubling coupled with HBT's self-reflexivity and *özenti*.

Dubbing and doubling in both HBT and Yeşilçam climax when Rasim and Zeki are seen twice in the same frame, with a split-screen image of two Zeki Mürens because, probably as a result of the technology of dubbing or editing, in these two scenes, Rasim's voice alters and it seems to be dubbed by someone else. In other words, Rasim is doubly dubbed, once by Müren and another time by someone else. Additionally, when either Rasim or Zeki moves in the split-screen image, parts of their arms vanish because Müren, as he moves, falls out of the split-frame. If Yeşilçam were analyzed through formalist arguments, the realistic illusion is nowhere to be found in this aural and visual doubling of Müren. However, this doubling of failures is what makes up Yeşilçam and its Turkification of a Western medium: it is not necessarily a failure but the very modality of Yeşilçam, placed in-between the non-illusionism, the direct address of traditional performing arts and the inherent realistic illusionism of the medium of cinema. However, Yeşilçam's filmmakers are also well aware of this as they carefully address their spectators; as in HBT, when the antagonist Semih is seen with another woman, Yeşim looks at the camera and winks, signaling the elimination of Semih as an obstacle to her and Zeki's coupling. With Zeki's rise as a singer and the revelation of his family background and subsequent elimination of class difference, Zeki and Yeşim were free to marry. But the problem of being cousins is never addressed in HBT—as may be seen in many cases in Turkey, including one of the richest business families, intrafamilial marriage does not carry the same stigma that it does in other cultures.

Considering the illusionistic, three-dimensional realism of Western cinemas, Yeşilçam faced the impossibility of success in its dream of making films like those of Hollywood. However, once it encountered the other, Yeşilçam lost its original self and produced Turkified tactics to register this Western medium in Turkey. Thus, though it did not follow the conventions of Hollywood cinema, it produced an ambivalent world of dreaming and mirroring, doubling and transforming. As much as Yeşilçam had a *hayal* (dream) of its other, it was itself a *hayal* (*Karagöz* shadow play or mirror image), and thus presented a world of *hayal* (dream/imagination/fantasy). In such a world of fantasy, then, things like a candied apple point to the bad, yet tasty apples of society.

Kara Sevda (Unrequited Love, 1968)

Similar to HBT, *Kara Sevda* (hereafter KS, dir. Seyfi Havaeri) belongs to the genre of "singer films" that introduces an already famous singer carrying his/her star persona into the filmic world rather than a film star who acts as a singer in the film. Singer films also offer a complete program of entertainment: not only pathos and action or emotions and spectacles but also music and performance. They introduce a migration from the periphery to the center through the rise of the singer and his/her heterosexual romance with an upper-class character. KS raises issues similar to those in HBT, while also using a folk singer to emphasize themes of modernization and westernization in a rural setting.

The 1968 version of KS is a remake, or rather a combination of two earlier films of Seyfi Havaeri, one by the same name (*Kara Sevda*, 1955) and the other *Gönülden Yaralılar* (Wounded through the Heart, 1949). In 1977, it was remade again in color, *Çeşme* (Fountain, dir. Temel Gürsu), but this time with the *arabesk* music singer Ferdi Tayfur. Havaeri mentioned that a producer who had thought him dead saw him by chance on the street in 1968 and asked him to remake the film with two stars, Nuri Sesigüzel and Hülya Koçyiğit (2002). While the original KS is not predominantly a singer film but rather a village drama with a sad ending, the 1968 version involves the folk singer Sesigüzel. The success of the 1968 version encouraged Havaeri to make another quickie, *Kara Yazım* (My Dark Fate), again with Nuri Sesigüzel. Much like its sequel, the story of *Kara Sevda* is based on an ill-fated love affair between the characters Hasan (Nuri Sesigüzel), the son of the farm's caretaker, and Selma (Hülya Koçyiğit), the daughter of the farm's landlord Rıdvan. Özgüç summarizes the first KS and *Çeşme* as the story of unrequited love between a farm lord's daughter and the son of the farm's caretaker, and the 1968 version as "a modern Layla and Majnun story" (1995).[2] Similar to Layla and Majnun, the protagonists in KS grow up together, but later are separated because of the girl's father's fears. Like Majnun, Hasan returns to Selma's grave to die and reunite with her in the afterlife. The similarities stop there. In KS, Hasan does not go mad and transcend from physical to spiritual love, hinting at religious spiritualism through which the lover and the beloved become one. Instead, staying true to its modern, post-sacred nature, KS's Hasan threads the melodramatic through vertical class movement, instead of madness and spirituality. In the materialistic world of the record industry, he becomes a famous singer, sells records, appears on the state radio, and is surrounded with beautiful women. Still his love, naturally unrequited, lingers in this materialistic world, as if it is the only moralistic thread that stops him from becoming entangled with individualism and capitalism.

KS's opening credits are accompanied by a folk song, sung by Sesigüzel, expressing the singer's unrequited love for Selma, a theme further emphasized by the scene in which, as children, Selma and Hasan plant a pine tree together, a symbol of their unity. The next scene shows them as teenage lovers talking under its fully grown branches. The class difference between them becomes an obstacle in the eyes of Selma's father, Rıdvan, who introduces himself as a businessman wishing to modernize his farm with the help of an agricultural engineer Necdet (Önder Somer), whom he wants Selma to marry. In line with Yeşilçam's melodramatic reproduction of the patriarchy and traditional family bonds, Hasan leaves the farm and Selma marries Necdet. At the end, Selma, unhappy because of the compulsory marriage and imagining Hasan seduced by the immoral girls of Istanbul, slowly dies of her unrequited love. Coincidentally, Hasan returns to the farm and sees his lover on her deathbed. He takes her to the base of their tall tree before committing suicide. In the next scene, their souls rise to heaven from their graves, located under the tree. In this scene, two figures in white clothes rise to the skies with the tree in the background—in reality, the actors are climbing the stairs of a soccer stadium with the background image of the tree superimposed on the footage.

KS's melodramatic modality invites discussion of two interconnected issues concerning republican modernization in agriculture, and the cultural politics and westernization of music. Similar to other Yeşilçam films, KS emphasizes the Kemalist educational discourse through Hasan, who is not allowed by Rıdvan to continue his education and is therefore unable to realize his dream of becoming an agricultural engineer. As Havaeri mentions, Atatürk set an example for Turkish peasants by forming a series of state farms and operating farm machinery (2002). Havaeri explains his use of tractors in KS to emphasize the modernization of agriculture, but such scenes also recall Atatürk's ride on a tractor at the Atatürk Forest/ Agriculture Farm in Ankara—though in Havaeri's film, the villain rides the tractor! While the rural, village film genre (both social realist dramas and melodramas) sided with Kemalist reform projects by portraying the traditional forces such as the landlords, imams, and feudal codes of honor as melodramatic obstacles and by supporting the agents and institutions of modernization, KS accommodates an implicit or perhaps an unintentional criticism of the republican cultural project. Among the stock types of rural films, the agents of modernization are teachers, soldiers, doctors, bureaucrats, and engineers. In KS, Necdet represents the center that reforms the countryside, the periphery: a modern, urban, and westernized center imposing its will over a traditional, rural, and Eastern periphery. However, Necdet allies himself with Rıdvan, the landlord, and thus runs

Figure 5.4. *Kara Sevda* (Unrequited Love, Seyfi Havaeri, 1969), the sentence on the lower left side of the poster states, "This film is made with cash money."

counter to an extent to the discourse of republican modernization. While Rıdvan's portrayal fits the mold of callous republican reformers, Necdet, through the end of the film, respects Selma's love for Hasan and consents to give her a divorce.

The arch-villain Rıdvan's attire further complicates KS's modernization and westernization discourse: Western-style clothing (hat, polo pants, binoculars, and a horse-whip in his hand symbolic of his role as landlord) that is markedly different from rural Turkish dress codes and instead reminiscent of the attire of the early republican elite. In avidly Kemalist village literature or films, the landlords form an alliance with other reactionaries to promote traditionalism. However, KS is confused in this respect because, like the republican reformers, the abominable landlord wishes to accomplish agricultural reform and a change in cultural taste from traditional to Western musical forms. Both the association of KS with a folk music singer, replaced by an *arabesk* singer in *Çeşme*, and the impressive success of KS at the box office, especially in the Anatolian towns where the allure of folk music was stronger, reflect the distaste of the public for the extreme measures of republican cultural projects, such as the ban placed on the broadcast of Turkish classical music on the state radio for a little over a year in the early 1930s. In this manner, KS's introduction of a contradiction between folk music and Western music is telling because Rıdvan forbids Selma to listen to Hasan's folk songs. In a sequence, Rıdvan, after hearing the voice of Hasan, who was supposed to go to town to pick up Selma's fiancé, Necdet, is enraged thinking that Hasan is still on the farm. Selma indicates a tape recorder and tells him that she recorded Hasan's song. However, by echoing the republican reformers who attempted to modernize and westernize, to polyphonize the monophonic folk music, Rıdvan yells at his daughter: "You will not listen to this music anymore. You will listen to tangos, waltzes!" But Selma replies that such folk songs remind her that she belongs to these lands; she stands up for the Turkish folk who would not acclimate themselves to Western musical forms. Thus, when Yeşilçam attempts to incorporate Kemalist modernization into its melodramatic modality, elements of traditionalism emerge at the expense of the very ideology the film attempts to promote. Although such asides seem contradictory, both the republican reform programs and the traditionalist opposition to them were partly successful and created a hybrid or ambivalent culture in Turkey that does not completely belong to either vision.

The transmitter of Western musical forms, the state radio, also broadcast programs such as "The Village Hour," which was intended to enlighten the rural masses with information on modern agriculture and farming. After his expulsion from the village, Hasan goes to Istanbul to find a job and is discovered by a talent scout who hears him while singing desperate songs of love at his hotel. As when Müren sings in the factory in HBT, here too all the people in the hotel listen to the singer's unself-conscious performance. Fame and fortune come to lower-class characters out of good luck or spectacular coincidence, provided they keep their integrity. Hasan, who remains faithful to Selma, wins the state radio's competition recruiting singers. Soon, the recently married Selma turns on "The Village Hour" in the hopes of becoming more educated and helping with the modernization of the farm. Instead, she hears Hasan singing songs of desperate love. Selma faces her "past" lover through his "dubbed" voice, which indeed is a live concert in a radio studio, and also traditionalism (folk songs about unrequited love) as aired by the very agent of modernization, state radio.

At the end of the film, Necdet proclaims that Selma is no longer his wife because he realizes that she loves Hasan. However, Yeşilçam's morality does not allow a woman in a rural setting to get remarried. Elaborating on the Turkification of Hollywood scripts, Oran mentioned that it was more difficult for him to Turkify than to write original scripts because they had to maintain the foreign film's formula for success despite radically modifying it to suit local morals and traditions. For instance, some Western films that he adapted included married women cheating on their husbands. For him, when Turkish spectators watched such foreign films, they thought that such things were possible because ultimately, the foreign film represented foreign women. They did not see a problem when both the husband and the wife were foreign. But in "stealing" such a film's successful storyline, if scriptwriters placed a Turkish woman in the same situation, the Turkified version was fated to be a box office disaster: "In our film, if the woman is Turkish, her husband is an honorable Anatolian man. When we adapt such a film and allow the man to be cheated on, he is perceived as a pimp and she is understood as a prostitute" (Türk 2004, 204). In this moralistic world of Yeşilçam's melodramatic modality, there was no exit for Selma and Hasan except death. Ironically, at the end of the film, a couple leaves flowers on the graves of Selma and Hasan in hopes of getting married themselves. A voice-over narration presents an epilogue to the film, signaling the nostalgia of a sacred love in materialistic modern world: "From that time on, all lovers who could not be together visited the graves of the lovers to eliminate the obstacles before them."

KS's ambivalent resistance to republican reforms is coupled with its fostering of sacred over secular values, its localism and ties to a rural identity. Keeping in mind that the original films were made in the early 1950s, KS's peripheralism may be seen as echoing the Democratic Party's overtaking of the government from the Republican People's Party, with rural and lower-class support. In KS, after Hasan's burial in the village, Rıdvan and Necdet's goals for the modernization and westernization of the farm remain possible. At this point, the spirituality of Layla and Majnun stories resonates with the lyrics of Nuri Sesigüzel's folk songs about divine love and the desperation of love. In KS, before Hasan leaves the farm, Selma's mother asks Rıdvan to respect the lovers. Rıdvan replies: "In what kind of an age are we living, wife? The age of Kerem and Aslı or Layla and Majnun was long ago....The son of a farm's caretaker cannot be my daughter's groom." Thus the film suggests that tradition is both passé and yet also continuing, reaffirming Yeşilçam's ambivalence regarding the republican reforms.

On the other hand, Hasan's father, the farm's caretaker, symbolizes the powerlessness of the lower classes. As he watches the departure of his son or the marriage ceremony of Selma and Necdet in the background, silent and almost in tears, he stands in for the spectators, imagining Hasan in the place of Necdet. However, pathos peaks in the bridal chamber, immediately after Necdet turns on the radio and Selma hears Hasan singing on the radio: "They ripped a raw fruit from the branch; they separated me from my lover." Beset by the connotations of this song, Hasan's father, wandering around the farm house, also hears the radio and calls out to his son: "Hasan, this is my son's voice." Indeed, what is heard on the radio is Hasan's voice as he sings, but unlike in HBT, where Zeki Müren speaks his own lines, this singing voice of Sesigüzel himself is different from his dubbed speaking voice. Regardless of how his father unproblematically perceives both voices, Hasan's voice is also cracked in two. However, this politics of voices, and thus silence, is interlaced with the voice-over narration and the state radio. Whereas the over-narration symbolizes the truth of film as such, the voice of the radio represents the potent voice of the state, as the father of all Turks.

It is, after all, not Hasan's presence, but his voice that makes the project of modernization unravel. In the end, it is the landlord father—associated with the state both through his costume and in his projects—who is the locus of blame and who, like the republican regime, tried to change people against their will, whereas the caretaker father is the one who could not voice himself and thus lost his son in the process. In this respect, Hasan and his father, who share the last name Kara (meaning black or dark, and denoting fate), represent the masses as subjects and as being subjected to "Turkification-from-above." Thus at this site of contestation where modernization and traditionalism are acted out and on the border between the two, the working of *özenti* persists as altercation and transformation. Nevertheless, KS also tells the story of Selma who is "ripped like a raw fruit" in this encounter between tradition and modernity, which in any case stays put in its patriarchal nature.

Bir Teselli Ver (Give Some Consolation, 1971)

While KS introduces the transition from rural to urban through rural modernization, another set of films, like Lütfi Ö. Akad's *Bir Teselli Ver* (hereafter BTV), handles this transition within an urban environment. Though not well known abroad, Akad is considered the first "auteur" director of Yeşilçam and Özön (1962), Scognamillo (1973b), Onaran (1990), and Özgüç (1995, 10) claim that he realized the transition from a theater-inspired filmmaking to cinema. Unlike the popular directors of various quickie "business films" such as Havaeri or Muharrem Gürses, Akad usually worked with Yeşilçam's majors and gained acclaim for several social issue films that also did well at the box office. Around 1970, when some filmmakers and critics were engaged in heated debates about what constitutes the "Turkish" cinema, with Refiğ and Erksan, he advocated the "national" cinema perspective. An influential group of Kemalist and leftist film critics promoted European movements like Neorealism and New Wave as models for Turkish cinema, with little consideration of Third Cinema or Third World cinemas, further endorsing the republican model of westernization and modernization from above. Thus, mostly siding with Second Cinema, these critics opened the Turkish Sinematek (Cinematheque), modeled on and in collaboration with its French predecessor and augmented by an awareness of Western art cinemas and film history.³ However, they considered Yeşilçam completely opiate and backward and called for its obliteration. Against these criticisms, Yeşilçam filmmakers vocalized two main responses: *milli* ("national") cinema, an Islamic outlook proposed by Yücel Çakmaklı and Mesut Uçakan; and *ulusal* ("national") cinema, the nationalist outlook of Refiğ, Erksan, and, partly, Akad. Çakmaklı deemed Yeşilçam "cosmopolitan" and impure, envisioning the cinematic retrieval of Turkish-Islamic identity through Ottoman culture, hence his choice of an Arabic word, *milli*, for national. Alternatively, inspired by Orientalist Marxian arguments on the Asiatic mode of production that suggest the impossibility of a leftist revolution in Turkey due to the absence of a class-based capitalist society, Refiğ envisioned a national cinema that would combine elements of the history of Turks, including the phase of Ottoman Empire; hence the fabricated, but authentic, republican word *ulusal*. Akad, participating somewhat in this perspective, produced various types of films and managed to remain in his words "between dark and light" of cinema (2004).

In 1971, Akad directed five films: he wrote scripts for the first two, *Anneler ve Kızları* (Mothers and Their Daughters) and *Bir Teselli Ver* (Give Some Consolation), while the other three were written by Yeşilçam's "serial killer" scriptwriters, Safa Önal (*Rüya Gibi* [Like a Dream] and *Mahşere Kadar* [Until the Day of Judgment]) and Önal and Erdoğan Tünaş (*Vahşi Çiçek* [Wild Flower]). For Akad, the last three are "ordinary" business films, with "ordinary" scripts and "ordinary" direction. Three of them are singer films: *Anneler ve Kızları* with Neşe Karaböcek, *Bir Teselli Ver* with Orhan Gencebay, and *Rüya Gibi* with Zeki Müren. Akad also noted that *Rüya Gibi* and *Mahşere Kadar* were essentially remakes of his *Kader Böyle İstedi* (Thus Spoke Fate, 1968) and that "he made the same film three times" (2004, 521). For Akad, scriptwriters Tünaş, Önal, and Oran "always had a couple of synopses in hand; they wrote fast; and they never wrote something outside the lines, something bad. Because they wrote a lot, they at times gave you masterpieces that fit the rules of mathematics and statistics" (2004, 522). In short, all five of them reproduced Yeşilçam's melodramatic modality through dramatic and spectacular contradictions to motivate the spectators with a give-and-take of pain and pleasure.

Turkification is also at work in Akad's *Anneler ve Kızları*, for the film is based on Douglas Sirk's *Imitation of Life* (1959), which was itself a remake of John M. Stahl's 1934 film, *Imitation of Life*, based on a Fannie Hurst novel. After being asked by producer Erman to Turkify Sirk's film, Akad felt that he was asking for a story based on the dramatic conflicts

Figure 5.5. *Bir Teselli Ver* (Give Some Consolation, Lütfi Ö. Akad, 1971)

between two girls and between them and their mothers (2004, 513–14). However, Akad supplanted the original's racial conflict with a contradiction between the center (Istanbul) and periphery (Anatolia). Remembering the wisdom of Anatolian mothers through a dictionary of proverbs and idioms, Akad introduced Fatma Bacı (Yıldız Kenter) to replace the black mother, who, for him, is realistic and farsighted and who aptly supplements the traditional sagaciousness of the ancestors of Turks. A mother who is a singer replaced the white actress mother in the original (2004, 515). Interestingly enough, the wise Anatolian woman character led Refiğ to make an *ulusal* film by the same name, *Fatma Bacı* (1972), depicting the courageous survival story of an Anatolian woman who escapes from a blood feud and migrates to Istanbul.

As examples of *ulusal* cinema, both Akad and Refiğ's films presupposed authenticity and Turkishness, while Fatma Bacı was a Turkification of the black mother in Sirk's *Imitation of Life*. Like Meriç and Ataç writing on *The Tempest* but blind to Caliban's blackness, the proponents of *ulusal* cinema also overlooked issues related to colonialism. For Akad, slavery was not an issue in Turkish history, unlike the United States: "The thing which separates the people of a society which has never been enslaved and in which it was possible to rise from shepherd to grand vizier is not so much class but money" (2004, 514). Akad's Turkey had not been a slave- and class-based society but instead allowed vertical movement across the socioeconomic strata. Islamist proponents of *milli* cinema also pursued the Weberian path and condemned cultural differences (between the Christian West and the Islamic East, and between the secular, western-ized portions of Turkish population and the traditional, religious ones) for creating the ills of Turkish society. Both Akad's BTV and Çakmaklı's *Oğlum Osman* (My Son Osman, 1973) share this outlook. While BTV addresses the socioeconomic and cultural transformations through an *arabesk* singer film, *Oğlum Osman* attempts to recuperate forms of traditional storytell-ing with Islamist sentiment, through various protocols of Turkification. In short, both *milli* and *ulusal* cinema perspectives, in responding to leftists and the severe westernization reforms of Kemalists, praise a particular understanding of Turkishness that is oblivious and amnesiac because, not only did slavery exist in the Ottoman Empire but also the very films these directors produced establish dramatic conflicts through class differences.

In addition to his "Turkified" *ulusal* film, Akad's other significant film in 1971 was BTV. Akad began this project at the behest of film producer, Kadir Kesenen, who asked him to direct a singer film featuring the rising *arabesk* singer Orhan Gencebay. Akad explains his choice of the story's setting in a poor neighborhood of Istanbul as an attempt to eradicate Gencebay's star image as a singer (2004, 517). Having its roots in Egyptian music and its Turkified examples and combining traditional folk music with Western ones, *arabesk*, as the "music of migration" belonged to urban peripheries, to shantytowns that enacted a social existence in-between tradition and modernity. For Akad, who grew up in Istanbul listening to Müren and other musics of the center, *arabesk* was a foreign music and culture. Apart from leading to his acclaimed migration trilogy, both BTV and *Anneler ve Kızları* explore themes of transformation and migration through youth culture and music.

Opening with a series of musical instruments used in *arabesk* music: *bağlama* (a traditional Turkish folk instrument, like a long-necked, small lute), *ud* (a lute-like Middle Eastern instrument used in Arab, Persian, and Turkish music), violin, guitar, tambourine, and other percussion instruments, BTV introduces Orhan (Orhan Gencebay) working on written notation signals. While Orhan is portrayed as a professional musician, the blacksmith Kadir calls him "*aşık*," which literally means a lover like Majnun, but also refers to traditional folk or religious troubadours. Accordingly, he is a modernizer of folk music in the urban modernity of a squatter settlement and his synthesis of folk and modern music and culture is called *arabesk*. Orhan, a blue-collar laborer, helps repair the car owned by the factory-owner's daughter, Nermin (Tülin Örsek), and forgets his notes in her car. At home, Nermin plays Orhan's song on the piano and records it. When Nermin is having a party at her place, her friends insist that she invite Orhan, who with his work clothes on, finds himself at an upper-class party ripe with rock music. When he is asked to perform a song on the piano, he replies, "I know nothing of this instrument." Despite his unwillingness, Orhan relents and starts to sing, but the urban youth get bored quickly. Feeling humiliated, Orhan returns to his peripheral neighborhood where he sings to his friends, accompanied by a *bağlama*. In this shot-on-location neighborhood scene, which introduces a realistic portrayal of peripheral Istanbul, Orhan realizes his rural background and recognizes his difference from Nermin. Stated differently, his *arabesk* music and he himself belong to this poor, peripheral neighborhood. Unlike the music of Müren or Sesigüzel, he and his music are excluded from legitimate, statist channels of communication such as the state radio.

Singer films, a significant subgenre of Yeşilçam melodramas, often introduce singing and dancing at nightclubs, music halls, and parties. While such locales serve as meeting grounds for two main characters of disparate class backgrounds, they also portray stereotypical themes and characters. The female or male antagonists of melodramas inhabit these immoral and illicit spaces where they search for their next victim. This world of alcohol and sex is rife with fallen women who once sang at such clubs in hopes of fame and fortune or femme fatales who could lead the protagonists into immorality. Alternatively, musical entertainment and party scenes at lavish upper-class residences portray youths dancing and singing. Such entertainment venues often present class differences and cultural conflicts through the introduction of a lower-class, peripheral character. By being humiliated and ridiculed by the rich youth, this character champions the honor and morality of the common men and especially migrants in cities, whose experiences involve such urban encounters in their daily travel from the peripheries of cities to their centers, a phenomenon that began in the 1950s but did not enter public urban consciousness until the 1960s.[4] Thus BTV emphasizes this urban visibility of migrants residing in squatter settlements and redefines the borders of cities and urban culture.

As the tension mounts within Nermin's family over her friendship with Orhan, her father fires Orhan and threatens the dwellers of the squatter settlement. But Nermin defies her family and moves to Orhan's neighborhood. Later, his elders are refused after visiting Nermin's father on behalf of Orhan to ask for her hand in marriage. Yet the neighborhood crowd, determined to get the upper-class Nermin married to the lower-class Orhan, successfully confronts Nermin's family. At the colorful marriage ceremony, Orhan and Nermin traditionally kiss the hands of their elders to show respect, but are not shown kissing each other. Then, as the couple walks away from the crowd, a Rome band plays an ironically "sad" Orhan Gencebay tune about reuniting with a lover. Considered in relation to other singer films, Akad's work attempts to portray real life while maintaining the same relationships between characters and classes as other Yeşilçam films. In other words, Yeşilçam's melodramatic modality is also at stake in the singer film that involves a standard plot with stereotypical characters, and the dubbed doubling of voices and music.

Oğlum Osman (My Son Osman, 1973)

Though attempting to eliminate Yeşilçam's tropes, Yücel Çakmaklı frequently reproduced them. In his Kızım Ayşe (1974), the Fatma Bacı character of the Akad and Refiğ films (as acted by Yıldız Kenter) reemerges under a different name as a wise and religious Anatolian woman trying to protect her daughter. Both ulusal and milli cinema introduce issues related to modernization and westernization: the Turkification of the Western cinemas that simultaneously mocks and mimics the West; the fostering of a Turkish-Ottoman and/or Turkish-Islamic identity in the name of a return to an essential or original state; and the claim of movement toward a "proper" nationality through securing traditions and cultural identity. The latter's increased emphasis on religiosity is their primary difference. Additionally, both perspectives affixed themselves to realistic, continuity–editing, and classical conventions of storytelling. However, as products of Yeşilçam, they were not successful at hayal, and instead reproduced protocols of Turkification and melodramatic modality.

The Koranic quotation with which Kızım Ayşe begins emphasizes both formal and spiritual education. For Çakmaklı, cinema is first a form of entertainment, second an art, and last a medium of education (i.e., reading and reciting) (2002).⁵ His films usually involve not only vertical class movement through formal education but also spiritual elevation through traditional, religious, and verbal education. Instead of the dramatic contrast between rich and poor, Çakmaklı claims to place the contradiction between two ways of living: one western(ized), the other Turkish and Islamic. However, his films, reproducing Yeşilçam's melodramatic modality, present the western(ized) characters among urban upper classes, while the Turkish-Islamic ones are lower-class and rural. Thus the dismantling of "cosmopolitan" or "westernized" cinema is considerably undermined by his own films, which, similar to Yeşilçam, give primacy to the spoken word over the image. Çakmaklı recalls his imam grandfather's stories told in mosques and the tradition of traveling storytellers who went from village to village in Anatolia and who, through a limited number of visual images, told moralistic stories. Thus combining religious education (reading/reciting) with moralistic storytelling and starting with his first successful film, a

Figure 5.6. *Memleketim* (My Homeland, Yücel Çakmaklı, 1974)

documentary about the annual pilgrimage to Mecca composed of footage taken from various fiction films and documentaries, his films attempted to deliver a moralistic and religious message. In this vein, while resonating with Akad and Refiğ's films, Çakmaklı's films such as *Oğlum Osman* (hereafter OO) and its sequel *Kızım Ayşe* focus on family relations through a presentation of contrasts between classes, cultures, and geographies.

Based on Raif Cilasun's story and Bülent Oran's script, OO introduces, accompanied by a religious hymn about a father's prayer to have a son, Osman (Aytaç Arman) who returns to Turkey after completing his industrial engineering degree in Germany. His father (Nuri Altınok) and mother Seniha (Şükriye Atav), though living in a modern apartment, do not seem typically westernized. Both Seniha and the nanny, wearing headscarves, are shown placing a Koran, a prayer rug, skullcap, and rosary in Osman's room. While his father wants Osman to immediately take over and improve the factory with Europe's science and technology, his mother wants him to get married to his neighbor's headscarf-wearing daughter,[6] Fatma (Fatma Belgen). When Osman says, "In Europe, there is no hurry to get married," his father replies that "while it is good to use the science and technology of Europe, we must not lose our lifestyle." While republican ideology offered modernization and westernization in the fields of technology, science, and culture, Islamic modernizers believed that technological innovation could be adopted without changing cultural traditions. Çakmaklı, in line with Islamic political discourse, imagined Europe solely as a purveyor of its Christian heritage and thus perceived it as culturally threatening. In OO, Çakmaklı identifies the shift in Osman's values with his education in Germany, where he lost his culture and thus clashed with his parents, by becoming "*özenti*" or "imitative." The Islamist alternative offers a return to an (irretrievable) "*öz*" (essence/origin), the Turkish-Islamic identity undisturbed by modernization and westernization.

The melodramatic plot is strengthened by Osman's pursuit of a decadent life of drinking and gambling and Fatma's dutiful wait to marry him despite her dislike of Osman's Europeanization. Çakmaklı's seeming departure from class-based, Marxist themes, on a rhetorical level, works through a refusal of the West and its difference essentially aligned with Christianity. Osman's westernization is also foregrounded by his use of the first name Kaya (meaning rock) instead of Osman. While this naming policy seems to counter an Islamic name with a secular one, it also identifies Osman with Christianity, loose morals, drinking, and gambling. His father says, "Now, your name is Kaya, huh? Just a piece of stone. I named you Osman to be as brave as Osman Ghazi [meaning "veteran of a war in the name of Islam," the first sultan of the Ottoman Empire after whom the empire is named], and as religious as the Caliph Osman." Thus Çakmaklı's film defines Osman's duty: to follow the Prophet Mohammad as the Caliph Osman did and to found a Turkish Empire like Osman Ghazi, the founder of the Ottoman Empire after whom it was named. In a flashback, Osman's father remembers naming his son with the help of the leader of a religious brotherhood; how he taught him to love his flag and his homeland, and to pray and recite the Koran. His project was clear: Osman was to be loyal to Islam, the traditions and mores of Turkish society, and aware of the progress of the century (Western science and technology). Much like the republican project of creating a modern, secular Turkey, Çakmaklı's "project" is to nurture an Osman who synthesizes nation, religion, and technology. However, Osman lost the former two in the process of gaining the latter.

Osman's loss of spirituality due to scientific realism (read: materialism) resonates with the Turkish Islamists' essentializing, Occidentalist view: Europe is a materialist, capitalist culture and thus a soulless Christian entity. However, Islamic intellectuals, like their secular counterparts, could only perceive Turkey in relation to the West. Instead of focusing on the discursive power inherent in the West's imagining of the East and its presentation of a model modernization for the non-West, they also essentialized the West and ignored its internal discrepancies. The West is thus "usable" in terms of its technology but Turkey already has the remaining intangibles, a religious and national sentiment. So Kaya, a snob and a brat rather than an Osman, is disowned by his father and goes back to Germany. There, his German girlfriend, Helga, her father, and Osman watch a religious documentary about the creation of life by Allah (not the Christian God!) on a fictional television channel for Turkish workers in West Germany. The ten-minute documentary sequence is intercut with images of these three characters. With footage from Cecil B. DeMille's religious epics and William Wyler's *Ben-Hur* (1959), the documentary is a mishmash of black-and-white and color footage and laterally compressed widescreen images accompanied by a voice-over narration about Allah and prophets. The footage about Muhammad's era is taken from an Egyptian film about the dawn of Islam and Çakmaklı's 1969 documentary about the Hajj, the annual pilgrimage to Mecca, *Kabe Yollarında* (On the Way to the Kaaba).

Having no problem understanding the documentary narrated in Turkish, Helga's "materialist" father questions Osman about religions and Islam. Later Helga tells Osman that she will go to church on Sunday with her family. Osman imagines Helga covered, but praying in a church; then, he recalls his childhood and the Turkish flag. Falling asleep in his German home, Osman dreams that he is running away from rocks (*kaya*) falling from a cliff. After a rock smashes him, the Caliph Osman approaches him and says that he is his namesake, the Caliph Osman. Then, Osman Ghazi approaches him, and says: "You have my blood in your veins. Your name is my name. You are a Turk; you are a Muslim. Return to yourself!" Then, both Osmans, the Caliph and the Ghazi, remove the rock that had fallen on Osman. Coming back from his death as Kaya (or should I say Lazarus?), and returning to his self as Osman, he wakes up from his dream. Thus the dream (*hayal*) of being a European is misguided and Osman returns to Turkey, where he visits Osman Ghazi's tomb. With the voice-over narration, the film again reverts to a documentary format showing us the sixteen busts of the leaders of the "Turkish" empires, including Attila the Hun, Kutluğ of the Uighurs, Genghis Khan of the Mongol Empire, and Seljuk of the Seljuks. Then, Osman goes to Mecca for the Hajj, where another documentary sequence is incorporated. Osman, and through him, the Turkish public, is informed about Hajj rituals. But Osman's informants are not speaking; they are not even moving their lips. Instead, the voice-ver narration is meant to stitch the discontinuous footage together. For instance, the Egyptian Arabic narration is audible in parts taken from an

Egyptian film, as the film continually shifts from black-and-white to color footage, creating an obvious mishmash of unrelated images.

After this twenty-minute-long combination of documentary, fiction, and fantasy, Osman's father wakes up from a dream and tells his wife that Osman is returning. However, Osman is still in Mecca, returning to himself, asking for Allah's forgiveness. Only then does he return to Istanbul where, after redemption, he marries Fatma. Thus, after a voyage through Çakmaklı's documentary, Egyptian films, and Hollywood films, OO restores its melodramatic ending with a traditionally proper marriage before the couple walks toward the setting sun. Çakmaklı thus presents a complete program of entertainment, art, and education despite its dismantling of illusionism and realism of filmic language by combining various image tracks (documentary, feature, color, black-and-white) and soundtracks (dubbing Turkish in Turkish; dubbing Arabic in Turkish; voice-over narration in Turkish; Germans not only understanding but speaking in Turkish; lip synch; no lip synch; and various music and sound effects that do not run parallel to the image track).

Islamists, Kemalists, and leftists all yearned to engineer cinema through their nationalist projects. What Yeşilçam produced instead, regardless of such projects, was a filmmaking that combined the spectacular clashes of good and evil and an *özenti* that was altered and transformed in the filmmaking process. Despite these engineers understanding of Yeşilçam's *özenti* as imitation, they were themselves embedded in Yeşilçam. Though they aimed to tell, or make cinema tell, things other than what they criticized Yeşilçam for telling, they ended up within the same mode of narration. They wanted their films to be issue films, sending messages to the masses; yet they repeated Yeşilçam's visual and storytelling conventions. If Yeşilçam is a cinema of dubbing, *Oğlum Osman* is doubly dubbed: not only by the dubbing artists voicing the actors but also by the voice-over narration in the documentary sequences. The film is neither a feature film nor a documentary; it is neither a secular republican nationalist film nor a traditional Islamist film; instead it is a combination, claiming the voice, controlling and re-presenting it to the masses. Yet it fits perfectly into Yeşilçam's melodramatic modality, its give-and-take of reality and fantasy, spectacularity and sentimentality.

Şeytan (Satan, 1974)

Although Yeşilçam is consistently marked by non-illusionism and mishaps of realism, these are perhaps nowhere more disturbing than in works that depend on the realism of special effects, particularly various remakes of Western films or adaptations of novels and comic books in fantastic genres. Metin Erksan's 1974 remake of *The Exorcist* (dir. William Friedkin, 1973) inscribes such difficulties in special effects and the dynamics of Turkifying. In a book on "fantastic" Turkish films, Giovanni Scognamillo and Metin Demirhan note that there were a variety of genres in Yeşilçam that dealt with the fantastic: fairy tale, superhero science fiction, historical fantasy, and Western films (1999). These Western films (or "*kebab*" Westerns, similar to spaghetti Westerns) and superhero science fictions produced a practice of "Turkification" that did not quite reflect the daily realities of the society. Alongside these, Scognamillo and Demirhan consider two horror films: *Drakula İstanbul'da* (Dracula in Istanbul, dir. Mehmet Muhtar, 1953) and *Şeytan* (Satan, dir. Metin Erksan, 1974). While there are only a few horror films produced in Yeşilçam, such fantastic films present examples of direct remakes of Hollywood films that emphasize in part what Yeşilçam is not and cannot be. The dynamics of Turkification are even more clearly woven into the texts of horror films that attempt to domesticate themes often nonexistent in Turkish culture.

Erksan, who disowned *Şeytan*, claimed in 1974 that it was not a "direct" remake of Friedkin's film but an adaptation of William Peter Blatty's novel: "I read the novel and saw the movie in England. I cannot say that I have used the film to a great extent. I was completely loyal to the novel, as much as I could be. I filmed it according to my own perspective" (Scognamillo 1998, 258). *Şeytan*, as a Turkified text, not only translates a full set of Catholic codes into Turkish and Islamic ones but also presents a mixture of filmic language and styles. It also employed a collection of novelties both in terms of its filmic narrative and language. The idea came from producer-director Hulki Saner, known for his various melodramas starring a young girl named *Ayşecik* ("little Ayşe") and comedies with Sadri Alışık, such as the *Turist Ömer* series. *The Exorcist* was not shown in Turkey until 1981 and, according to *Şeytan*'s lobby card, it was made to exploit the success of the original: "The blockbuster film based on the best-selling novel which has been playing to sold-out crowds in America and Europe and makes its viewers faint." Nonetheless, *Şeytan*, a big-budget production by a Yeşilçam major, did not do very well at the box office (Scognamillo and Demirhan 1999, 80). Still, its incorporation of the original's special effects, such as Regan's (Linda Blair) spider walk and its translation of Christian codes into Islamic ones point to Turkification.

Şeytan, like *The Exorcist*, opens with an archaeological excavation in the Iraqi desert and then moves to an Istanbul mansion. There, Ayten (Meral Taygun) and her twelve-year-old daughter Gül (Canan Perver) are introduced with the stock characters of a mansion in Tuluat theater: the cook, the maid, and the governess. However, Ayten is an upper-class, "single, divorced" mother, which is not a common theme in Yeşilçam. At the mansion, a couple of strange things take place: the psychologist, writer, and religious scientist Tuğrul Bilge's (Cihan Ünal) book *Satan: Under the Light of Modern Perspectives on Mental Diseases, the Case of Demon Possession and the Rite of Exorcism in Universal Religions* appears from nowhere. Yeşilçam's tropes are at work here: Bilge means "sage" and his melodrama originates in his unsuccessful attempt to cure his mother who worked really hard to pay for his medical education. As modern science could not offer any answers to Gül's "sickness," Tuğrul and the archaeologist turn to exorcism: Tuğrul speaks with Gül in Latin, while the archaeologist recites the Koran in Arabic and splashes her with the water of Zamzam (a sacred spring near the Kaaba in Mecca), rather than the baptismal water used in the original. As in *The Exorcist*, Tuğrul transfers the spirit to himself and dies with it.

While *The Exorcist* is based on a true story that took place in Maryland in 1949,[7] Şeytan is based on that story's cinematic and novelistic rendering and subsequent Turkification. Beyond its visual and narrational inconsistencies, Şeytan is also full of slippages. By at times speaking in Turkish and at other times in Latin, Satan is aligned with both the West and the East within a film that promises to bring the West to the East, where there is no belief in the earthly presence of, and thus exorcism of, Satan. Erksan not only presented what he saw in London but also promised to handle this as well as *The Exorcist* did. However, when Ayten (or the dubbing artist who voices Ayten) says the name Suzan, Gül's governess, she first says "Suzan," but the second time she says "Suzın"—much like the English pronunciation of "Susan." So she pronounces Suzan's name in two different ways; one pronunciation is as a Turkish name, the other is as a Turkified one. But the English original is nowhere to be found.

This doubling of names in dubbing resonates with other novelties of Şeytan, such as Gül's adoration of a statue of Satan, as if she is performing a devotional prayer to pre-Islamic idols. Although *The Exorcist* has a subtext contrasting modernity with premodern religious rites, this becomes the primary issue in Şeytan, which continuously emphasizes a theme of science, secularism, or modernity versus religion. As a counterpart to *The Exorcist*'s Father Merrin, the archaeologist in Şeytan, who seems to be a guru of exorcism, is never introduced to the spectators: we do not know his connection with the imam and other religious figures or his previous encounters with Satan. Unlike Father Karras in the original film, Tuğrul is an atheist who claims not to believe in Satan and who drinks alcohol, yet goes to a mosque to get information about exorcism from an imam. Tuğrul indeed fits well within Yeşilçam's crossing of borders, moving vertically between classes, or having a chance to be one's other, desired self in a world of fantasy or dream. This dream world also introduces its own contradictions. While choosing to be a penniless writer instead of a famous medical doctor or, in other words, by rejecting the world of the power of science in order to write about Satan and thereby coming to believe in the existence of Satan and thus Allah, Tuğrul not only passes from the world of science to that of the religion, but ultimately loses his life. Ayten and Gül, who are seen at a mosque at the end of the film, echo such a move from atheism to religion. Thus the religiosity of the female characters is reinforced while atheism, associated with science and modernity, is punished by death.

Şeytan attempts to present a filmic experience that had previously been unavailable to spectators in Turkey, but this was only possible through mirroring or Turkification both of the original novel, as Erksan suggested, and of the film, as Saner suggested. Probably knowing that he had to produce a "different" film in a genre that did not have a lot of relevance to Yeşilçam, Erksan attempted to use a very different filmic language. At times it is

Figure 5.7. *Sevmek Zamanı* (A Time to Love, Metin Erksan, 1965), *Left*: Müşfik Kenter, *Right*: Sema Özcan

reminiscent of his own "art" films such as *Sevmek Zamanı* (A Time to Love, 1965), in which he tried to articulate a Sufi theme with the introduction of a love of the image of the lover or the other, and with a filmic language reminiscent of Alain Resnais. Likewise, his 1976 film *İntikam Meleği— Kadın Hamlet* (The Angel of Revenge—Woman Hamlet) introduces not only a Turkification of Shakespeare's text but also involves a very surreal language that seems far outside of Yeşilçam. However, *Şeytan* incorporates aspects of his "business films" such as *Feride* (1971), in which he uses elements of Yeşilçam's conventional tropes such as party scenes, a singer rising to fame, and a melodramatic storyline.

Like some Yeşilçam films, especially those early color films of the 1970s, *Şeytan* uses various zooms that come unexpectedly after cuts. While at times the film shifts from an establishing shot to a close-up through a fast zoom, at other times it does the opposite. In fact, the film's excessive use of zooms probably exceeds all other Yeşilçam films. This creates an effect of estrangement—perhaps just reinforcing the film's specificity as a horror film. Director Atıf Yılmaz criticized the excessive use of zoom in Yeşilçam: "Our filmmakers used it mostly by zooming on actors' faces, for they were not used to this equipment" (1997, 22). However, the "novel" language of the film is not just limited to the excessive use of zoom, but also involves frequent use of alternating high- and low-angle shots, shot-reverse-shot sequences coupled with varying angles and distances, back and front lighting, blocking and movement, pans and tilts. In doing all this, *Şeytan*'s vocabulary ranges from Hitchcock-style shots and editing to film noir shots of the police officer and lighting reminiscent of German expressionism. The low-quality props and special effects also contribute to this

Figure 5.8. *Şeytan* (Satan, Metin Erksan, 1974), *From left to right:* Ahu Tuğba, Canan Perver, Meral Taygun

hybrid language of filmmaking, further complicated by dubbing and the use of music from *The Exorcist*. The majority of the film's actors are not usual Yeşilçam stars but theater actors who rarely acted in Yeşilçam films. Nonetheless, there are also some stock types, such as the cook (Ahmet Kostarika) who at times seem to present comic relief; a large photograph of the mother on the wall (a commonly used prop in Yeşilçam films); the typical party scene; and the dubbing of some characters done by regular voicing artists who also dubbed various Yeşilçam stars. However, a series of novelties ran counter to them: less-known actors; alternating ways of organizing shots, editing, and *mise-en-scène*; novel props (statues and statuettes of Satan); and the eerie realism of medical tests and operations.

Şeytan is presented in a world bounded by the film itself, since Islam has no practice of the "exorcism" of Satan, though perhaps of genies. This absence of the practice is signaled in the film first by the explanation of what "exorcism" is, and then by using the word *exorcism* in English. As such, it clearly presents the dynamics of *özenti* as it tries to be the other, that of a Hollywood film. While the other is to be mirrored, to be like, and to be desired, the pure or original self is lost in the process of the other's Turkification. Yet this is marked by slippages: Yeşilçam has to keep pronouncing "Suzan" as "Suzın." But "Suzın" is not "Susan." It is not the blond whom Osman, disguised as Kaya in Germany, is looking for; it is not *The Exorcist* that the Şeytan is looking for; it is not the world of Punch that Karagöz is looking for; and it is not Susan that Ayten is looking for. Instead it is "Suzan," which is pronounced as both Suzan and Suzın. It is this being in-between, neither one nor the other, but both. And Satan speaks neither in English, nor in Arabic, but in Latin and Turkish—in a language that cannot be uttered anymore as it once was, in a language that itself lost its original voice, and in a language whose pronunciation we can only guess. So it is not the voice of truth anymore, but rather the voice of slippages.

Turist Ömer Uzay Yolunda (Tourist Ömer on *Star Trek*, 1973)

In Turkey's contemporary revival of cinema, parody has become a common way of incorporating the Yeşilçam tradition while also maintaining a seemingly ironic distance from it. Writing on a contemporary Turkish film, *Kahpe Bizans* (Harlot Byzantium, dir. Gani Müjde and Tolgay Ziyal, 1999), a parody of Yeşilçam's historical adventure films, Selim Eyüboğlu notes that the aspects of parody in the film rely upon Bakhtinian carnivalesque practices of laughter, by creating a space where fantasy and popular culture are exchanged in Turkey's contemporary big-budget film market. With reference to Linda Hutcheon, Eyüboğlu differentiates between a modern parody, where there is a hierarchical relationship between the original text and its parodization, and a self-conscious postmodern parody that dislocates this hierarchy, blurring the lines between what is parody and what is parodied (2001, 83–84). The latter type of a parody of Yeşilçam melodrama started in the late 1980s with two films: *Biz Doğarken Gülmüşüz* (We Laughed as We Were Born, dir. İsmail Güneş, 1987) and the hit film of 1988, *Arabesk* (dir. Ertem Eğilmez, 1988). Both films are parodies of Yeşilçam melodramas, particularly of *arabesk* singer films. The former film's title is a direct reference to Yücel Çakmaklı's 1973 film, *Ben Doğarken Ölmüşüm* (I Was Dead when I Was Born), starring *arabesk* singer Orhan Gencebay. While the structure of the title signals *arabesk* music's fatalistic and dark worldview reliant on a world of sacred tradition, the film is actually a parody of such a film's stories and songs, and features Komedi Dans Üçlüsü, a popular comic singer and dance trio. The more popular *Arabesk* was written by humor writer Gani Müjde, who also wrote and directed *Kahpe Bizans*.

While both films revive Yeşilçam at a time when it was starting to wane and become more and more self-reflexive, many critics often forget that parody was already a staple of Yeşilçam during the 1970s when many genres, particularly Western and adventure films, were Turkified through a process of parody. Hulki Saner's *Turist Ömer Uzay Yolunda* (hereafter TÖUY) was one such film, which took an episode of *Star Trek* and used parody as a means of considering encounters between the East and the

West. Similarly, *Cilalı İbo Teksas Fatihi* (Shiny İbo, Conqueror of Texas, dir. Osman F. Seden, 1971) involves a famous comic character who finds himself in the middle of a cowboy world after having already appeared in various films since the 1950s. Again, *Çifte Tabancalı Damat* (The Groom with Double Guns, dir. Osman Nuri Ergün, 1967) is about a bank clerk who imagines himself as Lucky Luke. There were also fairy tales that placed the funny, peasant fairy tale character, Keloğlan[8] (bald boy)—a standard Turkish character—in the world of other, Western fairytales, which viewers would know of only through Western films and stories, such as *Keloğlan ve Yedi Cüceler* (Keloğlan and the Seven Dwarfs, dir. Semih Evin, 1971). Several sex comedies of this era either directly referred to Western science-fiction and film characters or altered them in various ways, introducing familiar superheroes or heroes from American action-adventure films and television series. For example, *Çarli'nin Kelekleri* (Charlie's Fools, dir. Günay Kosova, 1978) is based on the television series *Charlie's Angels* but turns the female angels (*melek*) into male fools (*kelek*). *Süper Selami* (Super Selami, dir. Yılmaz Atadeniz, 1979) is about a market delivery boy who escapes from a plot against him and hides in a cave where an Indian fakir suddenly appears and first utters the magic word *Shazam* and turns into a superhero with the mask of *The Phantom* and the costume of *Superman* (Scognamillo and Demirhan 1999, 55). Then the Indian fakir transfers his magical force to Selami, who then becomes Süper Selami. Later, post-Yeşilçam cinema utilized postmodern parody through *Kahpe Bizans* or *G.O.R.A.* (dir. Ömer Faruk Sorak, 2004), which is partly based on TÖUY.

While these examples evidence a variety of genre-crossings, genrification, and recycling, they belong to a familiar mode of comedy based on a male comic character who is poor, honest, and witty and who is usually paired with a more educated or reasonable character, a pairing reminiscent of shadow plays, where the uneducated Karagöz plays off of the more urbane Hacivat, as well as theater-in-the-round, where Kavuklu is coupled with Pişekar. Alternatively, this character may also appear as a solo fool like the İbiş of *tuluat* and Keloğlan of fairy tales. In HBT, Zeki Müren's alter ego Rasim is a comic character who functions against his more educated Zeki. The connection between this cinematic tradition and earlier theatrical traditions is not merely circumstantial or subconscious; it was often carried by actors moving from one field to the other. For instance, İsmail Dümbüllü, who had inherited the headdress symbolic of the traditional acting profession, the *kavuk* (a form of Ottoman headdress that preceded the Fez, a product of nineteenth-century Ottoman dress reform, itself outlawed during the republican era), from one of his masters in theater, simply performed his stage sketches or used his theater character within the narrative of the film itself. These were: *Dümbüllü Macera Peşinde* (Dümbüllü in Search of Adventure, dir. Şadan Kamil, 1948), *Dümbüllü Sporcu* (Dümbüllü the Sportsman, dir. Seyfi Havaeri, 1952), and *Dümbüllü Tarzan* (dir. Muharrem Gürses, 1954). Dümbüllü films introduced not only the tropes of theater-in-the-round within cinema but also began the practice of making a series of films about various adventures of the same comic character, much like Hollywood comedies with Laurel and Hardy or the Marx Brothers. Three such popular characters were Feridun Karakaya's Cilalı İbo (Shiny İbo), Sadri Alışık's Turist Ömer (Tourist Ömer), and Kemal Sunal's İnek Şaban (Cow Şaban). Like Dümbüllü, all three were originally theater actors. The female counterparts of such characters appeared mainly in romantic comedies and came to be identified with particular actresses such as Belgin Doruk's Küçük Hanımefendi (Little Lady) or Hülya Koçyiğit's Kezban who traveled to various European cities for each film in the series. However, unlike traditional narratives, these belonged to a more contemporary melodramatic narration with some traits borrowed from the *tuluat* theater.

TÖUY is the seventh and last film to feature Alışık's Turist Ömer character, the product of a traditional theatrical background. All seven films were directed by Hulki Saner, who ensured thematic continuity enmeshed with references to the ongoing issues of the time and who, perhaps in collaboration with Alışık, created the travels of the tragic-comic hero leading to his final, parodic installment in space. The first *Turist Ömer* (dir. Hulki Saner, 1964) introduced Ömer as a "tourist," a rural, poor, and foolish migrant in Istanbul. Thus with a standard comic plot that follows a traditional figure in a modern urban setting, the film reflects on modernization processes. Later comedies in this mold frequently introduced an unnamed Kurdish migrant character who is not explicitly identified as a Kurd but recognized as such through cultural cues. Ömer, however, is clearly identified as Turkish. In the second film, *Turist Ömer Dümenciler Kralı* (Turist Ömer, the King of Tricksters, dir. Hulki Saner, 1965), Ömer is mistaken for a foreign prince, placing him among the high society of Turkey. The film thus not only addresses class difference but also the relationship among Turks, former Ottoman "masters" of Arab lands, and legions of oil-rich Arab tourists arriving in Istanbul who were wealthy, but whose behavior was seen as "uncivilized" and attire as antimodern. By propagating a view of the Arab world as the "East" of Turkey, such a film also mimicked the Western cinemas' consumption of the Orient as opulent, premodern, and romantic, similar to the Kurdish "East" or "South-East" of Turkey within its geographic boundaries.

In the third film, *Turist Ömer Almanya'da* (Turist Ömer in Germany, dir. Hulki Saner, 1966), Ömer goes abroad to Germany as a low-class, rural Turkish worker and falls in love with the stereotypical German "Helga." Being an immigrant worker, Ömer joins the lowest rung of the workforce of the burgeoning postwar European economy.[9] The difficulties that immigrants experience both abroad and after their return to Turkey became a common cinematic theme during the 1970s and 1980s. Later, the post-Yeşilçam era featured an influx of films by diasporic Turks and Kurds.[10] As one of the first films in this theme, *Turist Ömer Almanya'da* puns on the often-overlooked lives of displaced workers in West Germany. While this first wave of immigrant workers came mostly from rural areas of Turkey, a second wave of immigrants went to Europe as ethnic and

Figure 5.9. *Turist Ömer* (Tourist Ömer, Hulki Saner, 1963)

political refugees, especially after the 1980 military intervention. Dealing mostly with serious dramas such as *Otobüs* (The Bus, dir. Tunç Okan, 1975), *Almanya Acı Vatan* (Germany Bitter Land, dir. Şerif Gören, 1979), and *Kırk Metrekare Almanya* (Forty Square Meters of Germany, dir. Tevfik Başer, 1986), Oğuz Makal argues that such films used realistic language to deal with the problems of communication and the search for identity

(1994, 123). While such social realist dramas of Yeşilçam dealt with these issues in relation to nation and national cinema, later films by diasporic filmmakers addressed issues of transnationality, ethnic and cultural mixing, and coproductions through the involvement of European production companies or television channels. Coinciding with the demise of Yeşilçam in the late 1980s, films like *Reise der Hoffnung* (Umuda Yolculuk, Journey of Hope, dir. Xavier Koller, 1990), a coproduction of Switzerland, Turkey, and the United Kingdom, tells the story of a Kurdish family who tries to immigrate illegally to Switzerland. While some critics deemed these films non-Turkish, others saw transnational films as a venue for transgressing the reactionary conceptions of nationality.

While the post-Yeşilçam era emphasizes transgressions and transnationality, Yeşilçam dealt with the Western countries and with Turkish characters in such lands in three ways. First is the travel to the West depicted in comedies and romantic comedies with dislocated Turkish characters, such as Turist Ömer, in the West or in melodramas with upper-class characters vacationing in Europe. The second category involves films from different genres introducing lower-class and often rural characters immigrating to Europe in search of a better life. Finally, there are some "issue" melodramas such as *Memleketim* (My Homeland, dir. Yücel Çakmaklı, 1975) and *Bir Türk'e Gönül Verdim* (I Fell for a Turk, dir. Halit Refiğ, 1969) dealing with cultural tension between the West and Turkey and with the ideological standpoints of the filmmakers that are delivered through spectacular encounters, as in OO, where the values and morality of the East are victorious over the "capitalist" West and where westernization causes the loss of "essential" traits of the Turkish identity.

The fourth and fifth Turist Ömer films raise further modes of displacement with travels to Arab and African lands. While *Turist Ömer Arabistan'da* (Turist Ömer in Arabia, dir. Hulki Saner, 1969) reiterates the Ottoman colonial presence in the Arab lands, *Turist Ömer Yamyamlar Arasında* (Turist Ömer among the Cannibals, dir. Hulki Saner, 1970) reproduces the imperialist gaze through a discourse on "primitiveness" and through ignoring the practice of slavery during the Ottoman times. Both films introduce shades of Orientalism in a country that is considered Oriental itself. After his voyages to such "dark" and "black" fantasylands of princes and cannibals, Turist Ömer returns to Europe for *Turist Ömer Boğa Güreşçisi* (Turist Ömer, the Bullfighter, dir. Hulki Saner, 1971), for a popular touristic attraction in an arena surrounded by bulls and matadors. Having already become a seasoned traveler, Turist Ömer's last voyage was neither to the East nor to the West, but to the beyond, to the future and extraterrestrial world of the *Star Trek* television series.

In this series, Turist Ömer, a tourist traveling to many lands, is an ill-mannered vagrant and bum who parodies affluent, capitalist, and westernized tourism. Starting out as a lower-class, rural Turkish character, Ömer quickly acquires Istanbul vernacular and manages to return to Turkey at the end of each film—recalling the working of *özenti*. The comic effect is then produced through displacement, by relocating Ömer on board *Star Trek*'s USS *Enterprise*. Ömer's visit to the world of American television series not only transforms him but also introduces the "first" cinematic rendition of the series, predating its first official film version, *Star Trek: The Motion Picture* (dir. Robert Wise, 1979). Based on the pilot episode of the series, which nonetheless ultimately first aired in the United States as episode 6, "The Man Trap," on September 8, 1966, apart from the introduction, TÖUY follows the original script of the Turist Ömer character and the exceedingly poor quality of sets, makeup, and special effects. While the latter aspect recalls trash film discussions, TÖUY was a fairly mainstream Yeşilçam production, considerably better quality than various other quickies featuring comic book heroes such as Batman, Superman, and the Italian costumed photo-novel hero, Killing. In the original episode, the crew of the USS *Enterprise* lands on planet M113 for a medical check of the only two residents of the remote planet, Robert and Nancy Crater. However, Nancy turns out to be a "salt vampire" who is the last survivor of a species that lived on the planet. "Salt vampire," according to one Web site, was an in-joke referencing the NBC censors demands for revisions to cut open-mouthed kisses (http://www.statemaster.com/ency-clopedia/Star-Trek:-The-Original-Series). Thus a female "salt vampire," standing for open-mouthed kisses, not only bites, but also sucks out the life force of the *Enterprise* crew.

Although TÖUY does not involve such an ironic intervention, Yeşilçam's double-edged relation to the West and its Turkification of extraterrestrials through parody is at stake. The opening credits, with "upholstered" music from the original series and other sources, make use of the original series' opening credits, overexposing them in yellow. The crew lands on planet Orin 7 to check Professor Crater's (Kayhan Yıldızoğlu) and Nancy's (Şule Tınaz) health and to take some scientific notes from the professor. Unlike the original's sterile studio set of an unearthly planet, the Turkish *Enterprise*'s pioneer crew is teleported to the historical city of Ephesus. True to Yeşilçam's tradition of shooting on location, which utilizes Istanbul's Archaeological Museum, Ottoman fortresses, Byzantine churches and cisterns, and other such historical buildings for historical adventure films, the majority of science fiction and fantastic films utilized eccentric geographical locations such as Cappadocia, the land of fairy chimneys, and the ruins of Greek or Roman cities such as Ephesus. While the *Enterprise* is referred to as *Atılgan* (enterprising or intrepid), the names of characters are kept intact with transliterations, in a Turkish accent (e.g., "Spak" or "Körk").

A cut to 1973 Istanbul introduces Turist Ömer, about to be forced into marriage and praying for a miracle. After he gets his wish, he finds himself in Ephesus (Planet Orin) staring lustfully at the two female guardian robots of the professor's house, and then Hercules, the professor's stiff and Tarzanish robot, arrives and takes him to the professor and Nancy. Ömer annoys everyone with nonstop talking and lame jokes. He asks the professor about Mr. Spock: "Is this also a machine? But the engineer did a bad job. Look at these pointed ears, smooth hair, and strange look."

Figure 5.10. *Turist Ömer Uzay Yolunda* (Tourist Ömer on *Star Trek*, Hulki Saner, 1973)

When beamed on board of *Atılgan*, Ömer, like a mischievous kid, sits in the captain's chair, plays with the gadgets, and gives orders like the captain: "Mr. Spock, send us four well-brewed glasses of tea." Ömer's culturally specific jokes create alienation effects among the crew who try to understand this Easterner from the past. The doctor's tests ascertain that Ömer has a limited brain capacity and "an excessive reaction in his sexual plasmas; a primitive remnant in which the normal cells are grouped."

Apart from the Westerners from the future, Ömer also asks questions of *Atılgan*'s main computer: "What does two times two equal?" The feminine computer replies: "Four." "Ah, the *whore* knows the answer." The captain, who sees Spock get angry for the first time, asks Ömer to apologize. Ömer extends his hand to Spock for a handshake. But he takes his hand back, saying "Zzzt!" Spock tells the captain: "So you see, Captain, this creature is beyond reason." Spock, unable to understand the phrase "Zzzt," decides to ask the main computer, which, after hearing the question, instantly starts to shake and put out smoke before laughing hysterically and going berserk. In short, Ömer is an Eastern character "beyond reason."

In addition to Ömer's presence and the introduction of meat-eating flowers from *The Little Shop of Horrors* (dir. Roger Corman, 1960), TÖUY further deviates from the original during the clash of *Atılgan*'s crew with the salt vampire, when Yeşilçam's poor technical capacity is revealed by an orange-costumed and gas-masked monster. Yeşilçam's fantastic films share a similar low-budget, quickie aesthetic, whereas Turkified family melodramas, comedies, or action-adventure films are adapted better into Turkish settings. On the other hand, genres that demand sophistication in *mise-en-scène* exposed Yeşilçam's weaknesses, making such films popular among trash cinema aficionados. However, the issue of verisimilitude, which turns such films into trash, has to be elaborated. While Yeşilçam is a cinema of imitation for many, it is also a cinema of "Turkification" involving a nationalist *hayal* and *özenti* enmeshed with a melodramatic modality. Spock's laser gun shot, which works through scratches on the film negative that create an X marking on the shot creature, is indeed conceivable as a part of Yeşilçam's film language. Certainly, such films, seen as "trash," could be disregarded or seen with an ironic or sarcastic detachment. Taking inspiration from a formalist rendering of film language, one may also consider Jeffrey Sconce's reading of trash cinema through Kristin Thompson's concept of "cinematic excess" (1999a). For Sconce, when a spectator's motivation is broken by elements of filmic discourse or narrative, gaps or breaks in film's realism produce excess (1995). Trash cinema is more prone to producing excess because of its exploitative mentality, bad acting, cheap sets, and low-quality special effects. Such moments of excess may lead spectators to lose their grip on filmic textuality and bring extratextual themes and issues into the textual world of the film. While such a reading of Yeşilçam is possible, it leads directly to a larger frame: what if a film industry is itself in excess? If not taken in relation to a relevant visual history and a general framework of particular entertainment practices that predated and went hand in hand with cinema, Yeşilçam, according to the universal formalist arguments, could be considered pure cinematic trash. Instead, Yeşilçam's Turkification practices, marked by cheapness, aggression, and novelties, seem crucial to understanding a national popular film industry rife with flaws and intricacies, but also intricately enmeshed with the attraction of melodrama and complex ideologies.

At the end of the film, after the doctor kills the body-transferring salt vampire, Ömer mistakes the doctor for the deceased creature, and Spock says: "Do not be afraid Mr. Turist, the monster is dead." Ömer replies: "The monster is dead but you live. Everybody is afraid of you." This deliberate extratextual reference indeed voices the Turkish spectators' perception, who are jokingly afraid of Spock's pointed ears. In other words, Ömer moves across the textual and extratextual worlds by changing roles: Ömer, as the main character of *Turist Ömer Uzay Yolunda*, belongs to the textual world of the film; Ömer, who carries his identity intact over a series of films and who becomes a part of the *Star Trek* television series, belongs to an intertextual world; and Ömer, who voices the spectatorial perception of the television series, belongs to an extratextual world. Such deliberate addresses directed toward spectators, as a common Yeşilçam trope, have their roots in the traditional performing arts of Turkey. Thus instead of being formalist excessive moments, these constitute Yeşilçam's filmic makeup that entangles the textual, the intertextual, and the extratextual. At the end of the film, when Ömer finds himself back at the marriage ceremony, Mr. Spock helps him by making his ears pointed: "Hey, Mr. Spock, bro, you are a great guy. You made me an ear-victim like you!" Apart from being victimized, Ömer borrows Spock's powers to immobilize the bride and others and greets the crew with his trademark gesture of good-bye.

Kara Murat Fatih'in Fedaisi (Kara Murat, Fatih's Defender, 1972)

Unlike deliberate Turkifications of fantastic films, the homegrown stories of historical action-adventure films commonly utilize comic books and render the past melodramatically. Yeşilçam's historical fictions involve three different themes: conflict with the Greeks and other countries during and after the First World War and during the War of Independence that led to the demise of the Ottoman Empire and the formation of the Turkish Republic; hostilities between the Ottomans and the Byzantine Empire; and the lives and battles of Central Asian Turks against the Chinese and others. To these, one may add a small number of films about the history of Islam, involving the clash between believers and infidels, and films about recent political and military clashes of Turkey in Korea and Cyprus. The genre of historical action-adventure frequently reproduces the nationalism of the republican models, especially in the historical dramas and adventures about the War of Independence. But those dealing with the Ottoman or early Islamic period provide an anti-Byzantine and thus anti-Christian ethos, bringing together national and religious identities.

Having their roots in comic books or pulp novels, heroes such as Karaoğlan, Tarkan, Kara Murat, and Malkoçoğlu fight against the existing or projected enemies of the Turks including the Byzantines, Greeks, Crusaders, infidels, Chinese, and even Vikings. The ("harlot") Byzantium of Yeşilçam is a feminized, all-in-one enemy to be overcome and conquered in all respects: "Byzantines are the enemies of Turks, Christians are the enemies of Muslims" (Scognamillo and Demirhan 1999, 139). Starting with *İstanbul'un Fethi* (The Conquest of Constantinople, dir. Aydın Arakon, 1951), the Byzantine Empire was depicted as truly *byzantine*, full of palace

Figure 5.11. Photograph taken during the filming of *Kara Murat Fatih'in Fedaisi* (Kara Murat, Fatih's Defender, Natuk Baytan, 1972), Bora Ayanoğlu as the Sultan and on his right Cüneyt Arkın as Kara Murat

intrigues perfect for adventurous melodrama. Though this film attempts a realistic and objective portrayal of Byzantium, later films simply regurgitated Byzantine stereotypes: intrigues, illicit relationships, dishonesty, and torture (Scognamillo and Demirhan 1999, 139). Byzantium is simply an element enriching the *mise-en-scène* of a melodramatic plot: a fixed iconography of types; evil; heroes and heroines overcoming evil forces; tortures by Byzantine lords eliciting pathos; the conquest of Byzantine lands by killing the enemy; dramatic and spectacular confrontations enriched by elements from sword-and-sandal epics and Westerns; last-minute rescues; and romantic relationships with Byzantine princesses who later convert to Islam. Another common melodramatic trope is a Turkish character captured by the Byzantines as a child who later discovers his true identity, either by meeting one of his relatives or by a sign noticed by his brother following a dramatic confrontation between two siblings, reminiscent of the Corsican brothers.

Opening with the image of the Fatih mosque in Istanbul, originally built by Mehmet the Conqueror (*"Fatih"*), and with a narration about Istanbul, which would one day be conquered by Muslims, and accompanied by a religious tune about the *hadith* (words believed to have been spoken by the prophet Mohammed), *Kara Murat Fatih'in Fedaisi* (dir. Natuk Baytan, hereafter KMFF) is based on Rahmi Turan's comic book by the same name. Though an earlier version was made in 1966, *Fatih'in Fedaisi* (Fatih's Defender, dir. Tunç Başaran), this second version became popular and triggered several sequels featuring the action-adventure star Cüneyt Arkın. The next shot shows a sign in both Arabic and Latin on which the *hadith* about Istanbul is written, implying that it is in the garden of the Fatih Mosque: "How happy the commander who conquers the city of Constantine and how happy for his soldiers." The march of Fatih with his soldiers, accompanied by Ottoman military band music (*mehter*), is seen, as a voice-over narration gives formal historical information. Then a map of the Ottoman Empire in 1453 shows the territories conquered by the Ottomans. To indicate the conquest, an animated arrow on the map moves from Edirne, the capital of the Ottoman Empire before the conquest, to Istanbul, and it starts burning in animated orange flames. The narration continues, intercut with shots of the army band, Fatih leading on horseback, and animated arrows indicating conquered areas surrounding the expanding empire.

But there is a gimmick to the animated red arrow: on the map, the territories surrounding the Ottoman Empire are painted with colors other than red. When the red arrow emerges from the center (Istanbul) of the fluorescent yellow Ottoman Empire, it first turns the color on the map blood red and then annexes that land to the fluorescent yellow color of the map of the Ottoman Empire. This cartographic action is accompanied by a narration: "The entire world bowed its head before the Turkish sword. The Turks, turning the map of Europe upside down, were rewriting history with golden letters." The republican dream of being equal to the Western world can never come close to equaling such nostalgia of Turkish might and power over fifteenth-century Europe, just as Yeşilçam markets popular nationalism through historical fictions of Ottoman-Turkish identity. After this long preamble, the map focuses on the Princedom of Wallachia, of Vlad the Impaler (Turgut Özatay), which is conquered by animated explosions. After this introduction (continual voice-over narration with intercut shots of the filmic present and past, and animated maps), KMFF shows Vlad's palace, the apse of St. Irene (Aya İrini), an austere church built next to Hagia Sophia during the tenth-century iconoclastic movement and used as an imperial armory during much of the Ottoman era. There, one of Vlad's servants announces the crime of a man, woman, and child: "To be Turkish and Muslim." Vlad tells the Muslim Turks to change their religion and nation, and kiss the idol. After they refuse to kiss the cross, Vlad orders, "Impale the man, and take out the woman's heart." In Yeşilçam's ahistoricism, the fifteenth-century Ottomans are "Turks" with full awareness of their nationhood.

Vlad's lust and cruelty is stereotypically represented in a scene where he kills his mistress as his femme fatale wife kills a young boy. Later Vlad's forces ambush a group of Turks, including two siblings; Vlad asks the younger one to cut off his older brother's arms and legs, which the younger one does, after his older brother approves it. Cüneyt Arkın plays both the older brother in this scene and the grown-up younger brother, Kara Murat, in later scenes. In other words, the same actor playing two different roles cuts his own arms and legs—metaphorically castrates himself—before his eventual act of revenge! Cüneyt Arkın, who began his career as a male lead of melodramas, during this period became the main action hero of all sorts of Yeşilçam's "male" genres, for example, historical, science fiction, crime, and Westerns that demanded action scenes with fights and spectacular duels. Arkın did all of these scenes without the help of stunt doubles and with his "fighter team," stunt players who got beaten by him in one film after another. This doubling of Arkın, as himself and his brother in the same film, is a common ploy in Yeşilçam, which often handles the aging of a character just by applying talcum powder to actors' hair. In the dungeon, young Murat meets his future "princess," the little girl, Zeynep. After Murat goes to Istanbul to inform Fatih about what happened, the Ottomans raid Wallachia and Vlad escapes to Hungary.

The voice-over narration signals the passing of time. An adult raider of the Fatih army, Murat is again sent to Wallachia to overcome Vlad. When Vlad and his soldiers are in a hunting party in the Wallacian "desert" (the dune of a small Black Sea town north of Istanbul often used for desert scenes in Yeşilçam), one of his soldiers attempts to rape Angela (Hale Soygazi), who is actually the grown-up Zeynep. Kara Murat, disguised as an Albanian, saves Zeynep and befriends the Serbian Mikhail (Erol Taş). At the palace, Angela/Zeynep notices Murat's necklace and does not identify him as a culprit. Vlad's wife asks the guards to bring Murat over to her room. After they have sex, Murat manages to thwart her bloodlust and escapes from prison. As Murat attempts to overcome Vlad, two duels break out between the two men and between Vlad's wife and Angela/ Zeynep. After Zeynep kills Vlad's wife, Murat impales Vlad—the impaler impaled! The film finally ends with the happy trio of Mikhail, Zeynep, and Murat on horseback while Murat holds a very poor-quality fake head of Vlad on a stick.

In keeping with Yeşilçam's melodramatic modality, KMFF's iconography is supported by a standard set of narrative elements: shot on-location scenes introduce historical monuments of Istanbul; visual codes of the genre such as crosses, bowing before the priests, and the colorful drapery of non-Muslim royalty are reproduced; the "Byzantine" palace is rife with sexual perversions, intrigue, spies, and torture; and the Manichean conflict

Figure 5.12. *Kara Murat Fatih'in Fedaisi* (Kara Murat, Fatih's Defender, Natuk Baytan, 1972)

between the protagonists and the antagonists is handled with masculine overtones, perversions, vampirism, and unlikely coincidences. Similarly, Yeşilçam's incoherencies are also at play, such as the blame for idolatrous (i.e., Christian) Wallachians and Hungarians not being argued for Serbians or Albanians. The Ottomans are not imperialist invaders, but Vlad's victims. Thus KMFF, through its quasi-historical narrative, augments the inherently good and victorious characteristics of the Ottoman Turks, similar to Yeşilçam's other historical narratives offering a communal bind for the nation and for its religion. Thus when Christians convert to Islam and accept Ottoman authority, they become members of this community defined by an allegiance that silences ethnicity: "How happy is he who says he is a Turk," one of the key mottoes of the nation, relies on a double entendre, in which, like religion, national identity can be taken on through a heartfelt conversion toward the good. Conversion thus provides a thinly veiled proposition concerning the shared nationalism of the multiple ethnicities that make up the Turkish nation.

Canlı Hedef (Live Target, 1970)

While the fantastic films dealt with above are mainstream Yeşilçam films made with considerable budgets that may be considered trash, there are many other quickies that may be trashier still. All of them are considered here as part of the Yeşilçam tradition. To be able to argue for Yeşilçam's excessive aspects, one either needs to look at classical Hollywood or has to define classical Yeşilçam. But what constitutes classical Yeşilçam and its deviant or excessive texts is excess itself. Like Ed Wood, who saw ideal cinema in Orson Welles's films, Yeşilçam dreamed of the Western cinemas, especially Hollywood. In this, Yeşilçam also produced an ambivalent set of practices in response to the West, to a Western medium offering the possibility of a realistic representation of the world.

Internationally renowned for his social realist films, Yılmaz Güney, the Kurdish Turkish filmmaker, first became famous as the "ugly king" of Yeşilçam's action films. But as the "ugly king" of Turkish cinema, he was initially presented as the antithesis of the handsome "king" of Turkish cinema, Ayhan Işık, who was "the modest, honest, handsome young man, well-liked by neighbors, and sporting a Clark Gable moustache" (Özgüven 1989, 35). While Işık was the king of family melodramas set in Istanbul's lavish bourgeois houses, Güney wandered in the dark and seedy streets of Istanbul full of crime and action. While one was a product of the center and its middle-class cultural makeup, the other was a peripheral badass of the "other" side, of the republican regime's others; one was the easygoing king, the other was the "Oriental macho," whose debut as a director was with At Avrat Silah (Horse Woman Gun, 1966). As a "decent" gangster, a contemporary Robin Hood, one of his early lead roles was Zorro in a Turkified remake, Kara Şahin (Black Hawk, dir. Nuri Akıncı, 1964). His star image inscribes a romantic bandit who, though inherently good, is always forced by evil powers into the crime-ridden underworld of society.

While he fits into this scheme in the majority of the hundred-plus films in which he acted, his social realist dramas undermined this star image. As a fiction writer, he also published short stories and a novel and, later in his film career, started to write and direct his own films. He directed more than twenty films, largely between 1967 and 1971, making eight films in 1971 alone. After being jailed twice, once for helping a leftist organization and then for killing a prosecutor, he escaped from prison in 1981 and immigrated to France. However, in all of his films, he recouped Yeşilçam's melodramatic modality at different levels through Manichean conflicts and a low-budget filmmaking mind-set.

One film that presents a wary Yeşilçam realism is *Canlı Hedef* (aka, *Kızım İçin*, For My Daughter, hereafter CH). Among the thirteen films Güney acted in in 1970, he himself directed four of them. The plot summaries for these reveal the melodramatic framework: a tough guy taking revenge for the rape of his daughter, a tough guy taking revenge against the smugglers who killed his older brother, the romance between an ex-safecracker and the daughter of a soccer coach, the story of two gangs and of the love between an ex-murderer and the sister of a gambler, the story of a jail-breaker and a girl who runs away from a compulsory marriage with a landowner, a tough guy, whose father is an imam, regrets his crime-ridden life, a young boy's fight against drug smugglers who kidnap his girlfriend, the story of a guard and the three daughters of a rich man, the revenge story of a safecracker on the lam, the love story of a Turkish boy and a Greek girl in a fishing village, the "hopeless" story of a carriage-driver with five children, the adventure of the fight between two bandits and seven small-town troublemakers, and the sad story of lovers who fall apart because of a blood feud (Özgüç 1998). Among these, the only movie

Figure 5.13. *At Avrat Silah* (Horse Woman Gun, Yılmaz Güney, 1966)

that received critical acclaim was *Umut* (Hope, dir. Yılmaz Güney)—the sad and hopeless story of a carriage-driver who is obsessed with finding a treasure. *Umut* is generally accepted as one of the best ten films of the history of cinema in Turkey and one of the best examples of social realist drama in Yeşilçam, in the footsteps of Italian Neorealist classics. While *Umut* reflects elements of Neorealist style with its on-location shooting, post-synchronized sound, open and simple *mise-en-scène*, camera movement, and nonprofessional actors, such stylistic elements were almost all present in other Yeşilçam films, ranging from family melodramas to historical adventures and superhero flicks. What makes the Turkification of Neorealism in *Umut* or Neorealist films different from other Güney films of the same year was its filmic narrative: it represents social life through the medium of cinema in a particular way and replaces the tough guy Güney with a poor and helpless carriage-driver. While CH, about a tough guy taking revenge against his enemies who raped his daughter, is similar to the Neorealist style of *Umut*, its narrative does not frame the social ills as products of the capitalist system.

Yet both films relate to the West, to Hollywood or Italian Neorealism, through different grades of Turkification. Güney's double public persona, one as the "ugly king" of Yeşilçam and the other as the "cult" leftist figure went hand in hand during these years. Moreover, the military regime banned all of his films throughout the 1980s, suggesting the intricate blending of two personas. After 1971, he directed only five films and wrote two more that were directed by his assistant directors. In these five films, he consciously tried to deviate from Yeşilçam's conventions. In *Arkadaş* (Friend, 1974), he did not present "a usual chain of intrigues" and said "drama is already a part of daily life. I did not try to create a strained dramatic narrative/editing. I just wanted to portray daily life" (Dorsay 2000, 93). Moreover, he wanted to dismantle his own star image as the "adventurous, fighting and swaggering tough guy" (Güney 1974b, 4) by going against the "molded Yeşilçam types of good and evil" (Güney 1974a, 3). However, Güney only had relative success in doing so. One Islamist writer even claimed in 1977, "If one does not consider some pornographic scenes in *Arkadaş*, the film's moral conception might easily belong to an example of *Milli* [National] Cinema" (Sütüven 1977, 8). In other words, in trying to dismantle Yeşilçam, he reproduced the traditional decency and moralism. Moreover, Yeşilçam's practice and tactics persisted in his later films, including his last film, *Duvar* (The Wall, 1983), which he shot in France before his unfortunate death from cancer in 1984.

While the endings of Yeşilçam's "issue" films vary over the political spectrum, its filmmakers belonged to the domestic filmmaking practice conditioned by Turkification, melodramatic modality, *hayal* and *özenti*, which led to various levels of textual responses to the West. CH is a "standard" Güney quickie, reproducing such elements in a gangster film. The film opens with fast-paced cutting of close-up shots of money, guns, and people shooting and enjoying killing others, accompanied by Rare Bird's song, *Sympathy*, which is commonly "upholstered" for romantic scenes and even action scenes like these. The cuts conclude with a mafia meeting and the camera zooms to the boss Bilal (Bilal İnci), who reads a newspaper story about Asım Mavzer's (lit. "virtuous/upright Mauser rifle," played by Yılmaz Güney) return to Turkey. Nicknamed the "black executioner," Asım killed all three of Bilal's brothers before leaving the country, leaving behind Elif, his daughter, whose mother has recently passed away. Bilal and his men, led by Jilet (lit. razorblade, played by Tarık Şimşek), are out for revenge, as is Belalı Çino (lit. troublemaker Chino, played by Erdoğan Vatansever). Asım's friends Aspirin Osman (Danyal Topatan) and Korsan Kemal (lit. pirate, played by Yıldırım Gencer) also start to look for Asım. These carefully chosen names and nicknames constitute the film's "stylish" construction of the criminal underworld. While this nomenclature follows Yeşilçam's convention of using actors' first names as the characters' names (Bilal İnci as Bilal), it also employs an "epic" feel that compliments the film's elements borrowed from Westerns (Çino), and has extratextual references thanks to the pleasant sound of the names adopted by various Yeşilçam actors (Yılmaz Güney's real surname is Pütün). Such stylish nomenclature also inscribes a cartoonish feel, for Aspirin and Korsan are Asım's sidekicks, similar to Italian comic books, where the character Zagor, "the spirit with the hatchet," is coupled with Tonka, the bold and smart Mohawk, and the comic Mexican Cico (Chico); or Mark, the Commander of the Ontario Wolves, is coupled with the pirate, adventurer Mister Bluff and the wise fighter and comic Sad Owl. This underscores the exchanges between popular cultures and cinemas in Turkey and Italy with coproduced Westerns and actions films, and Turkified sex comedies, comic books, and photo-novels.

Asım pays a visit to his daughter at a school, where he meets with her teacher, who is an orphan. When he signs his will leaving everything to his daughter, he reveals that he was born in 1932 in Siverek, a predominantly Kurdish town in southeastern Turkey. Güney himself was born in 1931 (though, according to Özgüç [1995], it was recorded as 1937 on his birth certificate) as Yılmaz Pütün in Adana, in southern Turkey (Güney means South). So both Güney and Asım Mavzer were born around the same time and both are presumably Kurdish. The filmic and the real also merge in the film's alternate title: *For My Daughter*. Like Asım, Güney's own life is inscribed by guns and women: he shot films and guns; he shot guns at mirrors in hotels and then did the same in his films; he used real bullets in one of his films while shooting at a glass positioned on his ex-wife's head. At the time this film was shot, Güney's real-life daughter, also named Elif, was seven years old. At the time, Güney was married to Fatoş Güney, and Elif was the daughter of one of his ex-girlfriends. Elif Güney Pütün lived with her mother, Can, in Istanbul until she was four years old: "I went to a boarding nursery school. I lived with a nurse in Ankara up until I was eight. I lived in Adana with my aunt until I was eleven, then two years with my mom. When I was thirteen, I went to Moda to stay with Fatoş Güney" (Pütün 1999). Then, with Güney and Fatoş, she moved to France. So when CH was made, Güney and Elif were living apart and Güney expressed his love for her by naming the film and Elif in the film after his daughter. Concerning his father's use of her name for film characters, Elif says, "My dad sent messages to me by naming little girls in his films Elif. I knew he was trying to reach me" (1999). Beyond the contrasts between quality films and quickies, and between social realist films and popular cinema, CH crisscrosses between Güney's own life and his film characters, and thus his films' reality as opposed to their realism becomes increasingly ambiguous.

As a romantic relationship develops between Asım and Elif's teacher, Bilal's men track down Asım's daughter who, melodramatically, knows Asım not as her father but as an unidentified uncle. As evidenced in the list of Yeşilçam films' one-liners, a child talks about an unidentified man (i.e., his/her real father), "Mommy, I liked this uncle very much. Can I call him daddy?" Similarly, Elif tells Asım, "Please do not leave me...I liked you a lot. I am an orphan...I wish you were my dad." As everyone starts crying, Asım asks Elif to call him "Dad" one last time before his duel with Çino. Elif replies, "Dad, my daddy." While Yeşilçam's standard melodramatic tropes are at work in this sequence, on an exactly non-diegetic terrain, CH's melodramatic realism has an extremely "real" reverberation. However, CH quickly moves to a classy duel where Çino misses Asım and then begs Asım to kill him. But Asım refuses to kill him. Then, after Aspirin and Korsan take off, accompanied by the "upholstered" song, "El Condor Paso," the Andean song made famous by Simon & Garfunkel, Asım is left alone with Elif's teacher and Rare Bird's *Sympathy* is upholstered again. Such non-diegetic music is augmented by Aspirin Osman's songs, which are played with *cümbüş*, a banjo-like musical instrument with connotations of carousal or revel implying drinking and singing. However, this *cümbüş* ends quickly with the kidnapping of Asım and Elif by Bilal's men, who tie up Asım and make him watch, like the film's spectators, shadows falling on a white curtain behind which a man rapes Elif. Then, Asım asks his daughter to forgive him, before both are taken to and hung from a railway bridge. After a passing train cuts the ropes, Elif drowns in the river. So Elif, who already lost her innocence, dies in the name of melodramatic resolution. As previously noted, in Yeşilçam, if a woman cannot stay pure, she eventually pays for it with her life. Alternatively, if a man saves a woman from a rundown life, the woman has to be cleansed, usually by taking a symbolic bath and leaving behind the sinful life. But Elif, a child, has no chance to redeem herself and even had she lived, she would have been the victim of honor killing because she was "defiled." So her death produces narrative resolution and spectatorial catharsis.

To augment the traditional patriarchal regime, a revenge plot takes over as the trio of Asım, Aspirin, and Korsan starts hunting for Bilal. When they attack Bilal's girlfriend's house, in yet another bizarre scene, Asım rapes a woman in the house with a "real" snake to learn where Bilal is hiding. After this phallic act of revenge, the trio, with Çino, attacks Bilal's hideout. The attack is accompanied by "upholstered" soundtrack music from Costa Gavras's *Z* (1969), composed by Mikis Theodorakis. A French-

Figure 5.14. *Canlı Hedef* (Live Target, Yılmaz Güney, 1970)

Algerian coproduction, *Z* is about the Greek junta's oppression of the left. Gavras's movie won the Golden Globe and Academy Award for the Best Foreign Language Film in 1970, as well as a Jury Prize at the Cannes Film Festival.

Strangely enough, when Yılmaz Güney and Şerif Gören's *Yol* (The Way, 1982) won the Golden Palm at the Cannes Film Festival, they tied with Costa Gavras's *Missing* (1982) and thus shared the prize with Gavras. *Yol*, which was made in the aftermath of 1980 military intervention and was banned in Turkey for many years, is about five prisoners given permission to visit their homes for a week. The film also involves confrontations with soldiers and a banner reading "Kurdistan," which one of the prisoners comes across on his way to southeastern Turkey. Gavras's film *Missing* tells the story of a conservative American father, who, in the search for his missing son, discovers that Latin American juntas are involved with the United States government's entanglement in Latin American politics. In later years, a leftist music group, Grup Yorum, also combined this Theoderakis composition with a Nazım Hikmet poem, *Farewell*. Thus, while various other Yeşilçam films used the same theme music, CH's use of the Mikis Theodorakis's theme from *Z* does not seem coincidental. Indeed, the action parallels the leftist themes of real life. After his friends surround the depot where Bilal is hiding, Asım, wearing black pants, a navy shirt, a red scarf tied around his neck, and a black hat with a red stripe around its cone, walks toward the depot on his own, as if he is a lonesome cowboy bringing justice to the town. Around the time of this film, Güney himself was helping leftist guerillas who initiated an armed fight against the Turkish government in an attempt to trigger a revolutionary movement. As desired in real life, in their fight against Bilal, Asım and his "comrades" are successful, although Aspirin is killed. CH thus introduced interesting relationships with "reality" by referencing autobiographical elements of Güney's life, including familial and political attachments. Also visible are the uncanny coincidences that linked the film to Güney's other films and his life, oscillating between familial guilt and social responsibility, as well as with the Gavras connection to a leftist political activism.[11] Yet CH is a typical Yeşilçam film. As I will elaborate with reference to *Demiryol* (Railway, dir. Yavuz Özkan, 1979), the theme of fighting against evil as a melodramatic element of Yeşilçam pervaded Yeşilçam's political dramas and thrillers.

What made Güney an exceptional Yeşilçam star was his appeal to both male and female audiences, channeled through a toughness that went against the grain and the use of Charles Bronsonian tactics to take revenge. Güney was a crowd-pleaser not because of his connection with masculine genres such as action-adventure movies, but because of his presence in these genres as a bandit figure, rebelling against the system and using means both good and bad to achieve his end. As one legal brothel (*genelev*) worker who responded to a question about Güney's release from prison said, "His best film is *Baba* (Father, 1971). In that film, he cleanses (*kırklamak*) his daughter and saves her from prostitution. We all wait for someone to cleanse us" (Çeviker 1974, 41).[12] Stated differently, Güney's combination of the filmic and the real reflected on his spectators' desires. However melodramatic, Yeşilçam touched upon the lives of at least some of its spectators who identified with the lives portrayed in the films. It was not just the stories told on the screen, but also a convergence between reality and fiction that moved its spectators.

It is those unexceptional and unnoticed filmic stories that have the potential to move us the most. Throughout CH, as a part of his comical act, Aspirin keeps talking about telling a story that we never get to listen to. He asks Korsan, "May I tell you a story, bro?" Korsan replies, "Is it obscene?" "Yes." "Then, don't!" This dialogue, which itself tells a story, is repeated several times. But this untold "obscene" story is resolved while Aspirin is dying in the arms of Korsan, who, hoping to ground Aspirin in life, asks him to tell his obscene story. Yeşilçam is very much in the mold of such stories that are never told because they are always repeated to the point of extinguishing themselves. Yet those who are like Aspirin, the storytellers, are the ones who keep reiterating Yeşilçam's connection to the shadow plays, to *hayal*. In CH, it is all about the veiled connection to reality, like that of the rape scene that takes place "behind" the curtain, not in front of it. It is that reality that is projected from behind the screen that conditioned Yeşilçam. Yet it is that reality of a dream that was actually a nightmare, a phantom experience for Asım who closed his eyes in order not to see that particular shadow play. Such was the other side of Yeşilçam's *hayal*, which not only dislocates the reality of the film, but also blurs the line between the filmic and the real through the dreams and the nightmares of Güney himself, who felt he had abandoned his daughter, the "real" Elif, and thus "sent messages" to her through his films.

Demiryol (Railway, 1979)

Also called *Fırtına İnsanları* (People of the Storm), *Demiryol* is a political thriller that comes close to Third Cinema, outside both mainstream filmmaking and the *auteur* films of international art cinema circles. In the Turkish film world, discussions of Brazilian and Argentine cinemas mainly found a place in the early 1970s through French cinema circles. Aydın Sayman, writing in 1973, noted that some of Güney's films involved a mainstream, conventional filmic language that mimics Western cinemas, and some novel and original elements (20). Sayman compared Güney with Glauber Rocha, who talked about finding a new cinematic language beyond traditional and colonialist film languages. While this introduced a struggle in the system despite oppression and censorship, Sayman noted that Güney's films did not involve any illegal struggle like those of Fernando Solanas. Thus Yeşilçam's leftist films, such as *Demiryol*, were in the mold of Cinema Nuovo in their employment of Yeşilçam's filmic language to address their message. Yet this was complicated by dynamism supplied through fast-paced cutting and visual movement inherent in handheld cameras. However, not only do discussions on Third Cinema not involve Turkey, the leftist Yeşilçam films in question emerged briefly in the late 1970s, at a time when Third Cinema had already lost some of its international influence. While, as mentioned above, Turkey's position in world cinema is not geographically ascertained, as Turkey may belong to East European, Southeastern European, Mediterranean, Balkan, and Middle Eastern cinematic categories, films such as *Demiryol* did not have an impact on "Third Cinema" or these geopolitical categorizations of cinema. But in line with the leftist cinematic movement starting with Güney's few later films, *Demiryol* problematizes late 1970s Turkey, where various ideological stances led to severe political violence.

Demiryol, aiming to create a "storm over Turkey," addresses the issue of political activism in cinema and opens at Istanbul's Haydarpaşa train station where workers of the state's railway company prepare for a strike. While the railway worker Hasan (Fikret Hakan) defends the strike to raise the revolutionary consciousness of the workers, his brother-in-law Bülent (Tarık Akan) criticizes him for not pursuing violent struggle. This political clash resonates with a melodramatic one between the rich and the poor, bourgeoisie and proletariat. Yet there is a major twist in this, too: the bourgeoisie, though depicted in opposition to the proletariat and the strike, is represented through the governess Sibel's (Sevda Aktolga) relation with a businessman. Sibel, dreaming of being rich, dates her student's father, Mete, who has questionable relations with foreign political and business figures. The preparations for the strike, Sibel's lessons, and Mete's meeting with the foreign group are all crosscut, giving not only an introduction to the two classes, but contrasting the two main groups through the intermediating Sibel.

However, Sibel has no relation to Hasan or Bülent until after Bülent, with two of his friends, hijacks a supermarket truck and takes it to a squatter settlement where they distribute the goods while yelling leftist slogans. After police arrive at the scene, the people find themselves in the middle of cross fire and one of Bülent's friends is killed while Bülent and his other friend hide in a middle-class apartment, kidnapping a young university student who sympathizes with the leftists. Thanks to a melodramatic coincidence, the kidnapped girl's older sister turns out to be Sibel who, after arriving at home, has a fight with her sister about the righteousness of the kidnappers. At the station, the police arrive to assure safe entry for the scabs. Bülent's friend leaves the apartment, calls Hasan, and gets shot dead by the police. Hasan and his wife take Bülent to a hideout where he stays for a few days before being tracked down and shot dead by police.

During the strike, leftist university students come over to show documentaries to the workers, leading to a documentary interlude reminiscent of *Oğlum Osman*. On the other hand, similar to Güney's *Arkadaş* (Friend, 1974), *Demiryol*'s star actor Tarık Akan, who plays Bülent, is not involved in a romantic relationship and is killed in the film. In the early 1970s, thanks to his boyish good looks, Akan was one of the most sought-after actors of romantic films, especially comedies, such as *Aşk Dediğin Laf Değildir* (What You Call Love Is Not Just a Word, dir. Safa Önal, 1976), *Çapkın Hırsız* (Playboy Thief, dir. Atıf Yılmaz, 1975), and *Yaz Bekarı* (Summer Bachelor, dir. Osman Seden, 1974). But after 1977, he started acting in social realist films with single-word titles, such as *Nehir* (The River, dir. Şerif Gören, 1977), *Kanal* (The Channel, dir. Erden Kıral, 1978), *Sürü* (The Herd, dir. Zeki Ökten, 1978), *Maden* (The Mine, dir. Yavuz Özkan, 1978), and *Yol* (The Way, dir. Şerif Gören, 1982). Although he did not revert to his "real" last name, such a change

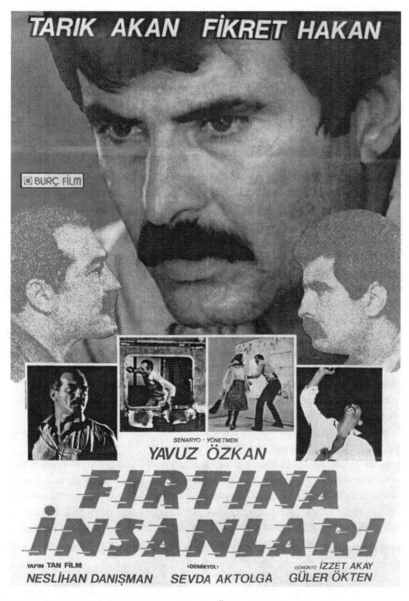

TARIK AKAN   FİKRET HAKAN

BURÇ FİLM

SENARYO · YÖNETMEN
YAVUZ ÖZKAN

*FIRTINA
İNSANLARI*

YAPIM TAN FİLM   ‹DEMİRYOL›   GÖRÜNTÜ İZZET AKAY
NESLİHAN DANIŞMAN   SEVDA AKTOLGA   GÜLER ÖKTEN

Figure 5.15. *Demiryol* (Railway, Yavuz Özkan, 1979), aka. *Fırtına İnsanları* (People of the Storm)

of genres signaled a brief spell of leftist, social realist films, which still were far from altering Yeşilçam's overall course. Among the 193 films shot in 1979, 134 of them were shot on 16mm film, signaling the mentality of low-budget sexploitative quickies. The genres of films in 1979 can be charted as follows:

Table 5.2. The Genres of Films in 1979[13]

1979	16mm Films	35mm Films
Sex Films	128	3
Realist Dramas	2	13
Romantic Films	4	21
Comedies	—	14
Action	—	8
Total	134	59

The comparatively few realist dramas belonged to two categories: left-ist realist dramas including *Demiryol* and mainstream realist dramas intended to exploit the market's potential demand. While approximately half of these fifteen realist dramas belonged to each category, approximately half of the twenty-five romantic films were singer melodramas, which as a trend continued in the 1980s with *arabesk* singers. Interestingly enough, only eight films, two of which were fantastic films with superheroes, could be considered action films, denoting to a decline in the early 1970s cycle that was recycled in the early 1980s.

While Bülent's death is portrayed as a wrongful attempt to eliminate the capitalist system controlled by Mete, his bourgeois friends, and their Western collaborators, Sibel's helpless position after her sister is arrested mirrors Bülent's situation. After Mete refuses to help her, Sibel asks for Hasan's help and starts feeling at home with the workers. While she seems to realize her class status, her offer to teach the workers English makes Hasan grin. While, for Hasan, workers should stay away from learning English, they indeed are under the influence of the West through television. Just before Hasan and his wife come to retrieve Bülent from Sibel's house, neighbors come over to watch *Love Boat*, an American television series that connotes the dream of wealth. This interlude reflects several trends typical of the late 1970s: both telephones and televisions were expensive enough that people would visit neighbors to watch television or to make a phone call, and yet the television that so absorbed their fantasies was a reflection of the United States, including the series *Star Trek*, *Love Boat*, *Roots*, and *Dallas* that were taking over from the waning reign of Yeşilçam. However, similar to Çakmaklı's reaction against the West and its use of voiceover narration and documentaries, *Demiryol* also reverts to a documentary on the history of leftist demonstrations shown to the workers. Here, one is tempted to conclude that Yeşilçam films, which claim to deliver a political message and which are unable to do so through the means of fiction, revert to documentaries and voice-over to compensate for their weaknesses.

Demiryol still marks an activist political language that entails dynamism, discontinuities, and unresolved plot elements, such as the situation of Sibel's sister or the invasive footage of demonstrations at the end of the film that is not directly connected to the plot. It presents a political application of Yeşilçam's quickie mentality, filmed on a low budget with a handheld camera, on-location shots, and many nonprofessional actors, especially in the sequences including crowd scenes such as those on the train, at the squatter settlement, and at the station during the strike. However, unlike Yeşilçam, the classes are segregated and vertical class movement is impossible. While Mete does not allow Sibel to be a part of his upper-class surrounding, the uncharacteristic absence of romance is undercut by whispers of a possible relationship between Sibel and Bülent. On the other hand, the film communicates its political message abruptly and relies on cardboard characters to represent evil. Besides, *Demiryol*'s centrist view punishes the leftists employing violent tactics within the narrative and becomes, in leftist terminology, a "revisionist" film, contradicting its own alternate title, *Fırtına İnsanları* (People of the Storm). Thus *Demiryol* conveys its message in a narrationally discontinuous seventy-minute film. An entry on Özkan in an online user-driven Turkish dictionary, *Ekşi Sözlük* (Sour Dictionary, http://sozluk.sourtimes.org/show.asp?t =yavuz+%C3%B6zkan&nr=y&pt=yavuz+ozkan, 2004), which is a cross between Wikipedia and the Urban Dictionary, introduces him as follows: "I would call him the Ed Wood of Turkey but I hesitate lest I disrespect Ed Wood by making this comparison... if one compares Ed Wood's films with those of Yavuz Özkan, the former would be like *Battleship Potemkin*" (*Bronenosets Potyomkin*, dir. Sergei Eisenstein, 1925). Though such a claim is overly hyperbolic, Özkan attempted to veer away from Yeşilçam only to find himself enmeshed in its poor production standards. Perhaps *Demiryol* may be seen in the mold of Eisenstein's *Strike* (*Stachka*, 1925), which ends with the working classes as the collective heroes contrasted starkly with the *agents provocateurs*, the bourgeoisie, and the police. However, after introducing many individual characters, *Demiryol*'s collective heroes come unexpectedly only at the end, unlike *Strike*'s concluding scene with high-angle shots of the strikers at the station, without undercutting its message. Additionally, *Demiryol*'s promise of a storm indicated through these demonstrations did not materialize and instead Turkey was shaken by the violent military intervention and junta government between 1980 and 1983. After the considerable tolerance toward political and sex films during the late 1970s (a time of democratic turmoil with coalition governments, early elections, and economic crises) the military intervention of September 12, 1980, put an end to such films.

Takma Kafanı (Don't Bother, 1979)

Nudity and the sexploitative potential of moving images have been used as an attraction from the earliest days of filmmaking. In Turkey, a similar history of female nudity, eroticism, and sexploitation has been a part of cinema. Of almost 7,000 films made in Turkey, Scognamillo and Demirhan list 576 films under the "basic index of films" in their book *Erotic Turkish Cinema* (2002, 279–87). Paying attention to Hollywood-style swimsuits and beachgoing in 1930s Istanbul, one film writer asks, despite the reactionary character of the Hayes code, "Is it not strange that the Americans were the first ones to show artists nude in cinema in contrast to now"

(Fuat 1934, 3)? The French, he notes, are the most courageous in terms of nudity, while American, German, British, and Russian censor boards act reasonably to ensure a movie's success with a beautiful body. As for nudity in Turkish cinema, for him, the first example is a stuntwoman wearing a slip in Muhsin Ertuğrul's *Sözde Kızlar* (Supposedly Girls, 1924). During the high Yeşilçam era, an article comments on sex in cinema as a permanently fresh subject and as an educational device. For the above-mentioned article, while Swedish sex films have an educational and aesthetic function, the ever-increasing nudity in Yeşilçam relies on seduction and attraction (Baydar 1967, 7). In other words, Yeşilçam is criticized as superficial and backward in comparison to Western sex films too. The same magazine is also optimistic about some Yeşilçam films that were "catching up with" the Western cinema by including footage of fully naked female bodies.

This page of Yeşilçam's history between 1974 and 1980 has generally been purposely forgotten and subjected to a moralistic reading. Though seen as the products of a *"lumpen-proletariat"* culture, sex films helped Yeşilçam to survive in the late 1970s. Especially during the earlier wave of sex comedies, in addition to Yeşilçam's filmmakers, various theater actors and other new faces, and some star actresses of low-budget Yeşilçam quickies went on to act in sex films. However, those who participated in the production of sex films, including the director of *Takma Kafanı* (hereafter TK, dir. Yavuz Özfigen/Figenli), usually avoid discussing them. Those who have spoken explain their participation as an economic necessity. In his memoirs, director Ülkü Erakalın, who questioned such excuses, under the subtitle "I am finding myself," explains, "Yes, when I started to make these films, I must have found my true self, with players whose acting was real, with real subject matters and realities as such" (1999, 206). Erakalın's remarks involve a process of questioning not only his own sexual identity through these films, but his underlining of the "reality" attached to sex films as a whole. What is that reality? Does it prevent the redemption of these filmmakers? Does it address a patriarchal society and film world that coincided with the socioeconomic and political demands of the era? Do his questions also address the realism of Yeşilçam's filmic language?

While many avoid remembering, unlike Erakalın, those who acknowledge their participation call it a mistake, though they interestingly underline sex films' role in the sexual enlightenment of the male population. If there was such a social value, then sex films indeed managed something that the Kemalist regime's own reform programs could not squeeze out of cinema. Yet the initial impetus behind sex films, which emerged from the European sex film wave and from Yeşilçam's low-budget action-adventures, was exploitation handled with an increased use of female nudity to rejuvenate the waning interest of male filmgoers. Even cinema magazines supported female nudity by underlining the Anatolian spectators' interest in striptease scenes, for they could not go to Istanbul's nightclubs. "Thus," says one article, "Anatolian film distributors are very careful about this fact when buying a film" ("Bu Sene..." 1966, 3). While female nudity was in demand for low-budget films, the success of the first few sex comedies started a wave of soft-core films, which later turned into 16mm quickie hard-core films. These films could be categorized as sex comedies, sex romances, sex action films, and even some fantastic, superhero sex comedies. Many of them are predictably either remakes of Yeşilçam, Hollywood, or Italian films, or even remakes of Yeşilçam films that themselves are remakes of Hollywood films. Sex films may also be differentiated as hardcore and softcore, 16mm ones with limited explicit scenes. Eleven films made in 1979 involved the word *Love* in their titles, while thirty-five referred to women or girls, some with adjectives such as "beautiful" and "loose." Many sex films ran shorter, around sixty and seventy minutes, allowing projectionists at sex film theaters to "montage" or "insert" separate hardcore scenes during the showing of regular erotic sex films.

In the 1980s, with the introduction of videotapes, sex films of the 1970s continued to be available on the video market, most of the time under the shelves, as well as in pocket theaters that showed new foreign and old Turkish sex films. The video market also offered a solution to Yeşilçam's crisis in the 1980s, when many films were not exhibited in theaters but marketed directly on videotape. Moreover, these 1980s Yeşilçam films often included scenes with female nudity that came in three different forms: a somewhat "arty," *à la française* nudity in the films of Yeşilçam *auteurs* (such as those starring Müjde Ar); a fairly standardized mainstream female nudity in romantic films or comedies (such as those starring Hülya Avşar); and a kitschy nudity of late Yeşilçam's low-budget films (such as those starring Banu Alkan). Nonetheless, these 1980s female stars did not act in the late 1970s sex films. Instead, those female stars of sex films found themselves no longer employable in the film industry, part of a patriarchal society that would not give, in the words of scriptwriter Bülent Oran's terminology, its cinematic "prostitutes" an opportunity to survive, but favored its "cuckolds" instead—a lot of male theater actors acted in films and plays after the 1970s. For Oran, this was a result of social structure: "When the girl does it, it is bad; when the man does it, it is good" (Demirci 2004, 156). Thus Scognamillo and Demirhan's book on erotic cinema presents a "basic filmography of some female actors in erotic Turkish cinema," but not of male players (2002, 261–77). One such actress, Zerrin Doğan, not only blames the film producers who forgot about these actresses in the 1980s but also criticizes Turkey for not having the concept of "sex star," and pocket-size cinemas showing sex films particularly in comparison with foreign cinemas (Demirci 2004, 70–71).

In this picture, sex films did not have a place in mainstream Yeşilçam histories, nor have they been considered outside of a moralistic framework. Following Erakalın's remarks, these films brought Yeşilçam's world of *hayal* down to earth, to reality, by presenting "prostitutes" and "cuckolds" as central characters. However, Yeşilçam, with its scriptwriters like Oran, was also at work in sex films that carry melodramatic plot structures. As a sex film actress, Zafir Seba said, "If one takes out the bed scenes from these films, they would be just another film which could be viewed as a family film" (Demirci 2004, 60). Yet the majority of sex film scripts do not uphold this argument. Even though sex films kept up with Yeşilçam genres and its practice of Turkification, the narrative worlds of these films are full of exaggerated sexual themes that carried most of the filmic action. For instance, an early sex comedy *Hayret 17* (aka *Vay Anasına 17*, Amazing 17, dir. Osman Seden, 1975) introduces a character with the "amazing" power of having sex nonstop seventeen times. While such are the joys promised for men, women were also portrayed as willing to get away from the "decent woman" frame to enjoy carnal pleasures with other men and women.

TK opens on a sunny Sunday in a public park where a man approaches a woman sitting alone on a bench.

> Man: May I sit next to you? The person you are waiting for did not come and you do not know how to spend Sunday.
> Woman: It seems the same has happened to you. And when you saw me, you had an idea.
> Man: Yes, that is true. I had a friend who did not come to our date and it is all over. She is the daughter of a rich businessman whereas I am a poor and simple young man. My name is Bülent. Would you like to hang out with this poor and simple young man?
> Woman: I see you are not shy.

Certainly, TK's Bülent (Hakan Özer) is not shy. Perhaps, like *Demiryol*'s Sibel, he realized that the melodramatic promise of vertical class movement is not realistic. A poor, simple young man living on the margins or periphery of the urban geography at a time of stark modernization and political turmoil, Bülent does not have the "consciousness" of his class. Instead, staying in the mold of *Demiryol*, he could easily be conceived of among the ranks of alienated workers, or as Özgüç puts it, in "such characters' *lumpen* pornographic world" (2000, 180).

In TK, the woman with whom Bülent speaks at the park is Aysel (Dilber Ay). For Özgüç, Ay acted in various courageous scenes, including lesbian intercourse, fellatio, and masturbating on a bathroom faucet, and was in one of the four truly hardcore porno films of 1979 among the 131 sex films made that year (2000, 180–81). In TK, Aysel thinks that Bülent is indeed a Casanova type and then dreams of him at home while touching her half-naked body and telling herself that she will not be like the other girls whom Bülent has deceived. Instead of marrying Kenan (Ata Saka) and having a proper life, Aysel falls in love and wants to enjoy life with Bülent. In this love triangle, Bülent represents a more modern and individualistic life based on Aysel's own decisions, whereas marrying Kenan implies a traditional role and a conservative lifestyle. However, unlike Yeşilçam's common trope of transitions between spaces of lower and upper classes, TK's story does not present upper-class characters or neighborhoods. Instead, beyond melodramatic fantasy of vertical class movement, TK's setting is a realistic one: a squatter settlement among newly rising apartment buildings of Istanbul. Additionally, the interiors of houses are also realistic, without any polishing, as some other Yeşilçam films do to the interiors of lower middle-class houses.

Yeşilçam's sexploitations introduced different tactics of Turkification for hardcore scenes. Because in many films like TK, there are no close-up shots of intercourse, but only close-up shots of women's genitalia, such explicit scenes were "montaged" (inserted) at film theaters. The projectionists kept the hardcore scenes taken primarily from foreign films ready to run on another projection machine and then, at proper times, they paused one projection machine before starting the other. Even at some theaters the ushers announced such scenes: "Hey guys, get ready to shift gears" (Demirci 2004, 107). Alternatively, some producers, in Özgüç's words, created *dönme* (convert or transvestite) films, which were basically edited compilations of scenes from earlier films marketed with a new name and poster. This was also the case for action-adventure film *Gaddar* (Cruel, aka *Şeytan'ın Oğlu*, The Son of Satan, dir. Mehmet Aslan, 1967) starring Güney through a compilation of scenes from three of his other films. Indeed some of the "thirty-seven" films in which Zerrin Egeliler acted in 1979, were *dönme* films. In the same year, Kazım Kartal was the lead actor in twenty-five films; Naki Yurter directed thirty films; Recep Filiz wrote the scripts for twenty-nine films; Sedat Ülker or Mükremin Şumlu was the cameraman of twenty-five films; and Oran made a deal with producer Necdet Barlık for fifty films, though while writing his eighth script, sex films were banned (Türk 2004, 301). Unlike the "upholstering" of music, a last tactic was upholstering that either involved the use of body doubles for hardcore scenes or stealing footage from different hardcore films, a practice made evident through the change of quality, color, and lighting of the different films. According to Demirci, while the majority of sex films were dubbed by the actors or by professional dubbing artists, some hardcore films made in 1979 and 1980 involved live-recorded soundtracks because filmmakers neither felt the need for dubbing nor wanted to deal with postproduction due to the timeliness and costliness of detailed plots, studios, and dubbing artists (2004, 109).

Aysel, "defiled" by Bülent, later finds relief with Kenan while Bülent and his boss's girlfriend have sex to the theme music of James Bond movies. As the tune stops, the dubbed moaning of the women is accompanied with an instrumental piece of pop jazz. After sex, a tenser tune signals the arrival of Necmi and his men, who attack Bülent. Later Aysel helps him to recover but Bülent wants to leave the neighborhood and Aysel is willing to follow him. Bülent (without moving his lips!) tells Aysel, "You are a good girl, a calm girl. But I am an energetic guy. I want a girl who will suit my lifestyle." Aysel (moving her lips) says, "What should I do to be the kind of woman you want?" Forty-four minutes into the film, its story ends at this point. The remaining twenty minutes of the film take place at a house of sexual fantasy: Aysel finds herself in the middle of an orgy, smoking weed, and enjoying life, accompanied by a pop rearrangement of a traditional folk songs signaling happiness. TK ends with Aysel on top of Bülent in bed as the camera zooms to Aysel's face as she speaks to Bülent. We cannot hear what she says, but as far as I can tell from reading her lips, she says "It is so nice to have sex with you." The real text, however, is carried by a pop song with the lyrics "People no doubt want to get pleasure from life."

TK's fantasy world does not belong to Yeşilçam's morality, but shares its melodramatic modality. Discontinuities, unuttered dubbed speech, uttered but unheard words, and inexplicable situations are all parts of TK, placing it firmly within the Yeşilçam tradition that rejects it. Yet TK ends not with marriage but another form of heterosexual relationship that Aysel freely chooses: Bülent and a free-willed life, over Kenan and a conservative marriage. So Aysel is the ideal candidate for male fantasy where pleasure wins out over decency. However, for many of the actors portraying roles like Aysel, the reality is grim. Many claim that they were drugged during filming and prostitutes were hired to act in some scenes. This underbelly of the clean, star-studded world of Yeşilçam came with its own reality that ran against the society's moralism. Like the nation-building process that attempted to erase untold, violent aspects of its emergence, moralist critics and historians have refused to acknowledge this underworld. In addition, while Yeşilçam was complicit on the surface with the nation's morality, it also hid many untold stories of stars on casting couches and shady deals between filmmakers, not only during the late 1970s, but throughout its history. However, after all sorts of political and sex films were ousted from the world of decency and political correctness and thus were "defiled" by the military regime, Yeşilçam's melodramas and comedies filled the void between 1980 and 1983. Once it was gone, even Yeşilçam's own sex stars conceived of the period through such moralism. Unlike Aysel, who chose pleasure over decency in the filmic world, Dilber Ay, who became a folk singer in the 1980s, chose decency over pleasure. According to Ay, all the sex films, even the pornographic ones, she acted in, did not involve penetration or "real" sexual intercourse. "I was a virgin from my first film... to my last film... I became a woman after the sex films were banned. That is, I shot all these porn films as a maiden. I can document this fact with dated medical reports" (Demirci 2004, 75).

A Last Word on High Yeşilçam

Yeşilçam's genres proliferated and evolved during the two-decade-long high Yeşilçam era, through various waves and cycles of films. As early as 1956, Yeşilçam was starting to understand the popularity of cycles and manipulate the films accordingly. The cycles were understood to be partial solutions to crises, such as the seasonal popularity of historical films, crime films, melodramas involving musical scenes, family melodramas, and village films ("Ebediyete Kadar" 1956, 17). While major production companies specialized in star-studded genre films, minors employed exploitative tactics with a quickie mentality. Yeşilçam's generic realism accommodated complicated and ambiguous practices on the part of both filmmakers and spectators. Yeşilçam's Turkification of a Western medium with three-dimensional realism is countered by its two-dimensionality.

As this doubled Yeşilçam, its aggressive expansion stigmatized all of its films, including social realist, *auteur*, and even sex films. While Onaran's 1994 survey of *auteurs*, who essentially produced social realist dramas and art films, distinguishes the films of mass culture through generic categories such as historical films, salon films, comedy films, and *arabesk* melodramas, it was those *auteurs* who produced films such as *Şeytan*, BTV, and CH. Although a conception of "true" and "proper" cinema that would enlighten the masses is at stake in such categorizations, cinema has historically been concurrent with fantasy and entertainment, *hayal* and *özenti*, and cinematic narratives involving generic formulations have determined the production and consumption network.

Both filmmakers and spectators communicated through such generic and cyclical references and are able to identify a multitude of genres. For instance, in a 1973 survey, spectators living in cities close to Istanbul emphasized their preference for domestic films over foreign films and then identified genres through gendered protocols (action as male and romance as female genres) ("Halk Soruşturması 3" 1973, 39-50). While young male spectators liked "(secret) agent," "comedy," "action-adventure," and "sex-adventure" films most, female spectators sought "sad" films and "love" films. On the other hand, genre identification has also a political dimension reproducing the formal ideology because state officials, such as teachers or low-rank clerks, preferred "realist dramas" and "educational" films. Echoing this responsibility, Yeşilçam re-produced the War of Independence in formal historical films or the republican fight against tradition in rural dramas. This confluence with official policies is also evident in the absences as well as the presences in Yeşilçam films. In a 1973 article titled "Turkish Cinema or Bazaar Mythology," translated from the French magazine *Cinéma 73*, Philippe Denizot notes the limited visibility of the Turkish police, army, and state on the screen, unlike the "daily reality [where] uniforms were a part of the visible," while the media portrayed the Turkish leftist rebels as bank robbers (1973, 6). A decade after Denizot's article was published, Yeşilçam star Hülya Koçyiğit criticized Turkish censors saying, "Look, there are some untouchable subjects in Turkey: A judge is never bribed, a policeman is never a murderer, and an industrialist is never corrupt. If you run against these in the story of a film, the film will be halted by the censors" (1984, 14).

In comparison with the distribution of Hollywood genres, biopics, hard-boiled detective films, and musicals were very rare in Yeşilçam, while singer films were produced in abundance. Initiated by the popularity of Egyptian singer films, various popular singers who produced music outside of the restrictions of the Kemalist cultural reform program made films in Yeşilçam, such as HBT, KS, and BTV. Singer films presented a complete entertainment program for spectators, through the coupling of songs, dances, and shows with romantic stories rife with tears, action, and laughter. Even the rise of television and video markets in the 1970s and 1980s did not put an end to these films that introduced musical classifications and taste politics. While HBT, as a "salon" film, presents an urban, upper-class environment, KS is a rural melodrama, and BTV is an *"arabesk* melodrama," introducing a squatter settlement in the urban periphery similar to *Demiryol* and TK. Whereas the melodramatic plots involve urban transitions between upper- and lower-class neighborhoods as in HBT, OO, and BTV, KS introduce a rural-urban transition and *Şeytan* belongs to the world of a modern, newly rising bourgeoisie. Although both TÖUY and KMFF introduce extraordinary spaces due to their temporal alterations, all films discussed in this chapter, thanks to Yeşilçam's practice of on-location shooting, introduce Istanbul in one way or another.

A conventional categorization of the ten films discussed above involves genre's relation to gender through action and romance. While the first four of them are closer to female spectatorial practice, the remaining six primarily address male spectators. All of them repeat a certain set of generic elements producing narrative predictability, as well as illustrating variations within their respective genres (Altman 1999, 21). For instance, despite their generic difference, both *Demiryol* and TK stray from Yeşilçam's modality in comparable ways. Still both films also present various melodramatic elements used to different ends. But because of their respective generic identifications, one as a social realist film that tries to stay away from a commercial star cinema, and the other as a sex film that goes beyond the moral prerequisites of a melodramatic fantasy world of romance, their narrative breaks reproduce their own generic characteristics. The predictability of *Demiryol*'s unconventionality resides in the killing of the star actor at film's end and its narrative's departure from love story, whereas TK's unconventionality relies on the introduction of free-spirited pleasure over moralism that serves male fantasy and sexploitation. Nonetheless, the subtexts of both films are fairly conservative, the one favoring orderly protest over anarchic revolution, and the other equating female virtue with virginity.

Finally, all of these films accommodate nationalist renderings through Turkification. While *Şeytan* and TÖUY are Turkified remakes of American films and television series, OO Turkifies footage from Hollywood and Egyptian films while KMFF and CH, respectively, render vampirism and Western-style duels from Hollywood films. One sense of Turkification introduces a violently constructed but unacknowledged identification with a national community that attempts to erase its others. Simultaneously, the meeting of Karagöz's two-dimensionality with Punch's three-dimensionality produces non-illusionism and non-representationalism through an illusionistic and representational medium. Although some writers, such as the former leftist, now Sufist scriptwriter Ayşe Şasa, claim that Yeşilçam is monophonic, without contradicting sound and image, image and meaning, and theme and anti-theme (1993, 8); in fact, Yeşilçam carries a multiplicity of voices, a mishmash of images, and a cacophony of soundtracks and image tracks where Turkification (translation and transformation) converges with *hayal* and *özenti* through the melodramatic modality of genre crossings. Yeşilçam is about movies, which move us; it is a movement from self to other and then back to a renewed self, and then to another other and so on. Karagöz had to enter the world of Punch, to experience it and then come back to find his own self already transformed and displaced by his movement. Then Karagöz moved again, went, and perhaps saw Punch one more time. Can there be an end to such movement especially in a world where the travel of cultural forms across international borders takes place with increasing speed?

6

Late Yeşilçam
Melting in the 1980s

Turkey and Yeşilçam in the 1980s

⊤he deaths and resurrections of Yeşilçam are numerous; many waves or cycles of films solved short-term crises during the high Yeşilçam era. Sex films of the late 1970s not only presented a similar solution, but with 16mm also introduced a shift in filmic equipment. In the 1980s, most films were shot on 35mm but rather than being exhibited in theaters were released directly to video. By the late 1980s, Yeşilçam went into an even greater crisis, with an enormous decrease in both ticket sales and the number of films made. While the annual number of films made under military rule between 1980 and 1983 remained approximately seventy, Yeşilçam produced more than one hundred films annually between 1984 and 1989, peaking at nearly two hundred films made in both1986 and 1987. However, in the early 1990s, the annual number of films made fell to around thirty, and more important, the distribution and exhibition networks of Yeşilçam were almost completely dissolved.

The early Yeşilçam of the 1950s started to flourish at a time when Turkey had just started to enjoy a multiparty regime and the gradual introduction of capitalism that accompanied Turkey's membership in NATO and concurrent U.S. aid. Strengthening ties between Turkey and the United States and the Americanization of Turkish culture both aided the film industry to an extent. The 1980s experienced a substantial shift from a state-run economy toward a more privatized, capitalist economy, or from the commercialization of the 1950s to the industrialization of the 1980s. Unlike the early 1950s, Turkey's integration into global capitalist markets after the 1990s and the close involvement of the U.S. companies in Turkey's film market initially had a negative effect on the film industry.

During its most successful years, Yeşilçam, with little state support, was the self-sufficient film industry of a still-traditional, semi-capitalist country whose industrialization and integration into the capitalist system were mainly triggered by the state itself. Thus, the Turkish economy started to abandon protective and subsidiary measures and the governments of the 1980s instituted reforms fostering economic liberalization. The institution of a free market economy involved measures such as privatization, increased exportation, and economic integration with other world markets. However, such measures led to a widening gap between the lower and upper classes, while chronic high inflation and tax increases aimed to manage the budget deficits put increasing pressure on the middle classes. In the 1980s, private enterprise played an increasingly central role and as civil societal organizations and institutions started to gain importance, the values and principles of republican ideology, especially those based on statism, populism, and laicism,[1] came under increasing scrutiny. At the same time, little by little, ethnic, religious, and gender-based identity politics came to the fore and created new issues for cinema to address.

While the high Yeşilçam era was concurrent with the period of the Second Republic, the late Yeşilçam and post-Yeşilçam eras coincided with the Third Republic, which started with the 1980 military intervention and the 1982 Constitution instigated by the generals (Zürcher 1994, 292). Freezing the political life for three years, the military regime concentrated power in the hands of the state apparatuses and, in putting an end to political polarization and suppressing violence, blocked almost all avenues of dissent and opposition. Throughout the 1980s, political freedom and rights were severely limited and the governments' enforcement of laws was very strict and at times violent, thus creating a semi-democratic and semi-authoritarian political regime. Even though some of the old politicians who were banned from politics returned to active politics through a 1987 referendum that changed the 1982 Constitution, communist politics continued to be illegal; those who escaped the military regime, including political figures and ethnic minorities, were for many years unable to return to Turkey, and some remain in exile.

Apart from such economic and political developments, after the 1980s Turkey experienced two important sociopolitical crises, one ethnic and the other religious. On the one hand, Kurdish militants started an armed rebellion under the illegal Kurdish Workers Party (PKK), which subsequently led to continual violent altercations between the PKK and the Turkish army that some consider a low-intensity civil war. On the other hand, the coalition governments with Islamic parties in the 1990s led the Turkish army to issue severe warnings regarding the indestructible *laicist* nature of Turkey's regime. In the early 1990s, Turkish nationalism and the project of modernization from above entered a crisis that led to an increased gap between the modernizing elites and the voiceless masses (Keyder 1997, 45). Through the new dynamics of economics and politics that involve globalization efforts and reforms for accession to the European Union, Turkey has become a player in global markets, and therefore not only has been forced to implement a "legal basis for citizenship rights and the foundational requirements for individual autonomy" but also has faced the challenges of ethnic separatism and Islamic fundamentalism (Keyder 1997, 46).

In light of such developments, the cultural field of the 1980s was marked by the increasing visibility of multiplicity in a capitalist market system under a repressive political regime. Thus, the 1980s were characterized by two contradictory tendencies: the suppression of the voice and the boom of different voices (Gürbilek 2001, 21). Despite the oppressive atmosphere, the previously unheard voices of decentered and fragmented portions of society became visible; and media and cultural industries underwent a transformation channeling their visibility. The cultural novelties of the era included aspects of a sociocultural modernization: a crisis of traditional patriarchy through discussions on the private sphere, foregrounding of issues of gender and sexuality, a growing discourse of individualism and liberalization, diversification of issues and images covered by independent media, visible dominance of *arabesk* culture of the migrant populations at urban centers, partial departure from republican linguistic reforms, change in significatory systems reminiscent of Baudrillardian simulacra and loss of the link between words and their cultural and sociopolitical meanings, and the continued growth of the cultural gap between the lower and upper classes paralleled by increasing economic inequality.

The 1980 military intervention marked a cultural break with the three-year-long junta government and subsequent elected governments, all of which had attempted to monitor the cultural life by controlling and censoring films with political or explicit content. Spectators, who in the late 1970s had already started to watch films on television and video instead of going to theaters, almost stopped going to theaters altogether during and after the military intervention. In the video boom of the 1980s, the main demographic comprised the middle classes and workers in Europe, both of whom could afford to buy VCRs and regularly rent videotapes from the rental stores that popped up throughout the country. However, this boom slowed down in the late 1980s and the rise of private television channels and satellite television in the early 1990s further hampered Yeşilçam's film production.

In the late 1980s and the early 1990s, film critics and writers commonly tied the end of Yeşilçam to the demise of another wave of "inflationary" filmmaking and considered state support necessary to resurrect the film industry. In 1986, a new law concerning the works of cinema, video, and music was passed and the Ministry of Culture started to be involved in matters concerning cinema initially through the control, and subsequently support, of films in the 1990s. Giovanni Scognamillo calls the years between 1987 and 1989 a period of "the last resistance, the last support for a demolishing wall" (1998, 423).

While Yeşilçam was losing its last castles, Hollywood companies were also attempting to control the Turkish market. After domestic films' almost four-decade domination, Hollywood films started to be seen more by Turkish spectators. Concerned about this, domestic filmmakers pressured politicians and in 1989 the Turkish government planned to limit the dominance of foreign films. The cinema law drafted by ruling Motherland Party's MP Gökhan Maraş to replace the one made in 1986 differed from its predecessor in four respects: it called for the funding of domestic films by transferring 40 percent of foreign companies' profits to a pool; implemented a minimum for domestic film exhibition (say, one-fourth of the films exhibited by a theater annually would have had to be domestic); banned the dubbing of foreign films in Turkish and showing them with subtitles to diminish spectatorial interest in them; and replaced the censorship board with a rating system based on age restrictions (1990, 10–12). Though that draft was never implemented, it could have helped overcome the crisis in the short-term, despite U.S. government objections. According to Maraş, one of the Motherland Party ministers, Güneş Taner, was informed of the U.S. government's concerns about the draft during his visit to the United States. According to columnist Yalçın Doğan of the Turkish daily *Hürriyet* (Freedom), U.S. President George Bush called the Turkish Prime Minister Turgut Özal at the time and said, "If you pass that cinema law draft through parliament, I will decrease Turkey's quotas of textile products" (Doğan 2004). Though it is very difficult to verify such a conversation, the failure of this draft marked the death knell of Yeşilçam cinema.

During its late era, Yeşilçam was marked by two principle tendencies: a continuing popular genre film production for the videotape market and a continuous self-reflexivity (as if Yeşilçam's directors had just figured out the language of modernist art!). With the ban on sex films, popular films started to deal with problems of sex and gender, mainly through male directors spicing up their films with female nudity. While Yeşilçam continued to produce family melodramas, romantic comedies, and action-adventure films, some "serious" Yeşilçam filmmakers began producing a new genre, loosely called "films about women," which were realist dramas about sexuality and gender issues. There were also a handful of films that indirectly touched on the period of the military regime or on filmmaking itself, through the tropes of a culture in stasis, shattered and frustrated by the loss of the ideological optimism of 1970s. These films' "self-reflexive" themes allowed filmmakers to analyze themselves and filmmaking, in a period when films were no longer as popular or future-oriented as they were the previous decade. Both genres were thus related to the sociopolitical and cultural conjuncture augmented by a sharp decrease in film consumption.

While there is no significant decline in the number of films made during the 1980s, filmgoing as a social experience and a family entertainment had withered away. Almost all of the theaters in small towns closed, while those that survived did so by exhibiting sex films. Major theaters in metropolitan areas persisted by showing mainly Hollywood blockbusters, which themselves emerged as a solution for Hollywood's crisis.[2] Certainly, this changed the spectatorial demographic toward a predominantly young, urban population of students or university graduates preferring Western films. Two recent surveys by Fida Film Company indicate that the average

age of spectators is twenty-nine. Additionally, 59 percent of these spectators are university graduates, 31 percent of them are students, and 72 percent of them are single (http://www.fidafilm.com/ffinc/tr/ff_03_03.asp).

During the late Yeşilçam era, post-Yeşilçam spectators and filmmakers became predominantly young and educated, with the influx of new directors producing both art and popular films after the early 1990s. While such films introduced novel themes commonly referred to under the rubric of "new" Turkish cinema, the roots of this shift date back to the late Yeşilçam era, to the intellectual overtones of some (art) films and to those filmmakers' involvement with international film circles. For instance, Genco Erkal, who won the best actor prize in the 1984 Antalya Film Festival, separated art films from those of Yeşilçam and mentioned the existence of a "young" or "new" cinema (Erkal 1984, 16). However, one of the most exceptional directors of Yeşilçam, Atıf Yılmaz, incisively criticized such arguments, for the films of "new" cinema defined themselves through and against Yeşilçam and they fell for a plot that the films festivals in the Western countries were forcing upon them. For him, such films satisfied the West's demand for exotic films about extreme and marginal events from Turkey and other non-Western countries (1984, 38). Similarly, after noting Yeşilçam's demise, which she takes as "being sympathetic toward the poverty, the culture, and the weaknesses of the people," Necla Algan claims that, because of the individualist, exotic, and self-orientalizing themes brought about in the films of the "serious" filmmakers of the 1980s, "the new Turkish cinema is a deliberate 'nightmare' if viewed from the perspective of the old Yeşilçam" (1996, 6). Despite such criticisms in the early 1980s, sixty-three directors made their first films between 1987 and 1996, which led Scognamillo to change the object of "inflation" from film numbers to directors: "Even though the motto 'Yeşilçam is dead, long live the Turkish cinema' has not yet become appropriate, indeed the trend is in that direction... especially in the eyes of the intellectuals" (1998, 478). Indeed, the demise of Yeşilçam marked the end of a certain type of Turkification and melodramatic modality with the influx of these films dealing with alternative narratives, focusing on different themes such as ethnicity or recent history, and with novel modes of visual narration presented through their educational background or awareness of international cinema.

Crises, Reflections, and Genres

Before becoming officially "late," Yeşilçam reproduced its earlier practices of filmmaking and storytelling. Even if women's films or self-reflexive films may be seen as new genres produced and consumed by educated, petty bourgeois circles, late Yeşilçam essentially recycled its generic constants through melodramatic storylines, typecasting, and low-budget filmmaking. However, during the 1980s, observation of the problems of film industry, compounded by a growing sense of isolation and alienation from active sociopolitical life, led to a sense that the word of the decade was *crisis*. Atilla Dorsay, a prominent film critic, talked of the 1980s as a period of recession leaving no room for optimism or hope, adding, "Towards its centennial, cinema was over, at least for Turkey" (1989b, 26). However, considering this mood of crisis as unique to the 1980s is shortsighted, since for many of its critics Yeşilçam had so often been characterized by crises. For example, writing in 1964, Hayri Caner noted that Turkish cinema had many problems: the crisis of finding new subjects, the need for new actors, the insufficiency of film theaters, censorship, cinema law, the decrease in technical competence, the increase in production costs, the low quality of films, and the commercialization of filmmaking (9). Indeed, such was Yeşilçam: no novelty, weak infrastructure, no state support, only control and censorship, continually increasing production costs due to inflation and the importation of equipment from Western countries, and a commercial industry that did not generally reinvest its profits into the industry. Such a mood continued well into the early 1990s, when various writers started to notice a potential for change.

Yeşilçam, which had found ways to handle different crises, ceased to produce films for theater exhibition after the 1980s and instead focused on producing and distributing for the video market and later in the 1990s for television channels. While many critics view these outlets as dead ends, others interpreted both video and television as beneficial to cinema, even providing a potential to advance the film medium (Türkali 1984, 69). Producer Türker İnanoğlu, who adapted well to the video and television serials market, underlined the issues of copyright created by the video market:

Figure 6.1. To protest Hollywood majors' control of film distribution and exhibition, director Korhan Yurtsever puts on fire his film *Zincir* (Chain, 1989)

the opportunity for public screenings done with VCRs at coffee houses and restaurants in Turkey, as well as the possibility of recording and marketing pirated tapes (1984, 68). Beyond such concerns about copyright, the decrease in the number of film theaters is striking: from almost 2,500 in 1970 to 1,350 in 1975, 938 in 1980, 767 in 1985, and approximately 300 in 1990 (Özön 1995a, 53; Dorsay 1995, 17). But this situation started to change after the demise of Yeşilçam. While the number of the spectators and film theaters has quadrupled since 1992, the number of films released for exhibition has also risen (http://www.fidafilm.com/ffinc/tr/ff_04_01.asp). However, this rejuvenation was concentrated in the three major metropolitan areas of Turkey: Istanbul, Ankara, and Izmir, which accounted for 75 percent of the ticket sales in Turkey.

Yeşilçam's distribution network had also weakened, eventually giving way to large Turkish import and distribution companies and Hollywood majors. While the production budgets were funded by video sales, some of the existing production companies also went into the distribution of videotapes. But the video market was also dominated by Hollywood films, further decreasing Yeşilçam's income and leading to its eventual crisis in the late 1980s (Dorsay 1995, 17). In both film and video markets, the competition between Hollywood and Yeşilçam started unequally because of promotional strategies and secondary market sales. Under such novel conditions, Yeşilçam's capacity to compete with Hollywood was severely limited, especially with the increasing popularity of television and the involvement of Hollywood in the distribution and exhibition of films in Turkey. In the end, Yeşilçam was a domestic industry of a semi-capitalist, "transitional," and belated country.

Yeşilçam's demise came with the early steps of a distinction between popular cinema and serious filmmaking. In a Fida Film survey, genres were listed as follows: adventure, emotional/sentimental, comedy, horror, science fiction, erotic, and animation. They also added a new type of category, that of "films with awards" (Scognamillo 1998, 426). While this survey included foreign films, it was indicative of the industry's outlook in the previous two decades. While those films with awards, auteur or art films, were seen as examples of "serious" filmmaking, they also found a spectatorial niche with young, educated urban audiences who demanded "quality" films and film publications. The concurrent opening of film production departments at various Turkish universities after the mid-1970s also aided in this change.

"Serious" films came with self-reflexive, individualist *auteur* films, and social dramas or films about women. On the other hand, the auteurist aspects of some of these also inscribed a shift from political reality toward an increasing state of fantasy within cinema. In this respect, the *hayal* aspect of Yeşilçam was carried to another dimension, where various characters of the 1980s cinema, through their dreams, escaped from the realities of daily life that offered a harsh and violent past and helplessness in the present. Thus, films dealing with the military intervention were characterized by themes including depression and amnesia, as well as daydreaming and fantasy. Alongside these films, popular cinema persisted in an utterly separate course, addressing the middle-class VCR owners in Turkey, and homesick, diasporic immigrant workers in Europe. Popular films, apart from working in various genres, ranging from family melodramas to action-adventure films and comedies, also continued to rely upon "Turkifications" of popular Western films such as *Star Wars* (dir. George Lucas, 1977) and *Lambada* (dir. Joel Silberg, 1990) or remakes of Yeşilçam films themselves such as *Kara Sevda* and *Sürtük*.

In order to account for the variety of genres and films and their relation to sociopolitical and cultural transformations in the 1980s, the next portion of this chapter will be devoted to the analysis of four late Yeşilçam films. The first film, *Öğretmen Kemal* (Teacher Kemal, dir. Remzi Jöntürk), which was released during the military rule in 1981, not only reflects various recycling from high Yeşilçam films but also reflects the mood and the conjuncture during when political oppression only allowed the expression of formal republican ideology. The second one, *Çarıklı Milyoner* (The Millionaire with Sandals, dir. Kartal Tibet, 1983), is a comedy that centers on the conflict between rural and urban cultures and attempts to situate itself in the tradition of fairy tales and oral narration. The third one, *Gülüşan* (dir. Bilge Olgaç, 1985), though based on a fairy tale and focusing on village life, is a film about women directed by one of the veteran female directors of Yeşilçam. Finally, an "individualist," "self-reflexive" *auteur* film, *Filim Bitti* (The Film Is Over, dir. Yavuz Özkan, 1989) portrays the ends of Yeşilçam, its filmic and narrational style, and its relation to a history of filmmaking that was based not only on a coexistence of the traditional and the modern but also on a "transition" from the traditional to the modern, from a Karagöz-style, two-dimensional, and oral narration to a more perspectival, modern capitalist culture, despite its low-budget aesthetics and discontinuous film language.

The significance of this shift not only inscribes the ends of Yeşilçam but also dispatches the novelty and modernity of the new cinema of Turkey. Though Yeşilçam's directors are not a big part of the post-Yeşilçam era cinema, they helped the rise of this new cinema as their films fell from grace due to their peculiarities and self-reflexivity. As Seçil Büker noted in 1990, Yeşilçam's late period involved "a questioning of itself. Our directors, and our players, are questioning what they and others did in the past. When the questioning starts, it means that self-criticism has also started" (Özdemir 1990, 12). In such a venue of self-criticism that embellished the cinematic world of those filmmakers who attempted to make serious films and other films different from those produced by Yeşilçam, there also appeared attempts at, as Engin Ayça put it, "individual narration" and "individual creators," a transformation from Yeşilçam's oral narration to more of a "written narration" (1985, 80). However, for Ayça, this distinction and the "age-old problems" of Yeşilçam continued to not only exist but also to determine mainstream popular cinema in Turkey. With the further capitalization and globalization of culture in the 1990s, such age-old problems became passé in the eyes of the new generation of filmmakers and spectators, who preferred to focus on the continuity of filmic discourse, the quality of filmmaking and special effects, and the sophistication of narratives.

Thus, when seen through the eyes of the contemporary spectators in Turkey, Yeşilçam, as framed by nostalgia, represents the innocence of remaining separate from the global and modern world of capitalism that has altered Turkey with increasing rapidity since the 1980s. Such a dream and imagination of happiness, romanticism, innocence, and purity, which was the quintessential makeup of Yeşilçam, was no longer able to disregard the very impure social and political history of Turkey in the 1990s. While Yeşilçam had actually been produced in a rather unromantic Turkey branded by brutal socioeconomic transformations, military interventions, political oscillations, and violence, this environment changed during the 1990s. The new social order was not about collective or communal *hayal*s and *özenti*s, or the protocols of Turkification, but about individual capitalistic *hayal*s and *özenti*s, the rendering and Turkifications of the West on a personal level, and the rise of Islamism. But such a conjuncture only came after the transformations and changes of the 1980s cinema detailed below.

Öğretmen Kemal (Teacher Kemal, 1981)

Produced immediately after the 1980 coup, *Öğretmen Kemal* (hereafter ÖK) illustrates the tensions within the military regime's aspirations, those who supported its claim to reiterate the republican ideology, and its double-edged relation to westernization. For Berna Moran, the main theme of the Turkish novel is westernization, especially during the late Ottoman and early republican eras. These novels created a hierarchical organization of characters based on their status: military and civilian bureaucrats were at the top of this scale, while peripheral, commercial bourgeoisie seemed to act as the ruling class, and the ruled were the workers, peasants, and small craftsmen (1994, 8–9). Though like early republican novels, the republican ideologues refused an understanding of a class-based social stratification, later social realist novels also used elements of a social hierarchy. These postwar novels, often called "village novels," were technically more sophisticated than the earlier ones; they offered detailed character development and psychological clashes, questioned the ongoing problems of rural life, and, loyal to the Kemalist project, portrayed modernization as the solution to many problems. The agents of modernization, such as soldiers, teachers, and other civilian bureaucrats, promised progress in their fight against reactionary, traditional forces. Even though they sometimes reflected on class conflicts, they remained schematic in their presentation of the village and melodramatic in the clash between good and evil forces.

Yeşilçam also reproduced the main themes of village novels, at times spicing them with Turkification. Known as the first rural drama in the cinema of Turkey, Muhsin Ertuğrul's pre-Yeşilçam film *Aysel, Bataklı*

Damın Kızı (Aysel, the Daughter of a Muddy Hut, 1934) is a "Turkification" of a Selma Lagerlöf story. While Yeşilçam's rural dramas took the village as a site of confrontation between traditional and modern forces, they often relied upon the village novels to melodramatize it. Similar to Moran's differentiation between early and later republican village novels, Scognamillo also reflects on "realist" village dramas, which he started with Erksan's *Aşık Veysel'in Hayatı* (The Life of Folksinger Veysel, 1952)

Figure 6.2. *Öğretmen Kemal* (Teacher Kemal, Remzi Jöntürk, 1981)

(1973a, 8). This so-called "social realist" rural drama emphasized the character's psychology and the conflict between the dominant and dominated classes. However, its scenes of arid fields and poor-quality crops were not well received by the censor's board and Erksan was forced to add scenes showing abundant fields worked by modern agricultural machines. Unlike social realist rural dramas, rural melodramas or singer films such as KS brought forward an ambiguous relationship to Kemalist discourse by, in a sense, hiding a critique behind such imagery. Rural melodramas, beginning with the pre-Yeşilçam films of director Muharrem Gürses, portrayed villages where "extreme emotions clash with each other in a bloody and deadly fight and its characters suffer, are furious, burn with violence and vengeance. Such was the 'melodramatic' village, not tied to reality" (Scognamillo 1973a, 11). Whereas their realistic or naturalistic characteristics are debatable, rural life in these films was a milieu of "suppression, difficult living conditions, traditional customs, static norms, and violence because of its structure" (Scognamillo 1973a, 13). Thus, even he considers these films melodramatic, calling them "*en marge*," simultaneously real and surreal. This marginal placement was due to the partial success of Kemalist reform projects, at least through the presence and visualization of its modernizing agents and the inevitability of change and modernization by means of agricultural technologies that demanded fewer workers, leading to migration and immigration.

Besides the "melodramatic" and "realistic" villages, Yeşilçam had a third, a "Kemalist" village where the state's modernizing forces engaged in ideological battles with the reactionaries and traditionalists. Whereas KS is the melodramatic example, ÖK reflects the Kemalist genre of rural dramas. ÖK, as a belated example of its genre, commemorates the hundredth anniversary of Atatürk's birth and praises the first year of the military regime. However, Kemalist phrases such as "the villager is the master of the nation," which seems to underline ÖK's mentality through the conception of a pure, innocent, and naive image of the village, did not come to life because the 1980 military intervention produced a model for a Turkish-Islamist synthesis that ran counter to the early republican model. More interestingly, apart from the 1980 military intervention's utter dissimilarity from the 1960 one in terms of its rendering of Kemalism, ÖK's attempt to present an idealized countryside with unwashed, backward, uneducated, primitive forces to be elevated by the modernizing agents produces nothing more than a *cliché*, a rehashing of Yeşilçam and positivist modernization. Not only does it attempt to present Kemalist ideology through identification with a "teacher Kemal," who is the devoted follower of Mustafa Kemal, it also schematically repeats and reproduces Yeşilçam's melodramatic modality. ÖK's modernization project, as expected, vilifies the religious leader, the feudal landlord, and the non-Muslim merchant—the regional upper classes—while offering the enlightenment of the unwashed masses: the poor villagers and especially their children.

Such national narratives of modernization, common to non-Western literature and cinemas, coincide with nation-building attempts carrying the tension between modernizing elites' westernization efforts and the traditional loci of power. In the early stages of nation building, such films often presented the themes for the foundation, institution, or development of a national cause and identity. For example, the 1950s Indian popular cinema offered "social justice and the formation of a new personality" through "a popular democratic perception which worked through some of the rationalist and egalitarian approaches of the liberal-radical intelligentsia" (Vasudevan 2000, 116). Republican Turkish intelligentsia also produced an image of a rural life modeled on Europe, especially in early republican novels and early and high Yeşilçam films. In offering social justice and a new identity for the masses, these modernizing narratives rely on the convergence of the melodramatic and the ideological to present the new nation's creators and supporters (teacher, soldier, doctor, appointed or elected village leaders, and other state officials) and their internal and external enemies (landlord, religious figure, traditional merchant, village elders, and bandits). Whereas some social realist films also present this distinction as a class difference, melodramas offer a distinction between poverty and wealth administered through a romance that inscribes a vertical class movement. Thus it is common to encounter the corrupted and traditionalist wealthy characters whose authority is threatened by innocent villagers and modernizing agents, especially in the biter bit narrative formulas. Additionally, these films almost always introduce comic figure(s) (village fool, beggar, or child) who commonly are naturally virtuous truth-tellers siding with the modernizing hero. Thus the voice of reason transferred into the voice of the wise fool helps communicate the modernizers' message to the peasants. Finally, the women in these texts are unanimously good. While it is common to find a strong mother figure who helps the modernizing hero's cause, there is usually also a young woman/girl figure who allows for a romantic relationship.

ÖK opens in 1980, in Karalar (lit. darks or blacks) village where teacher Hasret (lit. longing) and her students visit Teacher Kemal's grave, with a gravestone made of a blackboard that he used at the clapboard school he constructed. When an old and mad-looking woman Ayşe (Meral Orhonsay) starts crying beside the grave, their teacher Hasret (Funda Gürgen), who forty-two years ago was a child in the same village, replies: "Now I will tell you the story of Teacher Kemal, who was born in 1891 and has never died." In a blatant attempt to identify Teacher Kemal with Mustafa Kemal Atatürk, the teacher's birthday is exactly a decade after Atatürk's and the film takes place in 1938, in the year of Atatürk's death. In case this isn't obvious enough, in the credits the filmmakers not only thank the military governors of the city but also dedicate the film to "the memory of the eternal and the greatest teacher of all," Mustafa Kemal Atatürk.

Following these tawdry coincidences, the film's actual story introduces the bandit Durali (Fikret Hakan) and his lover Hasret, and the coming of a state official to Karalar. In the village, the zealot merchant Şerif (lit. sacred, descendant of Prophet Mohammed) is selling illegal tobacco to the villagers, before the "fool" of the village Çayır Mustafa ("grass-eating" Mustafa) criticizes him for asking exorbitant prices. When the shepherd boy Ali informs them of the coming stranger, the villagers hide their goods, thinking that the official must be a tax collector—implying, of course, that the only official they were accustomed to seeing during the Ottoman period was someone who would take from rather than provide for them. However, Şerif asks him to leave when they learn that he is only a teacher. Despite the poor welcome, Teacher Kemal (Cüneyt Arkın) is adamant about constructing a school building and he gets local support from an old crippled veteran missing an arm. Still wearing his military uniform sixteen years after the war, Gazi Dayı (Uncle Veteran) salutes Teacher Kemal and invites him to his house. Quickly, Teacher Kemal, Gazi Dayı, and Çayır Mustafa form an alliance to build a school where Kemal opens his first class by saying, "The state and nation are the same, single entity." The prime guarantor of this entity is the alliance because the combination of their names implies Gazi Mustafa Kemal; Gazi was the honorific he earned during the War of Independence and was used until 1934, when, with the institution of surnames, he was awarded the moniker Atatürk, father of the Turks, by parliament.

ÖK's cheap references do not stop there. Teacher Kemal responds to Hasret's longing for education by removing the cowbell from around her neck (her mother does not want her to get lost) and by literally saving her from being an animal. Teacher chooses to build a school on the landlord's field where there is a wishing tree, a site where people tie pieces of fabric to make wishes in a ritual considered superstitious. In this fight against the feudal regime and blind faith, Teacher cuts the tree, yelling, "I will bring you down, blind faith, collapse the sophistry that made my people illiterate; be gone the dark thought of the ages!" But, true to the Yeşilçam tradition, Teacher's lips do not move as he keeps chopping the tree with an ax. Against rioting villagers, Teacher says, "Look, my friends, I am against violence, I am a man of peace, and I am a soldier of Atatürk. Those who work are with me, those who are lazy are against me." Later, while leading villagers carry the coffin of a child who died of an epidemic disease, Şerif first stops the villagers and then starts his obnoxious overacting, pointing toward Teacher, shuddering with his entire body, and saying, "The wind of Satan is blowing from the hill of the wishing tree....The Satan is there, the curse is there!" Then, shepherd Ali throws stones at Teacher who says, "Sure, the rose thrown by a friend wounds us." This reply, taken from Pir Sultan Abdal, presents a subtheme of Alevites, the followers of Ali, similar to Shiites. As Ali realizes what he did, he cries and asks for Teacher's help to stop the epidemic. Instead of Şerif's talismans, Teacher cures the children with modern medicine.

The plot thickens (as thin as possible!) as Leon, the Jewish trader, visits the landlord at the beginning of the sap collection season. The evil trio— the landlord, Şerif, and Leon—are upset because children are at school instead of collecting the sap. They hire Durali to kill Teacher, but his life is saved by a watch in his pocket that blocks Durali's bullet, as happened to Atatürk during the war. Teacher then stops illiterate Durali from drinking a bottle marked "poison" and beats him up using his learned ability of boxing against Durali's beastly fighting manners. After befriending Durali, Teacher threatens the landlord by reminding him of the Courts of Independence, which were early republican courts of no appeal that persecuted many, especially dissidents. This reference is also telling in that ÖK was released during a junta government that jailed and executed its dissidents.

While struggling with these reactionaries, Teacher is deeply saddened upon hearing of the death of Mustafa Kemal Atatürk, after which he is further antagonized by the landlord's forced marriage to his fourth wife, Hasret. Both of these incidents drive Teacher crazy: "Now, I am leaving. I am punishing you. You will not learn and get an education. You will live like animals far away from running water, electricity, radio, and civilization. You will be dominated, exploited. If you do not want this, come to school!" After this agitating speech, the villagers follow him. However, after the landlord and the "gaiour" Leon rape Ayşe, she goes mad and falls from the bridge. After pulling the drowning Ayşe from the shallow water, Teacher administers artificial respiration, which looks more like he is cupping her breasts. Although the villagers, thinking that he raped Ayşe, beat Teacher with sticks, it is soon clear that the sticks are actually made of carved Styrofoam that break over his head! In a finely tuned last-minute rescue sequence, Durali arrives at the village, kills the landlord, his men, and Leon. Then, Durali asks Şerif what happened to Ayşe (as a 1980s minibus passes by in the background). Suddenly, Ayşe comes out of shock and tells Durali what happened. Having gotten rid of the Ottoman elements and ethnic minorities threatening the republican regime, Durali throws his knife and gun away, in a symbolic act reiterating the end of the war. Typical of a plot inspired by Westerns, in these closing sequences the gendarmes, symbolic of the good cops and state order, finally arrive bearing sheet metal for the roof of the school. Then, in the finished school building, Teacher asks everybody to turn their backs if they love him, and collapses, thus passing away. In a series of crosscuts, the sign of *Ataokulu* (Atatürk's school) burns as Teacher slowly falls to the floor. The closing credits are coupled with a folk song that is an ode to the war dead and a voice-over narration voiced by Durali saying, "Teacher Kemal, you need to see how our new school, our new village looks!" But alas!

ÖK's oddities and transgressions arise not from its compliance with modernization, but from its belatedness and overdoing of these. In part, this is intricately related to the military regime's claim to reiterate its version of Kemalism through sheer violence. As Dorsay noted, "The film is a half-western and half-comic book adventure of a Mustafa Kemal teacher" (1995, 362). Yet ÖK's awkward presentation of its ideology inevitably underscores the fear of the masses over which the military regime had taken power. ÖK's painstaking reproduction of Kemalist rural dramas is so "perfect" that perfection becomes overpowering and thus its ideologically informed representation turns into an unintentional parody of republican ideology's major themes (the paternalistic nationalist discourse; the Kemalist fight against Islam, Ottoman identity, and non-Muslim ethnic minorities; and the modernization from above). With its facile messages (education is civilization, illiteracy belongs to an animal-like state), slogan-like ideological statements (opening an *Ataokulu* in Karalar), simplicity (the trio of Gazi, Mustafa, and Kemal), banality (teaching how to write and read "Atatürk" in the first class), stereotypes (Islamic, Ottoman, and non-Muslim antagonists), and clichés (Hasret's longing for education and Şerif's zealotry), ÖK overuses everything available. While national narratives seem open to excesses given their own discursive ambiguities, such views generally underscore incompleteness in the signification of national narratives. In ÖK, there is instead an over-signification, an unwarranted clarity of its own discursive claims. Rather than creating ambivalence that could not completely reproduce its own origins, identity, or semantic network, ÖK not only creates a straight-forward taxonomy of "us and them" but also believes in and defends its own taxonomy through a series of binary oppositions: civilized versus primitive, human versus animal, modern versus traditional, science versus religion, British boxing versus Ottoman wrestling, Turk versus non-Turk, the evil Ottoman-Muslim-non-Muslim trio versus the crippled-mad-educating trio of Gazi Mustafa Kemal; in short, ominous evil versus omnipotent good.

With a military backdrop, ÖK's taxonomy offers not a national narrative to be willingly shared by the members of a community, but one to be violently instituted over them. Almost sixty years after the emergence of a nation-state with a claim toward a single ethnic identity and progressive vision, the moment of the military rule was no longer invested in claims of the righteousness of its existence, but in a state of emergency and martial law, as emphasized by the opening credits thanking the military regime. Yeşilçam cinema changed its tone during and in the aftermath of military interventions. The first Kemalist military intervention of 1960 likewise led to an end to the themes of religious exploitation in the films of the late 1950s, giving way instead to films that portrayed Turks as civilized city dwellers during the 1960–61 film season (Kuyucaklı 1961, 3). Similarly, military rule between 1980 and 1983 not only put an end to sex films and political films but also served as the catalyst for several films supporting the military regime's outlook. ÖK, seen from the milieu of a military rule and martial law, perfectly fits that bill.

ÖK's narrative and *mise-en-scène*, in the eyes of contemporary spectators, not only offers a trash film experience but also a parody of the ideology it is intended to defend. In contrast to the contemporary nostalgic view of the film conditioned by a concept of contemporary cinematic realism, late Yeşilçam films do not offer mimetic realism. Thus the film attempts to deliver its ideological message through placing the signifiers of Kemalism in an eclectic and self-contradictory syntax. Its offer of a "true" Kemalist village coincides with irony and parody of that image. Like the excessive, full-body overacting of Şerif, the film itself shivers and trembles because of its overconfidence and plodding deliberateness, opening itself up to carnivalesque laughter. Such was the secondary and ahistorical response of Yeşilçam to the military intervention.

Çarıklı Milyoner (The Millionaire with Sandals, 1985)

Introduced in its opening credits as "the first adaptation of traditional Turkish performing arts in which everything relies on imitation and jokes/gags," Ertem Eğilmez's *Şabanoğlu Şaban* (Şaban, the Son of Şaban, 1977) was one of the solutions that mainstream Yeşilçam found for its looming crises. Before this film, Eğilmez directed an extremely popular comedy series of four films, starting with *Hababam Sınıfı* (Keep-on Class, 1975), which included Kemal Sunal as a character named "Cow Şaban," who is basically a dumb and lazy student, a fact made ironic by his nickname, which also signifies a diligent and geeky student. Riding on the film series' popularity, the "Cow Şaban" character went on to star in seventeen "Şaban films" between 1977 and 1985. The Şaban character was also carried onto the private television channels in the 1990s through a couple of television series. In a master's thesis that he wrote on his own films, Sunal underscores two transformations in Yeşilçam as critical for the characters he played: the first was the introduction of color film in the early 1970s and the second is a move from "action comedy" to "situation comedy" in the mid-1970s (2001, 134). While the character Şaban is constructed against in a backdrop of traditional fairy tales and jokes that came through oral narration, Sunal sees his own character on the screen as an ordinary man with good intentions, pure, clean, clumsy, and moral because he rebels against unjust situations (2001, 136–37). The clumsy Şaban who triggers action comedy is indeed a product of traditional comedy characters and this characterization was also well established in Yeşilçam, for there are a variety of preceding characters such as Dümbüllü, Cilalı İbo, and Turist Ömer. Almost all of these characters relied upon the traits of traditional comics such as Karagöz, İbiş, and Keloğlan. Likewise, late Yeşilçam's mainstream popular comedies, using tropes of these earlier plays and films, created variations through some atypical inputs aligned with both action and situation comedy.

Just three years before making the previously mentioned statement about creating an "authentic" comedy based on traditional performing arts, Eğilmez had claimed that the Turkish audience was "dumb and watched every film presented to them." After mentioning that it was only possible to make "direct and natural situation comedy" in Turkey, Eğilmez added, "Our audience does not understand sarcasm, parody or 'absurd' jokes; for instance, they do not laugh at cold, American jokes... but they say, 'show us an exciting situation and we will laugh'" (1974, 33). A decade after that interview, Eğilmez not only parted ways with Sunal, who went on to star in his various comedies, but also claimed to change his stance in relation to comedy, saying, "It is generally reported that our people are fond of crude comedy and slapstick... I am not that inclined to give people such easy laughter" (1984, 37). The contradiction in these two statements emerges from the military intervention, which not only changed

Figure 6.3. *Hababam Sınıfı* (Keep-on Class, Ertem Eğilmez, 1975)

the outlook of the country but also that of filmmakers who made popular, mainstream comedies. Sunal also expressed a preference for his later "social realist" comedies made in the late Yeşilçam era. Simultaneously, he acted in "Turkifications" from Western comedies such as *Çarıklı Milyoner*, a Turkification of Frank Capra's *Mr. Deeds Goes to Town* (1936) and *Şabaniye* (dir. Kartal Tibet, 1984), a Turkification of *Tootsie* (dir. Sydney Pollack, 1982). At the same time, his homegrown comedies such as *Sahte Kabadayı* (Imposter Tough Guy, dir. Natuk Baytan, 1976), *İnek Şaban* (Cow Şaban, dir. Osman F. Seden, 1978), *İyi Aile Çocuğu* (The Child of a Good Family, dir. Osman F. Seden, 1978), and *Bıçkın* (Roughneck, dir. Orhan Aksoy, 1988) are all loose Turkifications of Alexander Dumas' *Les Frères Corses* (The Corsican Brothers, 1844) in which Sunal plays two identical characters, either twins or look-alikes.

Still popular among television audiences in contemporary Turkey, these Sunal comedies reproduce Yeşilçam's characteristic storylines and tropes. Frequently Şaban, as a migrant from a rural area or a lower-class bum, copes with the challenges of adapting to urban environments. However, mostly unsuccessful in this process of adaptation, such inhabitants of squatter settlements experience a divided, marginal everyday practice, no longer rural but not quite urban either. Within this experience of marginality, Sunal's characters search for a true path, purity, friendship, and love (Sunal 2001, 161). While urban upper classes set obstacles before them, Sunal's Anatolian heroes generally conquer the urban environment not just by eliminating evil but also by winning the heart of upper-class lead female characters. Thus, Sunal's comedies also rehash Yeşilçam's

ER - AR F İ L M YÖNETMEN ERTEM EĞİLMEZ
ARABESK
MÜJDE AR / ŞENER ŞEN
UĞUR YÜCEL
ÖZGÜN MÜZİK VE BESTELER ATİLLA ÖZDEMİROĞLU / ŞARKI SÖZLERİ AYSEL GÜREL
SANAT YÖNETMENİ ANNIE G. PERTAN / SENARYO GANİ MÜJDE / GÖRÜNTÜ YÖNETMENİ AYTEKİN ÇAKMAKÇI

Figure 6.4. *Arabesk* (Ertem Eğilmez, 1988), a Late Yeşilçam parody of melodramas featuring *arabesk* singers

melodramatic conflicts between good and evil, rich and poor, and rural and urban and augment the virtuous common man's morality and innocence, despite the clumsy, foulmouthed, and disorderly aspects of Sunal's characters.

Opening at a bourgeois mansion, *Çarıklı Milyoner* is quick to show the death of billionaire Hilmi Tok (Ali Şen) who leaves everything to his son, Bayram Tok (Kemal Sunal). Similar to Longfellow Deeds, Bayram is a good-hearted fool playing with his drum as the village children follow him. Then, his late father's assistant and lawyer come in a Mercedes to the village to inform him of his inheritance. After Bayram moves to Istanbul, a reporter, Suna (Necla Nazır), meets him by introducing herself as a poor, lower-class woman. Surrounded by relatives, his father's assistant, and his lawyer, all of whom are after his inheritance, Bayram finds refuge in Suna, who is not a "bounty hunter." While his relatives try various plots to control the inheritance, Suna starts publishing her reports in the paper titled, "The Millionaire with Sandals," referring to his rural rawhide footwear.

Unable to feel at home in the city, Bayram decides to return to his village and asks Suna to marry him. Feeling affectionate, Suna asks her head editor (Memduh Ün) to stop reports about the Millionaire with Sandals. But the editor publishes the report nonetheless, and Bayram, feeling betrayed after seeing the report, wears a pair of sandals and meets with Suna, chastising her for lying about her real identity. Then, in an attempt to distance himself from his urban identity, he takes off his clothes, puts on his drum, and starts to play. Still feeling rebellious, he throws some of his money from the roof of an apartment. Seeing this, his father's lawyer persuades the police to send him to an asylum and he is forced to prove that he is not mad.

Regardless of whether the Millionaire with Sandals returns to his village the film offers two simple traditionalist conservative messages: rural Anatolian men are by definition decent and virtuous and cities or modernization in general are evil and morally corrosive. Evil was not necessarily aligned with the upper classes or the bourgeoisie. Instead, Yeşilçam offered an alternative, melodramatic outlook in which mankind is already divided into good and evil; and evil was something related to morality and ethics. Those who are immoral could have been from any class or group, but the point is that in the end, good always prevails. Fairy-tale villains are commonly reproduced in Yeşilçam's mainstream comedies where the good-hearted, decent village boy fights against the monsters, witches, or giants, to win the hand of the princess. Sunal wrote in his thesis, "Kemal Sunal is the symbol of the crises of values and the transformations that have taken place in Turkey since the 1950s" (2001, 161). Far from problematizing such transformations and crises, Sunal's characters essentially offered Yeşilçam's melodramatic modality and morality. Though in their plots they open up an anarchic world, these comedies restore order and morality in their melodramatic resolutions. In this respect, comedies starring Sunal did not have many problems with the military rule or with contemporary television channels that add a number of "beeps" to mute his obscenity and rehash his films that combine traditional comic characters with action and situation comedies.

Gülüşan (1985)

As one of the rare female directors of Yeşilçam, Bilge Olgaç produced popular films that partially diverted from Yeşilçam's earlier conventions. Nonetheless, the late Yeşilçam novelties of her films, such as the issues borrowed from the high Yeşilçam era social realist films and the changing status of the migrant lower classes, are also visible in late Yeşilçam family melodramas starring *arabesk* singers. In this respect, a certain strand of *arabesk* singers' films, especially those with adolescent singers such as Küçük Emrah (Little Emrah) or Küçük Ceylan (Little Ceylan), were increasingly concerned with the impossibility of a melodramatic resolution, reminiscent of rural or folk music singer melodramas with tragic endings. The lower-class characters of these films were less and less exposed to high-class riches and augmented a sense of traditionalism, conservatism, and moralism through portraying the miserable conditions of migrant classes in urban peripheries.

As Selim İleri has noted, with reference to the popular romance writer Kerime Nadir, high Yeşilçam period "salon" (or romantic) comedies and family melodramas dealt with pathos and domestic sensitivities set in a foreign décor: "First domestic sensitivities are turned into pathetic cries. Then the tabloid aspect is introduced in a Western, lifeless, and detached atmosphere" (1973, 13). Instead of following this convention of 1950s and 1960s pulp novels, these late Yeşilçam *arabesk* singer films were marked

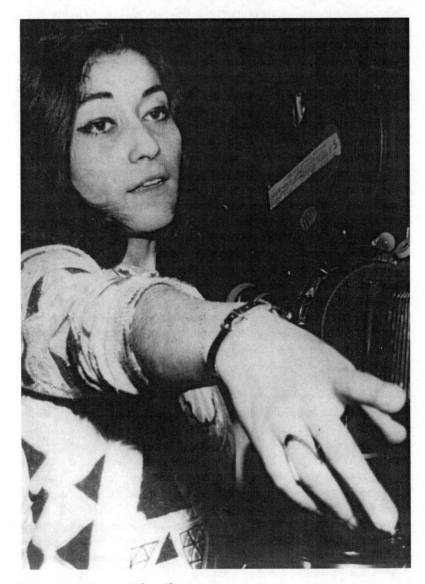

Figure 6.5. Director Bilge Olgaç

by increased pathos amplified through the bald visualization of prostitutes, addicts, and poverty. As indicated in one of Küçük Emrah's songs, these stories were about "the downtrodden, on their own, helpless, poor orphans, those who know no happiness, they always cry, never smile."

Two things may have triggered this change. The first is the socioeconomic transformations of the time that were increasingly felt by the lower classes, such as rising inflation, worsening economic conditions, and the increasing media representation of the socioeconomic gap between classes. Beforehand, the migrant population's visibility in urban centers was limited. As the new populace of the urban centers came to outnumber those who had been born there, both economic and sociocultural differences became increasingly apparent. Moreover, in the 1980s, as political or ideological voices were suppressed, the voices of *arabesk* singers, ethnic minorities, and women started to be more visible in the public realm. Such a multitude of individual voices was also conditioned by an erasure of collective voices in a depoliticized arena.

Some film writers have suggested that one could detect subtle political content in the films of some *arabesk* singers, such as the Kurdish İbrahim Tatlıses, who became particularly famous during the 1980s and was known for the "sweet voice" he adopted as a surname. For example, film writer Nezih Coş attempted to find a realistic approach, similar to that of Yılmaz Güney, arising from the "sincere pathos" and naturalism of Tatlıses's films. Coş imagined that the autobiographical aspects of Tatlıses's films, which depict his rise from construction worker to famous singer, could be turned into a realistic film language (1984, 19). In Tatlıses's *Yorgun* (Tired, 1983), his character, also named İbrahim Tatlıses, is a famous singer who is tired and bored of fame and individualistic, materialistic culture. The monotony is broken when by chance he meets and helps a teenager, and suddenly recalls his own youth. He then meets a working-class woman with whom he falls in love. Though such autobiographical elements, including the interweaving of real and filmic life, seem to offer a realistic approach, these films eventually restore traditional morality and adapt themselves to Yeşilçam in their rehashing of Güney-style "realism." What Coş has missed here is the melodramatic modality's adaptability and its use of realism to strengthen its own dramatic effects. Though in Hollywood, with the support of excellent sets and special effects, this generally involves an improved *mise-en-scène*, Yeşilçam has never been able to compete on such technical terms. While one strand of *arabesk* singer films revisited high Yeşilçam tropes, such as the love affair of a rich girl and a poor boy, the other more "pathetic" ones rehashed a more realistic language. The latter films did not necessarily involve two protagonists who differed in their class positions, but instead focused on the lives of lower-class characters. However, evil is always present in these films as well; their major difference was in their visualization of evil, as a precondition, unlike salon films, by being clearly, strongly, and sometimes violently visualized.

The evil characters of late Yeşilçam appeared through two different types who used different means to reach their ends. For instance, while Coşkun

Göğen is known as "Rapist Coşkun," Nuri Alço is known more for his sophisticated tactics in making "decent" women into "fallen" women (e.g., through getting women high on drugs or adding sleeping pills to their drinks). Among those women was a star actress of the 1980s, Ahu Tuğba, who also acted in a television series, *Esir Gönüller* (Captive Souls, 2005) with Alço. When the two discussed Yeşilçam of the 1980s in a recent interview, they gave a number of clues about how they conceived themselves as actors. When asked whether she has a special place in the fetishistic history of Turkish men with her leopard-skin bikinis, Tuğba replies, "I started a new era: I kissed, I made love.... After my parents got a divorce, I played in those roles for revenge. Suddenly I became an artist. My family was disgraced at the time. But nowadays the families themselves take their sons and daughters" to play such roles (Tuğba and Alço 2005). While Tuğba touches on how the conception of sexual and moral purity and cleanliness has changed in Turkey, she also remembers that in their films Alço always slapped her wonderfully, and she explains how she accepted the slaps with grace. In the same interview, Alço explains how, when they asked the producer-director Türker İnanoğlu to tell them about the script and what their roles were, İnanoğlu told them, "What script? One of you will play the prostitute, the other the pimp" (Tuğba and Alço 2005).

Thus while late Yeşilçam reproduced tropes of good and evil, they were modified through a series of developments. Mimicking nudity in the adventure films and the sex films of the 1970s, erotic scenes became common. In contrast to Oran's avoidance of protagonists who might be understood as "prostitutes" and "cuckolds" during high Yeşilçam, various late Yeşilçam mainstream films took advantage of such stereotypes and created salacious protagonists while maintaining a conservative moral stance. Nonetheless, while Alço was the villain, Tuğba was the heroine. Thus she, as the protagonist, offered her body for the male gaze and enjoyed the carnal pleasures of life as a woman, before finding her hero. Such popular action and romance films involved a move toward the presentation of female characters as "individuals," not oppressed by traditions or religion, but making their own decisions and living accordingly. Nevertheless, when asked about what Tuğba brought to Turkish cinema, Alço replies, "She kissed, made love. She gave a good reply to those who said that they do not kiss, they do not make love" on-screen. Though late Yeşilçam films involved "Turkish" female characters enjoying life, much like the late 1970s sex films, this did not change the resulting conception of these female characters in society. As in one of Tatlıses's films, *Günah* (Sin, 1983), which presented the drama of life as experienced by lower classes, the bus driver, who falls in love with a dancer in a nightclub, still needs to overcome the obstacle of loving a "fallen" woman. Thus, true to the Yeşilçam tradition of women washing away their sins, he takes her to a beach on a winter day and asks her to cleanse herself in the sea. A female character like Tuğba might be a protagonist, but in such a moral order she could never be a role model or offer social change in relation to women's sexual freedom. Instead she is proud to be an example of "what the young girls must not do." The inability of such films to produce a change underscores how, even as they created new tropes, they still functioned well within Yeşilçam's morality.

In the 1980s, some high Yeşilçam era female stars played roles in which they portrayed self-reliant urban individuals choosing their own trajectories and making love on-screen. While this indicates the partial change of women's roles both in society and in Yeşilçam, coinciding with the rise of feminist movement, such films also belong to an emerging category of late Yeşilçam's art house or auteur films. While deemed a new genre, "films about women" (or "woman films"), these films were essentially made by male directors. As Çetin Öner said, "The Turkish cinema has always discovered novel things. In the forties, it discovered the *efes* [bandit heroes of the Aegean region], in the fifties, the War of Independence, in the sixties, leftists, and in the eighties, women" (Özdemir 1990, 12). Like other genrifications of Yeşilçam, it was again the men or male directors who discovered the woman or femininity. Except for actresses portraying strong and free-willed female characters and a handful of female filmmakers, almost all of the producers, directors, scriptwriters, camera operators, and other film crew were male. Until 1990, only 66 of 5,514 films were directed by a total of 9 female directors (Öztürk 2004, 34). While there were no female directors before 1950, female directors are responsible for only 1.19 percent of cinema until 1990. However, between 1990 and 2002, this proportion rose to 5.76 percent, with a total of 16 female directors making 30 of the 521 films (Öztürk 2004, 34). Semire Ruken Öztürk divides these female directors into three different categories: the first female directors "who were not men" (i.e., not having a particular gender-based agenda) who made films between 1951 and 1980, the women directors of "the cinema of women" between 1981 and 1990, and politicized women directors, between 1991 and 2002 (2004). Though she talks about the late Yeşilçam period as "the cinema of women," she names only two directors in that category, Nisan Akman and Mahinur Ergun, who made a total of five films, while the remaining nine films were directed by two of Yeşilçam's female directors, Bilge Olgaç (eight films) and Türkan Şoray (one film), that is, by Öztürk's female directors "who were not men."

Of the ninety-six films listed by Öztürk, thirty-seven of them are directed by Bilge Olgaç who, for Öztürk, did not make a "cinema of women" because she did not address the problems of women as such, but instead saw them as a part of the system of "the problems of classes and the economic infrastructure" (2004, 87). For Öztürk, Olgaç did not create a "cinema of woman" because she problematized "the feudal system, the order of landlords and patriarchy"; in her films "women who marry older mean end up going mad or dying"; "the violence against women (concrete acts such as sexual assault, rape and beating) is shown and criticized"; and "honor is an important value and turns into an apparatus of power in the hands of men" (2004, 85–86). If these do not constitute a woman's cinema, then perhaps Olgaç, who started to direct films in 1965 and made a variety of action-adventure films in her early career, must be seen as a "male" director. Nevertheless, without being an ironic part of history or a woman disguised as a man, but instead being a sophisticated Yeşilçam director, Olgaç was very much aware of her position:

> We were doing our job. We had no idea of cinema being an art. At that time, we were in cinema to put bread on the table. Thus we did not think about the men and women in our films. I never thought about why I was making a woman take off her clothes. We did whatever the film demanded. (Öztürk 2004, 78)

While Olgaç's later high Yeşilçam films introduced social realist themes, she did not direct any films between 1975 and 1984 because of the popularity of sex films and the military intervention. Although she considered shooting sex films, she decided against it, not for feminist reasons but because she felt she could not understand their filmic mentality and dynamics (Öztürk 2004, 80). Her late Yeşilçam films, between 1984 and until her death in 1994, generally address the problems of women rising from tradition. As Deniz Derman Bayrakdar has noted, Olgaç "tells stories based on women, but unlike other women directors, she does not do so by turning the mirror on herself" (Derman Bayrakdar 1997, 32). Derman Bayrakdar interprets Olgaç as a director, a "woman director" of art cinema, and as someone who focuses on the problems of women in a patriarchal society (1997, 34), especially in terms of her "woman trilogy": *Kaşık Düşmanı* (One's Wife, 1984), *Gülüşan* (1985), and *İpekçe* (Silky, 1987). Olgaç summarizes *Gülüşan* as follows:

> This film takes place in a house with four people. One of the four is blind.... There is only one reason to make a film out of this story: polygamy (*kumalık*), barrenness, the relations between woman and man. In addition it has a different side to it: a little fantastic, fairy-tale like and its point of departure is a fairy-tale. Human beings may change due to the conditions of life. We are trying to look with a magnifying glass at a person's secret feelings. (Öztürk 2004, 83)

In other words, Olgaç sees her film focusing on power relations created in every relationship and social condition. In *Gülüşan*, a barren man—a character surprisingly different from Yeşilçam's multitude of characters—abducts a blind girl as his third wife and thereby generates a change in the hierarchy of relations between the members of his own household.

Inspired by a fairy tale, Osman Şahin wrote *Gülüşan*'s story and Olgaç, as in most of her films, wrote the script. With an original score by Timur Selçuk, the film's credits appear over a shot of long grass, indicating a rural setting. As the camera tilts up from the grass to the plateau, we see the miller Mestan riding his horse into the village where he lives with his two wives—the older, Cennet (Güler Ökten), and the younger, Zekiye (Meral Orhonsay). But because neither woman has given birth, Mestan plans to take yet another wife, and abducts a beautiful underage girl,

Figure 6.6. *Gülüşan* (Bilge Olgaç, 1985)

Gülüşan (Yaprak Özdemiroğlu). When he realizes that she is blind, he considers taking her back to her family, but accepts his destiny. After the wedding, Zekiye is angry about the situation but Cennet, who has already experienced a similar situation, looks comfortable, while Mestan feels bad about his fate with two barren wives and a blind third wife who later also turns out to be barren. Thus Mestan, who cannot accept or acknowledge his own barrenness and who simultaneously falls in love with Gülüşan, faces his castration, whereas Gülüşan's death at the hands of Cennet and Zekiye inscribes the film's tragic storyline.

Gülüşan, with its tragic ending and original musical score, despite being dubbed, departs from Yeşilçam's conventions and focuses on human emotions. While all women in the film are victims of polygamy, the power relations between them shift according to their conditions. Zekiye, who had enjoyed the status of favorite wife before Gülüşan's abduction, is forced to ally with Cennet, with whom she had not been in good standing. As the two turn from victims of polygamy to villains, Gülüşan is triply victimized, first by her blindness, then by her abduction, and finally through her persecution at the hands of the other wives. Making matters even worse, Mestan, who falls in love with her, initially enjoys this situation. Because Gülüşan is blind, "she is not ashamed of being naked. The visual pleasure that Gülüşan lacks becomes a richness that Mestan consumes and takes pleasure from" (Derman Bayrakdar 1997, 34). But this *belle captive*, as the prime object of Mestan's pleasure, is also enjoyed after her death. When Zekiye and Cennet watch Mestan crying and touching Gülüşan's dead body, they take pleasure from her death and Mestan's barrenness, for his dominance over his family vanishes. Mestan, who finds love in the pure, clean, and white but fragile and blind Gülüşan, in a "princess" as in fairy tales, cannot come across a magician who would open the eyes of Gülüşan or put an end to his barrenness. Instead, in this failed love story, Mestan is castrated and Gülüşan is victimized by the polygamous hierarchy, by patriarchy.

Gülüşan also offers elements of high Yeşilçam's "village realism" through its focus on traditional and feudal rural social structure. This realistic look at the village goes back to the early Yeşilçam, when such films were cut by censors, creating a "pink realism" according to Nijat Özön (1995b, 141). Discussing Metin Erksan's *Yılanların Öcü* (The Revenge of Snakes, 1961), Özön viewed the film's realism a departure from pink realism, despite the fact that it did not offer a "cold-blooded, objective quality of a document," in the mold of Italian Neorealism. Based on a novel by the leftist writer Fakir Baykurt, the film was exhibited only with a special permission from the president of Turkey, Cemal Gürsel, who also was the leader of the generals who conducted the 1960 military intervention. When the film was shown in Ankara, it led to anticommunist demonstrations, but was shown nonetheless and had a middling performance at the box office. Later, Özön found the "straightforward realism" that he was demanding from Erksan's film in Yılmaz Güney's film *Umut*, which he took to be very similar to Vittorio de Sica's *Ladri di biciclette* (Bicycle Thieves, 1948). In 1971, a month before the 1971 military intervention, Özön wrote, "*Umut*, without suspicion, is the most realist film that our cinema could have realized until today" (1995b, 206). While carrying elements of male melodrama, as in the case of Italian Neorealism, *Umut* points to the system as the source of poverty in a manner similar to *Gülüşan*. Though *Gülüşan*'s setting is a closed and limited world of four people, this not only allowed Olgaç to focus on the individual characteristics of her characters but also allows her to problematize power relations.

During Yeşilçam's lifetime, the majority of Turkey's population was living in villages where poverty, traditions, and a relatively feudal order continued to determine the lives of many people. Such a social "reality" was inevitably portrayed in literature and cinema, and villages presented a ready *mise-en-scène* for filmmakers. Unlike ÖK, which places the village as the location of the Kemalist dream, Olgaç's film, despite its realistic presentation of human relations in a patriarchal society, carries elements of fairytales within its symbolism, for example, the pure and clean princess like a white pigeon. Olgaç's films, though aligned with Yeşilçam, frequently employ such symbolic elements and thus are located on the margins of a patriarchal, moralist Yeşilçam, partly through distancing themselves from Yeşilçam's tropes.

Filim Bitti (The Film Is Over, 1989)

Such unraveling of the codes of Yeşilçam was hardly unique to *Gülüşan*. On the contrary, it is perhaps nowhere more apparent than in the painfully self-conscious *Filim Bitti* (hereafter FB), which raises the issue of the end of Yeşilçam. Özkan, who late in his career defended the idea that directors should also produce their own films, was well aware of the problems of filmmaking in Turkey. In an article, "The Adventure of a Film's Creation," he cited budgetary reasons for low technical quality:

> When you are planning your films, you are always limited by the conditions you are in.... You need to shoot the film in a set time frame. You work not at the locations you wish for, but at those you can find...the crew you work with is limited in productivity...and they do not have the conditions to renew and develop themselves.... The technology you have is used with minimum capacity because there is not enough knowledge.... While Western cinematographers work with a bag full of filters in each film they shoot, during the shooting of a film, two or three filters are enough for us. In the tradition of Turkish cinema, the idea of using light based on individual locations, the "lighting" of players, and the telling of a story have only been slowly left behind. After shooting a film under such conditions, a new adventure starts at the post-production stage. All films in Turkey are better when they are silent. During dubbing, you have to accept the unacceptable. At times, sound effects can make a film unbearable. In this country, I have not yet witnessed composed music adding anything to a film. (1993, 73)

In *Filim Bitti*, Özkan touches on many of these problems by relating the story of a film's shooting. Though he does not deal with the preproduction and postproduction of the film, *Filim Bitti* shows the process of shooting a film. The characters do not have names, and we only know them by their jobs such as *jeune*, *jeune damme*, director or producer. According to Özkan, the absence of names underlines an "independent attitude" and thus allows for a broader discussion of the problems associated with

Figure 6.7. Director Yavuz Özkan

filmmaking ("Filim Bitti" 1990, 14). For him, making a film within a film presents two sides of life, one real and the other filmic, and analyzes the human being in these two contrasting realms.

Starting with such premises, FB exhibits a self-conscious structure. It begins with a director (Halil Ergün) writing a script (the film's script is written by Özkan) on a typewriter at his office. The producer brings in a news story about the lead players, who have just divorced. On the set of the film, the prompter reads the script, and a man and a woman on a bed repeat their lines. In the film within the film (hereafter FB1), the *jeune* (Kadir İnanır) says, "I love you." *Jeune damme* (Zeliha Berksoy) says, "Me, too....Look outside." But the snow outside is not falling as it should, so the director yells at the special effects crew, which throw buckets of Styrofoam. As the woman and the man gaze at each other lovingly, we hear people talking and yelling, as well as noises generated by the crew trying to tear apart Styrofoam and shake the pine trees seen through the set's bedroom window. While FB1 is shot silently and we hear the prompter talking and the studio's noise, all of which mock this chaos made possible by dubbing, FB itself is dubbed! So what we hear is not the noise of the set but instead an artificial noise of the set created during post-synchronization.

Thus FB presents not only a low-budget mentality with cheap special effects but also a multitude of personalities as indicated in the chart below:

Table 6.1. Characters of *Filim Bitti* and FB1

Real Life	*Filim Bitti*	FB1
Kadir İnanır	Zeliha Berksoy	Meral Oğuz
Kadir	Zeliha (Kadir's Wife)	Meral (Kadir's Girlfriend)
K1	Z1 (K1's Girlfriend)	M1 (K1's Wife)

FB is about unexpected passages from itself to FB1 and a reversal of the relations in the frame film and the film framed. At lunch in FB, the director, Kadir, Zeliha, and Meral (Meral Oğuz) sit together while the film crew all sit at another table. The director asks Kadir and Zeliha whether their divorce will affect the film. It quickly becomes clear that it will, as they begin to fight when the director explains that FB1 is a love story. At her upper-class home in FB1, Z1 calls her boyfriend K1, who is married to M1. K1 comes over and his mistress Z1 kisses him just before the director stops them. He asks Kadir to be more enthusiastic while kissing Zeliha. But Kadir is not very willing, since the divorce is still very fresh. In FB1, Z1 and K1 are lovers, so Kadir needs to appear enthusiastic about kissing. But because his ex-wife Zeliha is the one kissing him, Kadir accuses her of getting his face wet. The director gets angry and asks a crewmember to bring in the producer to talk with the actors.

In FB1, K1, a conductor, behaves coldly to M1 and tells her that he loves Z1. Then, in FB, a fire breaks out on the set. The dance tune continues as the crew tries to stop the fire. After Zeliha refuses to speak to Kadir, he takes Meral on a boat ride. On the boat, Meral asks Kadir about his relationship with Zeliha but Kadir refuses to acknowledge that they are in a relationship. Zeliha tells the assistant director that she likes the "magical" love story of FB1, but she also adds, "Would such a story be possible in real life?" While FB shifts between its own reality and the story of FB1, to my knowledge, there is thankfully no gossip or any stories about Kadir İnanır and Zeliha Berksoy or Meral Oğuz having a relationship before, during, or after the shooting of FB. In FB1, as it snows Styrofoam outside, M1 arrives at a restaurant where Z1 and K1 have been eating. Accompanied by violin and accordion music at the restaurant, both M1 and K1 try not to look at each other. During the intermission, Kadir fights with Zeliha again and the director asks for a rehearsal of the scene in which K1 and Z1 talk in the restaurant's restroom. Again, the scene is not deemed suitably compassionate, and the director asks for romantic music to make them feel comfortable. During filming in Yeşilçam it was not very important which song of a particular singer was upholstered. Rather, sound editors considered the mood and the genre of the music and upholstered songs may be totally irrelevant to the content of the scene.

The next day, in a scene, K1 is about to conduct an orchestra in FB1, but FB's assistant director informs the director that the producer is not willing to pay for the extras who would act as the audience. Thus, the orchestra members of FB1 are also asked to act as the spectators for the music they perform. But in FB, this turns into a Felliniesque scene where the orchestra members perform as spectators, simultaneously listening to the music they make. Here, Özkan lays the blame for Yeşilçam's mistakes and discontinuities on the tight purse strings of meddling producers, who also get angry when the director uses a lot of negative film rolls: "You asked for ten more boxes of film.... You filmed each scene three or four times. Is this a Hollywood production? Even worse, is there not even one erotic scene?" As the director leaves to avoid a fight with the producer, Zeliha says, "But it is turning out to be a good film, an art film." The producer replies, "What am I going to do with an art film?" Zeliha says, "But boss, now the art films sell." The producer rushes behind the director and tells him, "This is what the audience demands: eroticism, violence, or comedy. You must tickle the audience, make them jump out of their seats, and arouse their nether regions." But the director asks the producer to leave the studio; the studio is his domain. As Özkan allows the producer in FB to make a comparison with Hollywood, he also takes part in that comparison because, knowing the conditions of filmmaking in Turkey, he should not have been making films. Nonetheless, he still writes, produces, and directs films and dreams of putting Yeşilçam into the world scene.

In FB1, M1 and Z1 befriend each other, while K1 is left alone. The next morning, K1 comes in, sees both Z1 and M1, and asks for coffee. But K1, played by Kadir, is indeed played by Kadir İnanır, who, as a film star, is known to be one of the most macho seducers of women. Naturally, K1 gets his coffee. After breakfast, M1 starts to pack her clothes and leaves K1's house. FB1 is about the sacrifice of a woman who loves her man. But in FB, during an intermission and sitting in her *jeune damme* chair, Zeliha appears to be flirting with the director while Kadir and Meral sulk. Zeliha is the *jeune damme*, not Meral.

During the filming of a long traveling shot, the director tells the crew to give full steam because they have one chance to shoot it for they are about to run out of negative film. The director yells for snow, K1 and Z1 partake in this love scene, and the producer arrives and starts to watch along with a film critic (Komet). While the crew keeps remounting a three- or four-meter-long piece of rail to create the effect of a traveling shot on a fifty-meter-long railing, the producer says, "This is acrobatics! If you are going to make them lovers, put them in a bed and let them make love." The critic, with the producer, nods his head, "You are right.... For some reason, our directors do not make do with their limitations and thus they end up being laughable." When the director comes to talk with them, the film critic hands him the pie he brought for the crew and repeats the same criticism. After the director thanks the critic for the dessert, the director throws the pie in the critic's face. This must be the not-so-secret desire of Özkan himself, who, in the article quoted above, goes on to blame critics and spectators:

As for the press, it continually refers to "the crises of Turkish cinema" and this clichéd feeling of "support" is fed by the "ooh, ah," exclamations written under the erotic photos of the players in the film. On the other hand, apart from those experienced film critics who sincerely follow the developments and attempted self-renewal in our cinema and its results, there is also another group who rejects and judges everything. I have not seen this group write a critique for a long while. They constantly, crudely attack Turkish films in particular. It is as if the condition of existence and acceptance as somebody important is through rejection. I have not yet read a single line from this group about the aesthetics, language or the form of a film. Having tasted blood, they make incessant war cries, "Not good," "a disgrace," "a disaster," "a travesty," "must be hung," "must be thrown away." I cannot understand where this hatred comes from and why it has been sharpened so much. Yes, it is possible to talk about a disaster in this country, but of what does this disaster consist? (1993, 73)

But in FB, there is also a silent character who watches the dynamics between the director and the producer, the players and other crewmembers. Though he does not talk, he is the studio's tea deliveryman who witnesses everything from his peripheral placement. As such, more like a nonprofessional player, he seems to be the "real" tea deliveryman of FB's set, representing the spectators, whom Özkan blames for being prejudicial. Because the spectators address domestic films saying "This is 'a Turkish film'," they are prejudiced: "The 'intellectual' spectators' faction watch the film to reject it, they do not care about any value in the film. Thus the extraordinary liberty of rejection and judgment is fully experienced" (1993, 73). In contrast to the "prejudiced," "fake-intellectual" spectators, Özkan's tea deliveryman stands for the "real" spectators for whom the film is made. It is because of this that rather than siding with the critic, he grins when he sees the director throw the pie in the critic's face.

The same day, the crew party together but Kadir stays outside without joining them, so Meral takes him a drink. Then, it starts raining outside in FB, and the crew goes out to dance in the rain. Similar to FB1's fake snow, here it is apparent that this scene was made on a sunny day and the rain is from watering cans and hoses, again emphasizing FB's impoverished special effects. After dancing in the rain, Zeliha comes back inside and lies to Kadir saying that she had repeatedly cheated on him. Kadir starts beating her up and Meral asks the crew to intervene. Zeliha steps on the stage made for the concert scene, Kadir follows her, and hits her with a metal pipe as the crew watches from among the chairs in the seating area. Divided from the action by a proscenium, all of the crewmembers are thus made into the spectators of the film, and Kadir stands alone on the stage while Zeliha lies on the floor, dead. So Kadir, who cheated on his ex-wife Zeliha himself, punishes her for lying by killing her. On the other hand, in FB1, it was M1 who was taking off, sacrificing herself to allow K1 and Z1 to be happy. While in the "art film" FB1, K1, and Z1 are the protagonists who lived happily ever after, in the self-reflexive, realist film, the "macho" Kadir, who sleeps with Meral, kills Zeliha because of her supposed indecency, while in real life, Kadir İnanır and Zeliha Berksoy did not have any relationship at all.

Writing from Özkan's category of "intellectual" critics, Kurtuluş Kayalı sees self-questioning as a widespread tendency in Turkish cinema and criticizes this tendency of self-reflexivity because he thinks such questioning is on the surface or superficial, without touching on social issues. Punning on the film titles, he notes, "Perhaps *A Big Solitude* [*Büyük Yalnızlık*] is being experienced. Maybe at some point it will be said that *The Film Is Over*" (1990, 7). Indeed the film was over in 1990 when, at the Third Ankara Film Festival, Kayalı criticized the directors of these two films, Memduh Ün and Yavuz Özkan, for belonging to the "old" Yeşilçam and demanded a reconsideration of post-1980 Turkish cinema. While Kayalı, through the majority of his statements, seems to fit Özkan's category perfectly, there is still some truth to them. The films of the 1980s were questioning themselves and at times, this questioning was esoteric and excessively self-reflexive, and a feeling of solitude was at hand. Though receiving awards at national film festivals, Yeşilçam's filmmaking practice was coming to a close, leaving more space for newcomers to the cinema world.

In the six-year period from 1991 through 1996, a total of 311 films were made, including 16mm films. Among these 311 films, only seventy-four were shown in theaters—a problem also experienced in the cinemas of European countries at that time. However, Agah Özgüç, who supplied the these numbers, mentions a series of novelties introduced in this period, such as an increase in the quality of filmmaking; cinema complexes with well-developed projection systems, modern interior design, and computerized ticket sales; newly opening film ateliers serving young people; and an increase in the number of short films (1997, 5). Özgüç also added that, except for these technically superior films generally distributed by Hollywood majors, the remaining films were mostly made for television, to some extent maintaining Yeşilçam's practices (1997, 6). As such, novelties in the production, distribution, and the exhibition network of cinema in Turkey were changing how cinema was made and conceived. In this respect, *The Film Is Over* was a timely film. Just around the time of the end of film as Yeşilçam knew it, or simply when *Yeşilçam Was Over*, Yeşilçam became excessively self-reflexive, by reflecting on its own reflection, by imagining its own imagination, by dubbing its own dubbing, and by dealing with its own fallacies while creating more of them. What remained hereafter was nostalgia and bereavement, irony and agony.

"The People of Our Street"

Following its persistent growth in the 1950s, Yeşilçam was very popular and dynamic in the 1960s, and it turned into "our street," a communal world of departure, from oneself or from other selves. As actor Ahmet Mekin noted in his 1961 article, "The People of Our Street," every street has its own characteristics (1961, 17). The name of the street is Yeşilçam (lit. green pine), but nobody knows why: there are no pine trees on the street. Mekin continues:

> The people of our street...do not live on their own street...the mornings are wild on our street. Yelling, shouting, conversations, and excitement....Cars, cameras, projectors stand in front of the offices of producers, and boxes and boxes of raw film are carried about. Stuntmen...snack on whatever they can find....Directors, reviewing their work plans for the day, determine the cast of players. At such moments there is nothing to say to the anxiety or the annoyance of the producers if one of the main players has not been seen yet....this is the cacophony just about every day on our street. No doubt one day, we will have big studios and a housing complex set up for the artists around it. And in this manner OUR STREET will become history. Even if this is a *hayal*, I like it.

When *Yeşilçam* was over, "our street" had indeed lost its dynamism. "The people of our street" did not go to a *Cinecitta alla Turca*; instead it moved to the studios of television stations or various production companies that popped up in the newer business centers of Istanbul. Yeşilçam, much like the republic itself, imagined in a constant state of crisis and thus being never good enough to compete with cinemas it imagined, gave way to a new practice of filmmaking. Until its demise in cinema, as shown in film theaters, Yeşilçam had always been expected to perform under the guises of intellectual and republican elite perspectives. But these demands were all based on comparisons to the West and to other film industries that were thought to be a step ahead of Yeşilçam. Thus, Karagöz had to have a *hayal* and *özenti*, he had to visit and learn from the world of Punch. That was his task, but before going to the world of Punch, Karagöz was not simply traditional or feudal. (Similar to Karagöz, Yeşilçam belonged to a masculine world, too.) Instead, Karagöz had already discovered ways of dealing with the Western medium in which he was, in his own right, a player.

Haunted by the late Ottoman period painter Şeker Ahmet Paşa's painting, *Woodcutter in the Forest*, John Berger writes that the painting involves a subtle strangeness in its use of perspective. After explaining the spatial ambiguities and perspectival problems of the painting, Berger notes that, "academically speaking," these are the painting's "mistakes"; "they contradict for any viewer...the logic of the language with which everything else is painted. In a work of art such inconsistency is not usually impressive—it leads to a lack of conviction" (1980, 80–81). Berger adds that these mistakes are not conscious, but unintentional, which leads him to ask two questions: "Why was the painting so convincing...how did Şeker Ahmet come to paint it in the way he did" (1980, 81)? While the farthest tree looks closer than anything else in the painting, Berger also thinks that this double vision has an authority about it. "Its precision is existential. It accords with the experience of the forest." For Berger, there is no horizon in the forest; as the forest embraces you, you are simultaneously inside it and seeing yourself from outside it. This situation in Şeker Ahmet Paşa's painting is due to the two opposing ways of seeing that Şeker Ahmet inherited: one European that he learned in Europe and the other Ottoman-Turkish. While the former relies on physical space and its perspectival representation, the latter, for Berger, is based on spiritual space, signs, and embellishment. "Light was not something which crossed emptiness but was, rather, an emanation. For Şeker Ahmet the decision to change from one language to another must have been far more problematic than might at first appear to us" (Berger 1980, 82–83). So for Berger, Şeker Ahmet had to have an ontological shift to a spatial perspective vanishing on the horizon of unilinear time. For Berger, Şeker Ahmet is distinct from Courbet or Turgenev in that he identified with the woodcutter and saw the forest as he does, instead of looking at it as a "scene" from the world as conceived by realists. Şeker Ahmet's is related more to earlier narrative forms that are "more two-dimensional, but not for that reason less real. Instead of choice, there is a pressing necessity. The only choices are about treating, coming to terms with, *what is there*" (Berger 1980, 83).

As I have tried to elaborate above, Yeşilçam's realism was of a different mold, one that is of the natural more than the real and one that is direct, dealing with "what is there." It is a realism that is "irrefutable, expected, and unexpected" in a combination of two-dimensionality, oral narration, and life despite its attempt to be realistic like Courbet or Turgenyev. So the failure and mistakes of Yeşilçam in this respect are not because it is less real than that of the Western cinemas, but a different experience of life (i.e., reality), introducing a double vision, that of Karagöz and Punch simultaneously. In a sense, Yeşilçam is like Şeker Ahmet who expressed himself in a Western medium but brought with him an Eastern makeup. Certainly such a clash of two separate entities, even the pairs of a binary opposition, could not have produced something other than an ambivalent synthesis. From the point of view of Westerners and the westernized elite, it would at times seem a facile and failed imitation and at other times a distorted imitation that offers various avenues of analysis. From the point of view of the majority of its historical spectators, it would combine entertainment with a sense of reality—it was not coincidental that many of the villains of Yeşilçam were sworn at or attacked when recognized on the streets. From the point of view of the contemporary spectators, at times it would be a good source of laughter, at times television entertainment, at times a source for the remakes of television serials, at times a field of study, and most of the time a nostalgic era that would be remembered with longing, and with a barely perceptible grin.

When asked whether Yeşilçam was determined by the feudal order and the rural populations of Turkey, Özön disagrees and talks about how Yeşilçam was acknowledged by the rural populations: "There is a tradition, an oral tradition; which I have called Karagöz cinema. That obliterates our cinema" (1996, 6). Indeed, Yeşilçam was not destroyed when it was telling these stories, but rather when the rural or urban spectators with rural origins were no longer paying for the tickets to go to a film theater and acknowledge these stories through the medium of cinema. However, these stories have not withered away; instead they keep being repeated on various television channels, not only through series and serials but also through reality and quiz shows. What happened in the meantime was a shift toward a younger, educated, urban, modern, and westernized demographic of film spectators. This new generation of spectators grew up watching Yeşilçam films on video or television, and in their minds Yeşilçam now belongs to these media.

Before these developments, the mood in the late 1980s and the early 1990s was dim and depressed, and many people in Turkey were hopeless, not only about the future of Yeşilçam but also about the future of cinema in Turkey. Nevertheless, there were some who had an instinctual belief in cinema itself. One such figure was FB's director, Özkan who said,

> The word hopeful would not suffice to explain my feelings. I believe that our cinema is getting ready for living through extraordinary times. The Turkish cinema has given the initial signs of leaving behind a period of search and transition. Now it is at pains to be a cinema that will be talked about more in Europe and then in the world. These days, when they say that our cinema is over, is ending, I feel like it is boiling like the mouth of a volcano. Nowadays, our cinema experiences the impatience of creating its own language, aesthetics, and a strikingness (*çarpıcılık*) that certainly will settle down soon. It is determined to quickly get rid of its insufficiencies of script, dialog, and rhythm. By solving these problems in a short time, it will first embrace our people and then flow outside its borders. That is what I think. You might question how it is possible to be that hopeful under such insufficient conditions. We have worn down the seemingly impenetrable shield of impossibilities enough. We will all see that this belief of mine is not merely a utopian vision. (1992, 65)

Yeşilçam was about rhizomatic growth, melodramatic modality, Turkification, *hayal* and *özenti*. To realize its *hayal* and *özenti*, and to grow persistently, aggressively, and violently, like Karagöz, it paid a visit to the world of Punch. There it made an agreement with Punch, with Hollywood in particular, that would later bring back some Hollywood majors. Upon Karagöz's return, however, Turkey was in sociopolitical stasis, under the violent repercussions of the military intervention. So during that standstill, coupled with an experience of the West, Karagöz reflected on himself and in his reflection he saw a void that reflected his own image to his own eye. As he kept reflecting upon his image, he became increasingly self-reflexive. Only after such experiences of Karagöz did it become possible to talk about a new cinema of Turkey, a cinema able to go beyond a particular mode of production, distribution, and exhibition beyond a nationalistic zealotry and a particular melodramatic modality. Though these changes have taken place, the age-old problems between popular and serious cinema, realist and melodramatic film, have not withered away. Instead they have taken a new form. On the one hand, new popular films have caught up with parts and portions of Hollywood's finesse, thanks to money coming in from Hollywood majors, private television channels, and corporate sponsorships. These films continue to be popular. However, the divide that has come to the fore is the distinction between popular films and art and auteur films, as well as with what one may call contemporary trash films. Though the second category does not generally do well at the box office, it has brought about a filmic discourse and narrative with fewer "flaws," with a particular economy of the image and of narrative, and with critical acclaim both in Turkey and abroad. Under the new global capitalist conditions of filmmaking, such is the state of cinema in Turkey. Connected with two bridges, one dating to 1973, the other to 1988, and with an undersea tunnel in the making, cinema in the hometown of Yeşilçam, in Istanbul, remains on the Asian or Anatolian side, or in the tunnel, while the looming question is about the strait in-between. In the next chapter, crossing one of the two bridges or yet-to-be-made tunnel will be at the center stage, while the strait in-between will demarcate one with the other.

7

Postmortem for Yeşilçam
Post-Yeşilçam, or the New Cinema of Turkey

> From one singular to another, there is contiguity but not conti-
> nuity....All of being is in touch with all of being, but the law of
> touching is separation; moreover, it is the heterogeneity of surfaces
> that touch each other. Contact is beyond fullness and emptiness,
> beyond connection and disconnection. If "to come into contact"
> is to begin to make sense of one another, then this "coming" pen-
> etrates nothing; there is no intermediate or mediating "milieu."
> Meaning is not a milieu in which we are immersed. There is no
> mi-lieu [between-place]. It is a matter of one or the other, one and
> the other, one with the other, but by no means the one in the other,
> which would be something other than one or the other.
>
> —Jean-Luc Nancy 2000, 5–6

Recent studies on national and transnational cinemas have attempted
to move away from the closures, limitations, and suppression of the
national to openings, transgressions, and liberations of the transnational.
However, in dissecting the nation, these studies have used catchphrases
such as "imaginary," "mythic," and "communal" to fix the nation and the
national into a totality that can only be challenged with tropes such as
"transnational," "hybrid," or "hyphenated." While reworking the concepts
of national cinemas, some scholars have criticized poststructuralist theories for disregarding nations or filmmakers and shifting their emphasis
solely toward texts. Alternatively, theories that emphasize the bridging
and connection between cultures are inclined to look for continuities and
similarities as they underline marginalities or transculturation as third
spaces or melting pots.

Rather than pursuing such critical positions, this chapter will underline
three singularities that inaugurate separations and touches: the national
and the transnational; popular and art/auteur cinema; and cinema and new
media. Instead of commenting on mediation or remediation, contemporary cinema and new media are singularities, already multiple and touching each other. While vernacularization and purification—what has been
described previously as "Turkification"—may be understood as cinematic

tactics to restore the national to which the transnational responds or transgresses, singularities work through separations and suggest differences and disjunctions. In this singular plural presence in a community of the world, each singularity is exposed, posited from its outside, without internalization and externalization, and thus without giving way to preconditioned cultural and racial purities and multicultural syntheses or hybridities. For Jean-Luc Nancy, "[A]ll of being is in touch with all of being, but the law of touching is separation" of "one with the other" but not "one in the other." Through rendering "post-Yeşilçam" or the "new cinema of Turkey" with this perspective, this chapter will first give a critical overview of theoretical discussions on national and transnational cinemas. It will then focus on the separation between popular and auteur cinema while tracing the cinematic developments. Finally, it will outline the changes and developments that have taken place during the post-Yeşilçam era, touching on the separation between cinema and new media, while maintaining the necessity for a novel understanding of cinema in Turkey.[1]

Contemporary Cinema: National with Transnational

The scholarship on the post-Yeşilçam period, called the new "Turkish" cinema or the new cinema of Turkey, is deeply inflected with the world and transnational cinema discussions and theoretical positions mentioned in the introduction. For instance, following Kevin Robins and Asu Aksoy's "deep nation" arguments, Catherine Simpson sees "Turkish cinema's resurgence," in terms of hybridity and bridging. She describes Fatih Akın's documentary *Crossing the Bridge: The Sound of Istanbul* (2005) as "a metaphor for a city in the throes of re-imagining its destiny and identity....Istanbul's hybrid identity is constituted through being on a 'bridge' that produces a perpetual state of 'crossing'" (Simpson 2006). However, this view, which attempts to pinpoint an identity for Turkey, is inclined to see "one in the other," instead of "one with the other." Instead, in writing on contemporary European cinema, Thomas Elsaesser notes the refusal of coproductions and contemporary auteurs to be seen as "artists" or "nationally representative figureheads" (2005, 491). "Fatih Akın, who let it be known that he prefers not to be typecast as a hyphenated ethnic director, and if he cannot be Fatih Akın, he would rather be the new Scorsese than represent the German-Turkish constituency" (2005, 498). Akın's remarks are significant in understanding a departure from national or transnational cinematic discourses. For Elsaesser, contemporary auteurs are interested in "how well local/national provenance can communicate with global/transnational audiences" (2005, 491). This places Akın and other contemporary directors working on a cross-national stage out of the boundaries of the national and transnational and within the ranks of world cinema, which should not been taken as a blank signifier but instead as a novel way of conceptualizing a group of filmmakers and an insightful opening for film theory.

In his preface to *Traditions in World Cinema*, after noting that both world (as a sign of cosmopolitan relativism) and cinema (as consumed through various media) are problematic concepts, Toby Miller argues that world cinema is a sign of "commodification and governmentality, dominated by the First World and subject to technological change, but at the same time as a way of transcending the categories of nations" (2006, xi–xiv). Elsaesser, who sees world cinema as a reworking of Third Cinema without its political agenda and as a term modeled on world music or fusion food, underlines that it is "adept at mixing idioms, more transnational" in terms of style, while often being "a star and genre cinema, where the star may be a director" (Elsaesser 2005, 496–98). For him, world cinema is more suitable for international markets and can be better understood through the hegemonic and imperial patterns of postindustrialist economies of scope, with its focus on niche markets, customized demand, global marketing strategies, outsourcing, and new forms of financing (2005, 499–500). In terms of its funding, world cinema relies on various sources of support, ranging from public funds to private sponsorships, both national and international. Thus Elsaesser takes world cinema not as a production category, but in terms of the distribution and exhibition patterns that determine its production process, through festival support and the induction of auteurs into world cinema circuits and video market shelves (2005, 504).

Elsaesser interprets these developments in relation to Hollywood and European cinema. After underlining Toby Miller's view of post-Fordist Hollywood in which its marketing determines the production at four levels ("sales" in all markets, "advocacy" through the promotion of the brand and acceptability, "surveillance" with intensive market and audience research, and "reassurance" through quality control and standardization), Elsaesser contrasts it with the European model with its focus on "representation" and "identity," and its mixed, small-scale, and hybrid production handled with a constellation of producers for a single film (2005, 506–7). In demarcating contemporary European cinema, Elsaesser uses the example of Akın's auteristic tendency to underline how Second Cinema's auteurism and artistic leanings have made the national converge with the nation-state. He indicates how its hostility to Hollywood has been undermined through Akın's defiance of national or transnational identities in the name of a kinship between his work and that of Scorsese (2005, 486–87). Thus like Hamid Naficy's "accented cinema" or the enlargement of its scope by Asuman Suner, according to Elsaesser, this new auteurism is a postindustrialist one that, as in the case of Asian cinema, offers elements of postmodernist self-conscious irony and references, eclectic or pastiche-like narrativity and style, as well as postindustrialist marketing through festival circuits (Elsaesser 2005, 496). While late Yeşilçam's auteurs and art films could be seen as fitting well within Elsaesser's earlier scheme of European cinema marked by a practice similar to Second Cinema, post-Yeşilçam's auteurs seem to fall into his category of European or world cinema.

Elsaesser's view of world cinema, which relies on "identity politics" with interplay and competition between national identity and local or regional themes through addressing a global audience, brings about narrativity focusing on spatial changes and displacement through journeys and travel due to changing conditions (2005, 508). He terms world cinema "art cinema light" due to its mix of mainstream narrative strategies with local or national themes and thus sees it as an upgrade over "post-national cinema prior to auteur status," which reflects the cultural sphere of neocolonialism through self-exocitization and auto-ethnography (2005, 509). The auteur tradition of Yeşilçam, which originates in Yılmaz Güney's late social realist films and which was subsequently continued by the self-reflexive and art films of late Yeşilçam auteurs such as Ali Özgentürk, Erden Kıral, and Ömer Kavur, may be considered in relation to Elsaesser's prior category. In contrast, post-Yeşilçam auteurs such as Fatih Akın, Ferzan Özpetek, Nuri Bilge Ceylan, and Zeki Demirkubuz are the auteurs of postindustrial, global cinema administered by the art house and festival circuits. For instance, while one film critic calls Ceylan and Demirkubuz's films "new auteur cinema" (Dorsay 2004b, 11), a study on Kavur that considers the director as an auteur—following Andrè Bazin and Andrew Sarris's criteria for auteur cinema and Peter Wollen's structuralist analytical tools—claims that during the late Yeşilçam era, Kavur's auteur status was strengthened by his films' failure at the box office, even if he worked with Yeşilçam's star actors (Kuyucak Esen 2002, 25). However, this guarantee of "popular failure" has, despite similar failures in the post-Yeşilçam era, been replaced by a fragmentation of audience market. Nowadays, auteur films are specifically marketed for niche spectators and auteurs have become stars in their own right. Even some first-time directors of the post-Yeşilçam era begin their films with the favorite phrase, "A [insert the director's name here] film," in an attempt to create the image of an auteur as a star. As Timothy Corrigan observes, "auteur film" has become "a critical tautology, capable of being understood and consumed without being seen" (1998, 50). The promotional use of auteurs as brand names implies an autonomous creative force that seems to contradict the system, by turning auteurism into "a marketing tool that coincided nicely with the rise of college-level film education among the industry's most heavily courted audience segment" (Cook 1998, 35). In contrast to this rendering of auteurs as brand names, avid supporters of auteur cinema keep demanding consistency, unified personality, and originality, as well as a leftist political edge from their favorite auteurs. However, this novel frame of global cinematic auteurism is commonly inscribed by inconsistencies, fragmented and diasporic identities, self-conscious references, and a departure from political activism. For instance, after noting that the sixty-three new directors who made their first films in the period between 1987 and 1997 constitute a new group, Giovanni Scognamillo, in reference to the director Ömer Kavur, terms the new generation of art cinema directors as "individualist" filmmakers who stay away from social issues and realistic dramas. For him, these art cinema directors modeled themselves on experimental European cinemas by remaining blind to the audience demands (1998, 478–79). More radically, some film critics and scholars have claimed that figures such as Fatih Akın or Ferzan Özpetek are not Turkish, that they are Orientalists or even traitors.[2]

Elsaesser maintains that European filmmakers should follow the diasporic auteurs' identification of themselves as auteurs by refusing to be recognized through their hyphenated identities, and proposes that European filmmakers should open themselves up to world cinema. He augments this argument through introducing "double occupancy," which underlines "the co-existiveness of symbolic and ethnic identities" and "the overlap of media representations, racial stereotypes, and day-to-day discriminations" (2006, 650–51). However, this search for an influence to come to the world of mainstream filmmaking through diasporic films, that is, the possible influence of minor economies of representation over the major ones, indeed reverts to the arguments of Third Cinema, which relied upon the dislocation of First and Second Cinemas through revolutionary films. However, this possibility of teaching from Akın's or other diasporic films, which, according to Elsaesser, are "at once tragic, comic, and utopian," respectively marking pathos and self-torment, irony and contradiction through mistaken identities. In offering a shared space, they constitute one aspect of contemporary film in Turkey and elsewhere.

This search for lessons from other sources, asking mainstream popular cinemas to learn from auteur films, and this idea of sharing through double occupancy reproduces a view of mélange and its discourse of mutual enrichment. In relation to arguments about multiculturalism, hybridization, exchange or sharing, Nancy notes that "this well-intentioned discourse... remains a discourse of intentions and exhortations" (2000, 148). The national learning from the transnational, the mainstream popular cinema sharing with the auteur or art cinema, and cinema becoming a hybrid through the new media, are all instances of such discourses. Identity, be it Turkish, European, or non-Western, is nothing but separation: no-*thing* for it is not a substance that can be "pinned down," and separation because "it is always the other of another identity" (Nancy 2000, 149). Thus, sharing, mutual enrichment or exchange between singularities is not a thing precisely because "cultures... do not mix. They encounter each other, mingle, modify each other, reconfigure each other" (Nancy 2000, 151). There are no melting pots that contain differences, nor spaces simultaneously occupied by two or more things, but instead, for Nancy, there is melee, which is of action, of fight and love, of meetings and encounters, of the two sexes in each one of us (2000, 150–51).

Of contemporary cinema, then, it could be said that it is neither national nor transnational, neither popular nor art, and neither cinema nor new media; instead, similar to culture, it is of these singularities, each of which is single and unique. As there is no pure and simple origin, as previously asserted through the discussions on the first Turkish film, both the culture and cinema of a nation should be seen as already multicultural, "because the gesture of culture is itself a mixed gesture: it is to affront, confront, transform, divert, develop, recompose, combine, rechannel" (Nancy 2000, 152). Taken in this sense, the identity of a cinema is already itself, "an ipseity, a 'being-its-self'," which is "necessarily impossible to identify" (Nancy 2000, 153). Then, in this community of films, which we call "cinema," the sense of common or "being-in-common excludes interior unity, subsistence, and presence in and for itself" because, as Nancy puts it starkly, unitary communities are responsible for death, not "the sort of death found in the cemetery...but the death found in the ashes of crematorium ovens" (2000, 154–55). Thus instead of digging for a national cinema by taking it as a unitary community of films, here it is maintained that these singularities touch each other in exposing their limits, and instead of inviting deep nations or double occupancies, touch leads to melee, with assault, rivalry, desire, dialogue, fear, pity, laughter, bifurcation, substitution, concurrence, and configuration. Thus this sense of community, the melee of singularities, is not mythical; it does not presuppose myths of learning lessons, prescribing mixtures, or practicing unities. Instead, unlike myth, which is "projected and pronounced," "what is written, and what is to be read...is the *mêlée* of the traces of a meaning that gets lost in looking for itself and inventing itself" (Nancy 2000, 157). In this chapter post-Yeşilçam, a postmortem to Yeşilçam, is "written" as a cinema featuring the national with the transnational, popular mainstream cinema with auteur cinema, and cinema with new media.

Tracing the Posts and Separations

While finding English-language sources on cinema in Turkey before 1990 is very difficult, what many film critics and scholars call the "new Turkish cinema" has been well-covered in both film magazines and journals (see Dorsay 1989a, Dönmez-Colin 2008, Erdoğan and Göktürk 2001, Robins and Aksoy 2000, Simpson 2006, and Suner 2009). In looking at this new phase of the history of cinema in Turkey, many of these scholars, like their counterparts who have published works in Turkish, argue that the new Turkish cinema is different from Yeşilçam and also introduces a separation between popular or mainstream cinema and art, auteur or independent cinema. The myth of origin of the new Turkish cinema is often considered christened by *Eşkıya* (The Bandit, dir. Yavuz Turgul, 1996), which is often taken as a "true" Turkish or domestic film. This sense of the validity of the national, which is deemed "new" through its resurrection or rebirth, implies a moment of Turkification, with which comes a sense of melancholic and nostalgic pathos construed in the renewal of the past. For instance, viewing Turkish cinema's "resurgence" through an unraveling of the "deep nation," one article invites "collective melancholy" to understand the cinematic and sociocultural transformations in Turkey (Simpson 2006). Similarly, another film scholar observes that a new generation of filmmakers has formed its "own language" despite the influence of tabloidization, sensationalism, and media attention. Thus the rejuvenation of Turkish cinema in the 1990s is not based on intellectual considerations so much as on an increase in film numbers and ticket sales (Pösteki

2004, 28–29).³ Alternatively, Dorsay titles his collection of film criticisms written between 1990 and 2004 "The Years of Collapse and Renaissance," taking this to be a "resurrection after death" and a comeback of Turkish cinema by "traversing even the fanciest American films" and sees "a generation of homegrown directors" behind this success (2004a, 11–14; 2004b, 11). Thus, perhaps, it has been the "homegrown" post-Yeşilçam directors who must claim the national more than, say, Yeşilçam directors. But what made the directors homegrown? How can one constitute the authenticity and validity of the nation? When did post-Yeşilçam's homegrown directors enter into the film scene?

From the mid-1980s to the late 1990s, Hollywood films dominated the market, spectators were mostly a young, urban population frequently disparaged as Americanized youth, and the majority of Turkish films did very badly at the box office or bypassed theaters altogether, going directly to the video market or television. Scognamillo has noted that between 1989 and 1996, from 485 films made, 385 were not shown in theaters (1998, 425). It is only in the last decade or so that some Turkish films have done well at the box office, but these films are mostly funded by new capital and frequently distributed by Hollywood majors. In the meantime, like the traditional newspaper industry of Turkey, Yeşilçam was undermined

Figure 7.1. *Selvi Boylum Al Yazmalım* (The Girl with the Red Scarf, Atıf Yılmaz, 1979), a High Yeşilçam melodrama which turned into a contemporary cult film

by a new economic order. As Turkey became more of a capitalist economy and integrated with the global capitalist system through the privatization efforts of the government, newly urbanized capital started to control the media. Private television channels that emerged in the 1990s supported films in return for broadcast rights, while sponsorship deals with big companies have also become standard for films. As an active exchange of personnel among cinema, television, and advertisement industries has appeared, filmmakers have started to work for television series and serials and some directors of television commercials have also made films.

Yeşilçam's demise and the beginning of post-Yeşilçam could be observed in yearly reports of cinema in Turkey. Since 1991, the magazine *Antrakt* (Intermission) covered these developments through Agah Özgüç's yearly reports that, for instance, compared the number of films made in 1951, thirty-six, with those in 1991, thirty-three (1992, 12). For 1992, Özgüç noted that while many theaters had closed down, the new ones opening were devoted to exhibiting Hollywood films, forcing out the domestic films and leading them to find other ways to reach their audience: "If a film is longer than ninety minutes, it is turned into a serial film by dividing it into two or three episodes. If there is hope for finding an open slot at a film theater, this time serials made for television are shortened and summarized into ninety-minute films" (1993, 79). Then, during the 1993 season, though new film theaters were opened and the festival scene was promising, and an unprecedented eighty-three films were made, only eleven were shown in pocket-sized theaters (Özgüç 1994, 12). The domination of Hollywood majors in the distribution networks of Turkey after the late 1980s not only signaled the eventual dissolution of Yeşilçam's distribution network but also marked the introduction of a novel economic infrastructure for filmmakers. The distribution and exhibition of domestic films in Turkey were done by U.S. companies Warner Brothers (WB) and United International Pictures (UIP), while the two other Turkish distribution companies in the market, Özen and Avşar Film, relied primarily upon imported films.

During the early 1990s, only four domestic productions were listed among the fifty films with the highest box office revenues. As a Yeşilçam-size blockbuster, *Amerikalı* (The American, 1993), a comedy starring Şener Şen and directed by Şerif Gören, with 354,656 spectators, was sixth on this list of highest-grossing films.[4] However, this did not mean that domestic films had a significant share of box office revenues. Along with a change in the profile of the spectators, who had become mostly young, educated, and urban, the balance between the box office revenues of foreign and domestic films also shifted. Scognamillo noted that while in 1978 domestic films were seen by 58.2 million spectators, this number fell to 3 million in 1992. While altogether only 7.8 million tickets were sold in 1992, this figure, which increased to 34.9 million in 2006, still falls short of the high Yeşilçam-era figures, especially when one considers the concurrent rise in population. For Özgüç, despite the domestic film producers' complaints, films with enough commercial and artistic appeal had a chance to play at the best theaters with the best promotion through advertisements handled by the Hollywood majors in Turkey (1994, 13). Similarly, discussing the "winds of change" in cinema, film producer Sabahattin Çetin said,

> The 1990s will bring about major changes...the media boom...has been promising....The filmmakers who are thinking through the conventions of the old production mode will have major difficulties because cinema has entered in a process of an organic integration with the other media. This situation will bring forward a new type of producer: this producer is a cultured man who knows foreign languages, who is familiar with world and European cinema, and who contemplates projects with his/her European counterparts. (Baran, Yavuz, and Arslanbay 1993, 77)

Indeed, such was the case with the integration of the Turkish economy to the global capitalist market that resulted in partial Hollywood domination of film distribution and exhibition, as well as with the introduction of European coproductions through Eurimages.[5] In the decade after 1992, both the number of spectators and film theaters quadrupled, while after 1997, every season at least 200 films have been exhibited in theaters (http://www.fidafilm.com/ffinc/tr/ff_04_01.asp). While the majority of these are Hollywood films distributed by the three major distribution companies (Özen, WB, and UIP), all of these companies also started to distribute and at times produce domestic films. During the apogee of the Yeşilçam era, Turkish distribution companies imported Hollywood films often at least a year after their exhibition in the United States because they waited for a decrease in the import costs of mainstream films. One extreme example was *The Exorcist*, which was not shown in Turkey until the early 1980s. Moreover, the copies of films that came to Turkey were generally scratched, old copies that had previously been shown in European theaters. Both the entry of Hollywood majors into the distribution market and the marketing tactics of global Hollywood changed this situation by leading the shortening or elimination of this time gap.

As film critic Mehmet Açar notes, this may also be related to the economic liberalization and changing structure of the spectatorship in Turkey (1995, 1189). The demands of young, educated urban spectators in the late 1980s prompted the improvement of film copies and theaters. As of 2006, while there were around 200,000 seats in 411 theaters with a total of 1,300 exhibition halls and/or screens, half of these seats were in three big cities, Istanbul, Ankara, and Izmir (Yavuz 2006). These three cities, which include almost one-third of Turkey's population, account for 63 percent of ticket sales. Moreover, three major chain theater companies, owned or partnered by global firms and operating mostly in these three cities, have over 300 exhibition halls holding 44 percent of the total number of seats. While the domination of the West in the global media industry eventually diminished the share of non-Western countries in their own domestic popular markets and raised the issue of cultural dominance, this domination of the film market has not eliminated non-Western film production altogether. Post-Yeşilçam reflects this new global cinematic dynamic very well, with a combination of local and international capital in production, distribution, and exhibition networks.

As indicated by three surveys done for Fida Film in 1999, 2002, and 2006, the majority of cinemagoers in Turkey are young, educated, and upper-class spectators. While 62 percent of film spectators are upper or upper-middle classes, the percentage of female spectators rose from 37 percent in 2002 to 49 percent in 2006. In 2002, 44.5 percent of all spectators were between the ages of 15 and 24 and 41.7 percent were between 25 and 39. In 2006, these numbers changed slightly to 40.1 and 47.8 percent, respectively. In response to a question about their film preferences, the 2006 survey participants indicated the importance of a strong cast (78.1 percent) and an attractive subject or genre (72 percent), whereas they indicated that the following would make them to go to film theaters more frequently: actors they like, 62.7 percent; cheaper tickets, 46.1 percent; directors they like, 32.7 percent; and European and festival films 31.7 percent. Apart from the expected star and genre appeal, this survey indicates an awareness of auteurs and art cinema in line with, as indicated above, the rise of global auteurs. Since the early 1990s, apart from overtly popular mainstream films, two nationalistic films, a fiction work by Ziya Öztan, *Cumhuriyet* (The Republic, 1998), and a documentary by Tolga Örnek, *Gelibolu* (Gallipoli, 2005), made the list of top fifty films as of 2008: thirty-fifth with 753,000 spectators and thirty-seventh with 673,000 spectators, respectively. An independent low-budget comedy by Yüksel Aksu, *Dondurmam Gaymak* (Ice Cream I Scream, 2006), came in forty-second with 636,000 spectators and the much-delayed 1999 release of Yılmaz Güney's banned film *Yol* (Road, 1981) gathered 459,000 spectators. However, the placement of these films in the category of post-Yeşilçam auteur or art films is very problematic because, except for Yılmaz Güney, who was a Yeşilçam actor and director, none of these directors are considered post-Yeşilçam auteurs.[6] Instead, the films of post-Yeşilçam auteurs such as Nuri Bilge Ceylan, Zeki Demirkubuz, or Yeşim Ustaoğlu sold tickets ranging from 2,000 to 73,000. The only exception to these trends are the films of Fatih Akın and Ferzan Özpetek, who perhaps as global diasporic auteurs, were able to gather more attention from the domestic box office with some of their films.[7]

However, among recent domestic blockbusters (generally made with a budget from close to a million dollars to as much as several million dollars), those that received wider attention relied on either stars or genres, and no auteur or art films were among the top-grossing films. The ten top-grossing films as of early 2008 are *Eşkıya* (2.5 million tickets), *Vizontele* (dir. Ömer Faruk Sorak, 2000, 3.3 million tickets), *Kahpe Bizans* (Harlot Byzantium, 2000, 2.4 million tickets), *G.O.R.A.* (dir. Ömer Faruk Sorak, 2003, 4 million tickets), *Vizontele Tuuba* (dir. Yılmaz Erdoğan, 2003, 2.9 million tickets), *Babam ve Oğlum* (3.8 million tickets), *Organize İşler* (Magic Carpet Ride, dir. Yılmaz Erdoğan, 2005, 2.6 million tickets), *Hababam Sınıfı Askerde* (The Class of Chaos in the Army, dir. Ferdi Eğilmez, 2005, 2.5 million tickets), *Kurtlar Vadisi: Irak* (Valley of the

Wolves: Iraq, dir. Serdar Akar, 2006, 4.2 million tickets), and *Recep İvedik* (dir. Togan Gökbakar, 2008, 4.3 million tickets). While the only Hollywood film among the ten top-grossing films in Turkey since 1996 is *Titanic* (dir. James Cameron, 1997, 2.8 million tickets), there are only three other Hollywood films in the list of the twenty top-grossing films. As for the ten top-grossing domestic films, four of them were distributed by Warner Brothers, and ten of the twenty top-grossing domestic films were distributed by Hollywood companies (nine by WB and one by UIP).[8]

While the picture above inscribes the globalization of the film market in Turkey, not only in terms of distribution but also through coproductions, European support, and international cast and crew, it also underlines a discord between popular and auteur cinema. These top-selling films were unanimously popular in the domestic market but, apart from *Kurtlar Vadisi Irak*, which became infamous for its anti-Americanism, others attracted little international attention. The majority of them were also released in European theaters in countries where there was a considerable Turkish migrant community, such as Germany, Austria, the Netherlands, and France. Instead, Turkey has recently been, as noted above, exporting "auteur films" to the scene of world cinema and festivals.

Others have also noted this change in filmmaking, film, and film culture over the last two decades, especially after the rise of private television channels that re-ran Yeşilçam films in the 1990s before starting to produce their own series and serials.[9] Engin Ayça, who pointed out that Yeşilçam is not over but has changed its medium, asks whether it is possible to argue that "cinema can only exist in film theaters...or is it time to have a different approach to the issue? Is cinema a different thing now" (1994, 51)? Ayça's explanation of the changes that came after Yeşilçam deals with film culture and how it adapted to television. For him, during the high years of Yeşilçam, those who watched foreign films (the westernized elite) were seeing a very limited number of Yeşilçam films. With television (and videotapes) Yeşilçam's spectators were introduced to foreign films dubbed in Turkish. For Ayça, these developments encouraged the elite and the masses, as the spectators of two different strands of cinema, to learn each other's language, thus increasing their tolerance of each other's tastes. He also notes that television exposed its viewers to different forms of narrative film, especially documentaries, which had been totally ignored by Yeşilçam. "Therefore their culture and the language of seeing cinema got diversified. So today's Yeşilçam spectators have not given up their tendencies, but have become more tolerant, able to have more perspectives and open to various products" (Ayça 1994, 52).

Post-Yeşilçam Era Clashes and Convergences

Turkey's rapidly changing socioeconomic profile points to a significant young workforce who can, at the same time, serve as a large audience for cinema in Turkey. Turkey's population has risen from 35 million in 1970 to 70.5 million in 2007. While 60 percent of the population was living in villages or rural areas in 1970, this number fell to 30 percent in 2007. The average age of Turkey's population is twenty-eight years and only 7 percent of the population is over sixty-five, whereas 26 percent of the population is under fifteen. While in 1970 only 1.7 percent had graduated from a university and 3.2 percent were high school graduates, as of 2006, 9 percent were university graduates and 18 percent were high school graduates (Erdem 2007). As Turkey changed from an agricultural economy in the early years of the republic to an industrial one (currently four-fifths of exports are industrial goods), the GDP per capita also rose from 538 dollars in 1970 to 10,472 dollars in 2008.

Concurrent with these changes and the increasing influx of global economic networks and technologies into Turkey, political life has also experienced various transformations and turning points: an ongoing process of democratization and privatization with which the main axis of political bifurcation in Turkey has become the separation between Kemalists and Islamists. While a series of Islamist parties became more and more visible in the political arena during the 1990s, two military warnings or memorandums also underlined the gap between the Kemalist military and the Islamist parties. The first of these memoranda, commonly referred to as a "postmodern" military intervention consisting of a military warning to the politicians in lieu of an outright coup, came in 1997 and led to the closure of one Islamist party RP (Welfare Party), which was then replaced by FP (Virtue Party). After FP was closed, it was replaced by two parties in 2001, the more traditional Islamist SP (Felicity Party) and the more moderate AKP (Justice and Development Party), which has been the ruling party in Turkey since 2002. In a manner reminiscent of the 1997 "postmodern" coup, in early 2007 the Kemalist military again warned the AKP government, this time with an electronic letter (thus the name "e-memorandum") published on the Turkish army's Web site. Despite echoing the horrors of previous coups, especially that of the 1980 military intervention, none of these coup "simulacra" produced the hardships of earlier coups, such as the freezing of political life, mass jailing, or capital punishment.

Leaving behind the often-unpleasant political history and various socioeconomic and political changes of the last couple of decades, the main axis of politics and society has shifted considerably. After the fall of the Berlin Wall and the end of the bipolar world system, Turkey has lost its critical role as an ally to the West through NATO. However, while the yearnings for a greater role in Central Asia did not come through, Turkey has still been able to integrate itself into the processes of globalization. On the other hand, despite various democratizing reforms, the rights of minorities are still more limited than European Union directives guiding Turkey's bid for membership.

These developments mirrored the influence of the world of cinema. Apart from opening itself up to the practices of global film business by coproducing with European countries and Hollywood, and apart from the recent influx of Bollywood filmmakers shooting films in Turkey, contemporary domestic cinema has also reflected on global capitalism (*Çinliler Geliyor* [The Chinese Are Coming, dir. Zeki Ökten, 2006]), its relations with the European Union (E.U.) (*Avrupalı* [The European, dir. Ulaş Ak, 2007]), the war in Iraq (*Kurtlar Vadisi Irak, Deli Yürek Bumerang Cehennemi* [Crazy Heart: Boomerang Hell, dir. Osman Sınav, 2001], *Maskeli Beşler Irak* [The Masked Five: Iraq, dir. Murat Aslan, 2007]), its international conflicts and ethnic minorities (*Güneşe Yolculuk, Yazı-Tura* [Toss-Up, dir. Uğur Yücel, 2004], *Büyük Adam Küçük Aşk* [*Hejar*, dir. Handan İpekçi, 2001], *Bulutları Beklerken* [Waiting for the Clouds, dir. Yeşim Ustaoğlu, 2003], *Salkım Hanımın Taneleri* [Mrs. Salkım's Diamonds, dir. Tomris Giritlioğlu, 1999]), and its discourses about religion (*Takva* [Takva: A Man's Fear of God, dir. Özer Kızıltan, 2006], *The Imam* [dir. İsmail Güneş, 2005], and *Anka Kuşu* [*Simurgh*, dir. Mesut Uçakan, 2007]). Such a constellation of films is neither surprising nor novel, for Yeşilçam too responded to Turkey's international conflicts with, say, the Korean War or Cyprus conflict films, or to its internal strife through social realist films. Instead, what is specific to post-Yeşilçam is auteur cinema's treatment of these issues, which remains outside the reach of popular filmmakers, as well as the separation between secularism and Islamism, which has found its reflection in the contemporary horror films of Turkey, as will be discussed below.

As part this recent snapshot of Turkey, the traditional middle classes, which had constituted Yeşilçam's family spectators and who had largely fallen by the wayside during the 1980s, made way for what could perhaps be termed as a new middle class. In this new urban existence, not only have the differences between lower and middle or upper classes become apparent and exist side by side, they have also allowed for the everyday visualization of cultural differences between what may be termed the new middle classes, nurtured by a global culture of professionals or internationalized work force, and the comparatively more traditional culture of the lower classes. This new middle class, referred to by some as "white Turks," has also been contrasted with another culturally different newly emergent middle class, which fosters an altered, globalized version of Islamic culture. However, these strands of the new middle classes converge in terms of their consumerism, which is supported by a move toward suburban, *site* life.[10] In this new middle-class milieu, there is "a powerful desire for escape from pollution, street life, and social heterogeneity, as well as an emphasis on family intimacy and rule-bound society and order" (Ayata 2002, 26). However, this novel everyday practice, confined by the self-enclosed apartment complex communities, has also produced segregation determined by the overriding identity of individual apartment complexes. For instance, research on the secularist Ankara suburbs indicates that the everyday life of these apartment complexes bespeaks class, gender, and culture differences (Ayata 2002). Despite higher levels of education among the women of this new suburbia, they are still strongly aligned with domestic roles. "The community is also defined by what it excludes: city life and its vulgar mix of the lower classes, the new rich, and the Islamists" (Ayata 2002, 30). In other words, while being integrated into global consumerism with shopping malls crowned by chain theaters, unlike the new rich, these residents of suburbia indeed are the republican elite version 2.0, who, with the extreme shifts in the economic makeup of the country, have partially adapted to postindustrial life while gradually losing the republican political and economic center to the new rich and the Islamists.

However, gated communities and *site* life are not limited to the secularist middle classes of yore. Instead, the new rich are also a part of this life, including the globalized, new urban elite, the Islamist bourgeoisie, and the nouveau riche with a rural, traditional background. Rather than assuming a cultural and civilizational gap between the secularist elite and their Islamist counterpart, Nilüfer Göle instead notes that the rise of the Islamic elite and intellectuals is tied to a historical backdrop that had been invisible to the republican elite until the outbreak of Islamism in the 1980s (1991, 132). While the republican elite has relied upon its own conservative, centrist version of modernization and westernization, the new urban middle classes' rendering of rural, traditional culture came in two forms: one is, as it is commonly termed in the 1980s, *arabesk* culture, and the other is Islamism. While both of these seemed to be alternative existences with, to some extent, oppositional and dissident voices, both of them also maintained their integral hierarchical and gender-coded segregations. For instance, by noting that the new, urban-style headscarves of Islamist women had become a political symbol marking Islamic opposition and resistance to the objectification of women by the male gaze, Göle notes that this dynamic of the separation of looking and seeing also meant a male privilege, because only those entitled to see had a chance to unveil the concealed privacy (1991, 135).[11] After noting that Islam's challenge of secularism was played out through women in the 1990s, another scholar argues that the justification of both secularists and the Islamist lifestyles of women, as argued by those women themselves, relies on narratives of "nativity to Turkey," "locality," or "authenticity" (Navaro-Yasin 1999, 60).

Post-Yeşilçam's cinematic world reflected similar tendencies in its mix of popular cinematic languages through a sophisticated visual narration and the ongoing but limited Turkification of Western films, whereas contemporary auteur cinema has represented the vernacular internationally. However, this does not mean that one of these ends dominates the other, nor are the stresses of globalization free of their discourses. Instead, as Çağlar Keyder comments on Istanbul as existing between the global and the local, and between the West and the East, while carrying the contrasts of extreme wealth and extreme poverty (1999), or as Deniz Kandiyoti notes the influx of global economic, social, and cultural schemes through an uneven mix of economic liberalization, the proliferation of goods and services, and the deterioration of traditional and mostly public service-based middle-class incomes (2002, 4), Turkey has opened itself and its cinema to the world, both globally and locally. With the rise of the nouveau riche, both secularist and Islamist, in private businesses and multinational corporations, Istanbul and other metropolises have started to present a proliferation of consumerism with chain theaters, malls, super-markets, international brands, and restaurants. "There is a polarization of space but also cohabitation of heterogeneous populations. There is a negotiation over cultural heritage, not outright war. Battles are waged, but compromises are also reached" (Keyder 1999, 26). In other words, such changes have led to the presence of the global with the local, secular with the religious, and rich with the poor.

In this era of post-Yeşilçam, the domestic film industry also opened itself to global cooperation and support schemes, especially that of Eurim-ages. With Turkish citizens living and shooting films abroad, the success of domestic films at international film festivals, and international film festivals hosted in Turkey, the post-Yeşilçam film industry has also pro-liferated through the division between popular cinema and auteur films. What all of these changes, in both popular and art cinemas, have put for-ward has been the long-postponed industrialization of the film market. Nonetheless, in the post-Yeşilçam world, Yeşilçam continues to exist in the quickies produced mainly for use as television serials. After the end of the Yeşilçam era, cinema has become a product integrated into the general frame of media industries and thus global capitalist markets, especially through distribution networks in Turkey. Thus contemporary cinema in Turkey is fundamentally different from Yeşilçam, even though its partly cultic reception is enmeshed with its projected and recollected nostalgic simplicity, innocence, and morality.

While the resurgence of cinema in Turkey implies an insurgence against Hollywood, it could also be viewed in terms of its uneven movement. In the preceding chapters, Turkification and Yeşilçam are, in one respect, placed as forces creating continuities and forcing alterities into unities. Post-Yeşilçam, though not free from Turkification and Yeşilçam, is also inscribed by unevenness and thus separation of one from the other. While its resurgence seems to cater to the visibility of ethnic minorities, such unevenness also indicates violent disturbances as films roll. Despite the limited visibility of others, the oscillation between highs and lows and the separations inscribed in contemporary Turkey seem to be veiled. In other words, contemporary popular cinema in Turkey has yet to account extensively for Islam and Kurds, both of which are partially visible but still outside of secularist parameters.

Secularist incursions into post-Yeşilçam have not yet been able to dis-tinguish themselves from its nationalism and identification with national cinema. While one aspect of Turkification fell into the confines of the sec-ularist republican projects, the challenges to contemporary renderings of Kemalism brought forward a competitive understanding of Turkish identity, subjected to mythic originary and unitary claims by Kemalists, nationalists, and Islamists, as well as by Kurds and other ethnic minori-ties. However, some scholars of cinema, such as Robins and Aksoy, also acquiesce to the limits of this search for mythic origins as they opt for the "multi-cultural, multi-confessional, multi-lingual" projection of the late Ottoman Empire by remaining obstinately blind to its calamities ranging from colonialism, slavery, violent oppression of the empire's others, and the dominance of religion in legal and political stratification (2000, 204). The Ottoman Empire, an *ümmet state* that identified itself in gathering the Muslim community of the world and was led by an emperor entitled to be the caliph, caters to the other side of contemporary melancholy and nostalgia reproduced by intellectual circles through a mythic projection attempting to diverge from the nation-state's vices and to search for its primordial state. Within the confines of this misconception, since the nation-state is taken to be a purifying and cleansing entity, whatever existed before its induction must be multicultural. While this postmodern nostalgia implies a longing for a supposed "valid" and "true" originary state, it can only be found in the past and thus cannot be retrieved. However, the defenders of Ottoman multiculturalism and multilingualism reproduce Francis Fukuyama's postmodern closures of history and Samuel Huntington's reiteration of civilizational clashes, remaining blind to the religiosity of the empire.

The global revival of religious discourses and civilizational clashes has coincided with three separations in Turkey: between the West (the European Union in particular) and the non-West (Turkey in particular), the secular (Kemalists) and the Islamic (identified with the ruling AKP), and Turks (nationalists and the Turkish army) and Kurds (Kurdish nationalists and the PKK). Despite the so-called transnationalist moves, nationalism is not withering away, but instead creating violent outbreaks against non-Turks and non-Muslims living in Turkey. "Nationalism is now kind of a protest on the part of those who have found themselves excluded from the contemporary global order, a movement of disaffected young men against an international 'regime of civility'" (Stokes 1999, 129–30). The killing of the Armenian Turkish intellectual Hrant Dink or the attacks against Christian priests in 2007 can be understood as instances of such outbreaks. While such xenophobic violence is unanimously criticized by the mainstream Turkish media, the media, and specifically cinema, also help augment the potential for such acts through nationalistic coverage of news and production of nationalist narratives, such as those of recent nationalist action-adventure films. Seen in this vein, the separatist discourses in Turkey about nation, religion, and culture have also been expressed cinematically through various reactions harking back to discourses of nationalism and Islamism and through openings pointing to alternative avenues.

Post-Yeşilçam, the new cinema of Turkey, inscribes these separations, their communality, and melee. While secularist media in Turkey continue to reinterpret and reproduce their version of Kemalist westernization and modernization, their Islamic counterparts, in addition to their usual religious propaganda, air documentaries on Leonard Cohen, do remakes of *My Name Is Earl*, and visualize the proliferating culture of Islamist bourgeoisie. If film theory, with regard to non-Western countries, were to attempt to understand what is going on in such worlds of cinema, it would have to leave behind its nationalist or transnationalist outlook in order to see how this unevenness converges and clashes through McWorld and Jihad. In other words, categories such as the national or the transnational and the film theory that reproduces them still presume clear-cut distinctions and segregations that cannot account for this unevenness of references and tropes. Such categorical imperatives are implemented with a theoretical violence compelling mélanges, without paying attention to the melee of singularities. However, this wildly contradicting programming is already about the mingling and modification of cultures in which meetings and encounters occur.

"Yeşilçam Film": *The Bandit*'s Postmortem to Yeşilçam

The success of Yavuz Turgul's *Eşkıya* (The Bandit), a nice surprise for many with more than 2.5 million tickets sold, reintroduced discussions of what constitutes "Turkish film." While Turgul deemed it a "Turkish film," underlining its domesticity and authenticity, *Eşkıya*'s popularity converged with nostalgia and melancholy, partly as a postmortem to Yeşilçam. "Yeşilçam film" or "Turkish film," a novel genre, offers various characteristics: marking Yeşilçam's irretrievability, this genre constructs an imaginary and mythic past that is communicated through nostalgia and melancholy. After noting that standard Yeşilçam films have recently been perceived as "a joke, synonymous with bad taste and banality,"[12] Asuman Suner claims that "the tropes of home and belonging" offer a thematic continuity between contemporary popular and art films, related to an anxiety of identity (2004, 306–7). For her, this "ghostly" house inscribes the trace of the past and the return of the repressed, as may be observed in the ghostlike female characters of contemporary films or popular nostalgia films' inability to turn their references to minority cultures into ideological or political issues (2004, 209; 2006a, 14–15). Unlike Frederick Jameson's sense of "nostalgia film," which entails the restructuring and projection of "pastiche" onto "a collective social level" and which "attempts to appropriate a missing past" through fashion and generational recuperations (1993, 75), and unlike Suner who considers *Eşkıya* a "nostalgia film" by placing nostalgia in relation to the freezing of the past as a "social childhood period" (2006a, 73), the genre of Yeşilçam film offers to fill, via melodrama, the modernizing moral gap opened between the past and the present. These films that claim to reiterate an authentic past offer the innocence and purity of a bygone era through the selective memory of the nostalgic gaze. After the various socioeconomic and cultural transformations that paved the way for the integration of Turkey into the global capitalist system after 1990, Yeşilçam film also indicated a further revival of the duality between the modern and the traditional, where the melodramatic storyline introducing unrequited love, as in the case of *Eşkıya*, served as filler. Thus following Linda Hutcheon (1998), the genre Yeşilçam film is not a postmodern genre, where nostalgia is "called up, exploited, *and* ironized," nor a clash of innocent childhood with an evil, grown-up present, but instead a "revivalist" genre, offering the melodramatic search for a lost authenticity.

The dynamics of this filler marked a shift in terms of gender identity through a new genre of masculine melodrama to which *Eşkıya* belongs. In the film, after serving thirty-five years in jail, the Kurdish bandit Baran (Şener Şen) discovers that his village has been deserted due to a dam project and then goes to Istanbul to find his beloved Keje (Sermin Hürmeriç). Despite managing to find her, he discovers that he cannot be with her and so throws himself from the top of a building toward immortality. Bringing together elements of Yeşilçam's melodramatic modality, this new genre of Yeşilçam film has also marked an important shift. Box office hit tearjerkers with high production values, such as *Babam ve Oğlum*, *Beyaz Melek* (The White Angel, dir. Mahsun Kırmızıgül, 2007), *Kabadayı* (For Love and Honor, dir. Ömer Vargı, 2007), and *Gönül Yarası* focus on new challenges faced by male characters, and thus could also be called male weepies or masculine melodramas. In this meta-Yeşilçam vocabulary of melodrama, men in search of identity voice a demand for recognition from women, who, as the loci of this conferring and powerful gaze, are pushed to the fringes of the narrative.

While male weepies fit into the general frame of new cinema in Turkey that is narratively male-centered, popular cinema's interest in the Turkish East is also inscribed through nostalgia and nationalism, which caters to a gap between modernity and tradition. The Turkish East constitutes not only the predominantly Kurdish areas in southeastern Turkey but also the underdeveloped parts of Turkey and the bordering countries that fell under the rule of the Ottoman Empire. *Eşkıya* and many other box office hits of the new cinema of Turkey such as *Vizontele, Vizontele Tuuba, Propaganda* (dir. Sinan Çetin, 1999), *Beyaz Melek, Maskeli Beşler: Irak, Deliyürek:*

Figure 7.2. *Eşkıya* (The Bandit, Yavuz Turgul, 1996)

Bumerang Cehennemi, and *Kurtlar Vadisi: Irak* deal with Turkey's Eastern problem, that of the Kurds, who in these films cannot speak in their own language. While the first four of these films deal with the internal East, the other three often point to external others through southeastern Turkey. However, carrying the persisting stains of urban Turkey's past, such films often refer to traditional and rural bonds, which are nowhere to be found in modern life. Thus the theme of travel is commonly found in these films through the internal or external spatial dislocations of the main characters. However, in line with the new urban culture, of which the rural and the traditional have become integral parts, these travels often voice the impossibility of a return to village life. Indeed, two years before *Eşkıya*'s release, a hit *arabesk* ode to village life by Ferdi Tayfur highlighted this impossibility: "Let's go back to our village/Dance at the wedding of Fadime." However, as the lyrics of the song also indicate, this return is like Baran's desire, only wishful thinking. Masculine melodramas are, in a sense, about a crisis of gender power, reflecting the rural Anatolian man's helplessness and castration in urban centers, because of the different credo of urban life, as may be seen through the duo of Baran and Cumali (Uğur Yücel), a petty mafioso character named after a character played by Yılmaz Güney in *İnce Cumali* (Slim Cumali, dir. Yılmaz Duru, 1967). In the city, the bandits are replaced by petty, lower-class criminals who cannot completely adapt to urban life, thus raising the impossible aspiration of going back and retrieving rural patriarchal dominance. Baran's main opponent, Keje's husband, represents a strand of the nouveau rich, which, despite its rural, traditional, and Kurdish background, does not aspire to go back to the village.

Seen by many as an epic film, *Eşkıya*, like the Yeşilçam films it tries to revive, is also about various silences and unutterable realities. Assuming that Baran the bandit was captured by gendarmerie on Cudi Mountain around 1960 or 1961, when the high Yeşilçam period started, in 1995 or 1996 that same mountain was a war zone where the Turkish army fought against PKK militants. This shift from premodern banditry to contemporary political violence is also underlined in Istanbul where Baran meets Cumali. While the rural bandit is replaced by the urban mafia, warfare, or violence, the film, despite the characters' obvious Kurdish names, does not make any deliberate references to Kurds and their sociopolitical situation. Instead, because of her love and forced marriage, Keje chooses to remain mute, not speaking to anyone, until she sees Baran. Keje's silence brings about issues in relation to the suppression of women through traditional patriarchy, echoing Gayatri C. Spivak's arguments about the dual suppression of subaltern women and their tactics of resistance through rejection. Hence when given voice in Turgul's film, Keje speaks in Turkish with Baran. This is the contemporary "Yeşilçam film" that revives Yeşilçam's cinematic narratives as well as its ideology and silences and its Turkifying aggression and violence, which become increasingly handy with the increase in the number of male-centered narratives of new cinema in Turkey.

Was *The Bandit* the Mythic Origin?

This second aspect of post-Yeşilçam, the predominance of masculine texts in cinema, has been a frequently discussed issue among film critics and scholars who note that there are no female-centered plots and no romantic comedies or melodramas with professional female characters. Post-Yeşilçam, in many of its regular dramas or comedies, relied on a formulaic repetition of male-centered plots that, in the case of comedies, indeed revive Yeşilçam's tradition of comedies, relying upon a rehashing of traditional comic characters. As a hit comedy before *Eşkıya*, *Amerikalı* (The American, dir. Şerif Gören, 1993) carries various tropes of male-centered plot, parody, and westernization. Şeref the Turk (lit. Honor, Şener Şen), who became rich in the United States, returns to Turkey in search of his childhood love Melek (lit. Angel, Lale Mansur). Whereas the parodic use of melodramatic overtures of evil plots by villains and fallen women inscribes the film's distanced relationship with Yeşilçam, *Amerikalı* is also a parody of Hollywood films incorporating episodic references to the hit films of the era such as *Pretty Woman* (dir. Garry Marshall, 1990), *Thelma and Louise* (dir. Ridley Scott, 1991), and *Home Alone* (dir. Chris Columbus, 1990). Relying on cultural differences to produce comic effects, *Amerikalı* again uses a journey between East and West in which the westernized Turk finds out how much Turkey had changed. In a song, Şeref says, "Bridge, tower, subway, pool/Watermelons sold by the slice/Burger, blue jeans, coke, ice/Man, we become Americans." Such an influx of objects and themes indicative of Westernization, concurrent with the globalization of Turkey in the post-Yeşilçam era, encourages a critical look at the changes in Turkey through an implicit criticism of the loss of authenticity and nativity.

Similarly, a few Islamist films such as *Minyeli Abdullah* (Abdullah from Minye, dir. Yücel Çakmaklı, 1989) and *Sonsuza Yürümek* (Walk toward Infinity, dir. Mesut Uçakan, 1991), the earliest box office hits of late and post-Yeşilçam, depicted similar themes related to this loss and westernization. While the secular and/or formal histories of cinema in Turkey often ignore these films that, despite the patchiness of statistics, were very popular in various peripheral metropolitan areas and Anatolian cities, such films with deliberate political messages and activist language supporting Islamism are also not considered "political films" (see Pösteki 2004; Özgüç 2005), but rather "white cinema." While this term, coined by Abdurrahman Şen (1995), attempts to account for the propriety and cleanliness, hence whiteness, of Islamist films, these films could also be seen in direct contrast to secularist films. In contrasting the evil Istanbul with the proper one, for instance, *Yalnız Değilsiniz* (You Are Not Alone, dir. Mesut Uçakan, 1990) opens with the female lead strolling through a modern part of Istanbul, seeing advertisements for beer or female stockings and Wendy's hamburgers or other fast-food vendors, which are set against proper Islamic attitude, such as buying dates from a street vendor to break fast (Arslan 2007, 169). Focusing on the story of a young girl who finds herself in a struggle over the headscarf, *Yalnız Değilsiniz* still carries Yeşilçam's tropes in its melodramatic storyline of stark contrasts between secularism and Islamism, between the misled westernized portions of the population and the true, proper path of Islamic enlightenment. Such religious hits of post-Yeşilçam brought the issue of covered women to the fore, thus joining the headscarf debates in Turkey.[13] The politicization of the headscarf issue in Turkey is an integral theme of these films. However, similar to the covered women's essentially solitary struggle to wear headscarves in public spaces such as schools and government offices, which is not a problem for Islamist men and which is not supported by the secularists at all, Islamist cinematic representations of the headscarf issue are handled by men, much as late Yeşilçam's women's films that were predominantly made by men.

In recent Islamist films, such as *The Imam* and *Anka Kuşu*, Islamist directors have not been able to reframe their outlook and have kept retrieving the melodramatic aspects of Yeşilçam. *Anka Kuşu*, considered a Turkish-Islamic response to *The Matrix* (dir. Wachoski Brothers, 1999), tells the story of a young film director's journey back to the small town where he grew up, which becomes an internal odyssey. In contrast, *The Imam* continues this trope of return to the village and small town as the irretrievable site of innocence and purity. Although it inverts the story of *Öğretmen Kemal*, it nonetheless reproduces the republican project's binaries, presenting the story of a Western-educated professional who finds himself a village imam as he dutifully fills in for his old friend.[14] This time, instead of the village teacher who brings enlightenment to the village, it is the "white" Turk who once was an Islamist who discovers and returns to his self and roots.[15] This neoliberal and neonationalist figure of the "new," "Euro-," or "white" Turk was introduced in 1992 by a veteran columnist, Çetin Altan, who placed their socioeconomically and cultural "civilized" characteristics against the "black" or "dark-skinned" Turks (including Kurds), who are perceived as constituting the "uncivilized," rural, or migrant lower classes (Sumer 2003, 114). However, *The Imam*'s treatment of this separation augments it with a recent, concomitant separation: the one between the secularists and Islamists. While Islamist nationalism shares a sense of anti-Westernism with traditional nationalism, its focus coincides with a nostalgic retrieval of the Ottoman imperial past as the leader of the Islamic world (Bora 2003, 450). The main character, *"the"* imam, initially seen as extremely westernized by the villagers and thus, as in *Öğretmen Kemal*, finds himself forced to communicate with the village's fool. Similarly, Islamic nationalism, or Turkish-Islamism, in contemporary Turkey still relies on the inverted vocabulary of Kemalist nationalism when presenting itself. However, as hinted by the title of the film, *"the"* imam cannot, in the world of contemporary globalization, stay away from the article "the," indicating westernization.[16] Instead, with the rise of Islamic bourgeoisie and lifestyle, contemporary Turkish Islamists have shared and enjoyed globalization.

The Horrors of Contemporary Turkey

While the early 1990s post-Yeşilçam Islamist hit films carried direct political messages, recent Islamist films, in line with post-Yeşilçam, focus on male characters. In this respect, masculine melodramas and their contemporary Islamic counterparts, like İsmail Güneş's *Sözün Bittiği Yer* (When Words Are Not Enough, 2007), are about the helplessness and fragility of fathers who cannot guarantee a good life for their sons—much like the republic, as imagined through the paternal figure of Atatürk (lit. the father of Turks). However, this is a gendered conversation between a father and a son, and here, in the world of male weepies, there is no space for women. While these masculine melodramas serve as moral filler for the contemporary crises of Turkey, their success in this task is open to debate. The male-centered narrativity of post-Yeşilçam is marked by the limited nature of romantic comedies or family melodramas where female protagonists occupy considerable narrative space. While the revival of religious culture may be handy in explaining the limitedness of family melodrama, as the religion and the sociopolitical reflections of proper religious life and attire may be seen as moral fillers, this could only be used to explain the situation of Islamists. Alternatively, televisual melodramas, immensely popular in the last decade, may be seen as additional filler. However, these points do acknowledge that post-Yeşilçam's filmic women are mostly absent or mute because of the ongoing patriarchal regime of the film world and the reflections of general sociopolitical and economic crises in relation to shifting dynamics male power and dominance, from traditional to modern, rural to urban, local to global, and heterosexual to homosexual.

Nevertheless, either because of all of these crises or because of the shift in the spectatorial culture in post-Yeşilçam with the influx of young, educated, and urban spectators who are increasingly aware of Hollywood genres and world cinema, horror films, a nascent genre of post-Yeşilçam, often introduce central female characters *Araf* (The Abortion, dir. Biray Dalkıran, 2006), *Gomeda* (dir. Tan Tolga Demirci, 2007), *Büyü* (Spell, dir. Orhan Oğuz, 2004), *Beyza'nın Kadınları* (Shattered Soul, dir. Mustafa Altıoklar, 2006), *Gen* (Gene, dir. Togan Gökbakar, 2006), and *Küçük Kıyamet* (The Little Apocalypse, dir. Durul and Yağmur Taylan, 2006). These female characters are the monstrous others, directly bearing evil or becoming the victims of evil forces, a characterization that indicates a ensuing threat to the male-dominated, secularist "white" Turk world. Thus these films inscribe an ongoing struggle between Islamism and secularism. In relation to post-Yeşilçam's women, there seems to be a convergence of pre-slasher female victimization and post-slasher monstrosity of women. With reference to Julia Kristeva, after noting that "the place of the abject is 'the place where meaning collapses'," and the abject as a threat to life that must be "radically excluded," Barbara Creed argues that abjection in modern horror texts utilizes religious "abominations" such as "sexual immorality, murder, the corpse, bodily wastes, the feminine body, and incest" and that, in horror films, abjection works in three respects (2000, 65). The first has to do with the crossing of the border between the normal and the monstrous, the second with the abjection of the feminine body, and the third with the construction of the maternal figure as abject. By focusing on Kristeva's differentiation between "maternal authority" as "mapping of the self's clean and proper body" and "a universe without shame" and "paternal laws" as "the phallic phase and acquisition of language" and "a universe of shame," Creed maintains that "virtually all horror texts represent the monstrous-feminine" through an interplay of disgust and pleasure, of bodily wastes and the breaking of the taboo (2000, 68–69). As Creed notes, if it is religion that purifies the abject, then horror films may be seen as a "modern defilement rite" (2000, 69–70). Seen from this perspective, unlike male weepies, which have to do with the paternal law and the shame of guilt in relation to the republican father who "Turkified" his sons, post-Yeşilçam horror films may be seen in relation to maternal authority. However, instead of a menstrual or excremental bodily fluid or waste, as in the case of Hollywood's horror films, post-Yeşilçam's secularist horrors point to another abjection, a metaphorical rendering of the headscarf. Through it, maternal authority, without shame and demanding the clean and proper body as a religious guarantee against all sorts of abominations, is being covered by concealing the "beauties" of the body and blocking the male gaze. In other words, post-Yeşilçam's monstrous females are concomitant with the covered women who are still left out of the state-controlled institutional public spaces and are not allowed to work at government offices or secularist private businesses.

While these films often utilize homegrown Islamic tropes, such as quotations from the Koran and djinns or other creatures of Islamic mythology, they often bring forward a more sophisticated Turkification than their Yeşilçam antecedents, in the sense that they combine the global cinematic vocabulary with homegrown narratives. Among these films, *Okul* (The School, dir. Durul and Yağmur Taylan, 2003) invites a close relation to *Scream* with its popular mainstream appeal and *D@bbe* introduces the vocabulary of Japanese horror cinema through its low-budget aesthetics. However, the majority of these films share their focus on the horrors of "white" Turks. *Okul* centers on upscale high school students; *D@bbe* mashes the Internet and Islam to present evil in the lives of affluent, secular small-town folks; *Araf* deals with giving birth and abortion in the upper middle classes; through the story of a group of archaeologists, *Büyü* introduces an age-old myth about the killing of all of the little girls in a village except one; *Beyza'nın Kadınları* focuses on a serial killer story through various personae taken by the upper-middle-class lead female character; and *Küçük Kıyamet* deals with the hysteria of an upper-middle-class woman about a possible earthquake that might take place in Istanbul. While the female lead characters are mostly uncovered, educated, and urban upper middle class, these films, directed by secular male Turks, involve a metaphorical horror, that of the Islamicization of Turkey. Their horrors, the threats against the secularist "white" Turk world come out of the closet in *Beyza'nın Kadınları*, where the schizophrenic lead female character assumes the identities of different females, especially those of the covered women, as she loses control of her main identity, the wife of a psychiatrist. Beyza's hysterical recollection of her past forces her to cover herself and thus brings to mind the secular mass hysteria about the threat of being forced to cover if the Islamists gain enough political power. However, while this secular mass hysteria imbricates a "white" Turk position, covered women, who are turned into monsters, are not only discriminated against by the secularists but also by the overt patriarchy of Islamist men. Thus the recent wave of horror films, mostly produced by secular young directors and intended for young spectators, often allegorically highlights the obsession with covered women.

Sexing the Differences: Sex Films and Comedies

If, as suggested by Linda Williams, horror is one of the three lowly, exploitative genres (the other two being melodrama and sex), the limitedness of female characters in other genres might be understandable because of the absence of othered monstrous women who are left out of this economy of representation (2000, 219). On the one hand, while horror films, through the abjection of the monstrous feminine, cater to the fears of "white" male Turks and their lust for blood and sadomasochistic urges, contemporary male weepies invite the despicable tears of male masochism and the shame and guilt of initiation to the paternal law in the search of a position between the West and the East, Islamists and secularists, and homosexuals and heterosexuals. On the other hand, one of the most sought-after and dangerous items in the pornographic underworld of Turkey, living through pirate VCDs or DVDs and various Web sites, are sex films featuring covered women, embedded in a locus of taboos and the ultimate danger projected by the Islamist males. As a result, the contemporary underworld of Turkish pornography's locus is the female body where meaning collapses and where the abject as a threat must be excluded. These films reiterate Yeşilçam's dilemma of cuckolds and prostitutes and its appalling contemporaneity with a discursive shift.

While Post-Yeşilçam's mainstream comedies, which will be dealt with shortly, use themes related to sex for marketing, and while there are currently many television stars and models who invite sexploitative (mis)uses of the media, there are no "publicly-known" porn films or stars in Turkey. Instead, the world of pornography, still aligned by the prostitute and cuckold double, is either maintained through pirated copies of porn films, the Internet, or through diasporic Turks, especially Sibel Kekilli and Şahin K (Yılmaz). While Sibel Kekilli, especially after becoming (in)famous after her lead role in Fatih Akın's *Duvara Karşı* (Head-On, 2004), received hypocritical media coverage as the "immoral" star of German porn films and the honorable star of contemporary postmigrant and auteur cinema, Şahin K became a veritable star among young, educated Turkish males (Arslan 2008). While obvious gender differentiation and segregation is at stake in the media coverage of the two actors, Kekilli's position is complicated from being disowned by her father because of her past in pornography. Marginalized by paternal authority, Kekilli's situation reflects the postmigrant duality and dilemma set in-between Germany and Turkey, the West and the East, and immorality and morality. On the other hand, Şahin K has become famous with a scene in one of his many porn films produced for a German company, in which he acts and of which he also is a part owner. In the scene, Şahin K, with his big belly, moustache, sandals, and half-erect penis, walks from the sea to the beach as if he is the Mark Harris (Patrick Duffy) of the television series *The Man from Atlantis* (1977) and asks the naked woman waiting for him whether she wants to have his ice-cold penis coming from the sea. After this clip was distributed via the Internet, Şahin K became a hit figure enmeshing his rural background and look as a "dark-skinned" Turk with "ironic" sexual power among young, educated males.[17] Whereas Şahin K, as a witty male star of pornographic films, is often seen with ironic interest, Sibel Kekilli epitomizes an immoral woman, demonized for her part in earlier porn films. However, both of these diasporic actors are understood, according to the ongoing myth of morality, concurrent with the oblivious Yeşilçam era of sex films, to be the others of the nation, living in a world free of the burdens of Turkey, and thus making such transgressions possible.

In addition to postmigrant cinema in which sex may become an overt theme, the digital and ethnic media and cinema underworld of Turkey offer two distinct avenues of consumption. Digital satellite receivers are very common, especially in rural Turkey and, despite sketchy data, these receivers account for one-third of television consumption in Turkey (Çolakoğlu 2006). While the domestic satellite service Turksat, which gives local television channels a chance at national and international broadcast, is the legitimate avenue for this, Hotbird offers two additional options: the Kurdish satellite television channel Roj TV and the porn and film channels. Kurdish-language broadcast in Turkey, which is supposed to be handled by the Turkish Radio and Television (TRT) institution, including feeds in other minority languages, has only been rarely practiced.[18] Instead, Roj TV offers an alternative feed diverging from the formal state ideology of Turkey.[19] In addition, encrypted pornographic feeds and movie channels on Hotbird are also widely consumed through illegal code breaking. Moreover, in the pirate DVD and VCD market in Turkey, both foreign and domestic porn films are widely bought and sold. Thus despite increasing attempts to control the sexual content of the Internet by blocking some Web sites and on television through the RTÜK (The Supreme Board of Radio and Television) by the current government, both ethnicity and sex are commonly consumed through alternative avenues.

While these media have brought about a partial normalization of nudity and sex in the media and in the post-Yeşilçam cinema, both secular and Islamist media in Turkey are open to representing uncovered women through a correlation between nudity and prostitution. However, when it comes to covered women, even the mere idea of women's rights moves one step toward the dangerous terrain of the terror and oppression of Islamist males.[20] Thus perhaps the contemporary counterpart of Yeşilçam's dilemma is another dilemma where the duality between the sexually liberated Western women and the morally decent Turkish women is replaced with one between the sexually liberated and therefore indecent uncovered women and the morally and religiously decent covered women. The looming question here, then, becomes that of the cuckolds and how they changed in the post-Yeşilçam era.

"Youth comedies" present another nascent post-Yeşilçam genre in which the disregard of traditional, Islamist Turkey and mild exploitation themes related to sex have come to the fore. Popular examples of such films include *Çılgın Dersane* (The Crazy School, dir. Faruk Aksoy, 2004), *Çılgın Dersane Kampta* (The Crazy School at the Camp, dir. Faruk Aksoy, 2008), and *Neşeli Gençlik* (Joyful Youth, dir. Mesut Taner, 2007). Both *Okul*, a horror comedy, and *Sınav* (The Exam, dir. Ömer Faruk Sorak, 2006), an action comedy introducing Jean-Claude Van Damme as a secret agent, converge with this genre. Additionally, the remakes of or sequels to the *Hababam Sınıfı* series, *Hababam Sınıfı: Merhaba* (The Class of Chaos, dir. Kartal Tibet, 2004), *Hababam Sınıfı Askerde* and *Hababam Sınıfı 3.5* (dir. Ferdi Eğilmez, 2006), with their usual cast of seasoned, slightly older students at a high school follows a well-known formula of comedy. However, the influx of new youth films indicate an interaction between the films and the spectators who consume them, through a juvenilization enmeshed with high-concept movies and with a redefinition of the cuckold-prostitute duality. Among these films, *Neşeli Gençlik*, a Turkification of *American Pie* (dir. Paul Weitz, 1999), with its slogan, "One day you will get laid, too," was marketed through sexploitative overtones, with scenes introducing nudity widely covered in the media during the release of the film.[21] Unlike 1950s Hollywood, which targeted and exploited teenage audiences with controversial and bizarre plots and substandard budgets (Doherty 2002), the juvenilization of post-Yeşilçam with exploitative teenpics is a co-effectual process, similar to the changes that took place after the blockbuster with high-concept films (Wyatt 1994). Like *Grease*'s (dir. Randal Kleiser, 1978) combination of stars, music, dance, merchandising, and proven formulas, *Çılgın Dersane* may be thought of in line with high-concept films that have a simple, straightforward storyline and that are also responsive to economic changes. Following Douglas Gomery and Robert Allen, Wyatt notes that high-concept films, as will be elaborated shortly, inscribe a due change in the cinematic mode of production through the influx of myriad factors (1994). Post-Yeşilçam's youth comedies, apart from their relation to high concept's juvenilization, offer a converging thematic structure that runs parallel to masculine desires and exploitation.

Various dramas dealing in part with the situation of Eastern European women either illegally coming to Turkey or being forced into sex slavery have also reflected this trend. Mainstream films such as *Balalayka* (Balalaika, dir. Ali Özgentürk, 2000) and *Rus Gelin* (The Russian Bride, dir. Zeki Alasya, 2003) have tried to deal with such problems through the lens

Figure 7.3. *Uzak* (Distant, Nuri Bilge Ceylan, 2002)

of social issues, by fixing the situation of Eastern European women in Turkey through pathological references. On the other hand, the Eastern European woman of *Azize: Bir Laleli Hikayesi* (Saint: A Laleli Story, dir. Kudret Sabancı, 1999) is teleported into the masculine underworld of the mafia before she turns into a locus of the representation of masculine desire and violence in *Gemide* (On Board, dir. Serdar Akar, 1998), *Azize's* sister film. These two films have converging stories through an East European female character who is forcefully captured by one group of males, the ship's crew, and from another group, the mob. These two intertwined storylines are seen by one scholar as "stylistic repetitions, without critical potential," whereas, for instance, Derviş Zaim's *Tabutta Rövaşata* (1996), Barış Pirhasan's *Usta Beni Öldürsene* (1997), Yeşim Ustaoğlu's *Güneşe Yolculuk* (1999), and Zeki Demirkubuz's *Masumiyet* (1997) and *Üçüncü Sayfa* (1999) are taken to deal with "hybrid forms" through "multi-centered" and "multi-vocal" spatiotemporal construction nurtured by an "expressionist" and *"film noir"* climate (Akbal Süalp 2001, 94–95). Similarly, after noting that the "new Turkish cinema" is a cinema of men, another scholar sees these two films as "aestheticizing the plundering of the female body" unlike Nuri Bilge Ceylan's *Uzak*, which makes the male world "estranged and disturbing" (Suner 2006a, 313).[22] In other words, while this inscribes a continuation of criticisms directed against Yeşilçam, in the case of post-Yeşilçam such criticisms cater to another distinction, that between popular and auteur cinema.

Post-Yeşilçam's Postclassicism and High Concept

What is more interesting in the case of *Azize* and *Gemide* is not their representation of male desire and violence, but that their fragmented and interwoven storytelling seems to fit into the mold of contemporary cinema while still maintaining the stylistic tradition of Yeşilçam, as was discussed in relation to *Canlı Hedef*. *Gemide* tells the story of a crew of a small coaster who, on land in Istanbul on a drunken night, find themselves in a deadly fight with the mafia and then capture an Eastern European girl and take her on board, where the plot thickens with lust, seduction, and the girl's eerie silence. *Azize*, on the other hand, is the story of three mobsters who try to find a virgin girl for a mafia boss but lose her in their encounter with the crew in the Laleli neighborhood of Istanbul.[23] Written by Önder Çakar, who also wrote the international award-winning *Takva*, these two films not only offer a glimpse into the masculine underworld of Istanbul but also introduce stylistic clashes, memorable quotes, and metaphorical references to the situation of Turkey. Apart from the stylish slang used by the coaster's captain, both his analogy between the coaster and the country and his emphasis on the destruction of the country either by earthquake or by adultery, caters to self-conscious references to the film itself, as the female saint (Azize), the *belle captive* of a masculine world, turns into the cause of the crew's apocalyptic end.

While it is possible to maintain that both *Gemide* and *Azize* seem to fit well into post-Yeşilçam's novel patterns of storytelling, this point becomes more debatable if one considers similar discussions in relation to classical and postclassical and/or postmodern Hollywood. The recent studies of David Bordwell (2006) and Kristin Thompson (1999b; 2003) propose that despite "novel strategies of plot and style," there is still a coexistence of "change and continuity" in contemporary Hollywood (Bordwell 2006, 1). By naming contemporary Hollywood "modern classicism," Thompson sees the "youthquake/auterist phase" between 1969 and 1977 as "a brief detour that has had a lingering impact on industry practice," but not "harbingers of a profound shift in Hollywood storytelling" (1999b, 4). For Thompson, "auteur" has become both a label and publicity tool of product differentiation for marketing, and led to "juvenilization" by moving minor genres into the mainstream (1999b, 7–8). Despite this detour, with reference to Warren Buckland, who finds the arguments about the new Hollywood's "loosely-linked, self-sustaining action sequences often built around spectacular stunts, stars, and special effects" as "overstated," Thompson maintains that contemporary blockbusters or high-concept films still have "well-honed" narratives, keeping up with a cause-and-effect chain of events marked by progression, clarity, and unity. Similarly, as Bordwell observes, while the basics of storytelling have been extended in three ways (dividing the plot into three acts, maintaining the consistency and plausibility of main characters by making them have a flaw, and the induction of a mythic journey), classical Hollywood's narrational techniques ("appointments, deadlines, causally dense scene construction, a balance of narrow and wider ranges of knowledge, passages of overtness balanced with less self-conscious ones") are still in effect (2006, 28–34, 50). Both Bordwell and Thompson, to support their point about the continuity of narrative forms from classical to postclassical Hollywood, underline the mode of production, the economic structuration of Hollywood as an oligopoly. To make this point, Thompson quotes Douglas Gomery, who underlines the continuing control of majors, while Bordwell notes, "Bazin was right: the 'classical' art of the American cinema is most demonstrable in 'its fertility when it comes into contact with new elements,' integrating them into its distinctive 'style of cinematic narration'" (Thompson 1999b, 4; Bordwell, 2006, 50). Though not openly stated, both of them refer in these arguments to fundamental Marxist theory: Thompson's is the premise that infrastructure determines superstructure and Bordwell's is about the working of capitalism that has the capacity to integrate its opposites.

While this formalist invitation of Marxism to place narration may also be employed in making sense of post-Yeşilçam, the new cinema of Turkey involves intensive changes in terms of the cinematic mode of production, interrelated with the postindustrial economic makeup of the contemporary world that seems to go unnoticed in these discussions. As Richard Maltby notes, postclassical Hollywood illustrates "the end result of the changes initiated by the Paramount decrees, the establishment of a new relationship with the television industry, and the switch of its attention to a younger audience" (1998, 23). For him, this new makeup turned Hollywood majors into financiers and distributors and led them to be more responsive to audience demographics, market fragmentation, and globalization. Similarly, after the departure of the wild capital of Yeşilçam from the movie business, new capital—which includes a mix of Hollywood and domestic majors, minors, media, advertisement moguls, independent producers searching for international collaboration, and to some extent old-style Yeşilçam producers—has appeared. With Eurimages funds and the regulations supporting domestic cinema administered by the Ministry of Culture, independent and first-time fiction and nonfiction filmmakers have also found financial sources and niches in which to make and exhibit their films, even if they may do so only in a limited number of theaters. For instance, two recent big productions, *Kabadayı* and *Beyaz Melek*, with almost 2 million spectators each, cost around 4.8 and 3.2 million dollars and were released in 400 and 260 theaters, respectively. A quarter of these theaters were in European countries with a considerable Turkish and Kurdish population. Both of these films are basically masculine melodramas following the tropes of "Yeşilçam film." *Kabadayı*, which literally translates as hoodlum or bully, is a remake of *Eşkıya* in terms of its narrative tropes and star appeal, again starring Şener Şen as an old-style hoodlum who encounters his new-generation counterpart. *Beyaz Melek*, on the other hand, follows Yılmaz Güney's popular films, with its Kurdish star actor-director Mahsun Kırmızıgül, who became famous as an *arabesk* singer in the last decade. While such well-funded domestic productions are released simultaneously in Turkish and European theaters, this is not the case for independent or smaller productions handled mostly by smaller distribution companies. *Kabadayı* and *Beyaz Melek*, on the other hand, were distributed by UIP and Medyavizyon, respectively.

These big-budget productions attempting to retrieve Yeşilçam's modality may also be seen in relation to high-concept films. While Yeşilçam's narratives marked various convergences and encounters between the traditional and the modern and the Eastern and the Western through non-illusionism, direct address, and reliance upon oral over visual narration, the contemporary genre of Yeşilçam film, with its high production values[24] and simple and direct storylines, marks a break with the Yeşilçam tradition. Visually, these recent films could be aligned with contemporary global popular cinemas and do not reflect Yeşilçam's characteristic non-illusionism or non-realism. Narratively, the genre of Yeşilçam film claims to reflect on contemporary Turkey through a nostalgic retrieval of the innocent and pure past through masculine melodramas offering to fill the moralistic gap. As Wyatt notes, linking a star's persona with a straight-forward concept is critical for the marketing of high-concept films (1994, 10). This is the case for *Kabadayı*, which links a passé bully figure, Şener Şen, with his contemporary version in Kenan İmirzalıoğlu, while the concept links a series of binary oppositions between the traditional and the modern, unrequited love and the happy ending, while dealing with these issues in the contemporary context of Turkey.[25] In addition to the nationalist action-adventures, this is also the case for such recent successful comedies as *G.O.R.A.*, *Hababam Sınıfı* and *Maskeli Beşler* series, market-driven films bringing together a new "look and sound" and "the match between a star and a project, a pre-sold premise (such as a remake or adaptation of a best-selling novel), and a concept that taps into a national trend or sentiment" (Wyatt 1994, 15). In terms of marketing, Wyatt notes that high-concept films offered product differentiation to exploit different market segments, "an emphasis on style" integrated with marketing and merchandising, the promise of a straightforward subject matter and the marketing of this with advertising campaigns, and a glitzy look. In other words, post-Yeşilçam's mainstream films also attempt to encapsulate "the look, the hook, and the book": quality images and visual style, well-defined marketing strategies, and the limitation and straightforwardness of narrative elements (Wyatt 1994, 22).

As Wyatt posits, high concept is a postclassical style of filmmaking "with strong ties to the classical cinema, yet with some significant deviations in terms of composition" (1994, 16). High concept is thus a conjunctural phenomenon that resulted from the convergence of various economic and aesthetic changes. Post-Yeşilçam's hyphenated belatedness, as indicated by the prefix "post-," could then be seen as a result of a myriad of phenomena that are neither limited to the filmic world nor national borders per se. Instead, similar to auteur films' inter-relationality with global film festivals and auteurs, post-Yeşilçam's mainstream also carries similar separations and relations. Aspects of the high-concept film, in the case of post-Yeşilçam, have also coincided with male-centered plots. If, on a very basic level, it is possible to propose a distinction, by looking at genre narratives between action and romance based on their focus on male and female protagonists and on their appeal for male and female spectators, respectively, or if, as John Cawelti notes, formulaic literature relying on archetypes focused on either "adventure and mystery" or "romance, melodrama," and fantasy (1976, 4), then, among the ten top-grossing films of post-Yeşilçam era Turkey, there is only one foreign film, *Titanic*, a romance, and two domestic films, *Babam ve Oğlum* and *Eşkıya*, both masculine melodramas, whereas the remaining are action and fantasy films or comedies, all focusing on male characters.

The masculinist discourse of nationalistic action-adventures has retained elements of Turkey's own past. As a culturally self-colonized country and an extension of an imperial past, Turkey harbors the separation of both colonial and colonized cultures. Similar to early Hollywood's image of the East, which conceptualized the Orient as a world of dream and nightmare, archaic wisdom and contemporary savagery, contemporary cinema in Turkey has dealt with images of the West similarly: while Americans' technological wisdom and power coincided with a portrayal of their savagery and corruption, these films imagined the southern and eastern Turkey and the Middle East similar to Hollywood's image of the East. These nationalist desires, enmeshed with an Ottoman past and its domination over these lands, created an image of the Turkish East and relegated the ethnic and religious minorities, neighboring countries, and women to a taxonomical fold similar to that marked by colonialism. The Turkish West, Turkishness, the nation-state, and men have been set in a hierarchically dominant position in this binary system. In consequence, post-Yeşilçam's high concept is not only made up of myriad factors indicating a particular economic and aesthetic ensemble but also indicates a conjunctural shift with the dominance of a masculinist discourse at different levels in different films. However, while one view of this male-centered narrativity urges for unitary communities, another view may underline the singularities made up ofmelee, of action and exposition and of touch and sharing.

Exposing Limits: Post/Migrants and New Media

The melee of post-Yeşilçam can also be observed through the influx and incursions of postmigrant, diasporic, or transnational cinema and novel forms of cinematic expression through new media and digital technologies, which offer alternative avenues of film production and consumption. These cinematic incursions have not only arrived through further separations acknowledging other forms of sharing and touches but have also posed multiple threats to unitary communities. Migrant or postmigrant filmmakers such as Ferzan Özpetek or Fatih Akın have been subjected to nationalist discourses that deem them as Orientalist or anti-Turkish or to transnationalist discourses that consider them responsible for the possibility or the creation of mélanges. Such transnationalist discourses depend on two historical moments. The first moment of diasporic cinema, or films about migrants in the 1970s and 1980s, such as Tevfik Başer's *Kırk Metrekare Almanya*, as maintained by Deniz Göktürk, is about "enclosure, oppression, and subordination" or about "claustrophobic spaces and scenarios of imprisonment" (2001, 143; 2000, 64). In a second moment, the Bosporus, which separates two loci of insulation, Europe and Asia, has supposedly been crossed by bridges or tunnels. As may be observed in Sinan Çetin's *Berlin in Berlin* (1993) or Thomas Arslan's *Geschwister* (Siblings, 1996), this second moment, for Göktürk, "opens up possibilities of traffic in both directions" and "encounters in 'contact zones'" (2001, 147). For her, this new genre may be described as "postcolonial hybrid films" (Shohat and Stam, 1994) or "independent transnational cinema" (Naficy 2001), which emphasizes a shift from "subnational" to "transnational" by offering "world cinema" that undermines separatist categories such as "third cinema" or "sub-state cinema" (Göktürk 2000, 66).

Whether underground or above the sea, bridges or tunnels are about intersections, about "constructed" connections between two loci of insulation. Fatih Akın's *Yaşamın Kıyısında* (The Edge of Heaven, 2007) illustrates this very well. As the recipient of the first European Parliament (EP) "Lux" cinema prize, it is both a critically and officially acclaimed film. In an *International Herald Tribune* article, Akın is presented as "a filmmaker who builds bridges across cultures" (Kulish 2008). While it is very possible to place Akın's films in relation to various filmic traditions, ranging from Fassbinder's melodramas to Yeşilçam's episodic and unruly melodramatic language or from new American cinema's violent realism to contemporary transnational or multicultural melodramas' self-conscious, stereotypical storytelling, what seems more interesting here is Akın's status as a "European" auteur, as indicted by the Eurocrats. His award-winning film is doubly Europeanized, with the ovation of Members of the European Parliament (MEPs) and with its subtitling in all twenty-three official EU languages. According to EP vice president Gérard Onesta, the prize is intended for "non-elitist films" that represent universality of Europe's values, its cultural diversity, or its integration debates and Lux indicates "a positive version of the tower of Babel, like the European Parliament (EP), a symbol of linguistic and cultural diversity" ("EP's First Lux Cinema Prize..." 2007). Then, the imagination, the myth, and the religious tale comes down to one metaphysical origin, that of the Judeo-Christian, of the Lux, and of the tower of Babel, where all nations and languages must merge in a melting pot, in the same language, in the same body-soul duality in which diversity becomes enslaved and subjected to the idea of a one nation, one God, and a unitary community, a communion. This is the European community that is to be constructed against something, against the domination of Hollywood, as indicated in the interview with the producer of *Yaşamın Kıyısında*, Klaus Maeck, who says European cinema has to "safeguard itself," has to resort to isolation ("EP's First Lux Cinema Prize..." 2007).

Burned by their fellow countrymen and still exposed to deaths reminiscent of those in crematoria, migrants or postmigrants, people of different ethnic backgrounds in different nationalist loci, experience political, social, economic, or cultural melting pots, in which they melt in or are victims of arson attacks as in those in Germany. If cinema has to help such nonelitist enclaves of unitary communities, it is in that imagination of Europe. What if, as Derrida asks in rereading *The Communist Manifesto*, "A specter is haunting Europe—the specter of communism....Haunting would mark the very existence of Europe" (1994, 2–3). Derrida argues that historically there are two specters: the old, mid-nineteenth-century Europe that faced a future specter, the threat of communism, and contemporary Europe faced with a past specter, one without body, "an illusion, a phantasm or a ghost" that also presents a future danger, the possibility of a comeback (1994, 47–48). Derrida offers "conjuration," a word Marx could have used had he written the manifesto in French, because he could have diagnosed conjuration in the new Europe, in the new world order. *Conjuration* means three things: "swearing together an oath to struggle against a superior power," "the magical incantation destined to *evoke*, to bring forth with the voice," and "the magical exorcism...that tends to expulse the evil spirit which would have been called up or convoked" (Derrida 1994, 50, 58). Thus for Derrida, a conjuration marks an alliance and a conspiracy to overthrow some power; for instance, a group of subjects sworn to "represent forces and ally themselves together in the name of common interests to combat a dreaded political adversary, that is, also to conjure it away" (1994, 59).

When the EP brought together filmmakers and the MEPs for "cultural diversity days" when Akın's film was announced as the winner of the first Lux prize, they also discussed the European film industry and its American competition. There, director Cédric Klapisch commented that European cinema was in crisis because of American hegemony and the lack of intra-European circulation of European films, and that European cinema will deteriorate over the next three years due to the digital revolution ("EP's First Lux Cinema Prize..." 2007). Thus the EP must conjure an alliance and conspiracy to overturn American dominance because the EP represents contemporary Europe, which is faced with both a past and future specter: the past of American domination and the future of digital revolution. Thus awards (which could also be thought of as "presents") are presented for films that conjure an alliance and conspiracy, "to exorcise: to attempt both to destroy and to disavow a malignant, demonized, diabolized force, most often an evil-doing spirit, a specter, a kind of ghost who comes back or who still risks coming back *post mortem*" (Derrida 1994, 59).

If it is time, at this end, to venture into exorcism, against a specter that haunts cinema, this would be of cinema's aesthesis, the rationality and positivity of its aesthetics, as Klapisch says, of a past, of the time when films used to be richer, of the days when they were watching Bergman and Fellini ("EP's First Lux Cinema Prize..." 2007). However, how much does Bergman or Fellini appeal to, say, more than 2 million citizens of Turkey living in Germany, who are "widely considered as the most 'alien' group of immigrants in Germany" and for whom the employment rate is the highest (Kosnick 2007, 11, 14)? Here it seems that there are no filiations or hierarchical cultural orders, but various instances of identity and iden-tification that underline bifurcations, contrasts, sharings, and encounters at various levels. For instance, one Turkish-language broadcast in Berlin, Radio MultiKulti, claims a multicultural Berlin just as films by migrant or postmigrant auteurs deal with the themes of travel, searching for or returning home, as well as multicultural and/or homosexual love affairs. In the works of "auteurs" one may observe various things: Akın's prob-lematization of Turkishness through not belonging and reversals of migra-tion between home and host nations, Özpetek's partially veiled refusal of "sexual normality" through queer films and his revisions of Italian identity (Anderlini-D'Onofrio 2004; Duncan 2005), Thomas Arslan's post-migrant characters carrying the stresses of diasporic or transnational identities (Mennel 2002; Gallagher 2006), and Kutluğ Ataman's transitional trans-vestites experiencing a multicultural underworld (Clark 2006). While these works explore these films in terms of border crossings, transnationalities, and postnational arguments, other Turkish-language radio or television feeds in Berlin reflect different ethnic, religious, and cultural claims. The Open Channel, supported by the German government's multicultural policies, was designed to present a televisual public space where migrant populations could voice their concerns. But the Turkish-language broad-casts, done through the Open Channel, reflect the home country's melee among groups like secularists, Islamists, Alevites, Turks, and Kurds (Kos-nick 2007, 183). This may be thought of as happening in "Deutschkei" (i.e., Deutschland-Turkei), which "may be envisioned as a self-contained Turk-ish *ecosystem*...[a] geographically imaginary, yet socio-politically very real sphere...an extension of Turkey than as a part of Germany" (Argun 2003, 6). In Deutschkei, each of these parties approaches Turkey and its intergroup relations differently and they also often find themselves in vio-lent encounters that are extensions of the clashes at home.

While this may reflect the melee of fight in Deutschkei, the melee of love could be observed on *Düğün TV*, a wedding channel broadcasting via sat-ellite and intended for the Turkish population living throughout Europe. As the one-of-a-kind wedding television channel, *Düğün TV* is not about weddings, but instead it broadcasts live or taped wedding ceremonies so that they can be seen by family and friends who could not attend the cer-emony. Advertising itself as the first and only wedding television of the world, *Düğün TV* offers two hours of airtime for a cost of several hundred euros. Those who have families in Turkey incorporate them into the wed-ding ceremony virtually, crossing borders and obstacles, both financial and visa-related. As an upgrade from the popular video film trade and consumption in the 1980s, such a television channel allows the Deutschkei to communicate with Turkey instantaneously. In addition, today Deutch-kei regularly watch Turkish television broadcasts. In addition to online shopping and various entertainment and talk show programs aired on *Düğün TV*, a new television serial, *İthal Gelin* (Imported Bride, 2007) is advertised on the channel's Web site (http://www.dugun.tv). In its unruly combination of jazz, rap, and Azerbaijani folk music, the trailer for the series introduces a theme song where people who are called *"auslander"* (foreigner) in Germany, and *"Almancı"* (Turkish resident of Germany) or *"gurbetçi"* (living abroad) in Turkey call themselves "human beings." Apart from this plea, the channel also airs text messages of Deutschkei people who are looking for partners and thus serves as a commercial community portal. In other words, wedding ceremonies are wed with further possibilities of coupling, as some messages indicate that those who watched the weddings viewed people seen on-screen as possible partners, much as they might look for matches at a live wedding.

Identity, Western or non-Western, could be pinned down to separation, which moves, slides, and takes up other identities by already being plural or multicultural. Virtual communities and new media offer instances of such encounters, minglings, and modifications, not only in Deutschkei but also in Turkey and elsewhere. The Turkish, often leftist or nationalist, criticism of Özpetek's *Hamam* as a self-orientalizing film that carries colonial subplots, or of Akın's *Crossing the Bridge* as misrepresenting Istanbul's music scene with an exotic, touristic gaze, often reflects the critics' understanding of what the Kemalist nation-state should look like rather than an examination of its shifting parameters. These films thus raise a discussion about the dominance of a totalitarian or omnipresent voice, whether secular or Islamist, that attempts to override all others. Akın's or Özpetek's voice is denied representation, denied the capacity to speech, as they see, imagine, or perceive Turkey. Similarly, the denial of the voices of others in Turkey, in the case of ethnic, non-Muslim, and gendered identities, is laced with such lingering claims toward hegemonic and monophonic sound. As noted above, dubbing has been interlaced with Turkification in Yeşilçam and there is still an ongoing practice of dubbing in almost all of the recent television serials, to which contemporary films often gives references. For example, the highly popular television serial *Kurtlar Vadisi* is not only dubbed, but unlike many other television series or serials, the voice of the tough nationalist protagonist of the serial, Polat Alemdar (Necati Şaşmaz), is dubbed by a professional dubbing artist as in high-era Yeşilçam films. Thus the voice in question, or the right to speak, belongs to a veiled dubbing artist in order to represent a character who often silences the minorities or enemies of Turks in the series.

On the other hand, in the post-Yeşilçam era and with the advent of digital technologies, dubbing of both Turkish and other films has left the hands of Yeşilçam filmmakers or the Kemalist elite. The new practice of the dubbing or subtitling of foreign films done by different television channels often censors or alters various dialogues ideologically or religiously. For instance, during dubbing, various Islamic television channels often translate "God" into "Allah" and, in extreme cases, characters such as *The Smurfs* have been turned into a community of Islamic believers. Alternatively, dubbing amateurs, with the help of the popularization of digital technologies, have also started to engage with various Turkish or foreign films by rewriting their stories by dubbing and distributing their dubbed, pirated copies. By producing a mishmash of voices and cultural references, such amateur translations not only glocalize Hollywood but also blur the lines between re-presentational economies. Unlike the muted accent of mainstream dubbing practices, these digital incursions into the world of cinema, which has become a product not necessarily consumed in film theaters, but through computers and other digital technologies, produced various instances of accented voice. Instead of the accented films of world auteurs, these local vernacularizations are known by the name of the place where the "accented" dubbing has been made such as the "Turcomen" version of *Braveheart* (dir. Mel Gibson, 1995) from Kars, the "Çorum" version of *Troy* (dir. Wolfgang Petersen, 2004), and the Turcomen versions of *Gladiator* (dir. Ridley Scott, 2000) and *Titanic* (dir. James Cameron, 1997) both from Elazığ. There is also the Dalga Dublaj Takımı (DDT, The Derisive Dubbing Team), formed by two brothers, Üsame and Sadık Ağırbaşlı, who produce Konya-accented works with religious overtones and local references associated with the culture of the city (Arslan 2006). To these, as noted above, one may also add Kurdish-language popular cinema including various sex films in Turkey that are in distribution in a seemingly underground market.

While these alternative dubbings produced various multiplications of the voice, the *getürkt* economy of pirated films also involves various instances of altered or vernacularized subtitling. These subtitles are often produced by amateurs and distributed through Web sites. Those who download illegal, often DivX format, copies of Hollywood films also download the Turkish subtitles for them and watch these films through computers or DVD players.[26] These subtitles not only introduce a multitude of mistakes but also multiple instances of Turkification or Islamicization, depending on the amateur translator. In a recent translation, when Will Smith's character Robert Neville in *I Am Legend* (dir. Francis Lawrence, 2007) says "There is no god," a note in parentheses followed by a smiley face states "Forswear it, dude" (*(Haşa de ulan :)*) (http://www.iha.com.tr/haber/detay.aspx?nid=8830&cid=11). Such ironic interventions into original texts could perhaps be seen as dismantling the logic of the original, its global bourgeois ideology of individualist creativity ascribed to an artist who has ultimate authority over his or her text.

Instead, such cases of dubbing or subtitling inscribe "remediation" (of both Yeşilçam and Hollywood) inscribing various convergences and encounters. "All current media function as remediators and that remediation offers us a means of interpreting the work of earlier media as well…ours is a genealogy of affiliations, not a linear history" (Bolter and Grusin 1999, 55–56). If remediation involves the remediation of older media, then one of the earliest cases of the postmortem for Yeşilçam is that of 2/5 BZ's work that, through sampling, uses dubbed dialogues from Yeşilçam films in their electronic music. Formed by Serhat Köksal in 1991 as a multimedia project, 2/5 BZ edited together found sounds and performed sound and images with an anarchic tone and is often seen as responsible for the earliest ironic renderings of Yeşilçam films (Altuğ 2008). In *Kurtuluş Yok* (There Is No Salvation), a 1994 piece from the album

Opua Dışın (Pow Bang), Köksal, similar to Mozart's *Rondo alla Turca*, puts together Ottoman Turkish janissary bands' march music with techno rhythms and dialogues and sound effects from Yeşilçam films: "Death is no salvation, there is no salvation for any of you, pow bang" (http://www. myspace.com/2serhat5bz). While this remediation acknowledges Yeşilçam as postmortem, it also remedies and repeats Yeşilçam, by supplementing it in a post-Yeşilçam world. Each origin and death is indeed multiplication, as the singular plural, as the separation and repetition: Thus, "death is at the dawn because everything has begun with repetition" (Derrida 2001, 378), be it spectral or real, be it spectral real…or be it *hayal*!

Notes

Preface

1. The translation of İlhan Berk's poem is mine.
2. Like Hollywood, Yeşilçam (lit. green pine) is also the name of a place that invites an analogy to trees. However, unlike Hollywood, where film companies created a new town, Yeşilçam Street was located in downtown Istanbul, at Pera/Beyoğlu, where the first public film screenings were held.

Chapter 1

1. *World Cinema* is available on Nuri Bilge Ceylan's official Web site: http://www.nbcfilm.com/3maymun/news.php?mid=2.
2. In this book, expressions such as the "cinema of Turkey," "Turkish cinema," or "Turkish popular cinema" and their respective histories are limited to feature films, except discussions of the first films made in Turkey.
3. Özön refers to those filmmakers who had a background in theater and who also continued to work primarily for theaters as *tiyatrocular* (theater-makers) as opposed to the 1950s generation of filmmakers who were solely interested in filmmaking, whom he refers to as *sinemacılar* (cinema-makers).
4. Özön refers to an interesting film while he is talking about religious exploitation films: *Hac Yolu* (The Path of Pilgrimage, 1952). This film was marketed as a Turkish film but it was indeed an Egyptian documentary film with added scenes. The original documentary, *al Hajj* (1936) was shot by Egyptians and a reedited version of it was shown in the 1937 Venice Film Festival, as *Le Pélérinage Musulman à la Mecque* (The Pilgrimage of Muslims to Mecca). However, what is particularly interesting are the rumors about this film that made it into a box office hit: watching this film seven times equals to a pilgrimage to Mecca, which is one of the pillars of Islam. Obviously, spectators had to pay for a new ticket in each of their viewings! (Özön 1962, 150). This story is very telling about the exploitative character of popular cinema and also about the practices of the "Turkification" of foreign films, as will be shown in the following chapters to be a common tactic of Yeşilçam.

5. Among the columnists who compared Ceylan with Pamuk are Fatih Altaylı, Oray Eğin, and Hasan Pulur.

6. Please see J. Timmons Roberts and Amy Hite (2000) for more on how development and social change is handled by the modernization theorists.

7. Throughout this text, I gave literal translations of some film titles when I was not able to find an available English title.

Chapter 2

1. Early histories of Turkish cinema did not dwell on non-cinematic processes and developments that influenced filmmaking. Rakım Çalapala wrote the earliest, though very short, history of Turkish cinema in a booklet prepared by the Domestic Filmmakers Association in 1947 (*Yerli Film Yapanlar Cemiyeti*). Two other short articles were written by Nurullah Tilgen in film magazines *Yıldız* (Star, 1953) and *Yeni Yıldız* (New Star, 1956). A third attempt at documenting the history of Turkish cinema was Zahir Güvemli's chapter "Cinema in Turkey" in his mostly translated and adapted history of cinema (1960). These studies name some filmmakers and list some films but neglect to do in-depth analysis or develop anything beyond rudimentary classificatory schemes.

2. See Salih Gökmen (1973), Mustafa Gökmen (1989), Alim Şerif Onaran (1994), and Giovanni Scognamillo (1998).

3. A recent study in English published after the completion of my manuscript also reproduces the existing periodizations and their respective discourses by disparaging what the author calls "commercial" cinema. According to the film critic Gönül Dönmez-Colin, the domination of Muhsin Ertuğrul is followed by the "hegemony of Yeşilçam in the 1950s and 1960s," whereas she claims that the 1970s introduced "experiments with social realism and neo-realism, *auteur* cinema in the 1980s, a serious decline in the early 1990s, and a new movement of independent art cinema...and a revival of commercial cinema" in recent years (2008, 56). Agreeing with Özön, Dönmez-Colin also argues that Turkey did not have a national cinema similar to, say, Japanese and Indian cinemas of Ozu and Ray, respectively. Rather than being able to create "a cinema that fed on the national culture," Turkish cinema has a "mimetic relationship with the West, following Western modes without attempting a synthesis" (2008, 56).

4. While public spaces in Muslim areas of Istanbul were often gender-segregated at that time, the non-Muslim areas of Istanbul, including Pera, were integrated.

5. In the same year as these early screenings, a French citizen by the name of Cambon started to show longer films, probably by the Lumière brothers, which then led Weinberg to bring better Pathé equipment and films the following year (Scognamillo 1998, 17). In addition, an Izmir newspaper, *Ahenk* (Rhythm) dated December 10, 1896, reported that through Edison's invention called "kinematograph," Apollon Theater in the Frenk (French and/or non-Muslim) neighborhood of Izmir exhibited animated pictures (Erkılıç 2003, 14). Interestingly enough, while Edison's invention is named not as a "kinetograph" or "kinetescope" but as a "kinematograph" (*cinématographe*), which was capable of projecting animated pictures on a screen. Moreover, the films that were exhibited were Lumière films with various scenes from Paris. Whether this exhibition is the first

one or not, it still resembles the characteristics of the one held at Salle Sponeck, by being placed in a non-Muslim neighborhood of Izmir.

6. *Wayang* is used to refer to the puppet and shadow theaters of Indonesia. Javanese and Balinese shadow plays often carry religious tropes and have connections to the world of spirits and imagination.

7. "Kemalism" is an ideological rendering of Mustafa Kemal Atatürk's ideas and early republican reforms focusing on modernizing and westernizing the country through a positivistic rendering of the Enlightenment idea of progress.

8. A late nineteenth-century list of the genres of the day is as follows: the prose genres are tragedy, old comedy, *haute* comedy, play (*pièce*), drama, melodrama, comedy *bouffe*, comedy *burlesque*, vaudeville, *farce anglaise*, *farce Italienne*, and pantomime; and the musical genres are *grande* opera, *opera legér*, lyrical drama, comic opera, lyric, slapstick opera *bouffe*, operetta, ballet, *comédie musicale*, and pantomime (And 1999, 185).

9. While Özön and others noted that the Austro-Hungarian Company was Sascha-Messter-Film, the Austrian count Alexander Joseph Graf Kolowrat-Krakowsky and the German Oskar Eduard Messter founded Sascha-Messter-Film Gesellschaft m.b.H. in 1916.

10. A recent article on the film argues that Tilgen claimed this as the first Turkish film by tying it to a national narrative in articles published between 1953–56, and that Özön legitimized the film by giving it a title (Mutlu 2007, 87–88).

11. After the revolution, the Soviet government founded the Moscow Film School to produce "*agitki*–newsreels edited for the purpose of agitation and propaganda…[which] toured Russia in specially equipped agit-trains and agit-steamers designed to export the Revolution from the urban centers to the provinces" (Cook 2004, 116).

12. Fourwalling involved the practice of booking specific film theaters in advance to guarantee the exhibition of the films distributed by a specific company. Please see chapter 4 for more on the fourwalling practice in Yeşilçam.

13. Nezih Erdoğan and Dilek Kaya state that there is little information about why these and many other films were banned in Turkey and several other countries.

Chapter 3

1. While the prefix "trans-" indicates a movement beyond or across and a mechanism of responding to the West, "trance" denotes how such a movement or how these responses create an in-between situation.

2. Please see Tekelioğlu (1996) on the rendition of *arabesk* music as a popular synthesis that offered an alternative and spontaneous route of modernization from below, rather than that of the republican modernization project.

3. A thirteenth-century Sufi, Nasreddin Hodja lived in Anatolia and is a famous figure throughout the Middle East. While the tales or jokes often introduce folk and village themes, he is best known for his witty and satirical humor enmeshed with irrational events and crisp judgments.

4. In an article on the acting style of Hülya Koçyiğit, Çetin Sarıkartal also deals with a rendering of Yeşilçam's melodramatic characteristics. However, he speaks of the "melodramatic mode" of Yeşilçam as an instance of melodramatic storytelling determined by the patriarchal order and

limits Yeşilçam's melodramatic character only to the genre of melodramas (Sarıkartal 2003).

Chapter 4

1. Nijat Özön suggests that the golden age of filmmakers was between 1950 and 1970, while 1971 through 1987 was the period of "young" or "new" cinema (1995a). Similarly, Giovanni Scognamillo calls this period "inflationary" filmmaking, because of the excessive number of films made, but extends it to a period between 1960 and 1986. Alim Şerif Onaran, who essentially follows Özön, offers an early period between 1896 and 1938, the year of Atatürk's death; a transitional period between 1938 and 1952; and a period of filmmakers between 1952 and 1963. He calls the period between 1963 and 1980 new Turkish cinema and the period between 1980 and 1994 contemporary Turkish cinema (1994; 1995). While Onaran's periodizations are inspired primarily by political markers, instead of the 1960 military intervention, he prefers 1963 as a turning point: the date of the preparation of a law concerning cinema and of the shifts in the films of particular directors. English-language literature on Turkish cinema accepts Özön's periodization, as do writers such as Ayşe Franko (1987), Atilla Dorsay (1989a), Yusuf Kaplan (1997), and Gönül Dönmez-Colin (2008). Nezih Erdoğan and Deniz Göktürk (2001), while reproducing Özön's periodization, situate Yeşilçam's specific mode of production between the mid-1960s and mid-1970s, without delving into its characteristics.

2. At the time, Italian and Turkish filmmakers produced several co-productions including spaghetti westerns and crime and horror films. One such co-production, which brought together the Yeşilçam star Ayhan Işık with Klaus Kinski, was *La Mano Che Nutre* (Ölümün Nefesi, Evil Face, dir. Sergio Garrone and Yılmaz Duru, 1974). Please see Özkaracalar (1998, 30–33) for more information on this film.

Chapter 5

1. Not simply a nationally renowned singer, Müren also created an aura around his celebrity persona that led to a publicly known but never uttered collective communal secret: he was a cross-dresser, and by implication a homosexual, in a country of intense homophobia. As "the Sun of Art" or as "the Pasha" ("Army General") of Turkish music, he linked earlier musical performance practices to later ones, including a taste for *arabesk* late in his career. Though the state's radio and television broadcasts had strict regulations regarding the music and attire of their singers, Müren was not subject to such rules—when he went to a ball at the Presidential Palace in the 1970s, his eleven-inch platform heels caused a sensation. Yet his diction in Turkish was always exemplary and he westernized the practice of musical performance at music halls or clubs by introducing uniform clothing for the instrumentalists, and by introducing a thrust stage to wander among the audience. Educated in fashion design, he made his own costumes, openly crossdressing with miniskirts, earrings, and heavy makeup. He also acted in the Robert Anderson play *Tea and Sympathy*, which revolves around a "suspected" homosexual college student. As this communal secret about his personal life was always kept in the closet, Müren was not subjected

to homophobic violence. Even after his heart failure during a televised award ceremony on state television and ensuing death in 1996, none of the messages by the leaders and artists of Turkey and none of the obituaries referred to his homosexuality. Instead, only a few obituaries briefly mentioned his "bitter" private life without giving further details. Even a book on him that appeared at the time of his death chose not to mention this "well-kept" secret (Gür 1996).

2. Based on the real story of a seventh-century young Arab, the story tells how Majnun, after falling in love with Layla, went mad because of his father who did not allow him to marry Layla.

3. As a founder and longtime director of the *Cinémathèque Française* Henri Langlois was born in Izmir and supported the foundation of the Turkish Sinematek Association, which exhibited various examples of world cinema between 1965 and 1980.

4. Many such shantytowns in Istanbul and other metropolitan areas are generally referred as *gecekondu* (meaning dwellings built in one night) and are often subject to demolition. Built without permission on state-owned, and at times on privately owned lands, they were later integrated into city plans through general exemption laws issued by governments. As a result, instead of a planned urban settlement and growth, urban areas developed in an initially illegal manner later legitimized by the populist policies of various Turkish governments.

5. To attain religious knowledge, reciting, as in the practice of reciting Koran, is as important as reading. In addition, Çakmaklı also talks about a tradition of Islamic knowledge, especially in folk culture, which is transmitted through oral narration.

6. In Turkey, there are multiple codes of head covering for women, ranging from a full-body veil to a mere headscarf. Until the 1990s, covering did not have clear political coding and Fatma's headscarf does not necessarily indicate a political choice, which could at that time only have been indicated by a full-body veil.

7. The original movie is adapted from William Peter Blatty's novel *The Exorcist*, which itself is based on a purportedly true story of a Catholic priest's rite of exorcism performed on a possessed Maryland boy.

8. Keloğlan is a fairy-tale character known for his pure but cunning ways. Often he is portrayed as living in a village with his mother and then he takes on big challenges to marry a princess. Unlike other heroes forcefully eliminating villains or monsters, Keloğlan is a trickster.

9. Immigration from Turkey to West Germany started in 1961 and then expanded to other European countries such as Austria, Sweden, the Netherlands, and France among others. Following a strict and degrading process of health control, documented in John Berger and John Mohr's book *A Seventh Man: Migrant Workers in Europe*, workers were taken by these countries as temporary "guest" workers to meet the labor demands of rapid postwar industrialization. Starting out in the most demanding sectors of industry with the lowest pay, without social security, and living in packed, small, workers' quarters with fellow foreign workers, these temporary workers or *gastarbaiteren* slowly turned into permanent workers by receiving their rights and bringing their families from home.

10. Oğuz Makal takes up this issue in his *Sinemada Yedinci Adam* (A Seventh Man in Cinema), inspired by John Berger and Jean Mohr's 1975 book *A Seventh Man: Migrant Workers in Europe* that documented the one-seventh of workers in Northern Europe who were immigrants from

wide-range countries including Turkey, Greece, Albania, Italy, Portugal, and Iran.

11. Even I experienced such uncanny events when I started writing on this film for this study: I started to watch *Canlı Hedef* for the tenth or fifteenth time on November 1, 2005. That day, I stopped the VCR for a break and started channel surfing and ended up seeing the film on Kanal 7 (Channel 7), which is a moderate Islamist channel known for its support for the governing Justice and Development Party (AKP). Certainly, much like what happened to *Yol* (the Kurdistan banner was removed even from the illegal video copies of the film that were found on the black market in Turkey during the 1980s) or many other Güney films, the *Kanal 7* version of *Canlı Hedef* was also stripped of portions of the rape scene and the "snaky" torture scene.

12. I would like to thank İlker Mutlu who made me aware of this interview.

13. This list is compiled from Agah Özgüç's dictionary of Turkish films (1998, vol. 2) by looking at their short synopses, directors, and casts. Though the numbers may not be extremely reliable (for instance, Demirci [2004] noted that there were 121 sex films in 1979), it still gives an idea about the trends of that year.

Chapter 6

1. While secularism may indicate a separation between human and religious activities or political processes and the sacred world, the term *laicism* or *laïcité* refers to a narrower sense of this, indicating a clear-cut separation between the state and religion. The Kemalist rendering of the French laicisim places the state as being neutral in terms of religious matters but at the same time organizes and monitors Islamic religious activities by the way of governmental institutions. For example, all mosques and the religious personnel working at them are determined and controlled by the Religious Affairs Presidency. Thus this sense of laicism indicates a direct state control over religion.

2. Richard Maltby notes that the financial crisis of the industry between 1968 and 1971 not only marked the end of the classical Hollywood era but also allowed the advent of postclassical blockbuster films of Hollywood, which indicated a reduction in the number of films while investing more in the production budgets and marketing of a limited number of films (2003, 160).

Chapter 7

1. While "post-Yeşilçam" was initially used by film critic Burçak Evren and then reproduced in various contexts, the choice of the noun "Turkey" rather than the adjective "Turkish" in the "new cinema of/in Turkey" is common among antinationalist and/or leftist circles. However, in this study, the move from Yeşilçam as Turkish cinema to the new cinema of Turkey is rendered not necessarily as a "political" choice but instead to indicate the historical and conceptual shift after the transformation of Yeşilçam's Turkification practices. Post-Yeşilçam also inscribes, for Engin Ayça, the process of the formation of a cinema that opens up itself to the world and that pursues individual creativity and expression (Vardar 2007, 28–29).

2. For instance, in an interview in November 2007, Fatih Akın said that he would not show up for the compulsory draft to serve in the Turkish

army, leading some newspapers to call him a "traitor." As for Ferzan Özpetek, who has been frequently stigmatized as a self-Orientalist in Turkey, please see Elisabetta Girelli's 2007 article for an alternative view.

3. Two different critical positions are at stake here. One is the didactic, social engineering-related discourse of Kemalism inherent in the Turkish intellectual discourse. This is also indicated in regular television or newspaper interviews with people who frequently voice the necessity of education and learning and the necessity of this in cultural products. However, when one asks what books they read, what films they see, and what television programs they watch, this picture alters, because not many such interviewees read books, watch boring, intellectual films and documentaries, or view news programs on television. The second position is related to a view of cultural products in relation to culture industries, through a distinction between high, "good" culture, and mass culture, the opiate. In this discursive violence against culture, there is no place for popular culture, globalization, and transnationality. Instead, popular culture is tabloidization and sensationalism; globalization is an American plot that leads to the import of Western culture without any reservations; and transnationality is a bastardization of national culture, a threat to the unity and integrity of the Turkish nation. When critics, scholars, and people offer solutions for these problems, they voice yet another violent measure based on the discourse of a central state that produces, manipulates, and dictates a particular cultural program. In the name of making people watch useful, intellectual films and television programs, television channels are asked or forced to air low-quality documentaries and programs. However, all such positions ignore a basic fact. Yeşilçam, which today is cinematically produced and consumed through the genre of "Yeşilçam" or "Turkish" film, is itself about the Turkification of foreign texts. Instead of this Turkification, still common in television series, game shows, and reality shows, which often buy the original format and adapt it to Turkey, post-Yeşilçam cinema often introduced authentic voices and indigenous texts. Simultaneously, a new term, çakma (nailing), similar to Turkification, adaptation, or upholstering has come to the fore in recent years. "Nailing" refers to borrowing the storylines, themes, or other aspects of films, television series, or reality shows and adapting them to Turkish cinema or television through vernacularization or indigenization. Similarly, some original soundtracks or theme music of contemporary films also practice "nailing," which may be softened as influence or inspiration. For instance, the theme music of two recent films, Cenneti Beklerken (Waiting for Heaven, dir. Derviş Zaim, 2006) and Zincirbozan (dir. Atıl İnaç, 2007) are highly reminiscent of the theme music of the television series Lost, for which there are also plans to be "nailed" for Turkish television.

4. If not indicated otherwise, all of the post-1990 box office figures are taken from http://www.sinematurk.com/film.php?action=goToBoxOfficeP age&firstLoad=1.

5. Founded in 1988, Eurimages is a fund intended for thirty-three European countries under the Council of Europe. The fund supports coproduction, distribution, and exhibition of films and film projects with money contributed by member countries.

6. For instance, while Ziya Öztan does not have any other top-grossing films and while Yüksel Aksu worked for the television industry without making any other films for release in theaters, Tolga Örnek's documentary Hititler (Hittites, 2003), which lacks the nationalistic urges of his other documentary, gathered only 73,000 spectators. Still post-Yeşilçam, con-

current with the rise of documentaries globally, experienced the production and exhibition of a handful of documentaries about soccer teams, music, and everyday stories.

7. While Akın's *Yaşamın Kıyısında* (The Edge of Heaven, 2007) and *Duvara Karşı* (Head-On, 2004) gathered 287,000 and 294,000 spectators, respectively, Özpetek's *Hamam* (Steam: The Turkish Bath, 1997) was seen by 200,000 spectators. However, both directors' other films gathered far fewer spectators.

8. In 2003, while ten top-grossing domestic films gathered over 13 million spectators, seven of these were distributed by Warner Brothers, two by Özen Film, and one by United International Pictures. Warner Brothers' success, which started with *Eşkıya*, led to its increasing involvement in the market. However, in recent years, this pattern has changed to the advantage of Turkish companies such as Özen Film, KenDa, and Medyavizyon. For instance, while in 2007 domestic films gathered around 9 million spectators, only two of the ten top-grossing films were distributed by Warner Brothers and United International Pictures. Despite their involvement in the Turkish market, the Turkish CEO of Warner Brothers Turkey emphasized the fact that Turkey is a very small market for the company (Ahmet Tulgar 2003). While the number of tickets sold in Turkey is a little under half of Turkey's population (around 30 million), in a lot of European countries this number is twice or thrice the country's population. Thus when one thinks along these lines, Turkey is still an expendable and small market in terms of global cinema. When one considers that a couple of hundred million dollars are invested in a sizable Hollywood blockbuster, the negligibility of annual ticket revenues for all films exhibited in Turkey, still well under 200 million dollars, becomes clear.

9. After the state broadcasting company, TRT, introduced its second channel in 1986, the first private television channel of Turkey, Magic Box Star 1, started broadcasting through satellite in 1990. Now in addition to more than twenty national channels and many more local channels on air and in cable, digital satellite receivers provide hundreds of television channels from Turkish and foreign satellites.

10. *Site* (lit. place or site) refers to (often gated) complexes with low-rise apartments and townhouses with other amenities such as small parks, sports complexes, and shopping malls. Especially in the last two years, with the stabilization of inflation rates and decreasing interest rates, various new *sites* have started to offer a combination of the Western urban, city center life in these enclosed communities, with fancy names such as Mashattan (combining Maslak, a neighborhood in Istanbul, with Manhattan).

11. As will be discussed shortly, this masculine obsession with privacy plays out very well in "lowly" genres such as horror and sex films through the abjection of covered women.

12. While an educated cinephile in the post-Yeşilçam era might have considered some low-budget Yeşilçam films in this vein, Yeşilçam films are still very popular among television audiences. Many such films are refered to as "classic" melodramas or comedies of Turkish cinema. Here Suner might be referring to a recent symptomatic interest in trash cinema by generalizing it to a whole body of films produced by Yeşilçam, among which are various social realist films.

13. The headscarf issue in Turkey started in the aftermath of the 1980 military intervention, led by General Kenan Evren, who then was transferred to the office presidency and encouraged a state-sponsored discourse of Turkish-Islamic synthesis coinciding with the rise of an educational

program that popularized Imam Hatip high schools that focused on religious education to prepare congregation leaders, or *imams*, for the centrally controlled mosques.

14. Unsurprisingly, an academician working for the state-controlled Presidency of Religious Affairs, Ömer Menekşe, strongly criticized the misrepresentation of imams and other religious officials in various films, while praising various late 1980s and early 1990s Islamist films (Ertürk 2007). For him, not only Kemalist and Marxist films but also a lot of comedies with Kemal Sunal or recent blockbusters like *Vizontele* portray religious officials pejoratively. While his arguments are partially understandable in terms of Kemalist films that have a direct antireligious message, the introduction of comedies into this list indicates a Yeşilçam-style confusion between fiction and reality. However, this is also a common aspect of the post-Yeşilçam world of Turkey where various people still criticize films for misrepresentation of their city or occupation.

15. For Tanıl Bora, Turkish nationalism was accelerated during the 1990s due to a number of factors: the threat to the nation-state brought about by globalization (changing borders and conflicts, minority and human rights discourses, and transnational economic deregulation) and the crisis of the socioeconomic self-confidence in the early 1990s due to economic and political crises (the failure of Turkey's potential economic control of the Central Asian Turkic states, and the Gulf War and the United States invasion of Iraq, which created the realistic possibility of an independent Kurdish state in northern Iraq, triggering Turkey's focus on its Kurdish problem, which oscillates between "military solution" and "democratization") (2003, 434–36). Talking of two dynamics of contemporary nationalism, one as a reactionary movement aligning itself with a myth of national survival and the other a pro-Western one pursuing republican civilization discourse through updating it globalization discourses (an upper- and new urban middle-class phenomenon, converging with big capital and the media elite), Bora separates contemporary nationalist discourses in Turkey into four strands: official Kemalist language, left-wing Kemalist nationalism, liberal pro-Western nationalism catering for globalization and civilizationism, and racist-ethnicist Turkish nationalism fed by anti-Kurdish sentiments (2003, 436). These could be related, respectively, to the bureaucratic elite, traditional urban and educated middle classes, the new middle classes, and the traditional and party peripheral lower and middle classes. However, as Bora also notes, this fourfold separation is complicated with a rising discourse, that of Islamism.

16. The Islamist stance of the film presents a facile duality between a "true" imam who got sick and his high school friend who chose a different career instead of being an imam. While the true imam lives in a village, his friend has instead turned into a "white Turk" who has lost his connections to his rural and religious past. However, after the true imam gets sick, he asks his friend to fill in for him. However, his friend goes to the village on a motorcycle and stereotypically presents various secular and urban characteristics that do not go well with the villagers—hence the name, "the" imam, specifying a westernized Turk who has lost some of his "true" traits. The film then focuses on how the imam finds his true self in the village as he also shows the virtues of westernization to the villagers.

17. This ironic interest in Şahin K is also reminiscent of "Internet Mahir" (Mahir Çağrı, http://www.ikissyou.org), who is said to be one of the inspirations for Sacha Baron Cohen's character Borat Sagdiyev. Moreover, as also indicated in previous chapters, while sex comedies often utilized

local rural characteristics, Şahin K's films are before everything else porn films, which only have been turned into comedies by cinephiles.

18. TRT has recently started broadcasts in minority languages, including Kurdish-language broadcasts.

19. To this, one may also add the local television broadcasts in southeastern Turkey that offered a nascent practice of low-budget, Kurdish-language filmmaking and television series production. Some of these low-budget films produced by the "Yeşilçam of the East" cost around 2,000 to 3,000 dollars, were shot on location with amateur or semi-professional actors, and sold over 25,000 copies (Güven 2004). Whereas these films either relied on popular genres such as comedy and melodrama or tried to touch on some social issues such as honor killings, sex films were also produced for local audiences. For *Xaşhiki Kaliki* (Grandpa's Fantasies, 2003), which was made right after the lifting of the ban on Kurdish-language media, a Turkish actresses got a crash course to learn to say yes and no in Kurdish (Korap, 2003; Arslan 2006).

20. For instance, in 2000, the Turkish Hezbollah terrorist organization murdered the covered Islamist feminist writer Konca Kuriş, who fell against the hardliner Islamist discourses with her feminist viewpoints.

21. A lot of post-Yeşilçam films, though utilizing Hollywood in a direct manner, offered a novel path of Turkification. Various recent films introduced self-conscious references to Hollywood films or they adapted Hollywood's genre conventions to domestic subjects. Even remakes such as *Neşeli Gençlik* have partly diverged from Yeşilçam's prostitute and cuckold dynamic by shifting Yeşilçam's imagination of youth as a yet-to-be-educated group or a bastardized and westernized group of wild parties. Additionally, contemporary films and especially television series are also monitored well in terms of copyright and when they use non-Turkish sources they often give reference to the source or are faced with court cases thanks to the American companies in the Turkish market or to the smaller global world. These recent Turkifications are also named differently, especially in the television industy: for instance the remakes of *Grey's Anatomy*, *Doktorlar* (Doctors) or *Bewitched*, *Tatlı Cadı* (Sweet Witch), or the Islamist remake of *My Name Is Earl*, *Hakkını Helal Et* (Take It with My Blessing) are directly "nailed" from American series.

22. After noting that Ceylan and Demirkubuz "articulate a horror of a different kind…mundane acts of violence lurking beneath the surface of normality," Suner proposes that "Ceylan's cinema" deals with homecoming and that "Demirkubuz's cinema" with homelessness. This theme of homelessness in Demirkubuz's films is then related to "entrapment" leading to a "desperate mood" augmented by "the excessive use of claustrophobic interiors" and the alienation of characters from their own voices, by making voice unable to testify to the subject's inner truth (Suner 2004, 314–15). Here, Suner seems to have in mind a scene from Demirkubuz's *Üçüncü Sayfa*, in which a character's speech is first seen with a proper lip synch before a self-conscious distortion of lip synch. However, given the fact that this film also shows the shooting of a television serial where dubbing is still practiced and that Demirkubuz's films often have references to Yeşilçam films seen on television screens, this use of sound, instead of being seen in terms of a dissonant relation between voice and truth, may well be seen as an inside joke. In other words, Demirkubuz's deliberate references to Yeşilçam films, in which sound is already "dissonant," already separated from the body of actor, may well be a self-conscious

reference to Yeşilçam, with which Demirkubuz's films perpetually suggest a relation.

23. Laleli had been the center stage of Eastern European "suitcase trade" (*bavul ticareti*), which in the post-Soviet era became very common with Eastern Europeans bringing in goods in their suitcases to sell in Turkey and then buying Turkish goods on their way back to sell in their countries. While this seemingly minor and individual form of transnational trade turned into a big illegal market—for the goods sold and bought were free of customs check—this trade is also coupled with a sex industry. Even to this day, although the trade of commercial goods has come to an end, Laleli remains a locus of the illegal sex market.

24. Concurrent with live recording of sound, a lot of contemporary films have used original soundtracks and worked with composers. For instance, *Kabadayı*'s initial press release emphasizes a composer, Benjamin Walken Beladi who supposedly composed the scores for *The Passion of the Christ* (dir. Mel Gibson, 2004) and *The Island* (dir. Michael Bay, 2005). Indeed, Beladi was only an assistant to orchestrator in *The Passion of the Christ*.

25. Except for Şener Şen, the majority of high or late Yeşilçam stars have not been able to adapt well to the world of new cinema or television series and serials. Instead, with the influx of new action and comedy stars, either they are relegated to secondary roles or the films or television series starring them did not do well at the box office or in the ratings.

26. In this respect, it also seems crucial to note that while mainstream global, electronic companies produce standard DVD players that only show standard, copyrighted formats, various non-Western electronics companies, including the Turkish Vestel, produce DVD players that show not only regionally based DVD formats but also VCDs (MPEG- or DivX-formatted CDs) and other mainstream computer-based image formats.

References

Abisel, Nilgün. 1994. *Türk Sineması Üzerine Yazılar* [Writings on Turkish Cinema]. Ankara: İmge Kitabevi.

Açar, Mehmet. 1995. "Türk Sinemasında Amerikan Hakimiyeti" [The American Dominance in Turkish Cinema]. *Cumhuriyet Dönemi Türkiye Ansiklopedisi* [The Encyclopedia of Turkey in the Republican Period]. Istanbul: İletişim Yayınları.

Ahmet, Nuri. 1929. "Amerikan Filmlerine Dair" [Concerning American Films]. *Sinema Gazetesi* [Cinema Newspaper] 3: 3.

Akad, Lütfi Ö. 2004. *Işıkla Karanlık Arasında* [Between Light and Dark]. Istanbul: Türkiye İş Bankası Kültür Yayınları.

Akbal Süalp, Z. Tül. 2001. "Türkiye'de Sinema: 'Film Noir' ya da Dışavurumcu İklimin İçinden Geçerken" [Cinema in Turkey: 'Film Noir' or Passing through the Expressionist Climate]. In *Türk Film Araştırmalarında Yeni Yönelimler 2* [New Directions in Turkish Film Studies 2], ed. Deniz Derman. İstanbul: Bağlam.

Algan, Necla. 1996. "80 Sonrası Türk Sinemasında Estetik ve İdeoloji" [Aesthetics and Ideology in the Turkish Cinema after the 1980s]. *25. Kare* [25th Frame] 16: 4–9.

Altman, Rick. 1999. *Film/Genre*. London: British Film Institute Publishing.

Altuğ, Evrim. 2008. "Çek Bizi İçine İstanbul: 2/5 Porsiyon Olsun" [Istanbul, Pull Us In: 2/5 Portions-worth]. In *Sabah Cumartesi Eki* [Morning Saturday Supplement] (February 2).

"Amerika Sinemalar Paytahtı Hollywood'a Birisi Erkek Diğeri Kadın İki Genç Gönderiyoruz" [We Are Sending Two Young People, a Man and a Woman, to the American Capital of Cinemas: Hollywood]. 1929. *Sinema Gazetesi* [Cinema Newspaper] 5: 8.

And, Metin. 1985. *Geleneksel Türk Tiyatrosu: Köylü ve Halk Tiyatrosu Gelenekleri* [Traditional Turkish Theater: Traditions of Peasant and People's Theaters]. Istanbul: İnkılap Kitabevi.

———. 1999. *Osmanlı Tiyatrosu* [Ottoman Theater]. Ankara: Dost Kitabevi Yayınları.

———. 2000. "Karagöz'de Muhavere" [Edited by Sevengül Sönmez]. Istanbul: Kitabevi.

———. 2001. "Çağdaş Tiyatro Açısından Karagöz ve Orta Oyunu" [Karagöz and Theater-in-the-Round in Terms of Modern Theater]. In *Orta Oyunu Kitabı* [The Book of Theater-in-the-Round], ed. Abdulkadir Emeksiz. Istanbul: Kitabevi.

———. 2002. "Traditional Performances." In *Ottoman Civilization 2*, ed. Halil İnalcık and Günsel Renda. Ankara: Ministry of Culture.

Anderlini-D'Onofrio. 2004. Serena. "Bisexual Games and Emotional Sustainability in Ferzan Özpetek's Films." *New Cinemas: Journal of Contemporary Film* 2 (3): 163–74.

Anderson, Benedict. 1991. *Imagined Communities: Reflections on the Origin and Spread of Nationalism*. Rev. ed. London and New York: Verso.

Arakon, İlhan. 2004. Interview by İlker Mutlu. Istanbul.

Argun, Betigül Ercan. 2003. *Turkey in Germany: The Transnational Sphere of Deutschkei*. New York and London: Routledge.

Arkın, Cüneyt. 2002. Interview by Savaş Arslan. Istanbul.

Arslan, Savaş. 2006. "Dubbing Hollywood: Turkification in the Electronic Age." *Yeditepe Journal of Communication Studies* 4 (Fall): 53–63.

———. 2007. "Projecting a Bridge for Youth: Islamic 'Enlightenment' versus Westernization in Turkish Cinema." In *Youth Culture in Global Cinema*, ed. Timothy Shary and Alexandra Seibel. Austin: University of Texas Press.

———. 2008. "Head-On, Head-Off: How the Media Covered a Former Porn Actress's Rise to Stardom." *Film International* 6 (6) (November): 62–71.

Atadeniz, Remzi Yılmaz. 1999. "Remzi Yılmaz Atadeniz'le Söyleşi" [An Interview with Remzi Yılmaz Atadeniz]. By Metin Demirhan. *Fantastik Türk Sineması* [Turkish Fantastic Cinema] by Giovanni Scognamillo and Metin Demirhan. Istanbul: Kabalcı Yayınevi.

Awde, Nick. 2005. "The Grass Is Always Greener: Karagöz Comes to London" (April 13). Available online at http://www.thestage.co.uk/reviews/review.php/7343/the-grass-is-always-greener-karagoz-comes.

Ayata, Sencer. 2002. "The New Middle Class and the Joys of Suburbia." In *Fragments of Culture: The Everyday of Modern Turkey*, ed. Deniz Kandiyoti and Ayşe Saktanber. London and New York: I. B. Tauris.

Ayça, Engin. 1985. "Yeni Türk Sineması ve Eski Sorunları" [New Turkish Cinema and Its Age-Old Problems]. *Video/Sinema* 11: 80–81.

———. 1994. "Türk Sinemasının Periyodizasyonu: Engin Ayça ile Söyleşi" [The Periodization of Turkish Cinema: An Interview with Engin Ayça]. By Zahit Atam ve Bülent Görücü. *Görüntü* [Image] 2: 43–52.

Baran, Tamer, Saim Yavuz, and Hülya Arslanbay. 1993. "Pek de Parlak Değildin '92" [You Were Not That Bright, 1992]. *Antrakt* [Intermission] 16:74–78.

Baydar, Tuncay. 1967. "Soyunan Kadın" [The Undressing Woman]. *Sinema Postası* [Cinema Post] 242: 7.

Bazin, André. 1967. *What Is Cinema?* Trans. Hugh Gray. Berkeley and Los Angeles: University of California Press.

Belgil, Vehbi. 1952. "Yerli Filmciliğimize Ait Meseleler" [Problems Concerning Our Domestic Filmmaking]. *Yıldız* [Star] 59: 20–21.

Bennett, Michael Todd. 1997. "Anglophilia on Film: Creating an Atmosphere for Alliance, 1935–1941." *Film and History* 27: 4–21.

Berger, John. 1980. *About Looking*. New York: Pantheon.

Berger, John, and Jean Mohr. 1975. *A Seventh Man: Migrant Workers in Europe*. New York: Viking.

Berk, İlhan. 2003. *Toplu Şiirler* [Collected Poems]. Istanbul: YKY.

Berman, Marshall. 1983. *All That Is Solid Melts into Air: The Experience of Modernity*. London and New York: Verso.

Bhabha, Homi. 1994. "Remembering Fanon: Self, Psyche and the Colonial Condition." In *Colonial Discourse and Post-Colonial Theory: A Reader*, ed. Patrick Williams and Laura Chrisman. New York: Columbia University Press.

Bolter, Jay David, and Richard Grusin. 1999. *Remediation: Understanding New Media*. Cambridge, Mass.: MIT Press.

Bora, Tanıl. 2003. "Nationalist Discourses in Turkey." *South Atlantic Quarterly* 102 (2/3) (Spring/Summer 2003): 433–51.

Bordwell, David. 2006. *The Way Hollywood Tells It: Story and Style in Modern Movies*. Berkeley and Los Angeles: University of California Press.

Bozdemir, Banu. 2001. "İki Güzel Sinema Olayı" [Two Beautiful Events of Cinema]. Available online at http://www.intersinema.com/yazar/filmografi/20011207.asp.

Brooks, Peter. 1976. *The Melodramatic Imagination: Balzac, Henry James, Melodrama, and the Mode of Excess*. New Haven: Yale University Press.

———. 1994. "Melodrama, Body, Revolution." In *Melodrama: Stage, Picture, Screen*, ed. Jacky Bratton, Jim Cook, and Christine Gledhill. London: British Film Institute Publishing.

Browne, Nick. 1994. "Society and Subjectivity: On the Political Economy of Chinese Melodrama." In *Melodrama: Stage, Picture, Screen*, ed. Jacky Bratton, Jim Cook, and Christine Gledhill. London: British Film Institute Publishing.

"Bu Sene Strip-tiz Türk Filmciliğinin Kurtarıcısı Olmuştur" [This Year Striptease Became the Savior of Turkish Filmmaking]. 1966. *Sinema Postası* [Cinema Post] 197: 3.

Caner, Hayri. 1964. "Türk Sineması Ne Olacak?" [What Will Turkish Cinema Be?]. *Sinema Ekspres* 7: 9.

Cantek, Levent. 2000. "Türkiye'de Mısır Filmleri" [Egyptian Films in Turkey]. *Tarih ve Toplum* [History and Society] 204: 31–38.

Cavell, Stanley. 1979. *The World Viewed: Reflections on the Ontology of Film*. Enl. ed. Cambridge, Mass.: Harvard University Press.

Cawelti, John G. 1976. *Adventure, Mystery, and Romance: Formula Stories*. Chicago: University of Chicago Press.

Cezar, Mustafa. 2003. Interview by Canan Suner and Sedat Balkır. In *Akademi'ye Tanıklık 1: Güzel Sanatlar Akademisi'ne Bakışlar, Resim-Heykel* [Witnessing the Academy I: Views on the Academy of Fine Arts, Painting-Sculpture], ed. Ahmet Öner Gezgin. Istanbul: Bağlam Yayıncılık.

Chow, Rey. 1993. *Writing Diaspora: Tactics of Intervention in Contemporary Cultural Studies*. Bloomington: Indiana University Press.

Cimcöz, Adalet. 1970. "Ferdi Tayfur'un Lorel Hardi'si" [The Laurel-Hardy of Ferdi Tayfur]. *Filim* 1: 8–9.

Clark, Christopher. 2006. "Transculturation, *Transe* Sexuality, and Turkish Germany: Kutluğ Ataman's *Lola und Bilidikid*." *German Life and Letters* 59 (4) (October 2006): 555–72.

Cohan, Steven. 2000. "Case Study: Interpreting *Singin' in the Rain*." In *Reinventing Film Studies*, ed. Christine Gledhill and Linda Williams. London: Arnold.

Constantinidis, Stratos E. 2000. "Greek Film and the National Interest: A Brief Preface." *Journal of Modern Greek Studies* 18: 1–12.

Cook, David A. 1998. "Auteur Cinema and the 'Film Generation' in 1970s Hollywood." In *The New American Cinema*, ed. Jon Lewis. Durham, N.C.: Duke University Press.

———. 2004. *A History of Narrative Film*. 4th ed. New York: Norton.

Corrigan, Timothy. 1998. "Auteurs and the New Hollywood." In *The New American Cinema*, ed. Jon Lewis. Durham, N.C.: Duke University Press.

Coş, Nezih. 1984. "Tatlıses Sineması ve *Ayşem*" [The Cinema of Tatlıses and *Ayşem*]. *Video/Sinema* 7: 18–19.

Creed, Barbara. 2000. "Kristeva, Femininity, Abjection." *The Horror Reader*, ed. Ken Gelder. London and New York: Routledge.

Crofts, Stephen. 1998. "Concepts of National Cinema." In *The Oxford Guide to Film Studies*, ed. John Hill and Pamela Church Gibson. Oxford and New York: Oxford University Press.

Çakmaklı, Yücel. 2002. Interview by Savaş Arslan. Istanbul.

———. 2007. "Sinemamız Dünya Sinemasıyla Rekabet Edecek Duruma Geldi" [Our Cinema Can Now Compete with World Cinema]. Interview by Coşkun Koçyiğit, December 24. Available online at http://www.sine-masinemadir.com/?ynt=haberdetay&id=33.

Çalapala, Rakım. 1947. "Türkiye'de Filmcilik" [Filmmaking in Turkey]. In *Filmlerimiz* [Our Films]. Istanbul: Yerli Film Yapanlar Cemiyeti Yayını.

Çeviker, Turgut. 1974. "Genelev Kadınlarıyla Sinema Soruşturması" [An Interview on Cinema with Women Working in Brothels]. *Yedinci Sanat* [Seventh Art] 18: 35–41.

Çolakoğlu, Nuri. 2006. "Gökyüzü Uydularla Dolarken Türkiye Seyirci Kalmıyor" [As the Skies Fill with Satellites, Turkey Does Not Watch Idly]. *Referans* [Reference (June 14)]. Available online at http://www.referansgazetesi.com/haber.aspx?HBR_KOD=43503&KOS_KOD=38.

Deleuze, Gilles, and Félix Guattari. 1994. *A Thousand Plateaus: Capitalism and Schizophrenia*. 5th ed. Trans. Brian Massumi. Minneapolis: University of Minnesota Press.

———. 2003. *Anti-Oedipus: Capitalism and Schizophrenia*, 11th ed. Trans. Robert Hurley, Mark Seem, and Helen R. Lane. Minneapolis: University of Minnesota Press.

Demirci, Cihan. 2004. *Araya Parça Giren Yıllar* [The Years of Montaged Scenes]. Istanbul: İnkılap Yayınları.

Denizot, Philippe. 1973. "Türk Sineması ya da Çarşı Mitolojisi" [Turkish Cinema or Bazaar Mythology]. *Yedinci Sanat* [Seventh Art] 4: 3–6.

Derman Bayrakdar, Deniz. 1997. "Yönetmen: Bilge Olgaç" [The Director: Bilge Olgaç]. *25. Kare* [25th Frame] 19: 31–34.

Derrida, Jacques. 1994. *Specters of Marx*. Trans. Peggy Kamuf. New York: Routledge.

———. 2001. *Writing and Difference*. Trans. Alan Bass. London: Routledge.

Doğan, Yalçın. 2004. "Silah Bir, Sinema İki" [Number One: Guns, Two: Cinema]. *Hürriyet* [Freedom]. (July 20).

Doherty, Thomas. 2002. *Teenagers and Teenpics: The Juvenilization of American Movies in the 1950s*. Philadelphia: Temple University Press.

Dorsay, Atilla. 1986. *Sinemayı Sanat Yapanlar* [Those Who Turn Cinema into an Art]. Istanbul: Varlık.

———. 1989a. "An Overview of Turkish Cinema from Its Origins to the Present Day." *Turkish Cinema: An Introduction*, ed. Christine Woodhead. London: University of London SOAS Turkish Area Group Publications.

———. 1989b. "Antalya 89, Elde Var İyimserlik" [Antalya 1989, What Is Left Is Optimism]. *Beyazperde* (White Screen) 1: 26–29.

————. 1995. *12 Eylül Yılları ve Sinemamız* [The Years of September 12 and Our Cinema]. Istanbul: İnkılap Yayınları.

————. 2000. *Yılmaz Güney Kitabı* [Yılmaz Güney Book]. Istanbul: Güney Yayınları.

————. 2004a. "Back from Near Oblivion: Turkish Cinema Gets a New Lease on Life." *Film Comment* 34 (6): 11–12.

————. 2004b. *Sinemamızda Çöküş ve Rönesans Yılları: Türk Sineması 1990–2004* [The Years of Collapse and Renaissance in Our Cinema: Turkish Cinema 1990–2004]. Istanbul: Remzi Kitabevi, 2004.

Dönmez-Colin, Gönül. 2008. *Turkish Cinema: Identity, Distance and Belonging*. London: Reaktion, 2008.

Dubuffet, Jean. 1988. *Asphyxiating Culture and Other Writings*. Trans. Carol Volk. New York: Four Walls Eight Windows.

Duncan, Derek. 2005. "Stairway to Heaven: Ferzan Özpetek and the Revision of Italy." *New Cinemas: Journal of Contemporary Film* 3 (2): 101–13.

"Ebediyete Kadar" [Until Eternity]. 1956. *Akis* [Reflection/Echo] 96 (March 10): 17.

Eğilmez, Ertem. 1984. "Ertem Eğilmez'le *Namuslu* bir Söyleşi" [A *Namuslu* (lit. honorable), interview with Ertem Eğilmez]. By Vecdi Sayar. *Video/ Sinema* 4: 36–39.

Eğilmez, Ertem and Sadık Şendil. 1974. "Ertem Eğilmez ve Sadık Şendil'le Konuşma" [A Conversation with Ertem Eğilmez and Sadık Şendil]. Interview by Engin Ayça and Nezih Coş. *Yedinci Sanat* [Seventh Art] 12: 16–33.

Elsaesser, Thomas. 1987. "Tales of Sound and Fury: Observations on the Family Melodrama." In *Home Is Where the Heart Is: Studies in Melodrama and the Woman's Film*, ed. Christine Gledhill. London: British Film Institute.

————. 2005. *European Cinema: Face to Face with Hollywood*. Amsterdam: Amsterdam University Press.

————. 2006. "Space, Place and Identity in the European Cinema of the 1990s." *Third Text* 20 (6): 647–658.

"EP's First Lux Cinema Prize Goes to Turkish-German Co-production." 2007. Available online at http://www.europarl.europa.eu/news/public/ focus_page/037-12748-297-10-43-906-20071107FCS12747-24-10-2007- 2007/default_en.htm.

Erakalın, Ülkü. 1999. *Film Karelerine Gizlenen Anılar* [Memories Hidden in Film Frames]. Istanbul: Arıtan Yayınevi.

Erdem, Tarhan. 2007. *Yeni Türkiye'yi Anlamak* [Understanding the New Turkey]. November 3. Available online at http://www.obmuze.com/2007/ docs/031107_tarhanerdem.pdf.

Erdoğan, Nezih. 1995. "Ulusal Kimlik, Kolonyal Söylem ve Yeşilçam Melodramı" [National Identity, Colonial Discourse and Yeşilçam Melodrama]. *Toplum ve Bilim* [Society and Science] 67: 178–98.

————. 1998. "Narratives of Resistance: National Identity and Ambivalence in the Turkish Melodrama between 1965 and 1975." *Screen* 39 (3): 259–71.

————. 2001. "Violent Images: Hybridity and Excess in The Man Who Saved the World." In *Mediated Identities*, ed. Karen Ross, Deniz Derman, and Nevena Dakovic. Istanbul: Istanbul Bilgi University Press.

————. 2002. "Mute Bodies, Disembodied Voices: Notes on Sound in Turkish Popular Cinema." *Screen* 43 (3): 233–49.

Erdoğan, Nezih, and Deniz Göktürk. 2001. "Turkish Cinema." In *Companion Encyclopedia of Middle Eastern and North African Film*, ed. Oliver Leeman. London and New York: Routledge.

Erdoğan, Nezih, and Dilek Kaya. 2002. "Institutional Intervention in the Distribution and Exhibition of Hollywood Films in Turkey." *Historical Journal of Film, Radio and Television* 22 (1): 47–59.

Erickson, Hal. 2005. "Biography of Hugo Haas," *All Movie Guide*. Available online at http://entertainment.msn.com/celebs/celeb.aspx?mp=b&c= 315796.

Erkal, Genco. 1984. "Genco Erkal." Interview by Osman Balcıgil. *Video/ Sinema* 1: 16.

Erkılıç, Ertan. 2003. *Türk Sinemasının Ekonomik Yapısı ve Bunun Sinema Sanatına Etkileri* [The Economic Structure of Turkish Cinema and the Influences of This on the Art of Cinema]. Unpublished diss., Mimar Sinan University.

Erksan, Metin 1989. *Atatürk Filmi* [The Atatürk Film]. Istanbul: Hil Yayın.

Erman, Hürrem. 1973. "Yapımcı Hürrem Erman'la Konuşma" [A Conversation with Producer Hürrem Erman]. Interview by Nezih Coş, Atilla Dorsay, and Engin Ayça. *Yedinci Sanat* [Seventh Art] 6: 22–37.

Ertürk, Ali Ekber. 2007. "Diyanet'ten Sakıncalı ve Sakıncasız Türk Filmleri Listesi" [List of Proper and Improper Turkish Films by the Bureau of Religious Affairs]. *Akşam* [Evening]. February 1. Available online at http://www.karakutu.com/modules.php?name=News&file=article&sid=2672.

Evren, Burçak. 1995. *Sigmund Weinberg: Türkiye'ye Sinemayı Getiren Adam* (Sigmund Weinberg: The Man Who Brought Cinema to Turkey). Istanbul: Milliyet Yayınları.

———. 2005. *Türk Sineması* [Turkish Cinema]. Istanbul and Antalya: TÜRSAK and AKSAV.

Eyüboğlu, Selim. 2001. "Düşük Yapan Parodi: *Kahpe Bizans*" [Miscarriage of a Parody: *Harlot Byzantium*]. In *Türk Film Araştırmalarında Yeni Yönelimler* 2 [New Directions in Turkish Film Studies 2], ed. Deniz Derman Bayrakdar. Istanbul: Bağlam.

Fanon, Frantz. 1967. *The Wretched of the Earth*. Trans. Constance Ferrington. Middlesex: Penguin.

Filim Bitti [The Film Is Over]. 1990. *Beyazperde* [White Screen] 5: 14.

"Filmcilik: Şimdi Ne Olacak?" [Filmmaking: What Will Happen Now?]. 1958. *Akis* [Echo]: 32–33.

Franko, Ayşe. 1987. "Turkey." In *World Cinema Since 1945*, ed. William Luhr. New York: Ungar.

Fuat, A. 1934. "Sinemada Çıplaklık" [Nudity in Cinema]. *Holivut* (Hollywood) 46: 3.

Gallagher, Jessica. 2006. "The Limitation of Urban Space in Thomas Arslan's *Berlin Trilogy*." *Seminar* 42 (3) (September): 337–52.

Gavin, Kit. [Date unavailable]. "Homo Eroticus." Available online at http://www.cinema-nocturna.com/homoeroticus_review.htm.

Gazetas, Aristides. 2000. *An Introduction to World Cinema*. Jefferson, N.C.: McFarland and Company.

Gellner, Ernest. 1983. *Nations and Nationalism*. Oxford: Blackwell.

Georgakas, Dan. 2002–3. "Greek Cinema for Beginners: A Thumbnail History." *Film Criticism* 27 (2): 2–8.

Girelli, Elisabetta. 2007. "Transnational Orientalism: Ferzan Özpetek's Turkish Dream in *Hamam*." *New Cinemas: Journal of Contemporary Film* 5 (1) (April): 23–38.

Gledhill, Christine. 1987. "The Melodramatic Field: An Investigation." In *Home Is Where the Heart Is: Studies in Melodrama and the Woman's Film*, ed. Christine Gledhill. London: British Film Institute.

———. 2000. "Rethinking Genre." In *Reinventing Film Studies*, ed. Christine Gledhill and Linda Williams. London: Arnold.

Gledhill, Christine and Linda Williams. 2000. "Introduction." *Reinventing Film Studies*, ed. Christine Gledhill and Linda Williams. London: Arnold.

Gökalp, Ziya. 1968. *The Principles of Turkism*. Trans. Robert Devereux. Leiden: Brill.

———. 1976. *Türkleşmek, İslamlaşmak, Muasırlaşmak* [Turkification, Islamization, Modernization]. Ankara: Kültür Bakanlığı.

Gökmen, Mustafa. 1989. *Başlangıçtan 1950'ye Kadar Türk Sinema Tarihi ve Eski İstanbul Sinemaları* [A History of Turkish Cinema from Its Beginning to 1950 and Old Istanbul Film Theaters]. Istanbul: Denetim Ajans Basımevi.

———. 2000. "Sponek Birahanesi" [The Beer Hall of Sponek]. *Klaket* [Clapboard] 13: 59–60.

Gökmen, Salih. 1973. *Bugünkü Türk Sineması* [Turkish Cinema Today]. Istanbul: Fetih Yayınevi.

Göktürk, Deniz. 2000. "Turkish Women on German Streets: Closure and Exposure in Transnational Cinema." In *Spaces in European Cinema*, ed. Myrto Konstantarakos. Exeter: Intellect.

———. 2001. "Turkish Delight—German Fright: Migrant Identities in Transnational Cinema." In *Mediated Identities*, ed. Deniz Derman, Karen Ross, and Nevena Dakovic. Istanbul: Istanbul Bilgi University Press.

Göle, Nilüfer. 1991. *Modern Mahrem: Medeniyet ve Örtünme* [Modern Privacy: Civilization and Covering]. Istanbul: Metis.

Gülyüz, Aram. 2004. "Erotik Film Çekmek Bana Zevk Verdi" [Shooting Erotic Films Gave Me Pleasure]. Interview by Aynur Erdem. *Sabah* [The Morning]. October 15.

Güney, Yılmaz. 1974a. "Yılmaz Güney *Arkadaş*'ı Anlatıyor" [Yılmaz Güney Narrates *Friend*]. Interview by Nezih Coş and Engin Ayça. *Yedinci Sanat* 18: 3–7.

———. 1974b. "Yılmaz Güney'le Konuşma II" [Conversation with Yılmaz Güney II]. Interview by Nezih Coş and Engin Ayça. *Yedinci Sanat* 19: 3–17.

Gür, Ceyhan. 1996. *Zeki Müren: Şimdi Uzaklardasın* (Zeki Müren: You Are Now Far Away). Istanbul: AD Yayıncılık.

Gürata, Ahmet. 2001. "Adolf Körner: Müteahhass mı? Şovmen mi?" [Adolf Körner: Expert or Showman?] *Geceyarısı Sineması* 9: 26–27.

———. 2007. "Hollywood in Vernacular: Translation and Cross-Cultural Reception of American Films in Turkey." In *Going to the Movies: Hollywood and Social Experience of Cinema*, ed. Melvyn Stokes, Robert C. Allen, and Richard Maltby. Exeter: University of Exeter Press.

———. 2008. "Translation and Reception of Indian Cinema in Turkey: The Life of *Awara*." In *The BFI Indian Cinema Book*, ed. Kaushik Bhaumik and Kila Jordan. London: BFI.

Gürbilek, Nurdan. 2001. *Vitrinde Yaşamak* [To Live in the Shop Windows]. 3rd ed. Istanbul: Metis Yayınları.

Güvemli, Zahir. 1960. *Sinema Tarihi: Başlangıcından Bugüne Türk ve Dünya Sineması* [A History of Cinema: Turkish and World Cinema from Its Beginning to Today]. Istanbul: Varlık Yayınları.

Güven, Özkan. 2004. "Doğunun Yeşilçam'ı" [Yeşilçam of the East]. Milliyet Pazar (Nationality Sunday, March 24).

"Haberler" [News]. 1961. *Artist* 49: 29.

"Halk Soruşturması 3: Balıkesir ve Sakarya" [Public Survey 3: Balıkesir and Sakarya)]. 1973. Interviews by Zeki Yusuf Borazan and Merdiye Akyüz. *Yedinci Sanat* [Seventh Art] 9: 34–50.

Hall, Stuart. 2000. "Cultural Identity and Cinematic Representation." In *Film Theory: An Anthology*, ed. Robert Stam and Toby Miller. Malden, Mass. and Oxford: Blackwell.

Hattox, Ralph S. 1996. *Coffee and Coffeehouses: The Origins of a Social Beverage in the Medieval Near East*. 3rd ed. Seattle and London: University of Washington Press.

Havaeri, Seyfi. 2002. Interview by Savaş Arslan and Ali Sekmeç. Istanbul.

Hayward, Susan. 2000. "Framing National Cinemas." In *Cinema and Nation*, ed. Matte Hjort and Scott MacKenzie. London and New York: Routledge.

Hjort, Matte, and Scott MacKenzie, eds. 2000. Introduction to *Cinema and Nation*. London and New York: Routledge.

"Hollywood'a Dönen Şu İstanbul" [This Istanbul Which Turned into Hollywood]. 1951. *Yıldız* [Star] 37: 9, 24.

Hutcheon, Linda. 1998. "Irony, Nostalgia, and the Postmodern." Available online at http://www.library.utoronto.ca/utel/criticism/hutchinp.html#N73.

Iordanova, Dina, J. Goytisolo, A. K. G. Singh, A. Suner, V. Shafik, and P. A. Skantze. 2006. "Indian Cinema's Global Reach: Historiography through Testimonies." *South Asian Popular Culture* 4 (2): 113–40.

İleri, Selim. 1973. "Kerime Nadir Adı Teminattır" [The Name Kerime Nadir Is a Guarantee]. *Yedinci Sanat* [Seventh Art] 2: 10–13.

İnanç, Çetin. 1999. "Çetin İnanç ile Söyleşi" [An Interview with Çetin İnanç]. Interview by Metin Demirhan in *Fantastik Türk Sineması* [Turkish Fantastic Cinema] by Giovanni Scognamillo and Metin Demirhan. Istanbul: Kabalcı Yayınevi.

İnanoğlu, Türker. 1984. "Video ve Sinema Birbirine Düşman Değil" [Video and Cinema Are Not Enemies]. *Video/Sinema* 1: 68.

Jameson, Frederick. 1993. "Postmodernism, or the Cultural Logic of Late Capitalism." In *Postmodernism: A Reader*, ed. Thomas Docherty. New York: Columbia University Press.

Jusdanis, Gregory. 1991. *Belated Modernity and Aesthetic Culture: Inventing National Literature*. Minneapolis: University of Minnesota Press.

Kamil, Şadan. 2000. "Şadan Kamil ve Bir Dönemin Sineması" [Şadan Kamil and the Cinema of an Era]. Interview by Ali Sekmeç and Okan Ormanlı. *Klaket* [Clapboard] 14: 14–22.

Kandiyoti, Deniz. 2002. "Introduction: Reading the Fragments." In *Fragments of Culture: The Everyday of Modern Turkey*, ed. Deniz Kandiyoti and Ayşe Saktanber. London and New York: I. B. Tauris.

Kaplan, Yusuf. 1997. "Turkish Cinema." In *The Oxford History of World Cinema*, ed. Geoffrey Nowell-Smith. Oxford and New York: Oxford University Press.

Kasaba, Reşat. 1997. "Kemalist Certainties and Modern Ambiguities." In *Rethinking Modernity and National Identity in Turkey*, ed. Sibel Bozdoğan and Reşat Kasaba. Seattle: University of Washington Press.

Kayalı, Kurtuluş. 1990. "Türk Sinemasında Med Manzaraları" [Views of Low Tides in Turkish Cinema]. *Beyazperde* [White Curtain] 6: 7.

Kenç, Faruk. 1993. Interview by Hülya Arslanbay. *Antrakt* [Intermission] 24: 25–27.

Keskin, Sacide. 1985. Interview by Engin Ayça. *Video/Sinema* [Video/Cinema] 11: 82–83.

Keyder, Çağlar. 1997. "Whither the Project of Modernity Turkey in the 1990s." In *Rethinking Modernity and National Identity in Turkey*, ed. Sibel Bozdoğan and Reşat Kasaba. Seattle: University of Washington Press.

———. 1999. "The Setting." In *Istanbul: Between the Global and the Local*, ed. Çağlar Keyder. Lanham, Md. and Oxford: Rowman and Littlefield.

Koçak, Orhan. 1995. "Ataç, Meriç, Caliban, Bandung: Evrensellik ve Kısmilik Üzerine bir Taslak" [Ataç, Meriç, Caliban, Bandung: A Sketch on Universality and Particularity]. In *Türk Aydını ve Kimlik Sorunu* [Turkish Intellectuals and the Problem of Identity], ed. Sabahattin Şen. Istanbul: Bağlam.

Koçyiğit, Hülya. 1984. "Hülya Koçyiğit." Interview by Osman Balcıgil. *Video/Sinema* 1: 14–15.

Konuralp, Sadi. 2004. *Film Müziği: Tarihçe ve Yazılar* [Film Music: History and Writings]. Istanbul: Oğlak Yayınları.

Korap, Elif. 2003. "Erotik Film için Kadın Oyunculara Kürtçe 'Evet' Demesini Öğrettik" [For an Erotic Film, We Taught the Actresses How to Say 'Yes' in Kurdish]. *Milliyet Pazar* (Nationality Sunday, November 2).

Kosnick, Kira. 2007. *Migrant Media: Turkish Broadcasting and Multicultural Politics in Berlin*. Bloomington: Indiana University Press.

Kudret, Cevdet. 2001. "Orta Oyununun Oyun Yeri ve Bölümleri" [The Playground and Parts of Theater-in-the-Round]. In *Orta Oyunu Kitabı* [The Book of Theater-in-the-Round], ed. Abdulkadir Emeksiz. Istanbul: Kitabevi.

Kulish, Nicholas. 2008. "Fatih Akin: A Filmmaker Who Builds Bridges across Cultures." *International Herald Tribune* (January 10). Available online at http://www.iht.com/articles/2008/01/10/arts/akin.php.

Kuyucak Esen, Şükran. 2002. *Sinemamızda bir "Auteur:" Ömer Kavur* [An "Auteur" in Our Cinema: Ömer Kavur]. Istanbul: Alfa.

Kuyucaklı, Orhan. 1961. "Geçtiğimiz Film Sezonuna Umumi Bir Bakış" [A General Look at the Last Film Season]. *Artist* 47: 3.

Maccinema: The Macedonian Cinema Information Center. [Date unavailable]. "Year 1905." Available online at http://www.maccinema.com/e_hronologija_detali.asp.

Makal, Oğuz. 1994. *Sinemada Yedinci Adam* [A Seventh Man in Cinema]. 2nd ed. Izmir: Ege Yayıncılık.

Maltby, Richard. 1998. "'Nobody Knows Everything': Post-Classical Historiographies and Consolidated Entertainment." In *Contemporary Hollywood Cinema*, ed. Steve Neale and Murray Smith. London and New York: Routledge.

———. 2003. *Hollywood Cinema: An Introduction*. Malden, Mass. and Oxford: Blackwell.

Maraş, Gökhan. 1990. "ANAP Kırşehir Milletvekili Gökhan Maraş: Amerika'daki Sığır Çobanlarının Kültürüyle Bizim Kültürümüz Kıyaslanamaz" [Motherland Party's MP from Kırşehir, Gökhan Maraş: You Cannot Compare Our Culture to That of American Cowboys]. Interview by Nilgün Gürkan Aslanbay. *Beyazperde* [White Screen] 3: 10–13.

Mekin, Ahmet. 1961. "Bizim Sokağın İnsanları" [The People of Our Street]. *Artist* 38: 17.

Mennel, Barbara. 2002. "Bruce Lee in Kreuzberg and Scarface in Altona: Transnational Auteurism and Ghettocentrism in Thomas Arslan's *Brothers and Sisters* and Fatih Akın's *Short Sharp Shock*." *New German Critique* 87 (Autumn): 133–56.

Miller, Toby. 2006. Preface to *Traditions in World Cinema*, ed. Linda Badley, R. Barton Palmer, and Steven Jay Schneider. New Brunswick, N.J.: Rutgers University Press.

Moran, Berna. 1994. *Türk Romanına Eleştirel Bir Bakış 2* [A Critical Look at the Turkish Novel 2]. 3rd ed. Istanbul: İletişim Yayınları.

———. 1995. *Türk Romanına Eleştirel Bir Bakış 1* [A Critical Look at the Turkish Novel 1]. 5th ed. Istanbul: İletişim Yayınları.

Mutlu, Dilek Kaya. 2007. "The Russian Monument in Ayastephanos [San Stefano]: Between Defeat and Revenge, Remembering and Forgetting." *Middle Eastern Studies* 43 (1) (January): 75–86.

Muvahhit, Bedia. 1973a. "Bedia Muvahhit'le Konuşma" [A Conversation with Bedia Muvahhit]. Interview by Atilla Dorsay and Engin Ayça. *Yedinci Sanat* [Seventh Art] 9: 90–93.

———. 1973b. "Bedia Muvahhit'le Konuşma" [A Conversation with Bedia Muvahhit]. Interview by Atilla Dorsay and Engin Ayça. *Yedinci Sanat* [Seventh Art] 10: 94–100.

Müren, Zeki. 1963. "Zeki Müren ve Renkli Filmi" [Zeki Müren and His Color Film]. Interview by Hayri Caner. *Yıldız* [Star] 12: 11–13.

———. 1992. "Zeki Müren'den bir Demet" [A Bouquet from Zeki Müren]. Interview reported by Ender Uslu. Available online at http://www.sanat-gunesi.com/bir_cift_soz_ender_uslu.htm.

Naficy, Hamid. 2001. *An Accented Cinema: Exilic and Diasporic Filmmaking*. Princeton: Princeton University Press.

Nancy, Jean-Luc. 2000. *Being Singular Plural*. Trans. Robert D. Richardson and Anne E. O'Byrne. Stanford: Stanford University Press.

Navaro-Yasin, Yael. 1999. "The Historical Construction of Local Culture: Gender and Identity in the Politics of Secularism versus Islam." In *Istanbul: Between the Global and the Local*, ed. Çağlar Keyder. Lanham, Md. and Oxford: Rowman and Littlefield.

Novell-Smith, Geoffrey (ed.). 1997. *The Oxford History of World Cinema*. Oxford and New York: Oxford University Press.

Nutku, Özdemir. 2000. "Tanzimat'ın Getirdiği bir Tür: Tuluat Tiyatrosu" [A Genre that *Tanzimat* Brought: *Tuluat* Theater]. Available online at http://www.tiyatronline.com/loca209.htm.

Okan, Tuncan. 1958. "Zam Kuyruğundaki Sinemacılar" [The Filmmakers in the Line of Price Rise]. *Kim* [Who] 12: 36–37.

Onaran, Alim Şerif. 1968. *Sinematografik Hürriyet* [Cinematographic Freedom]. Ankara: T.C. İçişleri Bakanlığı Tetkik Kurulu Yayınları.

———. 1973. "Muhsin Ertuğrul'un Operet Filmleri" [The Operetta Films of Muhsin Ertuğrul]. *Yedinci Sanat* [Seventh Art] 9: 74–82.

———. 1981. *Muhsin Ertuğrul'un Sineması* [The Cinema of Muhsin Ertuğrul]. Ankara: Kültür Bakanlığı Yayınları.

———. 1990. *Lütfi Ö. Akad*. Istanbul: Afa Yayınları.

———. 1994. *Türk Sineması: I. Cilt* [Turkish Cinema: Volume I]. Ankara: Kitle Yayınları.

———. 1995. *Türk Sineması: II. Cilt* [Turkish Cinema: Volume II]. Ankara: Kitle Yayınları.

Onat, M. Sami. 1990. "Yerli Filmlerimiz" [Our Domestic Films]. *Beyazperde* [White Screen] 3: 52.

Oral, Ünver. 2002. *İbişli Kukla Oyunlarımız* [Our Puppet Plays with İbiş]. Istanbul: Kitabevi.

Oran, Bülent. 1973. "Senaryo Yazarı Bülent Oran'la Konuşma" [A Conversation with the Script Writer Bülent Oran]. Interview by Atilla Dorsay, Nezih Coş, and Engin Ayça. *Yedinci Sanat* [Seventh Art] 3: 15–26.

————. 2002. Interview by Savaş Arslan. Istanbul.

Önal, Safa. 2002. Interview by Savaş Arslan. Istanbul.

Özdemir, Cüneyt. 1990. "Açıkoturum Notları: Seksen Sonrası Türk Sineması" [The Notes from Open Table: Turkish Cinema after the 1980s]. *Beyazperde* [White Curtain] 6: 12–13.

Özder, Musa. 1974. "Toros Dağlarında Sinema Soruşturması" [A Survey of Cinema on the Taurus Mountains]. Interview by Osman Şahin. *Yedinci Sanat* [Seventh Art] 19: 50–53.

Özdeş, Oğuz. 1951. "Bu Sezonda Yerli Film Olarak Neler Göreceğiz?" [What Domestic Films Are We Going to See in This Season?] *Yıldız* [Star] 37: 8–9, 24.

Özen, Mustafa. 2007. *De Opkomst van het Moderne Medium: Cinema in de Ottomaanse Hoofdstad Istanbul, 1896–1914* [The Rise of the Modern Medium: Cinema in the Ottoman Capital Istanbul, 1896–1914]. Unpublished thesis, Utrecht: Utrecht University.

Özerdem, Mahir. 1954. "İtalyan Filmciliği ve Biz" [Italian Filmmaking and Us]. *Yıldız* [Star] 60: 6.

Özgüç, Agah. 1974. "Beş Tavuk Bir Horoz" [Five Chickens, One Rooster]. *Yedinci Sanat* [Seventh Art] 16: 70.

————. 1992. "Bir Yılın '91' Ardından Türkiye" [Turkey after a Year, 1991]. *Antrakt* [Intermission] 4: 12–15.

————. 1993. "1992'de Türk Sineması" [Turkish Cinema in 1992]. *Antrakt* [Intermission] 16: 79–81.

————. 1994. "Türk Sineması '93" [Turkish Cinema, 1993]. *Antrakt* [Intermission] 29: 12–17.

————. 1995. *Türk Film Yönetmenleri Sözlüğü* [A Dictionary of Turkish Film Directors]. Istanbul: Afa Yayınları.

————. 1997. *Türk Filmleri Sözlüğü: 1991–1996* [A Dictionary of Turkish Films]. Volume 3. Istanbul: Sesam Yayınları.

————. 1998. *Türk Filmleri Sözlüğü: 1914–1973* and *1974–1990* [A Dictionary of Turkish Films]. Volumes 1 and 2. Rev. 2nd ed. Istanbul: Sesam Yayınları.

————. 2000. *Türk Sinemasında Cinselliğin Tarihi* [History of Sexuality in Turkish Cinema]. Exp. 2nd ed. Istanbul: Parantez Yayınları.

————. 2005. *Türlerle Türk Sineması* [Turkish Cinema through Genres]. Istanbul: Dünya.

Özgüven, Fatih. 1989. "Male and Female in Yeşilçam: Archetypes Endorsed by Mutual Agreement of Audience and Player." In *Turkish Cinema: An Introduction*, ed. Christine Woodhead. London: University of London, SOAS Turkish Area Study Group Publications.

Özkan, Yavuz. 1992. "Yavuz Özkan: Sinemamız Kendi Dilini Yaratmanın Sabırsızlığını Yaşamaktadır" [Our Cinema Experiences the Impatience of Creating Its Own Language]. *Antrakt* [Intermission] 4: 65.

————. 1993. "Bir Filmin Yaratılma Macerası" [The Adventure of a Film's Creation]. *Antrakt* [Intermission] 16: 73.

Özkaracalar, Kaya. 1998. "Ayhan Işık'ın İtalyan Korku Filmleri" [The Italian Horror Films of Ayhan Işık]. *Geceyarısı Sineması* [Midnight Cinema] 1: 30–33.

Özkırım, Çetin A. 1959. "Yeşilçam Sokağından" [From the Yeşilçam Street]. *Sinema* 59 (September): 3.

Özön, Nijat. 1962. *Türk Sinema Tarihi* [A History of Turkish Cinema]. Istanbul: Artist Yayınları.

————. 1970. *İlk Türk Sinemacısı Fuat Uzkınay* [Fuat Uzkınay, the First Turkish Filmmaker]. Istanbul: Türk Sinematek Derneği Yayınları.

————. 1995a. *Karagöz'den Sinemaya, Türk Sineması ve Sorunları I: Tarih, Sanat, Estetik, Endüstri, Ekonomi* [Turkish Cinema and Its Problems from *Karagöz* to Cinema I: History, Art, Aesthetics, Industry, Economy]. Ankara: Kitle Yayınları.

————. 1995b. *Karagöz'den Sinemaya, Türk Sineması ve Sorunları II: Eleştirme, Eleştiri Yazıları, Sinema ve Toplum, Denetleme, Sinema ve TV* [Turkish Cinema and Its Problems from Karagöz to Cinema II: Criticism, Film Critiques, Cinema and Society, Control, Cinema and Television]. Ankara: Kitle Yayınları, 1995.

————. 1996. "Nijat Özön'le Söyleşi" [An Interview with Nijat Özön]. *Görüntü* [Image] 5: 2–14.

Öztürk, Semire Ruken. 2004. *Sinemanın 'Dişil' Yüzü: Türkiye'de Kadın Yönetmenler* [The 'Feminine' Face of Cinema: Female Directors in Turkey]. Istanbul: Om Yayınevi.

Özuyar, Ali. 1999. *Sinemanın Osmanlıca Serüveni* [The Adventure of Cinema in Ottoman]. Ankara: Öteki Yayınevi.

Pösteki, Nigar. 2004. *1990 Sonrası Türk Sineması* [Turkish Cinema after 1990]. Istanbul: Es.

Pütün, Elif Güney. 1999. "Pof Pof Diye Yürür, Palyaço Hareketleri Yapardı" [She Used to Shuffle and Act Like a Clown]. Interview by Melda Davran. *Milliyet Pazar* [Nationality]. (February 14): page numbers. Available online at http://www.milliyet.com.tr/ekler/gazete_pazar/990214/haber/hab1.html.

Roberts, J. Timmons, and Amy Hite, eds. 2000. *From Modernization to Globalization: Perspectives on Development and Social Change*. Oxford and Malden, Mass.: Blackwell.

Robins, Kevin, and Asu Aksoy. 2000. "Deep Nation: The National Question and Turkish Cinema Culture." In *Cinema and Nation*, ed. Matte Hjort and Scott MacKenzie. London and New York: Routledge.

Roudometof, Victor. 1996. "Nationalism and Identity Politics in the Balkans: Greece and the Macedonian Question." *Journal of Modern Greek Studies* 14 (2): 253–301.

Sarıkartal, Çetin. 2003. "Voice of Contraction: Melodrama, Star System, and a Turkish Female Star's Excessive Response to the Patriarchal Order." *Performance Research* 8 (1): 83–93.

Sason, Leon. 1961a. "Bir Film Nasıl Çevrilir?" [How Is a Film Shot?] *Artist Yıllığı* [The Yearbook of Artists]: 101–5.

————. 1961b. "Türkiye'de Sinema" [Cinema in Turkey]. *Artist Yıllığı* [The Yearbook of Artists]: 19–50.

Sayman, Aydın. 1973. "Türk ve Dünya Sinemasının Konumu" [The Position of Turkish and World Cinemas]. *Gerçek Sinema* [True Cinema] 2: 11–20.

Scognamillo, Giovanni. 1973a. "Köy Filmleri" [Village Films]. *Yedinci Sanat* [Seventh Art] 4: 8–14.

————. 1973b. *Türk Sinemasında Altı Yönetmen* [Six Directors of Turkish Cinema]. Istanbul: Türk Film Arşivi Yayını.

————. 1973c. "Türk Sinemasında Yabancı Uyarlamalar" [Foreign Adaptations in Turkish Cinema]. *Yedinci Sanat* [Seventh Art] 9: 61–73.

————. 1991. *Cadde-i Kebir'de Sinema* [Cinema in Cadde-i Kebir]. Istanbul: Metis Yayınları.

————. 1998. *Türk Sinema Tarihi: 1896–1997* [A History of Turkish Cinema]. 3rd and exp. ed. Istanbul: Kabalcı Yayınevi.

Scognamillo, Giovanni, and Metin Demirhan. 1999. *Fantastik Türk Sineması* [Turkish Fantastic Cinema]. Istanbul: Kabalcı Yayınevi.

―――. 2002. *Erotik Türk Sineması* [Turkish Erotic Cinema]. Istanbul: Kabalcı Yayınevi.

Sconce, Jeffrey. 1995. "Trashing the Academy." *Screen* 36 (4) (Winter): 371–93.

Sekmeç, Ali. 2001. "Faruk Kenç'i Kaybettik" [We Lost Faruk Kenç]. *Klaket* [Clapboard] 15: 4–7.

"Sesli Filmlere Dair" [Concerning Sound Films]. 1929. *Sinema Gazetesi* [Cinema Newspaper] 7: 7.

Sevinçli, Efdal. 1990. *Görüşleriyle Uygulamalarıyla bir Tiyatro Adamı Olarak Muhsin Ertuğrul* [With his Views and Practice, a Man of Theater: Muhsin Ertuğrul]. Istanbul: Arba.

"Seyirci: Yaşasın Sesli Film!" [Long Live Sound Film!]. 1929. *Sinema Gazetesi* [Cinema Newspaper] 20: 4.

Shafik, Viola. 1998. *Arab Cinema*. Cairo: The American University in Cairo Press.

Shohat, Ella, and Robert Stam. 1994. *Unthinking Eurocentrism: Multiculturalism and the Media*. London and New York: Routledge.

Simpson, Catherine. 2006. "Turkish Cinema's Resurgence: The 'Deep Nation' Unravels." *Senses of Cinema* 6 (39) (April–June). Available online at http://archive.sensesofcinema.com/contents/06/39/turkish_cinema.html.

"Sinema Biletleri Pahalıdır!" [Film Tickets Are Expensive!]. 1929. *Sinema Gazetesi* [Cinema Newspaper] 19: 10.

"Sinema Kanunu Çıkmazsa 1968'de Türk Sineması Batacak" [The Turkish Cinema Will Go Bankrupt in 1968 if the Cinema Law Is Not Passed]. 1967. *Sinema Postası* [Courier of Cinema] 256: 9.

"Sinema: Meydanı Boş Bulanlar" [Cinema: Those Who Seized an Opportunity]. 1958. *Kim* [Who] 23: 30–31.

Sinema Yıldızları [Cinema Stars]. 1934. Istanbul: Akşam Kitaphanesi.

"Sinemalar ve Seyirciler: Sinemalardan Fransızca Kalkmalıdır" [Cinemas and Spectators: French Must Be Banned from Film Theaters]. 1929. *Sinema Gazetesi* [Cinema Newspaper] 20: 4.

"Sinemanın Para Babaları" [The Patrons of Cinema]. 1967. *Sinema Postası* [Courier of Cinema] 254: 10.

Singer, Ben. *Melodrama and Modernity: Early Sensational Cinema and Its Contexts*. 2001. New York: Columbia University Press.

Sklar, Robert. 2002. *Film: An International History of the Medium*. Upper Saddle River, N.J.: Prentice-Hall.

Solelli, Sezai. 1948. *Yıldız 1948 Yıllığı* [1948 Yearbook of *Yıldız*]. Istanbul: Türkiye Yayınevi.

Sorlin, Pierre. 1996. *Italian National Cinema: 1896–1996*. London and New York: Routledge.

Standage, Tom. 2002. "The Turk: The Life and Times of the Famous Eighteenth-Century Chess-Playing Machine." Available online at http://www.theturkbook.com.

Stokes, Martin. 1999. "Sounding Out: The Culture Industries and Globalization of Istanbul." In *Istanbul: Between the Global and the Local*, ed. Çağlar Keyder. Lanham, Md. and Oxford: Rowman and Littlefield.

Sumer, Beyza. 2003. *White vs. Black Turks: The Civilizing Process in Turkey in the 1990s*. Unpublished thesis, Middle East Technical University.

Sunal, Ali Kemal. 2001. *TV ve Sinemada Kemal Sunal Güldürüsü* [The Kemal Sunal Comedy in Television and Cinema]. Istanbul: Om Yayınevi.

Suner, Asuman. 2004. "Horror of a Different Kind: Dissonant Voices of the New Turkish Cinema." *Screen* 45 (4) (Winter): 305–23.

———. 2006a. *Hayalet Ev: Yeni Türk Sinemasında Aidiyet, Kimlik ve Bellek* [Ghost House: Belonging, Identity, and Memory in New Turkish Cinema]. Istanbul: Metis.

———. 2006b. "Outside in: 'Accented Cinema' at Large." *Inter-Asia Cultural Studies* 7 (3): 363–82.

———. 2009. *New Turkish Cinema: Belonging, Identity, Memory*. London: I. B. Tauris.

Sütüven, Seyit Ali. 1977. "Yılmaz Güney'in Sırrı" [The Secret of Yılmaz Güney]. *Mutlak Fikir, Estetiği ve Sinema* [Absolute Idea, Its Aesthetics and Cinema] 1: 7–10.

Şasa, Ayşe. 1993. *Yeşilçam Günlüğü* [The Yeşilçam Diary]. Istanbul: Dergah Yayınları.

Şen, Abdurrahman. 1995. "Milli Sinemadan Beyaz Sinemaya" [From National Cinema to White Cinema]. In *Yeşilçam'la Yüzyüze* [Face-to-face with Yeşilçam], ed. Burçak Evren. Istanbul: Açı Yayıncılık.

Şen, A. Fatih. 1977. "Bir Salgının Patolojik Anatomisi" [A Pathological Anatomy of an Epidemic]. *Mutlak Fikir, Estetiği ve Sinema* [Absolute Idea, Its Aesthetics and Cinema] 1: 11–13.

Şener, Erman. 1968. "Sözlendirme Sorunu" [The Problem of Voicing]. *Yeni Sinema* [New Cinema] 19-20: 35—39.

Tansuğ, Sezer. 1996. *Çağdaş Türk Sanatı* [Modern Turkish Art]. 4th ed. Istanbul: Remzi Kitabevi.

Taştepe, Nazif. 1974. "Set İşçileri ve Figüranlar Konuşuyor" [Stage Workers and Stunts Speak]. Interview by Osman Aslandere. *Yedinci Sanat* [Seventh Art] 12: 15–19.

Tayfur, Ferdi. 1985. Interview. *Video/Sinema* 11: 82.

Tekelioğlu, Orhan. 1996. "The Rise of a Spontaneous Synthesis: The Historical Background of Turkish Popular Music." *Middle Eastern Studies* 32 (2) (April): 194–215.

Teksoy, Rekin. 2007. *Rekin Teksoy'un Türk Sineması* [Rekin Teksoy's Turkish Cinema]. Istanbul: Oğlak.

"Tenkit." 1929. *Sinema Gazetesi* [Cinema Newspaper] 2: 3.

Thompson, Kristin. 1999a. "The Concept of Cinematic Excess." In *Film Theory and Criticism*, ed. Leo Braudy and Marshall Cohen. 5th ed. Oxford: Oxford University Press.

———. 1999b. *Storytelling in the New Hollywood: Understanding Classical Narrative Technique*. Cambridge, Mass. and London: Harvard University Press.

———. 2003. *Storytelling in Film and Television*. Cambridge and London: Harvard University Press.

Tuğba, Ahu, and Nuri Alço. 2005. "Ahu Tuğba ve Nuri Alço İkilisi Yıllar Sonra Kamera Karşısında" [The Pair Ahu Tuğba and Nuri Alço Is in Front of the Cameras after Many Years]. 2005. Interview by Şermin Sarıbaş. *Hürriyet Pazar Eki* [Freedom Sunday Supplement] (March 20). Available online at http://hurarsiv.hurriyet.com.tr/goster/haber.aspx?viewid=551951.

Tulgar, Ahmet. 2003. "Türkiye'de İyi Film Değil Popüler Film Seyredilir" [In Turkey, Popular, Not Good, Films Are Watched]. *Milliyet Pazar Eki* [Nationality Sunday Supplement] (November 3). Available online at http://www.milliyet.com.tr/2003/11/07/pazar/apaz.html.

Tulgar, Kunt. 2002. Interview by Savaş Arslan. Istanbul.

"Türk Film Dostları Derneğinin İlk Toplantısı" [The First Meeting of the Association of Turkish Cinephiles]. 1952. *Yıldız* [Star] 92: 11.

Türk, İbrahim. 2004. *Senaryo: Bülent Oran* [Film Script: Bülent Oran]. Istanbul: Dergah Yayınları.

Türkali, Vedat. 1974. "Vedat Türkali ile Konuşma" [A Conversation with Vedat Türkali]. Interview by Nezih Coş, Abdullah Anlar, and Engin Ayça. *Yedinci Sanat* [Seventh Art] 17: 44–62.

———. 1984. "Vedat Türkali ile Eski Filmler Üzerine" [On the Old Films, with Vedat Türkali]. Interview by Vecdi Sayar. *Video/Sinema* 3: 67–71.

Ülker, Erol. 2005. "Contextualizing 'Turkification': Nation-Building in the Late Ottoman Empire, 1908–1918." *Nations and Nationalism* 11 (4): 613–36.

Vardar, Bülent. 2007. "Türk Sinemasında Bağımsızlık Olgusu" [The Phenomenon of Independence in Turkish Cinema]. *Cinemascope* 13 (December): 28–29.

Vasilevski, Gjorgi. [Date unavailable]. "History of the Macedonian Film." Trans. Zaharija Pavlovska. Available online at http://www.macedonia.co.uk/client/index1.aspx?page=26.

Vasudevan, Ravi. 2000. *Making Meaning in Indian Cinema*. Delhi: Oxford University Press.

Wickham, Glynne. 1992. *A History of the Theatre*. 2nd ed. London: Phaidon.

Williams, Linda. 1989. *Hard Core: Power, Pleasure, and the "Frenzy of the Visible."* Berkeley and Los Angeles: University of California Press.

———. 1998. "Melodrama Revised." In *Refiguring American Film Genres: Theory and History*, ed. Nick Browne. Berkeley and Los Angeles: University of California Press.

———. 2000. "Film Bodies: Gender, Genre, and Excess." In *Film and Theory: An Anthology*, ed. Robert Stam and Toby Miller. Malden, Mass. and Oxford: Blackwell.

Wright, Jane. 2005. "Jewel Is Out of the Shadows." Available online at http://www.camdennewjournal.co.uk/030305/f030305_04.htm.

Wyatt, Justin. 1994. *High Concept: Movies and Marketing in Hollywood*. Austin: University of Texas Press.

Yavuz, Deniz. 2006. *Haftalık Antrakt Sinema Gazetesi* [Weekly Antrakt Cinema Newspaper] 6 (December).

Yerli Film Yapanlar Cemiyeti [Domestic Filmmakers Association]. 1947. "Cemiyetimizin Maksat ve Gayeleri" [The Aims and Objectives of Our Association]. In *Filmlerimiz* [Our Films]. Istanbul: Yerli Film Yapanlar Cemiyeti Yayını.

"Yerli Filmlerin Zaferi" [The Victory of Domestic Films]. 1954. *Yıldız* [Star] 60: 3.

Yılmaz, Atıf. 1984. "Atıf Yılmaz ya da bir Sinemacının Çeşitlemeleri" [Atıf Yılmaz or the Variations of a Filmmaker]. Interview by Sungu Çapan. *Video/Sinema* 3: 36–38.

———. 1995. *Söylemek Güzeldir* [It Is Nice to Tell]. Istanbul: Afa.

———. 1997. "Türkiye'de Yeniden Politik Sinema Yapmanın Zamanı Geldi" [The Time to Make Political Cinema in Turkey Has Come]. Interview. *Görüntü* [Image] 6: 20–23.

Zürcher, Erik Jan. 1994. *Turkey: A Modern History*. London and New York: I. B. Tauris.

Index

Manukyan, Ferdinand 104
Maraş, Gökhan 204
Marmara Film Studio 73
Marmara region 106, 107
Marquès, José Luis 115
Marshall, Garry 256
Marshall Plan 24
Marx Brothers 169
Marx, Groucho 49
Marx, Karl 269
Marxism 154, 160, 265, 283n
Maskeli Beşler: Irak (Aslan) 249, 254, 266
Masumiyet (Demirkubuz) 263
Matrix, The (Wachowski Brothers) 257
Mecca 159, 161, 162, 164, 275n
Medyavizyon 266, 282n
Mehmet V, Sultan Reşat 33, 35, 36
Mekin, Ahmet 232, 233
melodrama(tic) 14, 16, 19, 30, 56, 59,
    66, 67, 68, 70, 78, 86–96, 100, 111,
    115, 116, 120, 121, 127, 133, 134,
    137–138, 144, 148, 149, 157, 160,
    162, 163, 167, 171, 174, 175, 176,
    177, 178, 181, 184, 186, 188, 193,
    194, 196, 198, 209, 210, 211, 212,
    218, 219, 243, 253, 254, 256, 257,
    260, 267, 268, 277n, 278n, 282n,
    284n
  family/women's melodrama 9, 17,
    92, 174, 180, 182, 204, 208, 219,
    220, 258
  "issue" melodrama 171
  masculine/male melodrama 3, 226,
    254, 255, 258, 259, 260, 265, 266, 267
  melodrama and modernity 88–91
  melodramatic narration/storyline 17,
    165, 169, 205, 253, 257, 277n
  melodrama and nationality 94–96
  melodrama and realism xi, 17, 68,
    87–89, 92, 94, 137, 184, 186, 211,
    212, 236
  melodramatic modality 15, 17, 18,
    19, 64, 67, 68, 80, 82, 86, 90, 91–96,
    97, 102, 111, 115, 116, 121, 128,
    129, 133, 137–138, 141, 143, 149,
    151, 152, 154, 158, 162, 174, 178,
    181, 182, 196, 198, 205, 211, 219,
    221, 235, 254
  musical/singer melodrama 67, 70,
    190, 197, 198, 211, 219
Memleketim (Çakmaklı) 159, 171

Menjou, Adolphe 49
Mephistopheles 125
Meriç, Cemil 132
Messter, Oskar Eduard 277n
Metro 42
Mexica(n) 95, 183
Middle East 2, 36, 37, 79, 105, 156,
    187, 267, 277n
Midnight Express (Parker) 1
migration 20, 24, 69, 77, 94, 100, 101,
    102, 111, 134, 140, 148, 156, 211,
    270, 279n
Milestone, Lewis 51
military intervention
  of 1960 11, 98–100, 215, 226, 278n
  of 1971 11, 98–100, 226
  of 1980 10, 11, 98–100, 102, 114, 115,
    170, 182, 186, 191, 196, 201–203,
    204, 207, 208, 209, 211, 212, 214,
    215, 216, 219, 224, 235, 248, 282n
  of 1997 ("postmodern") 248
Milli Sinema (film theater) 31
milli sinema movement. *See* national
    cinema
miniature painting 28, 29
minority 29, 50, 63, 79, 80, 202, 214,
    215, 221, 248, 249, 251, 253, 261,
    267, 271, 283n, 284n
Minyeli Abdullah (Çakmaklı) 256
Missing (Gavras) 185, 186
Mithat, Ahmet 88
modern 2, 8, 18, 27–28, 29, 36, 45–46,
    52, 53, 56, 63, 66, 68, 78, 87, 88–90,
    92–96, 102, 119, 129, 130, 137, 148,
    156, 157, 160, 163, 164, 167, 169,
    194, 198, 208, 209, 210, 211, 213,
    232, 235, 253, 255, 256, 258, 259,
    264, 266
  modern and traditional 12–13, 82,
    121, 123, 126, 153, 208, 215, 254
  modernism/modernist 21, 28, 204
  belated modernity 36–38
modernization 7, 28, 32, 37, 45–46, 48,
    49, 60, 64, 66, 70, 88–90, 97, 99,
    100, 101, 108, 120, 124, 129, 132,
    133, 148, 149, 151, 152, 153, 157,
    158, 160, 161, 194, 202, 203, 209,
    211, 212, 214, 219, 250, 252, 253,
    276n, 277n
  cultural modernization 8, 28, 69,
    144, 151, 157

LaVergne, TN USA
08 March 2011

219265LV00001B/3/P